WOMEN, PHILANTHROPY, AND CIVIL SOCIETY

The eighteenth volume in the series

PHILANTHROPIC STUDIES

Dwight F. Burlingame and David C. Hammack,
general editors

WOMEN, PHILANTHROPY, AND CIVIL SOCIETY

Edited by
Kathleen D. McCarthy

INDIANA UNIVERSITY PRESS
Bloomington and Indianapolis

This book is a publication of

Indiana University Press
601 North Morton Street
Bloomington, Indiana 47404-3797 USA

http://iupress.indiana.edu

Telephone orders 800-842-6796
Fax orders 812-855-7931
Orders by e-mail iuporder@indiana.edu

The paper used in this publication meets the minimum
requirements of American National Standard for Information
Sciences—Permanence of Paper for Printed Library
Materials, ANSI Z39.48-1984.

Manufactured in the United States of America

Library of Congress Cataloging-in-Publication Data

Women, philanthropy, and civil society / edited by Kathleen D. McCarthy.
    p. cm. — (Philanthropic Studies)
  Includes bibliographical references.
  ISBN 0-253-33918-9 (cl : alk. paper)
  1. Women in charitable work—Cross-cultural studies. 2. Women—
Charitable contributions—Cross-cultural studies. 3. Women volunteers
in social service—Cross-cultural studies. 4. Civil society. I. McCarthy,
Kathleen D.

  HV541 .W64 2001
  361.7'082—dc21

                                    00-063425

1 2 3 4 5 06 05 04 03 02 01

Contents

Introduction

KATHLEEN D. McCARTHY

The growing interest that scholars have shown in women's political culture — the ways in which women built institutions and influenced public policymaking from beyond the electoral arena — is perhaps not surprising. During the 1990s, innovative work on theories of the role of the state, maternalism, women's roles in political processes and nation-building, and the economic roles organizations play has expanded our understanding of the scope and nature of civil society and mapped a direction for future research. To date, much of this work has focused on the United States and Western Europe, raising important questions about the representativeness of the experiences of women in industrialized nations.[1]

This volume, which grows out of a research project on women and philanthropy sponsored by the Center for the Study of Philanthropy at The Graduate Center of The City University of New York, expands our understanding of female beneficence in shaping diverse political cultures. The contributors examine the role of philanthropy — the giving of time, money, and/or valuables for public benefit — in shaping nongovernmental organizations (NGOs), civil society, and women's political culture world-wide. As in the US, this often enabled them to create "parallel power structures" that resembled, but rarely precisely replicated, the commercial and political arenas of men. From nuns who managed charitable and educational institutions to political activists demanding an end to discriminatory practices against women and children, many of the women whose lives are documented on these pages claimed distinctive public roles through the nonprofit sphere.[2]

The authors in this volume are from Europe, the United States, Latin America, the Middle East, Egypt, India, and Asia. Their essays cover nations on every continent, representing a variety of political and religious systems.

In approaching the subject of women as shapers of civil society through their donations of time and money, each of the contributors

1

shares certain basic understandings of the environment in which civil society is formed, much of their perspective being drawn from contemporary discourses on women's political culture. For example, historians have argued that women's organizations have tended to have more policymaking authority in weak (i.e., decentralized, as in the United States) rather than strong states, such as Bismarkian Germany. However, the authors in this volume have discovered that public-private partnerships between governments and women's organizations were pervasive in both weak and strong states.[3]

In the nineteenth century, middle-class and elite women coupled their private donations and their work as volunteers with public funding to foster an invisible — but often highly significant — form of political activity. In effect, female philanthropy helped to subsidize state programs. Several of the articles in this collection show clearly that the roots of state welfare organizations lie in volunteer and religious institutions — in France, for example — and that women (including nuns) acted on behalf of the state, at least implicitly, by cutting the public costs of caring for those in need.

Colonialism may have helped to foster separatist [i.e., single sex] organizations and female voluntarism in some areas, as local needs were identified and addressed in the community rather than at the level of state government. The consolidation of nation-states, on the other hand, often had a chilling effect on self-help organizations, curtailing advocacy, and encouraging service delivery in those areas of need approved by the state. In other words, some strong state systems worked, and in many places continue to work, to suppress the activities of volunteer or nongovernmental organizations.

In the 1980s and '90s, however, there has been a significant resurgence of civil society and NGOs around the world. This "associational revolution" has been fueled, in part, by women's organizations and the rise of feminist agendas, trends vividly illustrated in the United Nation's conference on women in Beijing and the U.N. population meeting in Cairo. The growing visibility of NGOs is related to the downsizing of government in many regions and the declining faith in the state's ability to do everything. The weakening of centralized nation-states has opened the door to nongovernmental organizations, and women have been quick to seize the initiative. These women's organizations are influential well beyond their levels of staffing and funding. Simply in terms of presence they have a substantial impact on the formation and implementation of government policy.

Moreover, although we still lack reliable data, anecdotal information suggests that women probably comprise a majority of volunteers and

NGO workers in many, if not most, countries. Certainly, the essays in this book suggest that their influence is pervasive.

There are economic implications as well. Research on the economic impact of women's nonprofit entrepreneurship and market activities carried out through voluntary associations reveals the previously invisible roles played by elite and middle-class women in creating wealth to sustain their services. In the process, they often helped to create a parallel, "subterranean economy" for the production, marketing and sale of artifacts produced by and for women.[4]

Frequently, women's philanthropic contributions to the state — their unacknowledged subsidies for social services — were delivered through religious organizations. Certainly, such organizations and the ethical behaviors they encouraged through religious teachings affected the ways in which women participated in social and political arenas. Catholicism, Islam, Hinduism, and Judaism all emphasize giving as a social and religious good. Islamic law and Hindu customs in particular enabled women to control some of their own wealth. Protestantism and English common law encouraged women to volunteer their time as well as donate funds. Many of the activities undertaken by women on behalf of the social and political economy can only be described as entrepreneurial. Such efforts can be found in many countries — in seventeenth-century French convents, nineteenth-century Irish lacemaking projects, and schools for teaching carpetmaking skills in twentieth-century Egypt. The role of women as entrepreneurs on the margins is clearly an area that merits further research across cultures.

Religion played a particularly important role in determining the contours of women's philanthropic activities in different cultures. Questions concerning the place of religious institutions within the nonprofit sector have reverberated through many of the discussions about the sector's scope and nature in recent years. While some scholars sought to include only the non-sacramental services delivered by religious groups, others argued that religious institutions were a vital part of the sector in and of themselves; these debates have profound implications for our understanding of the sector's scale and aims.[5]

In the United States, religious groups were legislated into the voluntary sphere beginning in the 1780s, as state after state followed Virginia's lead in disestablishing state churches and severing them from public support. The upshot was that every church had to compete for parishioners and funds, efforts that led not only to the exponential growth of the country's denominational networks, but also to expanded public roles for the women who collectively helped to underwrite this organizational explosion with their money and time.

In the US, as in many countries, different religious groups fostered distinct cultures of giving. During the nineteenth century, Protestant laywomen gave money and time, and were often active politically. They tended to be involved in social advocacy and organized charities. Similarly, the role of Protestantism in promoting voluntarism and female civil society in other countries has frequently been important (one of the most Christianized countries in East Asia, Korea, is a key example, as Lee's paper demonstrates). Jews also give and volunteer, but particularly in the nineteenth century the emphasis was on the delivery of services within the Jewish community. Certainly, the roots of Jewish philanthropy remain there.

Catholics tended to emphasize the delivery of charitable and educational services, for example through hospitals and schools. Laywomen tended to participate as funders, while nuns managed the charities.

These service systems provided important power bases for women who sought to remain independent actors, particularly within the Catholic hierarchy. Nuns have traditionally been effective in funding convents through dowries and in generating income through services and the skills of individual nuns and the dependents and deviants entrusted to their care. In time, the behavior of women religious was politicized with the rise of Liberation Theology and the liberalization of the church following Vatican II. A new emphasis on voluntarism in more open structures has freed many women to be more active in the arena between church and state. In some countries, particularly Latin America, these activities have highlighted church-state conflicts and invited suppression by both the state and church hierarchies.

Hinduism and Islam tended to emphasize the roles of women as donors. In the twentieth century, however, organizations such as the Muslim Sisterhood, and Gandhian protests, encouraged the rise of women's voluntarism. Conversely, Confucianism offered no public space for women, nor opened prospects for women to control funds for services.[6]

RESEARCH HYPOTHESES

The Center for the Study of Philanthropy initiated a research project in 1994 to elucidate the role of women in building civil society through their gifts of money and time in a variety of countries. These papers come out of that initial project. All of the writers worked with a common set of seven hypotheses that guided their inquiries. The papers included in this book all address some or all of these hypotheses to a greater or lesser degree, providing a useful ground for comparing the authors' findings.

Hypothesis #1: Religion was the most important factor in shaping women's philanthropy and civil society.

Hypothesis #2: Women's organizations made their greatest impact on public policymaking agendas through "maternalist" programs for mothers and children.

Hypothesis #3: Women's organizations historically had more authority in weak, decentralized states than in strong, highly centralized ones.

Hypothesis #4: Women's nonprofit organizations were heavily dependent on public funding.

Hypothesis #5: Participation in voluntary associations enabled women to build "parallel power structures" to those of men.

Hypothesis #6: The type of strategies that women's groups adopted [e.g., as separatist organizations, or in "assimilationist," mixed-sex groups] had a profound impact on the degree of authority and autonomy that they wielded.

Hypothesis #7: Transnational philanthropy played a crucial role in opening a "space" for indigenous women's civil society activities.

These hypotheses play through the essays in this volume in various, often subtle ways. In one way or another, all prove to have at least some validity in the countries studied. Organized according to the factors mentioned earlier that shape civil society — government, market, and religious structures — one can see in these studies significant variations on the themes, as the following summaries suggest.

In terms of government structures, for example, Maria Luddy's paper on Ireland shows how women's philanthropy aided the development of a conservative Catholic state, where Catholic laywomen had only a limited tradition of social activism and reform. Women in Australia were politically marginalized, as Shurlee Swain explains. The strong centralized state church in France, and the strong centralized state, blurred the lines between private and public activities (Evelyne Diebolt). The comparison between France and Brazil in this respect is instructive, as Leilah Landim demonstrates, although the Brazilian church and state were legally separated in 1889. The strong central state in Egypt created tensions for the development of civil society, but as Amani Kandil shows the 1970s and '80s witnessed a reemergence of independent women's groups. Ghada Hashem Talhami's paper examines the interesting development of hybrid women's organizations that mixed politics and social work in Palestinian areas. In Korea, NGOs reemerged as vehicles for active citizen participation after the end of the authoritarian regime in 1987.

Religion plays a central role in all of these essays. Certainly, in the United States, Australia and Norway, Protestantism has been a vital factor in the growth of women's organizations. Religion was also central in Ireland, although there was little cooperation between Protestants and Catholics and substantial differences in the way the two groups worked. Protestant groups were often auxiliaries to Bible societies; there were few Catholic lay women's organizations after 1850. There was a similar divide between Protestants and Catholics in Australia, where evangelical Christianity helped to spur voluntarism.

Religion was central to the rise of women's philanthropy in Brazil, providing legitimation and access to funds, for example. But as in France, the professionalization of social work broke the hegemony of the church in providing social services. In Egypt, the concept of philanthropy was tied to Christian and Islamic charity. Both Hinduism and Islam have strong doctrinal sanctions — Islam for giving via zakat and Hinduism for service via the Bhagavad Gita. The earliest female-controlled charities in India focused on women's rights and the abolition of traditional customs, such as purdah. Voluntarism came with secularization and the advent of Christianity.

The patriarchal culture of Korea and Confucianism combined to keep women from controlling money or even their own decisions. Women's philanthropy was a revolutionary idea in Korea, where Christianity had a powerful influence through its emphasis on education. Christian women leaders became the cornerstone of the Korean church — and formed the heart of the anti-Japanese movement during the period of occupation.

The articles in this book illustrate the extent to which government, the market, and religion have shaped the role of female philanthropy and philanthropists in different national settings. By shifting the focus from organizations to donors and volunteers, we can begin to assess the relative importance of each of these factors in creating opportunities for citizen participation.

The analyses that follow were commissioned by the Center for the Study of Philanthropy as part of a larger project that examined the record of women's philanthropy in over twenty countries. The decision to focus on women reflects the Center's long-standing commitment to studying multicultural philanthropy, including women's efforts and international trends. Rather than focusing on nonprofits or public policy *per se*, the Center has concentrated on the activities of different gender, ethnic, and racial groups, and institutions such as foundations, within the philanthropic arena. This project is an extension of that mission. Each of the essays here assesses the role of philanthropy in opening a "space" for women in the public sphere, enhancing our understanding not only of women's roles, but of civil society more generally.

NOTES

1. See, for example, Kathryn Kish Sklar, "The Historical Foundations of Women's Power in the Creation of the American Welfare State, 1830–1930," Seth Koven and Sonya Michel, eds., *Mothers of a New World: Maternalist Politics and the Origins of Welfare States* (New York: Routledge, 1993), 43–93; Theda Skocpol, *Protecting Soldiers and Mothers: The Political Origins of Social Policy in the United States* (Cambridge: Harvard University Press, 1991); Kathleen D. McCarthy, "Women, Politics, Philanthropy: some Historical Origins of the Welfare State," in John Patrick Diggins, ed., *The Liberal Challenge: Arthur Schlesinger, Jr., and the Challenge of the American Past* (Princeton: Princeton University Press, 1997); Sonya Michel and Seth Koven, "Womanly Duties: Maternalist Politics and the Origins of Welfare States in France, Germany, Great Britain, and the United States, 1880–1920," *American Historical Review* 95, no. 4 (October 1990); Kathryn Kish Sklar, "A Call for Comparisons," *American Historical Review* 95, no. 4 (October 1990). For definitions of civil society, see Jean L. Cohen and Andrew Arato, *Civil Society and Political Theory* (Cambridge: MIT Press, 1994).

2. Kathleen D. McCarthy, "Parallel Power Structures: Women and the Voluntary Sphere," in McCarthy, ed., *Lady Bountiful Revisited: Women, Philanthropy, and Power* (New Brunswick: Rutgers University Press, 1990), 1–31.

3. Michel and Koven, "Womanly Duties."

4. See, for example, Kathleen D. McCarthy, *Women's Culture: American Philanthropy and Art, 1830–1930* (Chicago: University of Chicago Press, 1991); Kathleen Waters Sander, *The Business of Charity: The Woman's Exchange Movement, 1832–1900* (Urbana: University of Illinois Press, 1998).

5. See, for example, Virginia Hodgkinson and Murray S. Weitzman, *From Belief to Commitment* (Washington, D.C., 1993) and Lester M. Salamon, *America's Nonprofit Sector: A Primer* (New York: The Foundation Center, 1992).

6. However, there are often great variations within these traditions, some but not all of which are captured here. For differences among Islamic countries see Clifford Geertz's classic study, *Islam Observed: Religious Development in Morocco and Indonesia* (Chicago: University of Chicago Press, 1968).

– 1 –

Women and Philanthropy in Nineteenth-Century Ireland

MARIA LUDDY

Irish women's experiences were far more diverse, complex and vigorous than might appear from the limited number of studies which have been published to date on their lives.[1] Part of that complexity was created by the extent of women's involvement in philanthropic organizations. There were various levels of charitable involvement, that of the poor to the poor, that of the landed lady providing for her tenants, and the traditional neighborly charity that was always considered a part of Irish life. There was also the more formal development of charitable endeavor, particularly in the nineteenth century. Here women played a leading role in establishing orphanages and schools, working in prisons, refuges and workhouses, and creating a myriad of societies and organizations which catered to the poor and destitute of all religious denominations. Through their voluntary work women made a significant contribution to the development of Irish society; they enhanced their own social role; and ultimately a number of women philanthropists claimed that the importance of their contribution earned them the right to partake in the formal political process.

In this paper I examine a number of issues relating to women and philanthropy in nineteenth-century Ireland. Among these issues is the importance of religion in women's philanthropic activity. Women's role in philanthropy in the nineteenth century was profoundly affected by their religious affiliations. Indeed a key element of philanthropy in Ireland was the denominational nature of its development. One of the consequences of this denominational aspect was its divisive impact. Charities of different religions competed not only for resources, but also

This is a revised and extended version of a paper originally published in *Voluntas* (vol. 7, no. 4), the International Journal of Voluntary and Nonprofit Organizations and the official journal of the International Society for Third-Sector Research (ISTR). The authors gratefully acknowledge *Voluntas* and ISTR for their permission to reproduce this paper.

for clients. This had a profound impact on the provision of welfare for the poor, and particularly for children. The denominational basis of philanthropy meant that while women of Protestant and non-Conformist religions often worked together to provide relief there was almost no cooperation between Catholic women and those of other denominations.

The importance of the religious element in nineteenth-century Irish philanthropy is further borne out by the institution of convents. The most extensive welfare provision was made by Catholic nuns. The expansion of convent networks throughout the century affected the extent to which lay Catholic women became involved in charity work. Among the consequences of this expansion was the takeover by nuns of lay Catholic charitable enterprises, and the removal of lay Catholic women from the public arena of institutional charity work.

This paper focuses on religion as the dominant feature in Irish philanthropy during this period. However, other issues also need to be examined, such as the relationship between state-aided welfare and voluntary activity. While lay- and religious-run charities developed on a broad scale in the last century, government-aided institutions also provided a substantial amount of relief. There was also, in a small number of instances, a direct link between women's philanthropy and state aid, which can be seen clearly in relation to workhouses, where nuns took over nursing in the attached hospitals, and in institutions organized to cater for children, such as industrial and reformatory schools.

While charities often provided physical, and spiritual, relief the impact of philanthropic women on Irish society also had much to do with the imposition of moral and religious values. This is especially true in the case of nuns who, by the late nineteenth century had socialized Catholic children and adults into obedience, and subservience, to a reformed and powerful Catholic Church. All philanthropists reinforced class divisions within society but nuns, through their educational and philanthropic work, played a major role in shaping middle-class Catholic mores throughout the nineteenth century. The extent of charity provided by Catholic agencies far exceeded that of other religious denominations. This had much to do with the availability of personnel but also with the level of funding available to charitable organizations. It seems clear that lay Catholic women provided substantial financial support to convents, and thus played a significant role in their expansion and in the maintenance of a welfare system. While the issue of funding reveals the generally unacknowledged wealth available to women, other issues regarding women's role in philanthropy are worth noting. It is significant that women of Protestant and non-Conformist denominations were much more likely than Catholic women to join or institute organizations which called for legislative changes in matters of welfare. These women also led the way in campaigning for women's access to the franchise at local and national levels. Philanthropic involvement had a profound impact on how Irish women viewed the world and their place in it. For a small minority of philanthropic women of Protestant or non-Conformist denominations, their charitable work led them to political activism for social change. For lay Catholic women their relegation to the secondary role of fundraisers blunted their political development and also aided the development of a conservative Catholic state.

THE EIGHTEENTH-CENTURY BACKGROUND

Penal legislation enacted in Ireland in the seventeenth and eighteenth centuries limited Catholic access to education, the professions, and property and placed restrictions on the practice of their faith.[2] Due to intermittent harassment, the Catholic Church was disorganized and remained structurally weak until the reorganization of the nineteenth century.[3] The last decades of the eighteenth century saw a revival in Catholicism, a revival in which women played a distinct role, evidenced by the beginnings of the expansion of native religious foundations and the rise of women's philanthropic endeavors. Nano Nagle, for example, later founder of the Presentation community, began voluntarily, and illegally, educating the poor in Cork city in the 1750s.[4] At the same time in Dublin, Teresa Mulally also began to educate poor Catholic girls.[5] Financial support for the enterprises of such women came initially from their own personal funds; Nagle came from a wealthy background and Mulally had won money in a lottery. However, funds were also sought from the public, particularly from other women, and it was as patrons to charitable enterprises that women played a key role in the late eighteenth century. Some of the supporters of Mulally's work were aristocratic ladies or members of the developing Catholic middle class.[6]

Catholic women were not alone in becoming involved in philanthropic enterprises. Protestant women such as Mary Mercer, who established Mercer's hospital in Dublin in 1734, played an important role in funding charitable enterprises.[7] Also, in the eighteenth century, numerous widows' almshouses were established, some of which were, if not managed by women, established and funded by them.[8] Lady Arbella Denny, who opened the first Magdalen Asylum in the country in 1766, played a vital role in attempting to reform the abuses which plagued the Dublin Foundling Hospital, which was notorious for its horrendous conditions.[9]

Religion was as much a primary motivating factor in engaging in charitable works in the eighteenth century as it was in the nineteenth century. Good works were a means toward spiritual salvation and were expected from members of all religious denominations. Women, through prescriptive literature and church teachings, were particularly encouraged to engage in charitable work. The eighteenth century then saw the beginnings of a tradition of voluntary female philanthropy which consisted of public and private benevolence. It was not, however, until the nineteenth century that voluntary charitable associations were organized on a broad scale by women and became an enduring and pervasive feature of Irish society.

RELIGION AND PHILANTHROPY
IN NINETEENTH-CENTURY IRELAND

Social class was an important factor in deciding who would become a member of a charitable society in the nineteenth century. However, religious affiliation was of equal, if not more, importance. While women of all religious persuasions engaged in philanthropy,[10] lay charitable initiative remained predominantly in the hands of women of denominations other than Roman Catholic. Indeed it is clear that lay female and, to a lesser extent, male Catholic initiative was restricted by the role allotted to nuns.

Three major religious denominations functioned in Ireland in the nineteenth century: Roman Catholic, Anglican, and Presbyterian. The most reliable early figures for affiliation with a particular congregation come from the census of 1861 which showed that Catholics made up almost 78 percent of the total population, members of the Church of Ireland (Anglicans) made up 12 percent, and Presbyterians 9 percent, the remainder being divided among non-believers, Methodists, Congregationalists, Unitarians, Baptists, Jews and Quakers, among others.[11] There is no doubt that religion played an important role in the lives of women during this period. Religion not only defined and limited women's place in society, particularly the place of lay women, but it also, ironically, opened a door on the world of work for those women willing to form and join religious communities. In many instances lay women were enabled by the demands of "Christian duty" to develop public lives and careers in philanthropy. For middle-class women philanthropy became an acceptable means of conducting a moral mission in public, and such activity brought them very clearly into the public realm where they controlled finances, raised funds, ran institutions and catered for the needs of thousands of the poor and destitute.

Religion, an affair of conscience and privacy, also had a very public face in Ireland: in the rituals of the various churches and congregations, and in the setting up of female religious congregations and congrega-tions of Christian Brothers.[12] In 1800 there were 6 religious orders with 120 nuns inhabiting 11 houses in the country; by 1851 that number had increased to 1,500 nuns residing in 95 convents and to over 8,000 by 1901 in a total of 35 religious orders or congregations.[13] The establishment of convents allowed a freedom for women far beyond what was available to lay women. Convent expansion provided a very large number of single women with the opportunity of engaging in socially useful work at a time when women generally were denied such opportunities.

Entering a convent was the ideal for Irish Catholic women in the nineteenth century. Becoming a wife and mother was considered a sec-ond best option for women. Convents were institutions of power. Within these walls women could, and did, create their own systems of labor and some had the opportunity of rising to positions of power and authority unmatched by lay Catholic women. The need for social compatibility al-lowed for the development of a class-based system of authority within convents, which was most obvious in the distinctions which existed between choir and lay sisters. Choir nuns came from privileged back-grounds and engaged in the public work of the community. Lay nuns were generally less well educated and from much poorer backgrounds. They carried out the domestic tasks of the community and had little say in the managerial structures of the community.[14]

While nuns describe, and have described, their entry to religious com-munities as the pursuit of a "vocation," this rhetoric should not blind us to other expectations which nuns, as women, might have had of convent life. From a social perspective, women's religious communities provided an esteemed alternative to marriage and motherhood. The extent of con-vent networks allowed women to choose the type of convent, and hence the type of work, that best suited their interests, needs, and abilities.

Nuns built up an extensive network of welfare organizations catering to the poor. They ran schools, orphanages, reformatories, and industrial schools, Magdalen asylums and homes for the elderly. There was no aspect of charitable endeavor in which nuns did not establish themselves as workers. The extent of their activities made them a powerful force in shaping Irish society, both through their educative work and their welfare systems.

CONVENTS AND CHARITY WORK

The major form of relief work carried out by nuns before 1850 was sick visitation. Thousands of visits were made to the homes of the poor every year. The Sisters of Mercy in Limerick, for example, visited 3,161 individuals from 1838 to 1844. During the famine years, from 1845 to 1850, they attended to 4,737 individuals. Institutions such as orphanages, asylums for the homeless, blind etc., industrial schools, reformatories and hospitals were all on the increase after 1850. Convents tended to be multipurpose, engaging in a number of charitable activities at any one time. For example, the Sisters of Mercy managed schools, orphanages, asylums for the "fallen," industrial and reformatory institutions, as well as shelters for the homeless and refuges for young women. Convents also availed themselves of opportunities to run government-funded institutions after the 1850s. The extension of the Reformatory Schools Act to Ireland in 1858 allowed nuns to manage a number of these schools. Nuns also took advantage of the funding provided by the government under the Industrial Schools Act of 1869, seeing it as a means of allowing them to care for a large number of destitute children, with full religious freedom and solely under their care. This was particularly important in the light of the bitterness that arose with regard to proselytism and the care of children in nineteenth-century Ireland. By 1899 there were 8,422 children in 71 industrial schools throughout the country.[15] Convents managed 22 of these establishments.[16] At times the initiative for organizing a charity and then seeking government aid came from the nuns themselves. For example, St. Vincent's Convict Refuge at Goldenbridge in Dublin, was organized, in 1856, by the Sisters of Mercy as an "intermediate prison." The Irish prison board was concerned at the time about the rates of recidivism among women and strongly supported the refuge which received funding from the government.[17] Nuns also used the money made available by the National Board of Education to fund their primary schools. The Education Act of 1831 allowed religious denominations to manage their own schools and receive government aid as long as they used non-sectarian textbooks provided by the government. Just over eighty percent of convents were involved in education throughout the century.

Convents also engaged in nursing, and in 1865 the Sisters of Charity opened their own hospital in Dublin to cater to a specifically Catholic clientele. Nuns also gained access to these hospitals after 1861; by the end of the nineteenth century roughly half of the workhouse hospitals were staffed by nuns, primarily Mercy Sisters. From the re-emergence of the conventual movement at the end of the eighteenth century nuns found their way into public institutions. During the cholera epidemic of 1832, for example, they worked in Townsend Street Hospital in Dublin. The first advance in establishing religious-run hospitals came in 1834 when the Sisters of Charity set up St. Vincent's Hospital in Dublin. Nursing, which had long been portrayed as a branch of domestic life, was taken out of that sphere by nuns and placed firmly in the public domain through the establishment of their own hospitals, but primarily by the duties they undertook in workhouse hospitals. In 1861 the Limerick board of guardians was the first to win permission from the poor law commissioners to allow nuns to nurse in their workhouse hospital. It was never easy for nuns to gain access to workhouse hospitals. There were a number of reasons for this. Often boards of guardians were made up of Protestant members who feared that nuns would interfere with the religion of any Protestant inmates. The fact that nuns did not engage in night duty was also a deterrent. Nuns were to make a greater impact on workhouse hospitals after the 1870s when boards of guardians, previously the preserve of the Protestant gentry, began to be dominated by Catholic, and nationalist, guardians.

Nuns had a high social status in nineteenth-century Ireland. Their work in institutions and their own schemes of benevolence gave them a moral and spiritual authority which was unsurpassed by any other group of women in society. The charitable work of nuns became the public face of private philanthropic enterprise and the funds secured for them, particularly by lay women, allowed convents to extend their enterprises while relegating lay women to the supporting function of fund raisers. It was often a very wise decision to hand over charities to the nuns. It is clear from the evidence that in many cases, through financial or managerial neglect, Catholic charities would have folded without the intervention of religious orders. The expansion of convent networks did not mean that lay Catholics ceased to function in the charitable sphere. However, the most prominent lay Catholic philanthropic figures were, and remained, intimately associated with religious congregations; others who engaged in charity work were firmly controlled by clerics. By mid-century lay Catholic women and men had handed over many of their enterprises to nuns. Only a handful of philanthropic societies were formed by lay Catholic women after 1850 and only two of these were not eventually handed over to the nuns. Lay Catholic women did not create enduring, independent societies as their Protestant or Quaker counterparts did.

LAY CATHOLIC WOMEN AND PHILANTHROPY

Among the most important of the lay Catholic philanthropists were women like Anna Maria Ball (1785–1871), Ellen Woodlock (1811–84) and Sarah Atkinson (1823–93). A number of common threads link all of these women. They were all connected in some way with members of religious congregations, or the work of such congregations. Woodlock had spent time in a convent novitiate. Anna Maria Ball was the sister of Frances Ball, founder of the Loreto Congregation, and Atkinson worked closely with the Sisters of Charity and wrote a biography of that community's founder.[18] Importantly, they were also women of wealth and independent means who had the financial resources not only to engage in philanthropy, but also to direct that charity into those areas that most interested or concerned them. Their work was primarily concerned with helping orphaned or destitute girls or young women.

There were strong links of friendship between these Catholic women; friendship and kinship ties also bound them to religious congregations. Unlike many philanthropists of other denominations who tended to limit themselves to one project, these Catholic philanthropists engaged in a variety of work. The fact that they eventually handed their work over to religious communities allowed them the time to engage in a number of projects.

There was a general insistence among the Catholic hierarchy that collective philanthropy by women be organized through religious congregations. This is particularly evident in the work of Catherine McAuley, founder of the Sisters of Mercy, and Margaret Aylward, founder of the Sisters of the Holy Faith. Neither woman was interested in forming a religious community. "I never intended," McAuley noted in later life, "founding a religious congregation, all I wanted was to serve the poor since that seemed to be what God expected of me."[19] From the 1850s only a handful of lay organizations were formed by women, and of these only two were not eventually given over to the care of nuns.[20] Nuns symbolized the perfect response of women to charity. The famous Dominican preacher, the Rev. Thomas Burke, writing of nuns in the 1870s, stated that "amongst the 'consecrated daughters of loveliness' whom Christ has engaged as spouses of His church — we find the golden garment of an organized charity. We find the highest, the best, and the purest, devoted to its service and its cause."[21]

FINANCIAL SUPPORT FOR ORGANIZATIONS

The extent of financial support provided by women to philanthropic organizations is difficult to discern from the available evidence. This is particularly the case with lay organizations. From the surviving small sample of subscription and donations lists available for charitable societies some generalizations can be made. In my examination of these financial details the total number of women subscribing to any charity is underestimated in subscription lists as anonymous donors; moreover, those whose sex could not be ascribed were not included. In the Irish case it appears that women made a significant contribution to charitable organizations and societies which dealt with women and children, and these types of charities were more likely to be supported by women than other charitable enterprises. For example, the House of Refuge, established in Dublin in 1802, had a total of 132 subscribers, of whom 79 percent were women contributing a sum of £215 or 78 percent of the total income from subscriptions in that year. Other charities were less well supported by women, especially those which aided men. Wealthy women were crucial to fundraising, for what they contributed themselves and also what they could raise through their connections.[22]

In terms of financial support and commitment to charitable organizations, the most profound impact was made by women who contributed to the founding of convents. Those women who founded convents in the late eighteenth and early nineteenth centuries were from wealthy backgrounds. Catherine McAuley, for example, founder of the Sisters of Mercy, was left a fortune of £25,000.[23] Women who entered religious communities also brought substantial sums of money with them as dowries. Some women brought thousands of pounds.[24] Sums of between £500 and £600 were common in the pre-Famine period, lesser amounts of between £200 to £300 after mid-century. One means of support for religious communities came from bequests left by lay Catholic women. Although no substantial work has been done on the level of financial provision made to convents by lay women, it appears from the available evidence that such provision was considerable. For example, in Clonmel in 1856 a Mrs. Cott left a legacy of £1,400 to the local Presentation convent for the benefit of the poor children of the parish. In 1865, when the Clonmel Presentation community were engaged in building new schools, a Miss Catherine Burke, who died intestate, left an estate valued at £2,800, which came to her three sisters who were members of the community.[25] Lay women were of enormous benefit to religious congregations, particularly in the area of fundraising. In Cork the Sisters of Charity received a sum of £3,500 from Miss Mahony and her sisters who were, incidentally, aunts to Ellen Woodlock.[26] Bazaars, subscriptions, charity balls, and charity sermons were among the many vehicles used by philanthropists in the nineteenth century to raise funds for their work; women played a vital role in organizing and contributing to such events.

PROTESTANT WOMEN AND PHILANTHROPY

The earliest form of organized charitable work engaged in by Protestant women involved them forming auxiliaries to Bible societies. Originally their function was to raise funds for such societies, but from the first

decade of the nineteenth century women began to visit the homes of
the poor and distribute Bibles. By 1825 women were acknowledged as
the "life" of Bible associations.[27] Another significant aspect of women's
charity work was the establishment and support of foreign missionary
societies.

The two largest societies organized by women in Ireland were the
Young Women's Christian Association, which opened its first branch
in Ireland in 1866, and the Girls' Friendly Society, established in Ireland in 1877. Both organizations were similar in aims and structure
but operated separately from each other. Thousands of young Protestant
women joined both societies. The GFS, for example, offered training to
young girls and also sought permanent employment for them. Members
of the YWCA were encouraged to involve themselves in charity work
and many engaged in prison visitation and were strong temperance
activists.[28] Both organizations were keen to turn out devout girls who
would create domestic happiness in their future family lives. Like most
religiously inspired philanthropic groups of the last century, both organizations were socially conservative and inactive in areas which urged
legislation regarding the working and social conditions of the poor in
society.

Generally, women in Protestant organizations appear to have been
more independent of clerical authority in their philanthropic work than
their Catholic counterparts. Their institutions and societies also operated on a much smaller scale than Catholic charities in the care of nuns.
Quaker women were to the forefront in organizing the most progressive charities of the nineteenth century. Quaker women and men were
politically active in a number of radical causes, such as the anti-slavery
and the anti-war movements, and they took the lead in campaigning
against the Contagious Diseases Acts in Ireland. The minority position
of Protestants in Irish society allowed a sense of community to develop
among these philanthropic women. For many, charity work also allowed
a more active social life, an element which should not be discounted in
the attraction of philanthropy.

PROTESTANT VERSUS CATHOLIC CHARITY

The Protestant charity network was well developed in Ireland in the
nineteenth century, particularly in the cities of Dublin and Belfast.
Those Protestant charities, which provided relief to Catholics or were
specifically aimed at converting Catholics to Protestantism, came under
increasing fire from Catholics as the century progressed. The growth
of the Catholic middle class, together with the reorganization of the

Catholic Church, led to a concerted effort to counteract the perceived proselytizing zeal of Protestant missionaries and charities. Women were an important element in both Catholic and Protestant missionary efforts. Among the most influential Protestant organizations was the Irish Church Missions, established in 1847 by the Rev. Alexander Dallas.[29] Dallas considered the institution of poor and ragged schools, where children were provided not only with a rudimentary education, but also with material relief would increase the numbers of converts from Catholicism. In Dublin, Dallas was ably assisted in his enterprises by Mrs. Ellen Smyly. Smyly became the most public Protestant female figure in mid-nineteenth-century philanthropy. She had opened her first Bible school in Dublin in about 1850 and by the 1870s had been instrumental in establishing at least six day schools and residential homes for poor and destitute children. The managing committees of each school were distinct, although the membership of each committee overlapped. Smyly and her daughters sat on all the committees, raised funds for their projects, and oversaw the management of the various institutions they founded.[30] In 1883 the number of children claimed to be cared for in Smyly's homes and schools was 1,578.[31] Smyly's motivation for establishing such homes came from strongly held religious convictions. For a number of Protestant philanthropists, the practice of Catholicism was blamed for much of the poverty and destitution experienced by children and their parents. The religious and humanitarian aspects of this charity work were so closely bound that it is difficult to assess which was more important as a motivating force.

The reported successes of these poor and ragged schools, together with the myriad of other Protestant charities, caused a degree of alarm among Catholics. Proselytizing activities were denounced from the altar and in the pastoral letters of Catholic bishops. The issue of proselytism became an openly bitter battle in Dublin, particularly from the 1860s. The care of orphan and destitute children was the main focus of proselytizing attention, and one of the consequences of the battle for the souls of children was a major increase in the number of institutions to provide for their care.

The most public battles between Catholic and Protestant women over the issue of proselytism and the care of children occurred between Ellen Smyly's ragged schools, which were closely associated with the Irish Church Missions, and the Ladies' Association of Charity of St. Vincent de Paul, under the management of Margaret Aylward, later founder of the Sisters of the Holy Faith. Members of the Ladies' Association kept careful watch on the activities of the ICM, going so far as to take the names of individuals who attended their schools or missions, distributing crucifixes to the children, and visiting the homes of parents who sent their children to the Protestant schools to try and induce them to remove their children.[32] The annual meetings of the Ladies' Association provided Aylward with a public platform to berate the activities of Protestant charities. In 1857 the Ladies' Association was instrumental in establishing St. Brigid's Orphanage, to counteract the work of Protestant orphanages. The Orphanage worked on the boarding-out system, placing children with families in country areas. The foster parents were carefully vetted and the children well looked after; the orphanage was considered a success.[33]

Margaret Aylward, who had twice attempted to persevere as a novice in two convents, had left the novitiate of the Sisters of Charity in 1836 and had engaged in charity work in her native Waterford before moving to Dublin. She was an important figure in the Ladies' Association of Charity of St. Vincent de Paul; she was also behind the establishment of St. Brigid's Orphanage. Saving children from "Protestant perversion" was the chief aim of Aylward and her helpers. Conviction on a contempt-of-court charge led to a six-month prison sentence in 1860. Aylward had been asked to bring before the court a child, Mary Mathews, allegedly abducted from St. Brigid's in order that it would not be returned to a Protestant mother. Aylward, apparently, did not know the whereabouts of the child. The case was widely reported in the contemporary press. Aylward and her supporters saw the case as an attack on St. Brigid's orphanage and its attempts to counteract Protestant proselytism. After her release from prison she formed the Sisters of the Holy Faith which was canonically approved in 1869.[34]

Fear of proselytism was also evident in the area of hospital visitations. In 1873 the Association for Visiting Hospitals was established in Dublin to visit patients in eight hospitals in the city. The visitors were women and the association had been initiated to counteract the "intrusive zeal of a host of Protestant visitors who enjoyed, naturally enough, free access to the wards in hospitals."[35] Concern about proselytism also led to lack of support among Catholic clerics for the Irish National Society for the Prevention of Cruelty to Children, which was set up in 1889.[36]

While proselytism was the main feature attributed to Protestant charities by Catholic workers in the nineteenth century, this should not hide the fact that such charity also extended to the relief of the Protestant poor. Unlike Catholic convent institutions which engaged in many different charitable functions, societies and institutions established by women of other religious denominations catered to specific needs and had limited objectives. The narrowness of their operations was determined by practical issues, primarily by their financial solvency. Few of these organizations dispensed charity unconditionally, and one of the major problems facing philanthropists was to provide relief to the "deserving poor." This category consisted of individuals who were willing, but unable through illness or other just reason to work. In many instances the charity devised schemes of work for their recipients, thus making them "deserving" in the public's view.

Lay women's charities, like many convent institutions, directed much of their energy to schemes to make women economically independent of charity. Needle and laundry work became the staple means of funding many organizations and also of developing self reliance among the recipients of charity. From the period of the Great Famine women philanthropists revitalized and reorganized lace making and knitting industries on a relatively large scale. Nuns became involved in industrial enterprises also, with the establishment of lace schools being the best known example of such endeavors.

WOMEN AND THE GREAT IRISH FAMINE

At times of particular crisis the means of all charitable societies were often stretched beyond their limits. Subsistence crises were a regular feature in nineteenth-century Ireland. Partial crop failures in the first half of the nineteenth century brought local distress to various parts of the country. The potato blight, which was the immediate cause of the Great Famine, was first observed in County Cork in September 1845. Government attempts to relieve the distress — establishing Relief Committees, soup kitchens, and work programs — proved generally inadequate. The difficulties became more pronounced in 1846 but the country was plunged into further distress in 1847. It is impossible to calculate the exact numbers of deaths, but historians tend to agree that at least one million people died as a direct result of the crisis. The majority of deaths resulted from fevers, typhoid, and dysentery.[37] As at other times of crisis, the Great Famine spurred many philanthropists to action, but the scale of distress made it difficult for relief schemes to have any lasting effect.

Among the organizations providing relief was the Cork Ladies' Relief Society for the South of Ireland, which was functioning by January 1847. This was typical of a host of similar societies managed by women in these years. Such associations generally had landed women as their patrons, and most aimed to provide support to the female members of a family, in the expectation that such aid, often in the form of work or the means to work, would benefit the whole family. Similar organizations were established throughout the country. One society worth mentioning is the Belfast Ladies' Relief Association for Connaught, which was organized under the direction of the Rev. John Edgar, a noted temperance activist, in 1847. The ladies of this association attempted to counteract the effects of the famine in the west of Ireland by aiming to "... improve, by industry, the temporal condition of the poor females of Connaught and their spiritual [condition] by the truth of the bible."[38] To this end funds were raised to establish schools where skills such as knitting and needlework could be taught. By 1850 the association had employed thirty-two schoolmistresses within the province who worked under the direction of resident ladies. In the same year the association claimed to have offered education and employment to over two thousand young women. In this project both temporal and spiritual redemption were entwined. This combination characterized a host of philanthropic societies throughout the nineteenth century. Nuns nursed in fever hospitals, and fed the starving at their convents. In Youghal, for example, the Presentation nuns turned the convent kitchen into a soup kitchen where they fed the starving, using their wealthy contacts to fund the project.[39]

One major aspect of women's involvement in philanthropy in the Famine years was the development of cottage industries. For example, a lacemaking school, which had been started in Limerick in the 1820s, was revived by Lady DeVere during the Famine years. By 1857 the industry employed 1,500 women.[40] The Presentation nuns started a lacemaking school in their convent in Youghal in 1847 to provide employment for girls pauperized by the famine. The industry was still operating in 1900 when it employed 120 women. The Ladies' Industrial Society of Ireland, which was set up in 1847, aimed to unite women "to carry out a system of encouraging and developing the latent capacities of the poor of Ireland."[41] Lady Aberdeen, wife of the Irish lord lieutenant, instituted the Irish Home Industries Association in 1887 which attempted to unite all these local industries throughout the country where "resident ladies" had encouraged knitting, sewing, and weaving among the female peasantry to bring them "into communication with those anxious to purchase the articles manufactured." She also organized a display of work carried out by the Association at the Irish Exhibition in London in 1888 and opened three shops, in Dublin, London, and Chicago where such work could be sold.[42] As yet no work has been done by historians to examine the economic impact of these industries on the lives of the poor. Similarly these industries need to be considered in the light of the role played by women in their management. Such industries called for financial and marketing skills which are rarely associated with Irish middle-class women of the nineteenth century.

CONCLUSIONS

A large number of middle-class and aristocratic women involved themselves in charitable enterprises. Landed ladies dispensed charity to their tenants in traditional ways, such as visiting the sick and opening schools for the children of their estate workers. They also organized institutions or acted as patrons to charitable enterprises. Lay philanthropic societies generally remained localized, and women rarely developed a network of societies to extend their function. Unlike nuns, most philanthropists undertook charity work in their spare time and did not have the financial support or the high status that nuns enjoyed. Although difficult to enumerate precisely, philanthropic lay women organized over three hundred independent charitable societies throughout the century, ranging from the Asylum for Aged and Infirm Female Servants (1809) and the Country Air Association (1886), which provided a convalescent home for the poor, to the Dublin Kyrle Society (1877), which had among its aims the decoration of working-class clubs and the securing of open spaces for recreation in Dublin.[43] They also organized nursing for the poor, orphanages, schools, and asylums which looked after inebriates, criminals, and prostitutes.

Philanthropic effort was organized on distinct religious grounds and this served as both a cohesive and a divisive force in regard to those institutions established by women. Religion proved to be a barrier between women who organized charities. There was almost no interaction between lay Catholic women or female religious with their Protestant sisters. The element of proselytism caused tensions between various organizations, and this was particularly true of those societies which looked after orphaned or destitute children. The denominational basis of many charitable societies with similar objectives prevented women from uniting to create larger, more extensive — and perhaps more efficient — organizations. Religious bias inhibited women from pooling not only their financial resources but also from building upon each other's experiences as charity workers. Referrals were never made across the religious divide. The religious basis of many charitable societies also hindered the development of a critique of the social origins of poverty and destitution. While it gave many women the impetus to organize voluntary societies, religion also in many cases defined the limits of their approach. Those societies concerned with moral reform, the penitent asylums, or criminal refuges, sought to change values by example, persuasion, and a belief in the possibility of spiritual regeneration. The women who ran these benevolent societies were remoulding the "sinner" rather than questioning or eradicating those conditions which gave rise to the "sin."

From the time of the Famine there was growing concern among the middle classes with the idea of respectability, particularly the concept of sexual respectability. While the institution of Magdalen Asylums and Rescue Homes had been a common feature from the mid-eighteenth century in Irish philanthropy, the late nineteenth century saw the provision of preventative institutions being made on a wide scale. Many charitable workers were concerned with the possible sexual corruption of young women and instituted refuges which offered young "respectable" women shelter and training for future employment. Those who were not considered "respectable" — prostitutes or unmarried mothers — found shelter in Magdalen asylums, penitent refuges, or the workhouse. The first lay association to deal specifically with the plight of unmarried mothers was the Catholic Rotunda Girl's Aid Society, which was established in 1880. In the following year a group of Protestant women organized the Dublin Hospital Girl's Aid Association. The justification for these societies lay in the belief that these unmarried mothers were not to blame for their situation and that help, provided at an early stage, would prevent their further degradation. The help provided was conditional and not all unmarried mothers were acceptable to the committees. Careful investigations had to be made regarding their circumstances to ensure that they could benefit from any aid provided. The societies put the babies out to nurse, and the mothers were expected to pay for this service. If such payment was not forthcoming the children were quickly placed in the workhouse. The recipients of charity had to prove their worthiness — in this instance by taking some responsibility for their children.

One of the outcomes of women's involvement in philanthropy in the nineteenth century was the development of the Irish suffrage campaign.[44] Women began to partake in reform societies from the 1860s. Societies, such as the Ladies' National Association for the Repeal of the Contagious Diseases Acts (1871), the National Society for the Prevention of Cruelty to Children (1889), the Philanthropic Reform Association (1896), and the Irish Workhouse Association (1896), were the most progressive philanthropic societies of the century. Each of them — all, with the exception of the LNA, having mixed executive committees — actively sought changes in the law with regard to the safety of children and the protection of the destitute. The women on these committees, through their philanthropic work, developed a new awareness of women's disabilities which encouraged them to attack discriminatory social practices. These reformist women associated the acquisition of the vote with social change. Indeed the pioneering figures of the Irish suffrage campaign — the Presbyterian Isabella M. S. Tod (1836–96) and the

Quaker Anna Haslam (1829–1922) — both had a long tradition of philanthropic involvement.[45] Lay Catholic women did not have a tradition of social activism and were much slower to organize for social reform. Catholic women who became politically active tended to join nationalist organizations which did not seek social reform as a first step but rather freedom from England. Nuns became the primary source of socialization for the Catholic Church in the nineteenth century. They were also socially conservative, their own social structures reflecting the social divisions which were deemed natural to society. They did not inspire social revolution nor encourage the political or independent aspirations of women.

The major link between women involved in the suffrage campaign in the late nineteenth century was their involvement in reformist philanthropic associations. Those women suffragists involved in reform societies used women's tradition of charity work as an argument for receiving the vote. Charity activists argued that the vote was a means to an end — the spiritual and moral regeneration of society — which they were already attempting to implement through their benevolent work. Only a tiny proportion of those women involved in philanthropy supported the suffrage campaign, but significantly those charity activists who initiated the campaign were of religious denominations other than Catholicism. A tradition of philanthropy is evident in those women most active in seeking the vote; such a tradition was not to be found among Catholic women, whose active philanthropic function had been assigned to nuns.

By the late nineteenth century women had a very public place in Irish life. Nuns, with their convents, occupied not only a significant part of the geographical landscape, but also played a major role in binding the Catholic poor and middle class to a revitalized Catholic Church. Nuns were also a very visible part of public life, working in their schools, going about their home visitations, and caring for the ill in hospitals and the destitute in their institutions. As noted, the provision of charity was not left solely to nuns. Protestant and non-Conformist women had, by 1900, a pattern of establishing voluntary associations for a variety of causes. Women's voluntary organizations had provided an acceptable framework for public action, and they allowed women to become effective agents of change in Irish society. Philanthropy had a major impact on the formation of Irish society, in terms of practical support for the poor, but also in shaping the values of Irish people and shaping public and political activities, particularly those of women.

NOTES

1. For a comprehensive bibliography on recent writings on the history of Irish women see Maria Luddy, *Women in Ireland, 1800–1918: A Documentary History* (Cork, 1995). See also, Maria Luddy, *Women and Philanthropy in Nineteenth-Century Ireland* (Cambridge, 1995).

2. Maureen Wall, *The Penal Laws* (Dundalk, 1961).

3. Sean Connolly, *Religion and Society in Nineteenth-Century Ireland* (Dundalk, 1985).

4. T. J. Walsh, *Nano Nagle and the Presentation Sisters* (Dublin, 1959), 44–55.

5. R. Burke Savage, *A Valiant Dublin Woman: The Story of George's Hill* (Dublin, 1940).

6. See, for example, Subscription list in respect of the school for poor girls at Mary's Lane, 1766–72 Archives of the Presentation Convent, George's Hill, Dublin.

7. See Robert Gahan, "Old almshouses of Dublin," *Dublin Historical Record* 5, no. 1 (September/November 1942), 18; G. D. Williams, *Dublin Charities: A Handbook* (Dublin, 1902), 72.

8. See Maria Luddy, *Women and Philanthropy in Nineteenth-Century Ireland* (Ph.D. Thesis, University College, Cork, 1989), appendix two, for a list of widows' almshouses operating in Ireland in the eighteenth and nineteenth centuries.

9. For Denny's work at the Foundling Hospital, see Joseph Robins, *The Lost Children: A Study of Charity Children in Ireland, 1700–1900* (Dublin, 1980), 23–27.

10. Luddy, *Women and Philanthropy,* passim.

11. Connolly, *Religion and Society,* 3–6.

12. The Christian Brothers were a teaching community of men who took religious vows. They were formed by Edmund Rice in 1802. See M. C. Normoyle, *A Tree is Planted: The Life and Times of Edmund Rice* (Dublin, 1976).

13. Tony Fahey, "Nuns and the Catholic Church in Ireland in the Nineteenth Century," in Mary Cullen (ed), *Girls Don't Do Honors: Irish Women in Education in the 19th and 20th Centuries* (Dublin, 1987), 7. The most important of the new congregations were the Sisters of Charity, founded in 1815 by Mary Aikenhead; the Loreto Sisters formed in 1820 by Frances Ball; the Sisters of Mercy established by Catherine McAuley in 1831; the Sisters of the Holy Faith created by Margaret Aylward in 1867; and the Sisters of St John of God, founded in 1871 by the Bishop of Ferns. The other foundation made by a bishop occurred in 1807, with the establishment of the Brigidine community in the diocese of Kildare and Leighlin. A large number of European communities also made foundations in Ireland in the nineteenth century. See, Caitriona Clear, *Nuns in Nineteenth-Century Ireland* (Dublin, 1987), passim.

14. Clear, *Nuns,* passim.

15. Robins, *Charity Children,* 105.

16. Clear, *Nuns,* 108.

17. Luddy, *Women and Philanthropy,* 163–67.

18. See Sr. M. Pauline, *God Wills It! The Centenary Story of the Sisters of St Louis* (Dublin, 1959); A Loreto Sister, *Joyful Mother of Children: Mother Frances Mary Teresa Ball* (Dublin, 1961); S[arah] A[tkinson], *Mary Aikenhead, Her Life, Her Work and Her Friends* (Dublin, 1878).

19. Sr Angela Bolster, *Catherine McAuley: in Her own Words* (Dublin, 1978), 30.

20. See Luddy, *Philanthropy*, appendix one for details of these charities.

21. Rev. Thomas Burke, "The Attributes of Catholic Charity" in idem., *Ireland's Vindication: Refutation of Froude and Other Lectures, Historical and Religious* (London, n.d.), 21.

22. For a complete listing of subscriptions to various charities see Luddy, *Philanthropy*, 503–10.

23. Bolster, *Catherine McAuley*, 17.

24. See Profession list of the Sisters of Charity Archives of the Sisters of Charity, Milltown, Dublin.

25. MS Annals, 1813–1970, vol. 2, Presentation Convent, Clonmel.

26. Typescript annals, vol. 2, 35–36. Archives of the Sisters of Charity, Milltown, Dublin.

27. *Address to Ladies on Bible Associations* (Dublin, 1825), 4.

28. Luddy, *Philanthropy*, 191–94.

29. Alexander Dallas, *The Story of the Irish Church Missions, Continued to the Year 1869* (London, 1875).

30. Miss Vivienne Smyly, *The Early History of Mrs Smyly's Homes and Schools* (Pamphlet, speech delivered May 29, 1976).

31. Rosa M. Barrett, *Guide to Dublin Charities* (Dublin, 1884), 11–15.

32. First annual report of the Ladies' Association of Charity of St Vincent de Paul, 1852. The report noted "to each district we appointed two members, to find out the children therein going to proselytising schools. We sought to induce the parents to remove them, and send them to Catholic schools. We moreover, kept a register of their names, with notes of the schools to which they were sent. We occasionally visited these schools, in order to see the attendance of the children, and we sought to secure their permanent attendance, by promises of clothes, which we distributed at Christmas and Easter. Our endeavors in this department realized discoveries of a fearfully extended and active organization of the perversion of the children of the Catholic poor."

33. See Jacinta Prunty, "Margaret Aylward 1810–1889," in Mary Cullen and Maria Luddy, eds., *Women, Power and Consciousness in Nineteenth-Century Ireland: Eight Biographical Studies* (Dublin, 1995).

34. See Prunty, "Margaret Aylward."

35. Anon. "The Association for Visiting Hospitals," *Irish Monthly*, 15 (1887): 80.

36. Luddy, *Women and Philanthropy*, 92–94.

37. Cormac O Grada, "Ireland's Great Famine," *ReFresh* (Spring 1993); idem, *The Great Irish Famine* (London, 1989); James S. Donnelly, "The Famine," in W. E. Vaughan, ed., *The New History of Ireland*, vol. 5 (Oxford, 1989), chaps. 12–19.

38. Rev. John Edgar, *Women of the West Helped to Help Themselves* (Belfast, 1849).

39. M. Raphael Consedine P.B.V.M., *Listening Journey: A Study of the Spirit and Ideals of Nano Nagle and the Presentation Sisters* (Victoria, 1983), 233.

40. See Luddy, *Philanthropy*, appendix seven, 497–502.

41. Report for 1852 of the Ladies' Industrial Society for Ireland for the Encouragement of Remunerative Labour Among the Peasantry, 1853, 3.

42. Helen Blackburn, *A Handy Book of Reference for Irishwomen* (London, 1888),

53–57; see also, *Englishwoman's Review,* November 15, 1887, 492–94; July 15, 1889, 311–15; May 15, 1890, 198–201.

43. For other charitable societies organized in the nineteenth century see Luddy, *Philanthropy,* appendix 1, 411–69.

44. See Luddy, *Women and Philanthropy,* 208–12.

45. See articles on Tod and Haslam in Cullen and Luddy, eds., *Women, Power and Consciousness.*

– 2 –

Women and Philanthropy in France
From the Sixteenth to the Twentieth Centuries

EVELYNE DIEBOLT

INTRODUCTION

Is the question of women and philanthropy in France relevant? Is the question distinct from that of French philanthropy in general? Is it specific?

A brief historiographical review of studies undertaken on the subject will show that this is not a question that has been considered up to now by specialists in the area. Nonetheless, it is possible to expose the question if it is removed from the muddied ground of the religious and patriarchal system in which it is hidden. French women's philanthropy is completely dependent on the structures of French society — a powerful Catholic religion and a strong, centralized state considerably delayed the emancipation of women due to the weight of paternalism in French society. We can distinguish several phases to this history.

Before 1901, the history of philanthropy paralleled that of religion. As early as the sixteenth century, participation in philanthropic organizations offered numerous women — not infrequently under the guise of religious life — the possibility of participating in various civic and public activities. This made it possible for them to exercise a certain authority in social, economic, and political life in France. Others acted alone without the slightest hint of permission from on high and with a remarkable sense of social awareness. These women invested their time and energy in the world of charitable or educational works, with a significant degree of influence.

After 1901 philanthropy developed in four stages. First it took advantage of the right to association conferred on civil society by law (1901–20); next, philanthropy would slowly free itself from the church (1920–45), which had been enormously involved in it. From 1945 to 1980, philanthropy became completely institutionalized and was absorbed by the

29

state. Finally, during the past fifteen years it has been reborn in the form of autonomous volunteer groups.

Before considering the question of French women's philanthropic activities, we must also define charity as distinct from philanthropy. In France we do not see a clear-cut cleavage between the two. Charity, which began with the church and continues to play a certain role within religious life, never led to the large secular philanthropic associations and foundations that developed in the English-speaking world. Philanthropy, which may include charitable works but is not limited to them (artistic, civic and other endeavors might be included in the term), remained muddled for many centuries with the good works of the church. This fact in turn limited the possibilities for women to emancipate themselves through philanthropic activities.

Thus, we must ask if we can speak of the emancipation of women in any real sense. The unfortunate answer is that at no time, with the possible exception of 1920–39 — the period when charitable works became secularized — has philanthropy been a sure route to the emancipation of women in France.

THEORETICAL ISSUES

The role of women in French philanthropy has never been studied specifically in any period — medieval, modern or contemporary. To fill in the picture we must look through studies of particular cities,[1] or of a charity[2] (or even conduct a search of works on social economy[3] or the birth of the welfare state[4]). Religious history, whether Catholic or Protestant, allows scant room for women. Individually they are relatively invisible and tend to be submerged in a congregation of nuns or among the women of a parish. However, when an individual stands out from the rest, we can then evaluate her influence.

To find a trace of this philanthropy we must study various good works, charities, benevolent and community societies, patronage, and the humanitarian activities of both nonprofit organizations and of society in all areas.

In *The History of Women in the West,* edited by Michelle Perrot and Georges Duby,[5] not a single chapter deals with the role of women in French philanthropy. This demonstrates how little attention historians have accorded this question. A study of the resistance to research in this field in France would be very instructive concerning what is left unspoken or unwritten in contemporary French society.

British and American historians, even though present in French historiography for their research on French women, have also never specifically dealt with French women in philanthropy.[6] Some very interesting work has been done on American women in philanthropy that is useful to a study on French women in philanthropy.[7]

After what we have just seen, it is easy to conclude that the problem of philanthropy has not attracted a great deal of attention among French historians, nor even among sociologists. This lack of interest stems from the historical conditions in the development of French society related to political and religious institutions. These institutions tend to mask a phenomenon that might appear to be secondary compared to problems that are more clearly in evidence.

In France, the state, beginning with the monarchy under the *Ancien Régime,* was and is strong and centralized. Following the French Revolution this centralizing tendency continued in the form of Jacobinism and was accompanied by a tendency toward state intervention in all areas of the political, economic, social, and cultural life of France. The presence of the state in all its forms, including territorial — support or repression of the poor and indigent, social welfare, health and labor measures, education, subsidies, the growth of bureaucracy and public service at all levels, support for the arts and the maintenance of the arts and of science and all the rest — did not start yesterday. We are not just speaking of a tradition; it is a structural mode and means of functioning that have existed for a thousand years. Certainly there have been highs and lows, progress and failure, but in the last analysis the overall expansion of a centralized state has been irreversible. Territorial and municipal authority was added to central authority. This power is extremely active and strong and is still responsible for the maintaining of all social cohesion and benefits.

Opposing the state, the Catholic Church is an equally, if not more, powerful institution, and more ancient, which would rival the state until the beginning of the twentieth century.[8] The church is extremely rich. Its real property, its economic and commercial power (labor power and capital), are considerable. Its moral weight, the quality of its elite, the vast clergy both in religious orders and in parishes, its international ties and its grasp on society — in brief, its presence on all fronts — make the church a sort of state within a state from which stem a thousand years of conflict with the secular state. The twentieth century saw the triumph of state over church, and in the process the state aggrandized itself even more. The image of the welfare state (in French *l'état providence*) — whether in health, education, the arts, sciences, or whatever — has long been an established, verifiable fact.[9]

Furthermore, France does not change rapidly. It is an old country solidly established on *patriarchal values* and on a hierarchical and inegalitarian society. The social changes and the Industrial Revolution did not engender rapid and colossal fortunes as was the case in the United States. Additionally, France saw the development of a strong labor movement that was well developed and that organized the interests of the working class for a long period of time. However, the emancipation of women developed extremely late, even if here and there we see numerous and valuable exceptions. France has shown itself to be very conservative regarding the relationship of the sexes.[10]

Confronted with such an image of a relatively enclosed society, it is legitimate to ask what the place of philanthropy is and in particular that of women involved in philanthropic works. This place appears *a priori* so tenuous that the question has not even attracted the attention of the specialists.

In reality women have a role of philanthropy but in *specifically French forms* very different from those found in English-speaking countries. Even today in the church, young women entering a religious order often do so with a dowry and not infrequently those who helped found an order leave their goods to that order. The practice of charity was considered by the rich to be a social duty, as well as good for the soul. They could not forbid their daughters such a practice, nor could they refuse money to the church. The community of religious orders for women in France covered the entire territory and undertook all varieties of social and charitable works. Along with the municipalities, the religious orders were the pivot point of a system of social assistance.

These female religious orders sought their vocations from all walks of life. Numerous young women from all social levels entered religious life. They did not all arrive with empty hands. Young women from the working classes were much sought after because they constituted a free labor pool to do one's superior's bidding. To this we must add the army of women of good works who functioned through the local parish church.

This invisible, philanthropic role of Catholic women — and French Protestants, although smaller in number than the Catholics — forms the armature of French feminine philanthropy. This philanthropic aspect has been cleverly hidden in the official religious history that, on this point, has never been able to distance itself from ecclesiastical discourse.[11]

An evaluation of the economic importance of this sector has never been undertaken. It compares with the importance of domestic work and the underground economy of modern societies for which we do not possess any viable studies.

Even more difficult to evaluate is the sociopolitical part played by female philanthropy in the municipalities. It was the nobility and local bourgeoisie who established a network of municipal institutions through their personal financial gifts. Not only were their personal fortunes involved, but those of the mothers, wives, and daughters of the family as well. Lay women, who did volunteer work in these municipal institutions were found side by side with the nuns who did most of the work.

The relationship between the Catholic Church and the state is complex, interwoven, and full of conflicts.[12] The monarchy, ever short of funds, coveted the wealth of the church.[13] An agreement was reached, by which the church would exercise public functions, in particular care of the poor and the sick. Here, above all, we find women playing a primary role and enjoying a real but "parallel power"[14] due in part to their sheer numbers. The age-old struggle between church and state resulted in a conflict which led to two major laws at the end of the nineteenth century. The law of July 1, 1901, placed religious congregations under the control of the state. Under threat of dissolution, they had to apply for authorization to exist. Additionally, this law gave the right to any private citizen to form a legal association with a fixed purpose, on the condition the group so formed be a nonprofit organization.[15] Finally, under the Third Republic, the law of December 5, 1905 — called the Separation of Church and State — guaranteed freedom of religion to all citizens, but did not officially sanction any particular belief.[16]

The role of women was revolutionized by this new legal form of philanthropy in France, which favored the secularization of society and the creation of nonprofit organizations. The ability to create such organizations would make it possible for women to progressively emancipate themselves from both the tutelage of the church and from male dominance, even though women officially remained legally and financially dependent on men. Women now had a space of their own where they could exercise their independence and gain real working experience. We now find women investing themselves almost exclusively in the area of social philanthropy.[17]

The rise to power of women in philanthropy was a long development. At the beginning of the rise of nonprofit organizations, women like everyone else had to find means of support. Inevitably they turned toward the Catholic Church, whose power was still enormous. Instead of intervening directly in the affairs of nonprofit organizations, the church assumed the role of support provider. We find the same phenomenon among the Protestant churches. Not wishing to remain prisoners of religious support, the heads of nonprofit organizations turned toward the state, which became the target of all their demands — for example, for the recognition of their public usefulness. They also put pressure on government to obtain new legislation. The state responded by promulgating a certain number of laws (social insurance, family allocations, and professionalization of the health and social sectors). Strengthened by this new legislation, French women could emancipate themselves from supporting institutions such as the church. This emancipation, however, was not linear. It was full of ideological hesitations, advances and retreats, and internal struggles.

After a few decades, the nonprofit movement, which had grown in size and stature, was completely secularized and had moved progressively closer to the state. Nearly entirely funded by the state, charity was institutionalized to the point of becoming a para-governmental structure. This evolution was aided by the professionalization of the health professions. Philanthropy itself was diluted by the establishment of medical and other professional schools, of diplomas, of well-defined professional limits and responsibilities. Female philanthropy in the first half of the twentieth century ran the risk of loosing its importance as it grew ever closer to the state, even as it emancipated itself from the church. Simultaneously, new social needs developed — brought about by immigration, pandemics, and so on. These needs immediately the willing service of women who returned to the old pattern of unrecognized voluntarism.

The theoretical framework of female philanthropy in France evolved out of the Catholic Church (and the Protestant churches) toward state intervention by way of nonprofit organizations.

FRENCH WOMEN AND PHILANTHROPY BEFORE 1901

From the Sixteenth Century to the End of the Eighteenth Century

Between the sixteenth and the end of the eighteenth centuries, the essential question is that of the relationship of women to money. As a matter of fact, they had no control over either their fortunes or their revenues. They were always under the financial guardianship of men, father, and husband. Young girls were free to dispose of their dowry if they entered a religious order. When they married, it was the man who managed their fortune. Widows had more freedom. They could choose between the convent and a secular life in which they at last had control of their patrimony. Unmarried women remained under patriarchal tutelage within the bosom of the family. Stemming from the nobility or the bourgeoisie, women generally preferred to invest their resources in family estates, usually rural, where the ancestral château or principal residence was to be found. Thus they contributed to the efforts of their ancestors.[18]

In the absence of a connection to some form of public financial philanthropy, these women became involved in private charitable activities which, although hard to ascertain and difficult to quantify, absorbed a large part of their energy. The ties between the nobility and the bourgeoisie with the peasants who toiled on their lands had always been very strong; consequently, these women often cared for the population that lived on their estates. For them, such charity was infinitely superior to what might have involved selling lands to invest in discernible and expensive philanthropic enterprises. Such a decision would have been contrary to the mentality, traditions, and family interests in France.[19]

It seems that French women in general accepted this way of doing things and for the most part did not demand the autonomy and freedom to engage in monetary transfers to charitable institutions or educational or cultural endeavors. However, a minority of women proved an exception to the rule, particularly in arts and letters, and especially regarding charitable activities.

In the former case, only the queen of France or a member of the royal family, or at the very least a descendent of a very distinguished lineage, could hope to have musicians, painters, architects, or men of letters in her entourage (Marguerite de Navarre, la "reine Margot," Catherine de Médicis). The royal mistresses — Madame de Maintenon (mistress of Louis XIV), Madame de Pompadour (mistress of Louis XV) — played a preponderant role in the world of arts and letters. However, those who had benefited from their generosity fled when they fell into disfavor. In any case, their influence was fluctuating since it was for all intents and purposes linked to their masculine protector. Beautiful and intelligent, they attracted the clever and the talented in their salons and helped their protégés to obtain success. Frequenting their company was an obligatory rite of passage for those who wished to arrive. Some among these women dedicated their time and money to support a writer, a musician, or a poet — for example, in the eighteenth century, Madame du Chatelet and Voltaire, Madame Dupin and Jean-Jacques Rousseau.

Madame de Maintenon had the novel idea of educating the poor daughters of the nobility. In 1686 she opened a boarding school at Saint Cyr. She wanted the teaching done by secular ladies and not by nuns. Despite all her power, she was forced to give in to pressure, and in 1692, Saint Cyr became a convent school like the others. Madame de Maintenon did manage to retain a certain spirit favorable to its boarders. The nuns had to adapt to the needs of the children, contrary to other establishments where the pupils had to adapt to convent life. This experiment remained isolated, but the school still exists today.

Regarding charitable activities, the situation is more complex. The monarchial state delegated (or left) to the Catholic Church the mission of assisting the poor, caring for the sick, and educating the youth. However, the state firmly intended to oversee and even to reorient church-led activities in light of its own objectives and preoccupations of the moment. The state as well as the municipalities did not hesitate to intervene. Catholic activities were sometimes supported, sometimes hindered or forbidden, in particular regarding education. Dialogue was continuous, but we find as well confrontation and power struggles. In their beginnings, both private and public assistance were tightly interwoven. Thus assistance was conceived under the tutelage of two powers, church and state.[20]

Charitable works led to the mobilization of most of the women who became involved in philanthropy in France during this period. These women worked within a religious, monastic, or secular framework. Their activities were almost always controlled by the Catholic Church. They were not autonomous, although there were some notable exceptions, which are cited below. Such activities were restricted not only by monarchical authority and the police, but also by municipal administrators as they assumed increasing responsibility for public assistance.

The Convent Structure

Regarding female philanthropy within the church, a large contingent of both noble and bourgeois women joined the regular orders.[21] This trend extended in the nineteenth century to the middle and working classes.

Women of the nobility or the bourgeoisie brought their dowries. Widows brought with them their revenues and their properties.[22] From the sixteenth century on, the obligation to bring a dowry, unknown at the beginning of monarchism, began to be widespread at the moment when the endowments furnished by the founders no longer sufficed to maintain religious communities. The custom of the dowry, specific to feminine orders, shows very well that the religious profession took marriage as its model, since woman was meant to be maintained while man was meant to live from his labor. Nuns also frequently exercised a paid activity. It had become a vital necessity for religious communities in financial difficulties to have this supplementary source of revenue. In order for the convents to survive, they had to undertake works of public interest, such as care for the sick, education for girls, and asylums for women.

These institutions had to adapt to all situations, wars, famines, natural disasters, and epidemics. These women devoted time not given to prayer to the management, administration, and functioning of these institutions. They worked ceaselessly for centuries to assure these services within the framework of very different religious orders.

Nuns played an important role in educating and proselytizing young girls. They educated them while trying to convert young Protestants following the revocation of the Edict of Nantes in 1685. The most important order, the Ursulines, expanded rapidly.[23] Charity and necessity were intertwined. To open a free school for poor children, it was also necessary to create a boarding school for the daughters of the wealthy.

The example of Madame Louise de Marillac is extremely interesting, although of another nature. In 1633, aided by Saint Vincent de Paul, she founded the Daughters of Charity and became the mother superior of the order.[24] This is an example of an individual initiative within the framework of the church. The founder wrote the rules of life for this community, which expanded rapidly and developed a real competence in caring for the ill. It was with this congregation that Florence Nightingale would choose to complete her training before her expedition in Crimea. The nursing orders were not always as efficient as this one, but they constituted a solid structure that crossed the entire country.

Women were attracted to this kind of convent structure to freely participate in charitable and educational ventures that they, themselves, organized and controlled. We have a good example thanks to the work of Yvonne Turin.[25] Reading local archives in Auvergne, Velay, Lyonnais, and the center of France, she uncovered an exemplary phenomenon of female philanthropy from the beginning of the eighteenth century to the middle of the nineteenth century. Here we see the birth of female lay communities which were transformed into religious communities.[26] In the beginning of the eighteenth century, unmarried peasant women living in the same village formed groups of three or four that would establish a civil contract before a notary. These contracts regulated their communal life, stipulated the goods of each one, the mutual aid for which they were responsible, and what tied them together: common work, opening a school, a pharmacy, a hospice, or a hospital for the village. In these contracts they kept their own property but left it to one another upon their death. Often they could leave the community and retrieve their goods. They lived on premises that they bought and kept this property under their own name to prevent co-option by religious bodies. These small female communities, which formed around tasks like silk- or lace-making, as well as services for the community that harbored them, were autonomous associations stemming from the initiative of women, among women, and for women. They lived on the financial resources they procured: dowries which produced investment income; gifts; part-time work that complemented local donations (for example in exchange for instruction or nursing); loans to acquire or enlarge property.[27]

Numerous unmarried women were involved in similar activities, often acting out of a desire to create a structure for independent lives of their own. However, to do so they needed to gain the approval of the parish priest, if not the mayor, to confirm their independence as unmarried women. Most attached themselves to religious congregations, but some actively sought to maintain their autonomy. These groups lived by doing outside work, and they tried to improve their situation by seeking support from the village priest and the mayor, two independent forces that helped one another on a parish level in the face of two superior authorities — the religious congregation and the bishop of the diocese.[28]

These female entrepreneurs displayed a great deal of freedom of action, drawing opportunities for promotion, for self-affirmation, and even leadership from their congregations, while serving in areas that touched upon society as a whole, and not just religious life.

The Parish Structure

Women of all ages who did not join religious orders devoted their time to good works within the limitations of their parish. This sort of volunteer work was an integral part of the social obligations of women. Catholic discourse assigned a minor social role to women. It is she who cares for, consoles, and heals. She dedicates herself in total abnegation and gives her time and her person to the works of the parish.

The founder's will was not always respected however. For example, Anne de Tauzia donated 90,000 livres in 1624 to a religious order to create a general hospital in Bordeaux. Despite the dispositions in the founder's will in favor of a female religious order, the nobility and bourgeoisie of the city of Bordeaux claimed the responsibility for managing the hospital.[29]

The revocation of the Edict of Nantes in 1685 forbade the Protestant religion, and it was not until the French Revolution of 1789 that Protestants were recognized as a social group. Consequently, only then could a Protestant philanthropy develop. The most classical example of Protestant charity in the post-revolutionary period is Madame Necker who, with the consent of her husband, a banker and minister of the former king Louis XVI, founded a hospital in Paris which still bears her name.

When the French monarchy decided to open and finance institutions such as *les Invalides* (1670) to recompense its good and loyal servants of the state and to shelter, nourish, and care for these brave soldiers wounded in the service of the king, the monarchy was fulfilling a function that could have been undertaken by women philanthropists. Municipalities also restrained private philanthropy when they exercised their police functions in the poor quarters — for example, efforts by the police to clean up the *Cour des Miracles* in Paris in 1656 were accompanied by a policy of enclosure of the poor.

The case of the *Société de Charité Maternelle* (1774) is an exception.[30] It was an organization composed of those in high society, the brainchild of Madame Fougeret. This organization was independent of the church.

Its goal was to aid legitimate children of the poor to prevent their being abandoned. The society was chartered and placed under the patronage of Queen Marie-Antoinette and of the Princess de Lamballe. It was under the guardianship of the highest ranking women of the kingdom and lived off donations, which did not exclude the help of municipal subsidies. These subsidies remained secondary, however. Above all, this was a private charity.

THE NINETEENTH CENTURY

The revolutionary upheaval of 1789 shook all French cities and villages, even the most backward. The revolutionary period did not cause a rupture with the past regarding philanthropy, neither in terms of attitude nor behavior. Following the French Revolution, there is a multiplication of municipal public intervention. The poor and the sick were often lumped together both in theory and in practice, and large French cities began to be equipped with institutions for them. In Paris, the *Assistance Publique* hospitals were founded in 1848. We find *Hospices Civils* in Lyon and Marseille.

Female philanthropy functioned within the same religious framework as before. Although women's religious communities were forced to disperse in 1789, they were reconstituted after 1814. With the industrialization of France, the social structure changed. New forms of female philanthropy appeared, and perverse side effects resulted, as we see below in the example of "providences."

Financing of any philanthropic activity was most often mixed between private and public sources. In the mind of the women donors, no antagonism existed between the religious sector and the public municipal sector. We see this in the wills of Protestants who sometimes endowed as sole legatee the Consistory of the Reformed Church, and other times the municipalities, to found hospitals.[31] In any case, the state kept an eye on such transactions since government authorization was necessary, under the ordinance of August 2, 1817, for any establishment, public or private, to receive a grant or a legacy.

With the changes brought by the industrial revolution in the nineteenth century, French women from the poorer classes went to work in factories "before the machine," as unskilled laborers. Their salaries were 50 percent lower than those of men, and the legal duration of their workday was still eleven hours in 1892. At the turn of the century, more than 30 percent of the women between the ages of fifteen and sixty-five were active in the work force. The organization of the female work force was one objective of women's philanthropy, best illustrated by the example of the so-called "providences" — that is, orphanages, workhouses, and schools. French working-class women had little time and few resources to become involved in either giving or voluntarism. On the contrary, they were themselves the object of philanthropic and social efforts because they constituted a high risk group in terms of health and childbearing.[32] Nevertheless, they acted philanthropically whenever they could (visiting prisoners, for example).

The perverse side effects of philanthropy are most apparent in the organization and surveillance of female work by the female congregations. Nuns took children into "providences."[33] These communities lived off of donations and the earnings of the children and young women they sheltered, who often worked in silk in competition with the silk workers, the "canuts." During the revolution of 1848, in both Lyon and Saint Etienne, all the providences were sacked by silk workers. There was no violence against individuals, but the tools of the trade were destroyed. Few of the providences were rebuilt.

Women who were acting in these associations voluntarily subordinated their personal needs, often working to the point of exhaustion in order to construct schools or hospitals. It was this labor that provided their sustenance and gave the satisfaction of serving the present to prepare for the future. Obviously, in this context, the notion of a just salary did not exist, for these women wanted only simple nourishment and lodging for themselves and wished any profits from their labor be used to continue and even expand their philanthropic efforts. Consequently, in such cases, philanthropic intervention could lead to injustice.

Stemming from very modest origins, lay workers depended on no one but themselves and on the generosity they solicited through collections to finance their charitable works. Working-class women visited prisons. From 1800 to 1814 there were some fifty such prison visitors in Lyon. At first they visited women's prisons exclusively, adding male correctional facilities after 1811, cleaning cells and distributing soup (four thousand bowls of soup a day in Lyon in 1811).[34]

In 1814, Napoléon I was defeated and exiled, and King Louis XVIII took power. These political events disorganized the fragile women's movements. One of the prison visitors, Louise Juliand, thought to join a religious congregation to assure the continuity of prison visits. The archbishop directed her toward the Congregation of Saint Joseph. We see clearly here how difficult it was for these women to maintain important work in a purely lay framework since the ecclesiastical structure provided a support that sheltered them from the instability of changing circumstances. The church functioned as a support for initiatives that it had not solicited. The case of working women visiting prisons is rarely acknowledged and in any case seems to have died out before 1840. Thus in the long run, it was difficult for working-class women to participate in charitable activities.

A similar case occurred in 1838 when women from the bourgeoisie founded an institution to help women prisoners, inspired by the British model of the Society of English Ladies United for the Extension of Prisoners Reform, founded by Elisabeth Fry. The French institution was called the *œuvre des dames de Saint-Lazare*. Sustained by the Protestant churches, it became very important in the nineteenth century.

In France, the extreme poverty of the working class opened up numerous debates on how to create mutual aid societies, which would provide genuine compensations and benefits in case of work-related accidents, sickness, or death. Workers wanted to organize their own support and formed groups according to their political affinities, cooperatives, unions, or insurance associations, from which women were practically excluded, either as members or militants. In 1855, 345,128 workers joined mutual aid societies, but only 41,736 women workers joined them. From the worker's point of view at this time, a woman's place was in the home, and working women were simply competitors who "stole work." Once men took over class interests, a potential field of women's philanthropy was removed.

Bourgeois women's philanthropy in the nineteenth century was deemed moralizing and conformist in character, and caricatured in the "lady of good works."[35] Nonetheless, this view was criticized by some of its participants in the name of social Christianity. The working-class movement loathed bourgeois philanthropy and preferred to emphasize working-class solidarity in order to prevent the bourgeoisie from interfering in their affairs. We see the tenuous transformation of a social Christianity toward Christian socialism.[36] The "ladies of good works" were becoming very uncomfortable in their situation as their detractors grew in number.

Yet such criticisms did not discourage them. Indeed, bourgeois women's philanthropy in the nineteenth century showed great vigor and a good deal of initiative. It was responsible for creating charities in two new areas, infancy (with shelter rooms) and day-care centers. In 1826, together with her friends the Marquise de Pastoret and Madame Delessert, the Baroness Emilie Mallet, daughter of the wealthy industrialist Oberkampf and spouse of banker Mallet, founded a committee for shelter rooms, to take care of children between the ages of two and seven. The committee founded by Baronnes Mallet operated under the patronage of the curate for foreign missions. In 1837, these shelter rooms were placed under the responsibility of the Ministry of Public Instruction, but the organizers and inspectors were still women, and the care of the children was in the hands of paid female personnel.[37] In 1847, there were fifteen hundred such rooms in all of France, which sheltered a hundred thousand children a day. Finding that these rooms were very useful in freeing female workers from their maternal duties so that they could work in the growing industry, public authority thus transformed a charity initially privately created by a woman into an official institution. In this way, shelter rooms were transferred from the tutelage of female philanthropists.[38]

Day-care centers were opened around 1845. Sometimes they were founded by women, as in the case of Corbeil which was created in 1847 at the initiative of Queen Amélie, the wife of King Louis-Philippe, together with five bourgeois women. Sometimes they were initiated by a majority of men, such as that in Versailles in 1847. These centers opened early in the day and closed late at night so that female workers could drop their legitimate children there — illegitimate children were rarely accepted. Women who managed these institutions fought malnutrition rickets in children and tried to moralize women workers by encouraging them to legalize their relationships through marriage. The status of these creches varied — they became municipal in Paris, for example, whereas in the provinces they remained at the heart of parish philanthropy.

Around 1880, an originally English Protestant organization, the Salvation Army, took root in Catholic France under the influence of an evangelical renewal. The Salvation Army provided an important shelter for the impoverished. Women gave funds to the Salvation Army. For example, as late as 1930 the barge "Louise-Catherine," named after its generous donor, was moored on the Seine to welcome the homeless. The most generous benefactress was the Princesse de Polignac, the American Winnaretta Singer, widow of Prince Edmond de Polignac. In 1929, she hired a young architect, Le Corbusier, as the designer of the *Cité du Refuge,* which is today a historic monument and still the largest Salvation Army center in France.[39]

A tableau of female philanthropy from the sixteenth century to the end of the nineteenth century reveals its strength and its importance in the formation of the whole country. If we try to characterize the philanthropic strategies used by French women,[40] it appears that their efforts were mainly assimilationist: "women working within male-controlled institutions" in the framework of the Catholic and Protestant churches up to the separation of church and state in 1905. It is because of this religious framework that philanthropic institutions were able to survive to this date. Inside these assimilationist structures, two distinct strategies emerge simultaneously: individualism,[41] the most striking examples of which are Madame de Maintenon and Louise de Marillac;

and separatism, "women working together with other women to develop nonprofit organizations" — e.g., the convents.[42]

The Secularization of Female Philanthropy

Beginning in the mid-nineteenth century, education for girls was established in each municipality outside of the convent. Sisters or lay women taught. These municipal schools were inexpensive and enrolled many young girls after 1850. The access of girls to education was now open and raised the hopes of many women.

From 1850 on, the women referred to as "the first to breech the walls of the socially forbidden," refused the roles and the tasks to which they had been delegated and confronted the taboos. They demonstrated their prowess in a series of successes: Julie Daubié, the first French woman to receive a baccalaureate degree (secondary school) in 1861, was also the first to be awarded the degree of *Licence* (university) in literature in 1871; the first French woman doctor, Doctor Brès, born Gibelin, obtained her diploma in medicine in 1875; the first French woman lawyer, Jeanne Chauvin, followed in 1900. Others were to follow.[43] Among their company we find French women who do not correspond at all to the classic model of the charitable lady who cares for the poor out of piety. These women believed that to remedy poverty one must call on the technical and financial resources of the state. They were ready to exploit the new possibilities which French legislation offered them in the law of 1901, concerning associations which had been opposed by most French politicians until that time.

This legislation provided for a contract under private law which was easy to establish. To establish an association, it was sufficient to have at least three individuals who stated their aims and objectives at their departmental Préfecture of Police. Organizations thus created were for the self-development of citizens, who could express their opinions and common beliefs in them. Even though women were not yet fully considered citizens — they did not have the right to vote and on several legal points were considered as minors — they were not excluded under the law of 1901. They would use this law to rise to full citizenship and create a political linkage between women and the state.[44] The law of 1901 would literally revolutionize the relationship between French women and social philanthropy.

WOMEN AND PHILANTHROPY AFTER 1901

Following 1901, the type of philanthropy in which we find women active in France is almost exclusively concerned with social endeavors and good works, since French women still could not dispose freely of their own money. Thus we only rarely find French women as charitable donors or patronesses of the arts. The only field of action left to them that required little or no money, at least initially, was social action. Typically, they formed associations under the law of 1901 that fixed the limits of French women's philanthropy to the present, although it evolved considerably through the twentieth century. The French context implied a constant jockeying for position by women philanthropists between those two key institutions, the church (both Catholic and Protestant churches) and the state.

Traditional Catholic philanthropy, however, continued to exist and to occupy a dominant place in female social philanthropy. Married women from the leisured classes were free to dedicate themselves to good works within their parish. It was, however, the clergy who were responsible, at least in principle, for the work of the parish, while women took care of the menial tasks. Women from the working classes, on the other hand, labored long hours for a pittance in order to meet their daily needs. As of 1890, each large city in France published an annual directory of charitable organizations, some of which were covered by the law of 1901, and none of which were directed by women. The patriarchal hierarchy of the Catholic Church oversaw this type of philanthropy. Convents, themselves under the patriarchal control of the church, no longer grew as rapidly in the twentieth century as they had in the nineteenth, but they did continue to seek young women with a calling to join their ranks. This recruiting slowed considerably during the twentieth century, although convents did conserve their properties and financial goods and continued to fulfill certain philanthropic functions in the social domain. They represented a conservative function on which the church still relies to this day to defend its notion of charity and good works.

Simultaneously, in four different stages, an independent feminine minority in philanthropic works would develop in the health and social services. These women made use of the possibilities inherent in the law of 1901, which did not exclude women from the right of free association. Under the law of 1901 people gained the right to form common interest groups regardless of class or sex.

Phase One: The Renovation of 1900–1920

The legal status of women was not changed by the law of 1901. Wives continued to be financially dependent on their husbands. The case was not the same for unmarried women or widows, both of whom were freer to manage their own goods and to participate as they wished in organizations and associations. The main difference from the former period is that women were more and more determined not to let themselves be excluded from social and political life.

In any case, French society was still so impregnated by Catholicism (and Protestantism) that even the strongest female figures were not able to rid themselves of its influence.[45] Those who, in a genuine spirit of reform, attempted to found organizations that broke away from traditional patterns were forced to rely on the religious structure. The religious establishment furnished them with premises, the support of ecclesiastical personnel, and connections with generous benefactors (that is to say the network of political connections of the church). Doctrinal Catholicism valued spinsterhood and chastity for women. This is why, at the beginning of the century, a new generation of French women involved in social philanthropic organizations had two reasons not to get married: their legal status on the one hand, and their obedience to the precepts of the Catholic Church on the other hand.[46]

Although they were pious believers, these women were not attracted by convents.[47] They were modest about their religious convictions and extremely discrete about their religious practice. They belonged to third orders. Third orders are not religious congregations, but organizations composed of lay people and secular clergy who, to the extent possible, follow the rule of an order — Franciscan, Dominican, Carmelite, for example — while remaining in the world. It should be noted that the organizations founded and directed by women were legally independent of the church.

The women most representative of this tendency were: Léonie Chaptal,[48] who founded numerous philanthropic societies; Andrée Butillard and Aimée Novo,[49] who headed organizations taking care of Catholic women workers; Marie-Jeanne Bassot and Mathilde Giraud, who founded the *Résidence Sociale de Levallois-Perret,* the first French "settlement house."[50] In 1914, the Marquise de Ganay, Marie Diemer, and others created the *Association des Infirmières Visiteuses de France,* an organization that led large-scale initiatives against tuberculosis and infant mortality.[51] We find five women at the origins of the *Ecole des Surintendantes d'Usine* (f. 1917), whose goal was to train women to keep watch on female factory workers in order to help improve their lives generally and their hygiene and their working conditions in particular.[52] These women were often supported and encouraged, morally and materially, by a few members of the clergy well-known for their social convictions.

Quite often, the latter provided these new organizations with working space and equipment. The organizations usually began operation on a small scale and at low cost (what funds there were coming from the founders) and were staffed by volunteer women. However, as the organizations began to develop, they required ever more important sources of money. The women in charge thus found financial support among fathers, brothers, uncles or husbands of their friends, disciples, or followers, who were convinced of the merit of the projects.

Given the scarcity of money available, and aware that they fulfilled an indispensable social role with a new competence and efficiency, these organizations and their founders began to think: first, that their work could be paid and, second, that their professional qualifications could be recognized through specific training programs and diplomas. This would indeed change the nature of philanthropy. In the beginning, the services they offered — i.e., nursing, instruction — were paid for at ridiculously low prices by the private or municipal institutions that employed them. Only more social recognition followed by more substantial wages could allow them to lead a decent life and make themselves heard. It was the battle they fought for professionalization.

They were in conflict with the Catholic hierarchy about possibilities for training, professional qualification, and salary. Only a minority of persons within the church supported the growing organizational network, or were even interested in the novelty of its ideas. The forces that opposed it, including numerous women, regrouped in a female professional Catholic organization, the *Union Catholique du personnel des Services de Santé* (UCSS), very much influenced by the traditional notion of Christian charity developed in women's religious congregations and based on volunteer work, piety, humility, charity, and obedience.[53] As a matter of fact, the church intended to keep the reins of social philanthropy in its hands through the sisters of the healing orders, although this would not be such an easy task.

Indeed, in addition to the revolution led by Catholic women who did not hesitate to create and head their own associations, Protestant women constituted a force to be reckoned with. Although they only represented 2 percent of the French population in 1900, Protestants were very active in the field of social philanthropy.[54] Starting with the French Revolution, they had set up an important network of aid and solidarity made up of orphanages, hospitals, nursing homes, and parochial aid.

In the same way as Catholic women, French Protestant women seized the opportunities opened up by the law of 1901. Their legal status was the same as that of Catholics. They thought that there was an incompatibility between the position of a housewife and that of a woman philanthropist; therefore, they opted not to marry.

Let us now discuss the main Protestant organizations and their innovative founders. Around 1900, one of the first women doctors in medicine, Dr. Anna Hamilton, taking her model from the teaching hospital introduced by Florence Nightingale, reformed a charity founded in 1863, the *Maison de Santé Protestante de Bordeaux*.[55] In Paris, the widow of a banker, Madame Alphen-Salvador, financed the *Association d'Aide aux Malades*. Many Protestant women worked with Reverend Doumergue to create the *Association Foi et Vie*, which opened the *Ecole Pratique de Service Social de Paris*, one of the first professional training centers in the social field.

The Protestant churches lent moral support to these projects and helped them start up through modest material donations. French Protestant women had to look for the funds that would allow them to continue in Protestant circles. Faced with the deficiencies of French Protestant philanthropists, these women turned toward American philanthropists, who responded in various ways. American nurses thus financed Dr. Hamilton and the Bordeaux Protestant nursing home. Anne Morgan, the daughter of John Pierpont Morgan, and her American friends financed the *Association d'Aide aux Malades*, which became, thanks to American money, the *Institut de Service Social de Montrouge*. Miss Curtis from the American Red Cross found American funds for the Reverend Doumergue's organizations. American financial intervention was crucial for the survival of these institutions during the interwar period.[56] Neither the French philanthropists, nor the church, nor municipal or state authorities were prepared to come to the aid of these associations in a decisive way. Without the aid of American philanthropy, these associations would have died out and with them the hope for any professionalization for this sector.

These Protestant institutions constituted a focal point of opposition to charity as conceived by the Catholic Church. As early as 1901, they were strongly influenced by American social philanthropy. They became places where American techniques and work methods, formerly ignored in France, were introduced and diffused (through case work, teaching hospitals and superintendents).[57] The American women who arrived in France during World War I were surprised and pleased to find that the Protestant institutions provided an organizational structure open to their approach.

Paradoxically, Catholic philanthropists were not hostile to the Protestant model. On the contrary, they sought an alliance with the Protestants in order to obtain recognition for the technical value and visibility of their social work that was denied to them by the church.[58] In doing so, there was a tendency to become laicized and to become closer to those who, within the state, worked for a true health and social policy.[59] This rapprochement, scarcely visible in the first phase, would blossom during the interwar period. Thus it is here that we see the first move from philanthropy under religious control to state-controlled philanthropy.

Phase Two: The Professionalization of 1920–45

During the following period, 1920–45, female philanthropic societies changed in nature to become professional.[60] Indeed, with some exceptions, the women did not possess fortunes; in order for their organizations to survive, they were obliged to compete in the wage market. In order to do this, they had to demand payment for part of their services. They raised funds in the form of dues by the users, income paid for by worker or employer contributions and managed by mutual fund groups, or municipal subsidies, gifts, and private legacies. These salaried women got married and provided for their families, but their salary was too low for them to be able to make financial contributions. Some among them, usually those who remained unmarried, were volunteers either for their association or for other associations.

One notable exception to the preceding picture is that of Olga Spitzer who had no particular religious affiliation, but who relied on the support of the Protestant women trained by Reverend Doumergue. Her husband, a banker, placed at her disposal vast sums of money, millions of francs, which she used to finance an organization, the *Service Social de l'Enfance en Danger Moral*. This society provided social workers to assist children's judges, whose tasks included finding placement and care for youth in order to provide an alternative to the children's incarceration. Arthur Spitzer's fortune fed this service from 1923 to 1939.[61] It was copied by every judge for youth in every French city and constituted a solid network of associations, originally funded by private money and then, little by little, by the Ministry of Justice. Today, all of these private associations established under the law of 1901 are entirely funded by the Ministry of Justice.

The pioneers of the first period were still active, although aging: Anna Hamilton, Marie-Jeanne Bassot, Léonie Chaptal. They inspired others, whose names are less well known, to follow their example: Juliette Delagrange, factory superintendent and director (from 1926 on) of the Nursing Office of the Ministry of Health; Jeanne de Joannis, director of the *Institut de Service Social de Montrouge;* Madeleine Hardouin, factory superintendent, founder and director of the social service of the family welfare subsidies for the Paris region. As we can see, these women were not only in charge of organizations that we can still qualify as philanthropic to the extent that they were partly supported by private gifts (45 percent private gifts and 9 percent subsidies for the *Résidence Sociale de Levallois-Perret* in 1936), but they also accepted positions as administrators and managers at the municipal, regional, or national level. Increasingly, they became internationally recognized. Their work can still be considered philanthropy since, when paid, their salaries were minimal and did not correspond either to their professional qualifications or to the time spent on the job. They generally worked round the clock, seven days a week, and their salaries were just enough to support ascetic poverty.

The need for health care and support for war widows and orphans, together with the great social scourges of the time — syphilis, tuberculosis, infant mortality, professional illnesses such as black lung disease, alcoholism, and unsanitary housing — all created an urgent social need, which was met by an explosion of organizations founded on the pioneer model, which became a common phenomenon. Let us take the example of the *Résidence Sociale de Levallois-Perret,* the first French settlement house, founded in 1909. In 1922, there were fifty-eight such centers throughout France and in 1932, their numbers had grown to 140.[62]

The pioneers, philanthropists from the beginning, responded conscientiously to the invitation by the members of the newly founded French Ministry of Health (1920) to participate in national governmental committees in charge of drafting the professional regulations in health and welfare. The debate lasted years. Conservative Catholics launched an offensive that prevented the passing of a law by the National Assembly that would make it obligatory to have a diploma to practice in health or social welfare professions. Training, qualifications, and professionalization would be imposed by the state at a later period. Women favored the law, relieved to see that in the long run it would result in the opening of a specifically female field of endeavor. It was also expected to bring about an end to spinsterhood and volunteer work. This trend was in accordance with the reality of French circumstances. Indeed, in France, female labor was always important. It was absolutely necessary to the family economy, given the modest male salaries (in 1921, married women made up 49 percent of the female work force; in 1936, they comprised 55 percent).[63] Between the wars, health and social services constituted a steady source of female employment.

During the period 1920–39, French women philanthropists indicated a propensity to ally themselves with politicians who were favorable to the state reform policy. The Third Republic (1870–1939) was a period during which reformers and advocates of a massive state intervention in social welfare progressively succeeded, not without internal struggles, in establishing a legislative state that organized social security. This can be seen in the law of 1928, providing for the partial reimbursement of medical care for workers, and the law of 1932, stipulating that family allowances be paid to the head of households based on the number of children and placing social services at the disposition of family members.[64]

This type of centralized and compulsory system was not favorable to the development of private philanthropy. French philanthropists who had escaped the conservative Catholic hierarchy were now absorbed into the bureaucratic cogs of the state. They had to give up part of their pre-rogatives and freedom of decision to public authority. Thus, in France, for some women philanthropy was a means of moving from the private sphere to the public, even though they had neither the right to vote, nor legal equality with men. These women opened up a specifically feminine field, that of social work.[65] The problem was that with time the power of women in this area was entirely taken over by men.

In the interwar period, social philanthropy had essentially taken up the entire expanse of female philanthropy. This being said, we can evoke a few philanthropists, coming from diverse social milieus, exceptional cases who strayed from the beaten path.

Suzanne Deutsche de la Meurthe, unmarried daughter of the bour-geois industrialist, inherited her father's fortune in 1919. Sharing her father's passion for aviation, she created a racing competition with a cup bearing the family name and founded the tourism section of the French flying club. At her château at Boullains, she installed a "home for wings" to receive civil pilots.[66]

Marguerite Durand, a feminist journalist, donated her archives on the history of women, her personal library, and several objects to the city of Paris. In 1932, a library bearing her name was opened to the public, where it is possible to consult the materials she donated to the city. These archives specializing in women (23,000 volumes) were originally installed in the Fifth Arrondissement's City Hall, located in front of the Panthéon, a sanctuary reserved for great men. The library subsequently moved in 1989.[67] Marie-Louise Bouglé, a simple employee with meager resources also collected important archives concerning women, which can be found at the *Bibliothèque Historique de la Ville de Paris*.

These disinterested gestures had no economic importance, but on the other hand, their ideological impact was very important, especially these last two which helped conserve the memory of French women.

Louise Cognac-Jay and her husband made their fortune founding the department store "La Samaritaine." A childless couple, the Cognac-Jays donated an important sum to the Académie Française in 1920, which was used to make awards to families with many children. They left their art collection to the city of Paris, now displayed in the Cognac-Jay Museum.[68]

Such cases, although interesting, are rare. On the other hand, it would be worthwhile to speak at length about American women philanthropists who chose France as the recipient of their efforts. It might seem strange in a study on women and philanthropy in France to refer to Americans. However, even if it has not yet been studied exhaustively, we cannot ignore the role of American philanthropy in France during the interwar period, in particular that of women. The women in question donated either their professional competence in the social sphere (Anne Morgan, Chloe Owings) or invested a part of their fortune in the arts and letters (Winaretta Singer, Madame Edward Tuck, Peggy Guggenheim, and somewhat later Florence Gould). Almost all of these women were extremely wealthy heiresses and Francophiles. The total amount of money invested in France by American philanthropists has unfortunately never been calculated. If we add to this not insubstantial although unknown figure the hours of anonymous volunteer work by American nurses and doctors during the two World Wars on French soil, as well as the philanthropic activities of American wives residing in France, we would no doubt arrive at a considerable total. In gratitude, France has awarded the medal of the *Légion d'Honneur* to numerous American women philanthropists.

Phase Three: The Institutionalization of 1945–80

At the end of World War II, French women having obtained at last the right to vote (October 5, 1944) continued the struggle on other fronts. They still demanded equal pay for equal work, which demonstrates a change in mentality and a real desire to be recognized as equal to men. They still had to submit to marital authority, however, in order to exercise a profession, open a bank account, or dispose of their properties. It was only in 1965 that these obstacles were lifted, but it was not until the law of 1985 that complete equality between spouses regarding communal property went into effect. This situation in France was not favorable to women's philanthropy.

Furthermore, French women went to work in ever greater numbers. Only with difficulty could a family live without two salaries. As women's numbers in the service sector grew, there was little time left for volunteer work and less money for philanthropy.

From 1945 to today, female philanthropy has actually shrunk. Many women work in the health and social welfare fields for very modest salaries and dedicate all their time to their work. They often are devoted and show exemplary competence. Thus, the philanthropic spirit survives for the moment in these sectors, thanks to these women. Yet as they come into contact with women who perform such work without any special sense of mission (as they might any other), this is changing increasingly. The philanthropic origins of this sector are generally denied by the newcomers in the work force and this creates tensions within these professions. Furthermore, the whole sector, together with the organizations that carry out its work, have largely been taken over by men. The hierarchical, paternalistic relationship between men and women has been surreptitiously and progressively reintroduced into the sector.

All the private social-service organizations were regrouped in 1947 under one confederation, the *Union Nationale Interfédérale des œuvres Privées Sanitaires et Sociales* (UNIOPSS).[69] The most innovative associations of the beginning of the century gave birth to new associations modeled on the first one, joining together in federations or important groups, such as the *Fédération des Associations d'Aide aux Mères* or the *Fédération des Centers Sociaux.* Men took control of these groups while women stayed in the field to work. There were only one or two women on the administrative board of UNIOPSS,[70] for example, and the decisions were made by men. It was evident to the men there that women were just carrying out orders and that it was not necessary to consult them about important decisions, new rules, social laws, new work conditions, raises in salary, etc. This new union was totally outside the control of women or the scope of philanthropy.

Furthermore, Protestant female philanthropy had already abandoned this sector as early as the interwar period. There were no further Protestant organizations created after World War II.

As for the Catholic Church, religious congregations in the health services were encouraged to organize themselves separately in a federation called REPSA (*Religieuses dans les Professions de Santé*) with the intention of modernizing the functioning and hospital structure of their organizations. This was a way of taking things in hand and isolating convent sisters from lay people working in other groups. The *Association Professionnelle Catholique* (UCSS) that brought together conservative forces and which represented the voice of the hierarchy crumbled in the 1950s, due to lack of membership. The professionalization of the sector and the state support which ensued has satisfied even the most reticent Catholic women. Today we find these women in Christian unions or non-confessional professional organizations.

It sometimes happened that an organization evolved to the point where it was barely recognizable. Let us mention the case of the *Union Féminine et Sociale,* founded in 1925 by Andrée Butillard.[71] The original motto of this organization was to "bring autonomy and community to women." Its goal was to aid working women and, above all, to promote laws such as that of family allowances which encouraged women to stay in the home. This organization remained denominational until 1950. It was not a social service association but a discussion group where limited actions were organized. Consequently, it could not join UNIOPSS but stood on the fringe of social movements. After many internal debates and discussions, the association became a consumer movement in 1961, while maintaining training programs in the field of civic life and professional and social rehabilitation. Nowadays, the organization is very dynamic and led by numerous volunteer workers.

In 1963, all the associations regrouped in the *Offices Centraux des œuvres de Bienfaisance* joined the UNIOPSS. The circle of Catholic philanthropy still exists, even though it no longer claims its religious character and has merged with the French organizational scene. Women's philanthropy in France likewise disappeared in the middle of the wide ranging and gradual movement towards laicization and state control which the social sector experienced.[72] In fact, it is in this very same field that French women made their first entry into public life at high governmental levels. It is not by chance that, in 1936, Léon Blum appointed Suzanne Lacore, a former school teacher, as Under-Secretary of Public Health, and Cécile Brunschwicg, one of the five founders of the above mentioned School for Factory Superintendents, as Under-Secretary of Education. These women had indeed become public figures through their philanthropic works. The case of Germaine Poinso-Chapuis is also exemplary. A lawyer, a mother, and a Christian-Democrat, she was the epitome of the movement of Catholic women who advocated a strong, professional social sector independent from the religious hierarchy. She was called by Prime Minister Robert Schumann, himself a Christian-Democrat, to become Minister of Public Health and Population in November 1947. She was the first French woman to occupy a position of such importance. In 1974, the same portfolio was entrusted to the second French woman minister, Simone Veil, who, as a member of the Edouard Balladur government, oversaw the recovery of the Ministry of Health, Social Affairs and Urban Development in 1993. Between 1974 and today, a few rare women have made their way into politics, but they always were kept well away from the important ministries of Finance, Foreign Affairs, or Defense (a lone exception is Edith Cresson, who served as Prime Minister in 1991). France is still next to last in Europe in terms of the representation of women in political institutions.

Regarding the health and welfare field, it is clear that, within the space of a century, we have moved from private female philanthropy to state intervention. At the same time, women no longer play the principal role, but are incompletely represented in, and above all confined to, this field.

Today, organizations still control 50 percent of the welfare sector and 11 percent of the health sector.[73] This situation is the final trace left by feminine philanthropy from the beginning of the century. Together, the health and welfare sectors constitute a formidable financial power. The social security system, which includes health services in France, is intended to redistribute the national wealth. In France, the budget of Social Security is equal to that of the state.

Phase Four: The *Benevolat*'s Revival: 1980–95

In the last few years, a new type of female philanthropy made its appearance. We are witnessing an explosion in the number of organizations in all circles of society. The state is a ponderous machine that moves all too slowly, especially when new needs are making themselves felt on a daily basis. Birth control, the AIDS epidemic, blood donation, poverty, immigration, education, protection of consumers, protection of women and children — all call for urgent reactions. The organizational network — a mobile, innovative, and efficient intermediary between society and the state — is in a privileged position to fulfill the citizens' expectancies. Women take part in large numbers in these new organizations. They do volunteer work on an equal basis with men. It is well known, for example, that the government's plan against poverty and "precariousness" (law of 1988, *Revenu Minimum d'Insertion,* R.M.I.) was effectuated by the organizations themselves, an endeavor which mobilized many volunteer women. In effect, the French government had failed to allocate sufficient budget lines to the R.M.I. plan.

Exceptionally, women head such organizations. However, there is no female specificity to this type of volunteer work, apart from the fact that women are mostly present in subordinate positions, just as they still are in French society at large. We are talking here of an increasingly mass phenomenon of unnamed volunteers of all ages.[74] Volunteer work and militancy are not mutually exclusive. In some of these organizations, it is sometimes hard to distinguish between a volunteer worker and a militant. Indeed, a woman who is involved in an environmental protection organization no doubt performs volunteer work, but is she not first of all a militant? These women have to live through this duality. French volunteer work today stems as much from the determination to see one's ideas put into practice as from the desire to serve society. Let us add that since the concept of volunteer work was irremediably linked to the caricatured image of the "lady of good works," it still bears negative connotations. "Volunteer work is neither present nor taught in school, nor preached in church any more."[75]

This is not to say that women are no longer attracted to volunteer work. Given the current level of unemployment, which strikes them proportionally harder than men, and job instability, women find in volunteer work a means of fighting marginalization, of finding community, and creating social relationships around values that are not those of the work market — in short, a means of asserting themselves.[76]

In the 1990s, there is still a form of female philanthropy that is alive and well, that of the spouses of the Presidents of the Republic. This philanthropy is akin to that of the queens of France. These women use their public status and notoriety to create and promote foundations in areas that affect them particularly. Let us mention the work of Claude Pompidou on behalf of the elderly and the disabled, and the Foundation for Childhood of Anne-Aymone Giscard d'Estaing on behalf of children in jeopardy and families in trouble. Similarly, Martine Aubry, a young woman and former Minister of Labor, recently founded an organization called *Agir Contre l'Exclusion* whose aim is to aid the unemployed and the homeless.

Today, with such organizations as Doctors without Borders or Doctors of the World, we can discern philanthropy and volunteer work evolving toward greater humanitarianism. However, here again we do not find any specific-female characteristics.

GENERAL CONCLUSIONS

At the end of this brief presentation of French women's philanthropy, are we now in a position to single out the specific characters of this philanthropy over a period of four centuries, from the seventeenth century to the present?

Women's philanthropy was a determining factor in the economic, and social development of France during these four centuries. This fact is not emphasized enough in historical, economics and social studies. This is why I refer to this philanthropy as invisible and I demonstrate how the secularization process in the twentieth century with its growing professionalim made philanthropy more visible.

French women's philanthropy developed a "parallel power structure" in the face of religious and state authorities which was structurally assimilationist: "women working within religious male-controlled institutions." French female philanthropy was never able to keep its independence except on the local level or in certain specific institutions for short periods of time. These women, who dedicated themselves to philanthropic works, lived among themselves. Separatism (the small rural and urban communities of the eighteenth and nineteenth centuries) and individualism (creation of a religious order or association by a charismatic woman) coexisted in every epoch of feminine philanthropy; these movements were not the result of a linear evolution.

Such philanthropy allowed women to have a public role and to timidly emerge from the traditional position in which society had confined them. As early as the eighteenth century, some women philanthropists anticipated the right of women to dispose of their goods and to lead lives independent of familial and patriarchal structures. Furthermore, their claims to economic independence involving funds acquired outside the confines of family seem thus almost unusual and excessive. However, French society, so patriarchal, with rigid laws reasserted in the civil code of 1804, tolerated communities of women because they met a public need. These women were able to establish contact with the municipal and religious hierarchies. Thus they got their foot in the door of public life, when they were needed! Nonetheless, they did not transgress or step out of the feminine role of maintaining social ties, nourishing and caring for life. They never had sufficient financial means, but they knew how to make the best of their opportunities.

Women's philanthropy in France was born and developed within a religious and patriarchal framework, with a few exceptions which only prove the rule. It had to wait till the Third Republic in order to become more visible and autonomous. With the right to found organizations granted by the law of 1901, female philanthropy went through a brief stage of freedom in the health and welfare sector. However, it was rapidly brought into line by the state and male power. Women today are salaried employees in a tertiary sector dominated by men. Yet it should be noted that French women reached high levels in government for the first time in the health and social sector. An important and dynamic philanthropy explains this breakthrough into political life. Women always met with many obstacles and a lot of opposition, but they never gave up. In recent years women have again volunteered in answer to calls from the organizational network. Undoubtedly, female philanthropy has left its mark on the French social scene, but who sees it, who knows it, and who is willing to acknowledge it? In effect, no one — neither the women currently in charge of the health and welfare sector, up to the highest governmental level, nor the French feminist movement which has a very negative image of philanthropy because of the connotations of religious submissiveness that are still attached to it.

NOTES

1. Jean Pierre Gutton, *La société et les pauvres, exemple de la généralité de Lyon (1534–1789)* (Paris: Les belles Lettres, 1971); Roger Chartier, "Pauvreté et assistance dans la France moderne: l'exemple de la généralité de Lyon," *Annales Economies Sociétés Civilizations* no. 2 (mars-avril 1973): 572–82; Cissie C. Fairchilds,

Poverty and Charity in Aix-en-Provence, 1540–1789 (Baltimore: Johns Hopkins University Press, 1976); Colin Jones, *Charity and Bienfaisance: The Treatment of the Poor in the Montpelier Region, 1740–1815* (New York: Cambridge University Press, 1982); Yannick Marec, *Pauvres et Philanthropes à Rouen au XIXe siècle* (Recueils pédagogiques d'histoire régionale, Rouen 1981); Bernard Allemandou and Jean-Jacques Le Pennec, *La Naissance de l'aide sociale à l'enfance à Bordeaux sous l'Ancien Regime* (Bordeaux: Editions de la Maison de Sciences de l'Homme d' Aquitaine, 1991); Catherine Duprat, *Le Temps des philanthropes, la philanthropie parisienne des Lumières à la monarchie de Juillet* (Paris: Editions du C.T.H.S., 1993); Olivier Wernier, *L'assistance privée dans les Alpes-Maritimes au XIXe siècle (1814–1914)* (Serres, 1993).

2. Michel Foucault, *Surveiller et punir* (Paris: Gallimard 1975); Olwen Hufton, *The Poor in Eighteenth Century France, 1750–1789* (New York: Oxford University Press, 1974); John H. Weiss, "Origins of the French Welfare State: Poor Relief in the Third Republic," *French Historical Studies* 13 (1983): 47–78.; Robert M. Schwartz, *Policing the Poor in Eighteenth-Century France* (Chapel Hill: University of North Carolina Press, 1988); Alan Forrest, *The French Revolution and the Poor* (New York: St. Martin's Press, 1981); Katherine A. Lynch, *Family, Class, and Ideology in Early Industrial France* (Madison: University of Wisconsin Press, 1988); Ann-Louise Shapiro, *Housing the Poor of Paris, 1850–1902* (Madison: University of Wisconsin Press, 1985); Catherine Rollet-Eschalier, *La Politique à l'égard de la petite enfance sous la IIIe République* (Paris: Thèse d'Etat I.N.E.D.-P.U.F., 1990); Rachel G. Fuchs, *Poor and Pregnant in Paris* (New Brunswick, N.J.: Rutgers University Press, 1992).

3. Edith Archambault and Xavier Greffe, *Les Economies non officielles* (Paris: La Découverte, 1984); Edith Archambault, C. Bon, M. Le Vaillant, *Les Dons et le bénévolat en France* (Paris: Laboratoire d'économie sociale, 1991); Edith Archambault, "Defining the Nonprofit Sector: France," Working Paper No. 7 (Baltimore: Johns Hopkins University Comparative Nonprofit Sector Project, March 1993); Dan Ferrand-Bechmann, "Le phénomène bénévole," (Thèse de doctorat d'Etat és lettres, I.E.P., Paris: CESOL, 1991).

4. Henri Hatzfeld, *Du paupérisme à la Sécurité sociale, 1850–1940* (Nancy: Presses Universitaires de Nancy, 1989); François Ewald, *L'Etat providence* (Paris: Grasset, 1986); Sonya Michel and Seth Koven, "Womanly Duties: Maternalist Politics and the Origins of Welfare States in France, Germany, Great Britain, and the United States, 1880–1920," *American Historical Review* 95, no. 4 (October 1990): 1076–1108; Gisela Bock and Pat Thane, ed., *Maternity and Gender Policies* (London and New York: Routledge, 1991); Susan Pedersen, *Family, Dependence, and the Origins of the Welfare State, Britain and France 1914–1945* (New York: Cambridge University Press, 1993); Evelyne Diebolt, "Les associations face aux institutions. Les femmes dans l'action sanitaire, sociale et culturelle (1900–1965)" (Thèse de doctorat d'Etat és lettres, Université de Paris VII, juin 1993); Marcel David, *Les Fondements du social: de la IIIe République à l'heure actuelle* (Paris: Anthropos, 1993).

5. Michelle Perrot and Georges Duby ed., *Histoire des femmes en Occident*, 5 vol. (Paris: Plon, 1993).

6. Joan W. Scott, Louise Tilly, Stewart-McDougall, Coffin, Wishnia, Chenut, Bidelman, Hause, Moon, Moses, Sowerwine, G. Sussman, etc.

7. Kathleen D. McCarthy, ed., *Lady Bountiful Revisited: Women, Philanthropy and Power* (New Brunswick, N.J.: Rutgers University Press, 1990); Kathleen D. McCarthy, "Women and Philanthropy: Three Strategies in Historical Perspective," Working Paper (New York: Center for the Study of Philanthropy, CUNY, 1994); Lester M. Salamon, *America's Nonprofit Sector: A Primer* (New York: The Foundation Center, 1992).

8. André Latreille and René Rémond, *Histoire du catholicisme en France, tome 3, la période contemporaine du XVIIIe siècle à nos jours* (Paris: Spes, 1962); Jean-Marie Mayeur, *L'histoire religieuse de la France, XIXe et XXe* (Paris: Beauchesne, 1975); François Lebrun, *Histoire des Catholiques en France du XVe siècle à nos jours* (Toulouse: Privat, 1980).

9. As Rachel G. Fuchs very pertinently states: "By the decade before the First World War, France was becoming what François Ewald accurately describes as the 'provident state.' The French phrase 'l'état providence,' referring to the welfare state, indicates the secular appropriations of a religious term, and underscores the merging of private Christian charity ideals with secular public welfare goals, where the prior is subsumed under the latter. The secular, anti-clerical French state assumed the paternalistic charity which had been the hallmark of Christianity." In Rachel G. Fuchs, *Poor and Pregnant in Paris* (New Brunswick, N.J.: Rutgers University Press, 1992), 234.

10. Maité Albistur and Daniel Armogathe, *Histoire du féminisme français* (Paris: Edition des femmes, 1978); Jane Rendall, *The Origins of Modern Feminism: Women in Britain, France and the United States, 1780–1860* (London: Macmillan, 1983), Laurence Klejman et Florence Rochefort, *L'Egalité en marche. Le féminisme sous la troisième République* (Paris: Presses de la Fondation nationale des sciences politiques, 1989); Christine Faure, *La Démocratie sans les femmes* (Paris: P.U.F., 1991).

11. Two exceptions: Claude Langlois, *Le Catholicisme au féminin. Les congrégations françaises à supérieure générale* (Paris: Le Cerf, 1984); Yvonne Turin, *Femmes et religieuses au XIXe siècle, le féminisme en religion* (Paris: Editions Nouvelle Cité, 1989).

12. The Concordat of Bologna signed in 1516 by Pope Leo X and Francis I gave the king the right to name the bishops as well as abbots and abbesses in his kingdom. This gave the king the upper hand in who really ruled the convents. Claude Michaud, *L'église et l'argent sous l'ancien régime* (Paris: Fayard, 1991), 8.

13. In 1561, the Third Estate of the Estates General of Pontoise, i.e., the bourgeoisie, demanded that the wealth of the clergy be put at the disposition of the state (this would occur in October 1789 during the French Revolution). The state helped the Catholic Church to put down this Protestant reform. Thus after 1561, the Catholic Church would give financial aid to the state in return for keeping its supremacy. Claude Michaud, *L'église et l'argent sous l'ancien régime* (Paris: Fayard, 1991).

14. Kathleen D. McCarthy, "Parallel Power Structures: Women and the Voluntary Sphere," in Kathleen D. McCarthy, ed., *Lady Bountiful Revisited: Women, Philanthropy and Power* (New Brunswick, N.J.: Rutgers University Press, 1990).

15. Jean-Claude Bardoux, *Les Libertés d'association-Histoire étonnante de la loi 1901* (Paris: Edition Juris-Service, 1991); Marie-Thérèse Cheroutre, *Exercice et*

développement de la vie associative dans le cadre de la loi du 1e Juillet 1901 (Paris: La Documentation Française, rapport CES, 1993).

16. Jean Marie Mayeur, *La séparation de l'Eglise et de l'Etat* (1905) (Paris: Julliard, 1966).

17. Evelyne Diebolt, "Les associations face aux institutions. Les femmes dans l'action sanitaire, sociale et culturelle (1900–1965)" (Thèse de doctorat d'Etat és lettres, Université de Paris VII, juin 1993).

18. Michelle Perrot and Georges Duby ed., *Histoire de la vie privée du Moyen Age à nos jours* (Paris: P.U.F., 1988).

19. In the countryside, as Fernand Braudel emphasizes, "Bullion is rarely a true form of capital, it is used in the purchase of land and,... even more it was hoarded..., let us consider the coins of the women's necklaces in Central Europe..., the gold crosses of the peasants of France on the eve of the French Revolution," as quoted by Marie-Françoise Hans, *Les femmes et l'argent* (Paris: Grasset, 1885), 49. In other words, gold and silver were a means to acquiring land but were neither used in daily transactions nor parted with lightly. The church also bought land with the money from the dowries of young nuns.

20. "They cannot easily be separated," Rachel G. Fuchs, *Poor and Pregnant in Paris* (New Brunswick, N.J.: Rutgers University Press, 1992), 101.

21. Albert Giraudin, *Marie Thérèse Charlotte de Lamourous, fondatrice de la Miséricorde de Bordeaux (1754–1838)* (Bordeaux: Delbrel, 1912).

22. In the eighteenth century, the dowry of a professed nun in a Parisian convent could vary between 2,000 and 10,000 livres. Most often it amounted to 6,000 livres, which was the equivalent of a dowry for a marriage in the bourgeoisie. In higher circles, a young woman who wanted to marry an "auditeur des comptes, trésorier de France ou payeur des rentes" had to bring between 30,000 to 45,000 livres. She could not expect to marry a "président à mortier, vrai marquis" for less than 300,000 to 600,000 livres, see Geneviève Reynes, *Couvents de femmes* (Paris: Fayard, 1987), 47.

23. The first of these monasteries were established at the beginning of the seventeenth century. There were a hundred by 1650 and more than three hundred at the end of the century. A single convent in Saint Denis, which was founded in 1628, had close to four thousand pupils in 1657. Geneviève Reynes, *Couvents de femmes* (Paris: Fayard, 1987), 248.

24. Louis Abelly, *Vie de Saint Vincent de Paul, Instituteur et premier supérieur de la congrégation de la Mission et des filles de la Charité* 6 vols. (Clermont-Ferand: Thibaud, 1835).

25. Yvonne Turin, *Femmes et religieuses au XIXe siècle, le féminisme en religion* (Paris: Nouvelle Cité, 1989). Yvonne Turin obtained the right to read the archives of the Congrégation de la Doctrine Chrétienne in Nancy, the Congrégation Saint Joseph du Bon Pasteur in Clermont-Ferrand, the Congrégation des Sœurs de Saint Joseph du Puy and of the Congrégation des Sœurs de Saint Joseph de Lyon. Her documentation covers south-eastern, eastern and central France.

26. Ibid., 9.

27. Ibid., 65.

28. Ibid., 28.

29. Bernard Allemandou and Jean-Jacques Le Pennec, *La Naissance de l'aide*

sociale à l'enfance à Bordeaux sous l'Ancien Regime (Bordeaux: Editions de la Maison de Sciences de l'Homme d' Aquitaine, 1991).

30. François Gille, *La Société de charité maternelle de Paris* (Paris, 1887); Catherine Duprat, *Le Temps des philanthropes, la philanthropie parisienne des Lumières à la monarchie de Juillet* (Paris: Editions du C.T.H.S., 1993), 75–80.

31. André Lemery, "Les fondations hospitalières protestantes en Normandie," *Bulletin de la Société Française des Hôpitaux,* no. 34 (1977): 71–81.

32. Paul Leroy-Beaulieu, *Le travail des femmes au XIXe siècle* (Paris, 1873); Evelyne Diebolt and Marie-Hélène Zylberberg-Hocquard: *Marcelle Capy-Aline Valette: Femmes et travail au dix-neuvième siècle* (Paris: Syros, 1984); Yvonne Knibiehler and Catherine Fouquet, *Histoire des mères du Moyen Age à nos jours* (Paris: Editions Montalba, 1977).

33. Turin, *Femmes et religieuses au XIXe siècle,* 164.

34. Ibid., 149.

35. Bonnie Smith, *Ladies of the Leisure Class; The Bourgeoisie of Northern France in the Nineteenth century* (Princeton: Princeton University Press, 1981); traduction française, *Les Bourgeoises du Nord* (Paris: Perrin, 1989).

36. Jean-Baptiste Duroselle, *Les Débuts du catholicisme social en France, 1822–1870* (Paris: Presses Universitaires de France, 1951); Henri Rollet, *L'action sociale des catholiques en France (1871–1914),* 2 vols. (Paris and Bruges: Desclée de Brouwer, 1958).

37. This is the first example of a philanthropic activity which becomes a female profession. See also, below, under the section: The Professionalization of 1920–45.

38. Evelyne Lejeune-Resnick, *Femmes et Associations (1830–1880)* (Paris: Editions Publisud, 1991), 182–90.

39. Michel Allner, "L'Armée du Salut; armée, église, œuvre sociale: l'adaptation d'une institution victorienne aux cultures nord-américaine et française au XXème siècle," (Thèse de doctorat d'État és lettres, Université Paris VII, 1994), 512.

40. Kathleen D. McCarthy, "Women and Philanthropy: Three Strategies in Historical Perspective," Working Paper (New York: Center for the Study of Philanthropy, CUNY, 1994).

41. Ibid., 15–18.

42. Ibid., 2–8.

43. Laurence Klejman et Florence Rochefort, *L'Egalité en marche. Le féminisme sous la troisième République* (Paris: Presses de la Fondation nationale des sciences politiques, 1989).

44. Kay Lawson and Peter H. Merkl, "When Linkage Fails," chap. 2 in *When Parties Fail. Emerging Alternative Organisations* (Princeton N.J.: Princeton University Press, 1988), 13–38.

45. The French clergy was considerably enriched during the nineteenth century. In a fifty-year period its land-based wealth multiplied tenfold. Philanthropic possibilities within the church developed alongside this growth in wealth. QUID (Paris: Robert Laffont, 1990), 539.

46. Evelyne Diebolt, "Les femmes catholiques: entre Eglise et société," in *Catholicism, Politics and Society in Twentieth-Century France* ed. Kay Chadwick (Liverpool: Liverpool University Press, 1996).

47. At the beginning of the eighteenth century, France counted 90,000 religious for 22 million inhabitants. In 1836, there were 127,000 nuns for 33 million inhabitants. In 1970, there were 111,500 nuns for 50 million inhabitants and in 1990, 67,000 nuns. QUID (Paris: Robert Laffont, 1990), 978.

48. Madeleine Pelletier, *Mademoiselle Chaptal, ses principales activités sociales* (Paris: Editions Spes, 1937); Evelyne Diebolt, *Les œuvres de Léonie Chaptal dans le XIVe arrondissement de Paris 1900–1938* (Paris: Rapport Ministère des Affaires Sociales, 1988).

49. Henri Rollet, *Andrée Butillard et le féminisme chrétien* (Paris: Spes, 1955); Henri Pascal, *Monographie sur l'Ecole normale sociale* (Document dactylographié, 1988).

50. Sylvie Fayet-Scribe, *La Résidence sociale de Levallois-Perret* (Toulouse: Erès, 1990).

51. Evelyne Diebolt, "L'Association des infirmières visiteuses," in "Les associations face aux institutions. Les femmes dans l'action sanitaire, sociale et culturelle (1900–1965)" (Thèse de doctorat d'Etat és lettres, Université de Paris VII, juin 1993).

52. Paul Gradvohl, "Les Premières Années de l'association des surintendantes (1917–1939)" *Vie Sociale*, 8/9 (1986).

53. Evelyne Diebolt, "Une association catholique: l'U.C.S.S.," *Pour une Histoire des soins et des pratiques soignantes,* Cahier de l'A.M.I.E.C., 10, Lyon: Association des amis de l'Ecole Internationale d'Enseignement Infirmier Supérieur dite AMI(s) EC (ole) (mai 1988): 141–58; Michelle Barrot, Evelyne Diebolt: "Des services de soins congréganistes au Mouvement des centres de soins," *Cahier de l'A.M.I.E.C.*, 10 (Lyon, mai 1988): 235–56.

54. André Encrevé, *Les Protestants en France de 1800 à nos jours: Histoire d'une réintégration* (Paris: Stock, 1985).

55. Evelyne Diebolt, *La Maison de Santé protestante de Bordeaux (1863–1934). Vers une conception novatrice des soins et de l'hôpital* (Toulouse: Erès, 1990), préface de Jacques Ellul; Simone Crapuchet, *Bagatelle 1930–1958. La Maison de Santé protestante de Bordeaux: présences et développements récents* (Toulouse: Erès, 1992).

56. Evelyne Diebolt, Jean-Pierre Laurant, *Anne Morgan, une Américaine en Soissonnais (1917–1952)* (Soissons: A.M.S.A.M., 1990); Evelyne Diebolt and Nicole Fouché, "1917–1923, les Américaines en Soissonnais: leur influence sur la France," *Revue Française d'Etudes Américaines* No. 59 (Nancy: Presses Universitaires de Nancy, février 1994): 45–63; Evelyne Diebolt, "Association pour le Développement de l'Assistance aux Malades," in "Les associations face aux institutions. Les femmes dans l'action sanitaire, sociale et culturelle (1900–1965)" (Thèse de doctorat d'Etat és lettres, Université de Paris VII, juin 1993).

57. Marie Richmond, *Les Méthodes nouvelles d'assistance* (Paris: Alcan, Traduction française, 1926).

58. Evelyne Diebolt: "80 ans d'associations professionelles infirmières en France (1906–1984)," *Pénélope*, 11 (automne 1984): 122–30.

59. Gérard Noiriel, "Du 'patronage' au 'paternalisme': la restructuration des formes de domination de la main d'œuvre ouvrière dans l'indusrie métallurgique française," *Le Mouvement Social* (July–September 1988): 17–35; Alisa Klaus, "Women's Organisations and the Infant Health Movement in France

and the United States, 1890–1920," in Kathleen D. McCarthy, ed., *Lady Bountiful Revisited: Women, Philanthropy and Power* (New Brunswick, N.J.: Rutgers University Press, 1990), 157–75; Anne Cova, "French feminism and maternity: theories and policies, 1890–1918," in Gisela Bock and Pat Thane, ed., *Maternity and Gender Policies* (London and New York: Routledge, 1991); Evelyne Diebolt, "Les laïcisations hospitalières d'influence protestante," in Jacques Poirier, Jean-Louis Signoret ed., *De Bourneville à la sclérose tubéreuse* (Paris: Flammarion, 1991), 82–89.

60. Roger-Henri Guerrand, Marie-Antoinette Rupp, *Brève histoire du service social en France (1896–1976)* (Toulouse: Privat, 1978); Jeannine Verdes-Leroux, *Le Travail social* (Paris: Edition de Minuit, 1978); Jacques Donzelot, *L'Invention du social* (Paris: Fayart, 1984); Francis Bailleau, Nadine Lefaucheur, Vincent Peyre, ed., *Lectures sociologiques du travail social* (Paris: Les Editions Ouvrières, 1981).

61. Evelyne Diebolt, *Le Service social de l'enfance en danger moral, association Olga Spitzer, 1923–1939* (Paris: Rapport ministère de la Justice, 1993).

62. Jean-Marc Dutrenit, *Evaluer un centre social* (Paris: L'Harmattan, 1994). Note that in 1994, one million persons made use of the services in all of these centers.

63. Annie Fourcaud, *Femmes à l'usine: ouvrières et surintendantes dans les entreprises françaises de l'Entre-deux-guerres* (Paris: Maspéro, 1982).

64. Daniel Ceccaldi, *Histoire des prestations familiales en France* (Paris: U.N.C.A.F., 1957); Catherine Rollet-Eschalier, *La Politique à l'égard de la petite enfance sous la IIIe République* (Paris: I.N.E.D.-P.U.F., 1990); Karen Offen, "Body politics: women, work and the politics of motherhood in France, 1920–1950," in Gisela Bock and Pat Thane, ed., *Maternity and Gender Policies* (London and New York: Routledge, 1991); Susan Pedersen, *Family, Dependence, and the Origins of the Welfare State,Britain and France 1914–1945* (New York: Cambridge University Press, 1993), 224–28.

65. Yvonne Knibiehler, *Nous les assistantes sociales, naissance d'une profession* (Paris: Aubier, 1980); *La femme soignante* Evelyne Diebolt ed., *Pénélope*, 5 (Paris: Association Pénélope, 1981); Marie-Noëlle Valls-Lacroix, *Practiciens du secteur sanitaire et social, qui êtes-vous?* (Paris: Editions ouvrières, 1989).

66. Florence Montreynaud, *Le XXe siècle des femmes* (Paris: Nathan, 1989), 277.

67. Ibid., 222.

68. Ibid., 185.

69. Evelyne Diebolt and Sylvie Fayet-Scribe, "L'Union Interféderale des œuvres Privées Sanitaires et Sociales — L'UNIOPPS a 40 ans," *Union Social* (décembre 1987); Evelyne Diebolt, "Historique et dynamique d'une association interfédérale: l'Union Interféderale des Œuvres Privées Sanitaires et Sociales (UNIOPPS) 1947–1987," *Recherche sur les associations gestionnaires du secteur sanitaire et social, organisation et thèmes porteurs du mouvement fédératif* (Paris: Fonds national de développement de la vie associative FNDVA, 1988), 1–47; *UNIOPSS, Catholicisme, Hier, Aujourd'hui, Demain* (Paris: Letouzey et Ané, 1959) tome XV, fascicule 71.

70. At the founding meeting of UNIOPPS on April 15, 1947, only one woman was present. Here is the list of members: Mme Aubert-Picard representative of the Mouvement Populaire des Familles; M. le Rabbin Pellois, representative of the Grand Rabbin de France; M. le Pastueur Vidal, representative of the Fédération Protestante de France, M. Blondel; M. le docteur Courcoux, representative of the Fédération des Établissements Hospitaliers de France; M. de Novian, president

of the Fédération des Établissements Hospitaliers; M. Guérin de Vaux, president of the Secrétariat Catholique des œuvres Charitables et Sociales d'Hygiène et de Santé, also representative of the œuvres de Protection Maternelles et Infantiles, M. Lockhart, representative of the rural milieu; M. George Michel, representative the Union Nationale des Secrétariats Sociaux; M. Bonnaud, director of the administrative services of the Secours Catholique; Doctor Oberlin, M. Poindron representative of the Office Central des œuvres de Bienfaisance.

71. Sylvie Fayet-Scribe, *Associations féminines et catholicisme* (Paris: Editions ouvrières, 1900), 117.

72. Susan Pedersen, *Family, Dependence, and the Origins of the Welfare State, Britain and France 1914–1945* (New York: Cambridge University Press, 1993), 357–411.

73. In 1989 in the health and social sector there were 90,000 associations. The health sector showed 80,000 salaried employees and the social sector 200,000. In the health sector, the associations managed 11 percent of the global accomodation capabilities for a turnover of 16 billion francs and the social sector, 51 percent for a turnover of 30.5 billion francs. Marie-Thérèse Cheroutre, "L'essor et l'avenir du bénévolat, facteurs d'amélioration de la qualité de la vie," *Journal Officiel* no. 19 (12 juillet 1989): 11.

74. Dan Ferrand-Bechmann, *Bénévolat et Solidarité* (Paris: Syros-Alternatives, 1992).

75. Ibid., 28.

76. J. Van Til, *Mapping the Third Sector* (New York: University Press of America, 1988).

– 3 –

Women and Philanthropy in Brazil:
An Overview

LEILAH LANDIM

INTRODUCTION

The Nonprofit Sector Issue

In Brazil, only recently has there been talk of a "nonprofit sector" or "philanthropy" in the sense of "giving of gifts of time or valuables (money, securities, property) for public purposes," according to North American usage.[1] With the exception of a set of more recent organizations called NGOs, there is a scarcity of statistical data and studies on the role of voluntary or nongovernment organizations in Brazilian society. It is only in the last four or five years that the international debate on the third sector has penetrated the country's academic and political circles.

This absence has to do with the Brazilian national context where, contrary to historical experiences like North America's, society was "created" by the state. The story of Brazil's colonization is the story of how economic and political intervention by the Portuguese Crown laid the foundations for a society based on signorial authority and the immobilization of land, by constituting economic units based on slave labor and directed to external markets, characteristic of the plantation system, with an incipient domestic market and with a strong tendency to marginalize free men, both economically and socially.

The state's partner in this undertaking, the Catholic Church, was the official religion for nearly four centuries and played a decisive role in forming civil society. Until the republic was proclaimed in 1889, only Catholics were recognized as citizens. The principle of subsidiarity — through which civil organizations have gained strength — did not hold here as it did in other nations with a strong Catholic presence. On the contrary, church, state, and the landowning class (and, from 1930 onwards, the industrialist class) were allies in a history of centralization and authoritarianism, complemented by tardy constitution of a domestic market and the enfeeblement of civil society.

Although the history of private organizations acting in the public benefit does not have the same kind of presence and visibility here as it does in other national contexts, nonetheless this does not mean that organizations of this kind were not present in Brazilian society under the most diverse historical circumstances. Rather than being a nonexistent history, this is a history mistold by a sociology with an obsession for the state. It is surprising, for example, to discover that there are 190,000 organizations registered with the Inland Revenue authorities as "nonprofit" (1991 figure). A large part of this universe, which is quite diversified, is long-standing and forms part of the structure of non-explicit strategies (or strategies which were never transformed into clear policies) for public assistance to immense masses of the population, as well as for producing leisure, sports, or culture for those masses.

It should be added in this connection that, although centralized and strongly present throughout society, the Brazilian state is notable for being highly ineffective. Its social policies have, as a rule, been faulty and exclusionary, historically leaving the majority of the population beyond the reach of any benefits. This was an ample field for the development of philanthropy — which grew up alongside official social policies (but was not for this reason diminished or lacking in social importance) — where the presence of the Catholic Church (and, in the twentieth century, other religions) makes itself felt.

The voluntary organizations and initiatives in which women have been involved in Brazil's history were to bear the marks of this Catholic and/or governmental influence, whether by alliance or opposition, in their values, ideas, and types of activity.

The Women and Nonprofit Sector Issue

Given that debate about a "philanthropic sector" or "nonprofit organizations" has begun to emerge only recently in Brazil, imagine what this means for the issue of relations between women and philanthropy. As might be expected, there is even less data and thinking on women's presence or role in forming this field. Here, we are starting practically from scratch.

In addition to this double vacuum — the lack of discussion of either the nonprofit sector or of women's role therein — there is a third omission, which occurs in the field of women's studies itself. Despite the existence of a vast literature on gender that has built up in recent decades,[2] the specific issue of the role played by philanthropy and voluntary work in shaping Brazilian women's social existence and their entry into public affairs is overlooked by this area of research and debate. Raising this issue means investigating a relatively unfamiliar object.[3] For that reason, this study intends to take only a generic approach to the subject, suggesting certain questions and avenues for future inquiries into the correlations between gender and nonprofit organizations.

These avenues seem quite promising. As old stories are reviewed or phenomena familiar to common sense are reconsidered — as in the case of the "discovery" of a nonprofit sector in Brazilian society — so attention is drawn to the obvious, predominant presence of women as agents in vast numbers of voluntary organizations. Two issues present themselves, as to women's role in constituting a third sector in Brazil and as to what the many forms of the female presence in Brazilian society owe, for better or for worse, to women's activities as donors of time and money or creators of charities or institutions for social promotion, development, or reform.

As in other parts of the world, the literature on women's voluntary activities is uneven. In recent decades, Brazilian studies on women have focused basically on the question of women's emancipation and on the creation of citizenship and civil rights for women, thus giving greater visibility to organizations and movements for social reform, where women took positions as political actors in public affairs. There is a well-understood path from women's participation in the abolition movement through the suffrage movement to women's autonomism of the 1970s (although international models are often followed with no consideration for social and cultural factors specific to the Brazilian context).[4] Although these studies are interested not in the "nonprofit issue" but rather in emancipation, there is considerable information in the former area.

By comparison, the field of charities or social assistance organizations receives scant attention. It is generally discarded as an object of study, usually because "it reproduces traditional roles and, thus, female subordination," or "it also reproduces the subordinate position of the groups affected." This approach (which has its measure of truth) simply bars from scientific and political scrutiny a vast field of female presence in Brazilian society, which has generated profound cultural identities to be taken into account in any analysis of women's issues — and also of Brazilian society and the particular place of voluntary organizations in it.

Of the 190,000 nonprofit organizations in Brazil registered with the Inland Revenue, almost one third (or 55,396 organizations) are "beneficent, religious or assistance," an area with a massive women's presence, as evidenced by some localized research studies. This little known universe is internally differentiated and, over the years, has been changing in terms of relations with religions, society, and the state. It makes perfect sense to inquire into the effect of these organizations, down through history, on the positions assumed by women in Brazilian society (for example, in establishing specific women's powers outside the home, in leaving a very particular mark on movements for social change, in creating public policy, collective identities, or certain professional fields). We are here on ambiguous ground as to emancipation, where the domination of women and the perpetuation of their traditional roles in the private sphere are reproduced side by side with processes of empowerment and a firmer presence in the public sphere.

This paper takes a chronological approach to the emergence of and changes in certain patterns or "models" for women's action in society through voluntary organizations. Relations with the state and, especially, with the church constitute important variables to be examined. Another factor is the cultural background of this society, in which Afro-Brazilian religions and Iberian Catholicism, race, slavery, liberal ideas from France and the United States, the rural patriarchy, and urban western culture have blended to create singular syncretic forms.

The first part analyzes the colonial period, which saw the creation of female stereotypes, the roots of personalized Christian charity, and the model of voluntary action through religious organizations. The second deals with pioneering women's initiatives directed to social reform, from the late nineteenth century to the 1930s. The third is devoted to the role played by women and voluntary associations, from the 1930s onwards, in implementing the corporatist project of a Brazilian "welfare state" and laying the foundations for the profession of social worker. The last section considers autonomous associations marked by the feminism of the past twenty years, a period of reaction to the dictatorial regime, and the move to build civil society and democratic order.

The analysis also highlights three "models" of women's action in society through nonprofit organizations: charitable action, social assistance, and action for social reform. In each of these areas, we shall consider the initiatives of women as voluntary workers, as donors of material resources, and as creators of institutions. This universe of voluntary initiatives comprises different strategies by women, whether in building organizations composed solely of women, in participating in ventures dominated by men, or in the individual creation of institutions "of their own, on their own," as described by McCarthy (whose observations will be of use here too).[5]

In this historical analysis, which will disclose "models" of women's voluntary action, it is tempting to fall into an evolutionist approach, since we begin with charity organized via church channels and end with autonomous social development and reform initiatives in the public sphere. These different modalities of action through nonprofit organizations co-exist throughout history, down to the present. Often they are woven into a single initiative—more than their agents suspect or would like to think—and often they form part of the same individual or institutional history.

In summary, in this paper I shall endeavor to show:

1. As Brazilian society historically is closed to women's entry into the labor market and public life, voluntary organizations have represented significant, at times the only, opportunities for women to make their presence felt in society outside the home. The idea of "parallel power structures," which refers to the ways in which women can use "their participation in voluntary associations to carve out public roles for themselves in ways that paralleled, but rarely precisely replicated the political and economic prerogatives of men" (McCarthy, 1994, 6) can be useful to analyze these issues. These social spaces, like many others, in fact, were almost all loaded with ambiguities, since they also reproduce traditional stereotypes.

2. It would be impossible to understand the characteristics and the shape assumed by women's philanthropy in Brazil without taking into consideration the central role played by religion in this field, specially by the Catholic Church. I intend to show how religion provided basic values, legitimated and shaped issues and practices, and provided various spaces for women's activities in the public arena through voluntary organizations. Their access to funds (generally, scarce) came more easily through religious channels. Regarding women's voluntary action, there is a continuous thread running from charity through assistance to activism, facilitated by the permanent, formative presence of the Catholic Church. Nevertheless, in the past thirty years, this church hegemony has occasionally been broken; at the same time, women's traditional positions in society have changed significantly, a process in which the non-governmental organizations have played a role.

3. A significant place must be reserved, in the history of women's voluntary organizations in Brazil, for international philanthropy organizations of various kinds. Through the transnational channels opened by international agencies not only does money circulate, but also ideas and agents, giving their contribution, at different moments and under different contexts, in support of women's initiatives in the field of voluntary associations. Organizations linked to the churches are also operative in this field.

4. Although women had a place in the development of the welfare policies in the thirties—mostly, through the professionalization of so-

cial work and employment in government organizations — their power was reduced. The background of state centralization and authoritarianism must be considered in analyzing the limited authority of women's organizations (and civil organizations generally) in shaping public policies at that time. Only in the last ten or fifteen years has it been possible to see an effective impact of women's NGOs on public policymaking.

The importance of nonprofit organizations on the social, economic, and political Brazilian scene — both the service provision and civic activism wings — has been highlighted in recent times. This will certainly have consequences for the position of women in society, resulting from the centuries in which they have been centrally present and active in this area.

ROOTS: WOMEN IN THE COLONY, FRONT ROOM, AND BACKYARD

Primary Identities

"As for women in Brazil, they are of an idleness that defies all imagining; they are also crueler than the men; they beat their blacks — men and women — for the slightest faults;... they spend their time squatting on mats, from where they do not stir to get anything" (V. A. Gedrin, in 1817). "In the interior, one can spend a whole week under someone's roof without even glimpsing the host's wife and daughters. Brazilian women enjoy fewer privileges than those of the Orient. Relegated mostly to living with the slaves, they lead an entirely material life. They marry early and are soon deformed by the first childbirths, thus losing the few attractions they may have had. Their husbands are quick to arrange black or mulatta slave substitutes" (Conde de Suzannet in 1845).[6]

This image of lazy, fat, unattractive women, consigned to the interior of the greathouses, surrounded by children and slaves and subjected passively to the patriarchal domination of husbands among throngs of concubines, comes to us through numerous travelers' chronicles by visitors to Brazil in former times. These reports of foreign perceptions — important sources for a historiography of customs and day-to-day life — have contributed to building up what has become a standard stereotype of the identity and place of women in the centuries when Brazilian society was being formed.

First of all, of course, in reading these descriptions, one must make allowance for the cultural filter at work. It is well known, for example, that standards of female beauty vary from culture to culture. Also, the perceptions are not unanimous, as shown by one description written at that time, not incidentally by a woman: "One of the most widely held opinions about Brazilian women is that they are lazy and spend their days in idleness. This is a mistake. The Brazilian woman does nothing for herself, but she has things done. She makes every effort never to be seen to be busy. Meanwhile, those who are granted intimacy will find her, in the morning, ... presiding over the preparation of sweets, coconut ice, arranging them on the trays of negro men and women who will take them to sell around the city.... As soon as these leave, the ladies set the mulattas to sewing, since almost all the children's clothes and those of the lord and lady of the house are cut and sewn at home. They also make drawnwork handkerchiefs and napkins, which they send out to be sold as well.... This means pocket money for Brazilian women and allows them to satisfy their fantasies.... A Brazilian woman would be ashamed to be caught at any kind of task, because they all claim the greatest disdain for anyone who works.... No other professions are admitted in Brazil, besides those of doctor, lawyer and bulk trader" (Adèle Toussaint-Samson, 1815).

This description shows that there is more variety than supposed in women's apparent indolence and total dependency inside the closed units of the great plantations under patriarchal domination. It turns out that, even where this would seem to be impossible — without setting foot outside the home or dealing with strangers — the women endeavored to gain their own incomes with cottage crafts.[7]

As to the differences of opinion about "women's laziness," the texts are suggestive of ideas that have developed over the years and still people the Brazilian social imagination. This is the case with the idea, or ideal, of the reclusive woman who does no manual work. The female French visitor saw activity and restricted power where others saw idleness and absolute powerlessness. Nonetheless, the women who were observed did not do things directly; rather, they had them done by slaves, since they considered it unbecoming to be seen working.

In fact, this situation, which so shocked and drew value judgments from European or North American travelers, reflects and reproduces the broader cultural dimensions of a society polarized between slaves and owners, which aspired to aristocracy, marginalized the middle classes, and held a prejudice against manual work. As for women, a diffuse idea grew up that work and the street were for slaves and prostitutes. Leaving aside the moralist debate about the sloth or behavior of "Brazilian women," there is no denying that these stereotypes are solidly grounded in the reality of a society centered on the great plantations, relatively closed worlds ruled by the logic of the fief.

Recent historiographical studies of Brazilian women, which focus on mentalities and "invisible" daily practice, seek to break with this image of women as submissive recluses, contrasting it with the many stories of conflicts and resistance by wives and daughters against male domination in the colonial period. This research is also bringing out the cases of wealthier women, generally widows, who, on becoming the head of the family, administered plantations and entered local politics (cf. Freire, 1977).[8] These would have been "heroines" of the resistance against a radical situation of subordination.

Rebels or victims? Some authors point to the fact that these studies, while important for dismantling outdated stereotypes and unveiling possible deviations from standards of female behavior and identity, nonetheless raise this kind of dilemma. More promising, I feel, are those approaches that consider forms of female behavior in their multiplicity, remembering that "breaking with the stereotype of women's reclusion may mean excluding the less daring — possibly the great majority — from history" (Algranti, 1993).[9]

This brings us back to the reports mentioned earlier, also rich in suggestions regarding another dimension of women's social position in Brazil: the diversity and inequality of positions. In fact, for these texts, the "Brazilian woman" is only the white, upper-class woman. This will constitute an issue to be faced by later feminist projects and studies. In a society marked by centuries of slavery and profound social asymmetries, there will be a particularly acute need to discuss the intersections between class, gender, and ethnicity, as well as to bear in mind the diversity of situations. Here, the social hierarchy is reproduced in the hierarchies of sub-disciplines in the field of sociology, there being a smaller stock of studies of poor women — whether white, black or mulatta, free or otherwise — during the colonial period. As in the sources of information that come to us from travelers, the literature concerns itself chiefly with white women from the wealthier classes. From the beginning, however, Portuguese colonization imposed profound distinctions between categories of women in Brazil, like those glimpsed above, which have helped mold different patterns of relationships with men and different expectations as to women's social roles. Women from the lower classes not only worked, they were also able to exercise greater freedom.

In fact, if we proceed to examine poor — generally mulatta or black — women, who came increasingly to live in the urban centers, we shall arrive at the obverse of common-sense notions about a feminine identity subject to parents and proprietors. Recent authors have endeavored to throw light on areas in which women participated in colonial society by studying the history of women engaged in traditionally female functions, as midwives, confectioners, laundresses, seamstresses, etc. What is stressed here is their economic function, especially as small traders. Itinerant women food-sellers proliferated in the colony (the "black tray-women"), as did women proprietors of small stores, generally unmarried women or heads of families. There was a contingent of women who contributed to tax revenues and played a significant role in supplying food to the more urbanized areas, like the mid-west mining region in the eighteenth century (Figueiredo, 1993). Also being rediscovered here, besides their for-profit activities, is their role in developing the spheres of leisure and sociability in colonial society (as we shall explain later). They bring other images of women onto the stage of Brazilian society — albeit by the back door — which will also count in constructing a collective consciousness with regard to gender.

Women and the First Volunteer Organizations

What is the place, in this society, of volunteer associations or associations for the provision of public services by private initiative? In what way did women's social life depend on these associations, or how was it affected by them?

From what has been said, it can be seen that the terrain was not favorable to the emergence of this kind of organization. The plantation system is known to be averse to the construction of a democratic society. There, free men occupied an economically secondary position and had to depend on personal, client relations with someone prominent in order to survive and rise socially. The society so created was ruled by the logic of personal favors and loyalties, leaving little room for individual associations to flourish.

Another characteristic of Brazil's historical formation was, however, to be fundamental to understanding the issue of women and philanthropy — the weight of the Catholic Church in molding that society. For almost four centuries, the church was the institution most responsible for managing the opportunities, initiatives, and values linked to what we may call philanthropic activities. At least until the mid-eighteenth century, wherever there were social assistance, health, or education organizations, the church was also there, with a mandate from the state to promote them. Particularly noteworthy here are initiatives from two fields, the religious orders and the brotherhoods.

Although bound to the church structure, the religious orders nonetheless enjoyed a great deal of autonomy, considerably helped by their economic independence. Their funds came less from royal donations than from private bequests and donations — a "lordly philanthropy" which was quite active in the Colony (Russel-Wood, 1968). These orders — chiefly the Jesuits, but also Franciscans, Benedictines, and Carmelites — amassed great patrimonies and secured a close relationship with society, being responsible for founding schools, hospitals, hostels, asylums, etc.

In Brazil, then, philanthropic activity by women inevitably emerged in close association with Catholic Church groups, above all the women's religious orders that brought hundreds of Sisters of Charity (of the Immaculate Conception, the Franciscans, Carmelites, etc.) to Brazil. Gradually, convents, retreats, and women's schools were set up (the latter, as of the nineteenth century).

The convents and retreats — generally run by nuns from one of the orders, aided by lay volunteers — emerged as the first institutions of and for women. These institutions, set up in Brazil for the purpose of ensuring honor, devotion, and education — in keeping with the European tradition — multiplied particularly from the eighteenth century onwards. They housed both women who had opted for the contemplative, religious life (note that the position of nun carried status in this society) as well as those who were in some way socially displaced — orphans, widows, spinsters, or those who had transgressed against custom (women's honor was a central value in family structure).[10] The honor of honorable women was preserved, while the dishonored were punished. Indians, slaves, and prostitutes did not fit these categories (Algranti, 1993; Russel-Wood, 1968; Leite, 1993). Note also that, until the nineteenth century, these institutions were also the only education option for women.

The study by Algranti, mentioned above, draws a profile of the recluses in convents and retreats, showing that most were single women between sixteen and thirty years of age, the daughters of legitimate marriages within the colonial elite. Many took their slaves with them. In their interiors, the retreats reproduced the feminine culture of the epoch — music lessons, books of saints, flowers, sewing, and cookery.

A wide range of situations led women to enter these retreats. Families of the rural aristocracy would commit their daughters to prevent them from entering into socially unequal marriages. Parents who were unable or unwilling to provide dowries, a precondition of marriage, also committed their daughters. Women involved in family conflicts, widows, or spinsters also sought shelter. Girls from good families who had "lost their honor" were taken in. There were also special refuges for orphans where they would remain under social control awaiting marriage. The donating of money, goods, and bequests to these institutions, so as to provide these girls with the dowries that would enable them to marry, was one of the oldest practices in Brazilian philanthropy.

These women's institutions thus fulfilled a general function in maintaining order as concerned the possible places that women might find for themselves in society. The dominant image throughout their history is one of male violence against daughters and sisters, where forced internment was used frequently as a control strategy. On the other hand, women's repeatedly "opting" for the retreats can be seen as a form of flight from extreme situations of patriarchal family domination. When analyzing the role of these pre-industrial "separatist" organizations, we cannot lose sight of their ambiguous nature as the only leeway left for sociability and even social survival in an intolerably domineering society.

In the early centuries of Brazilian society, it is the brotherhoods or fraternities, however, that provide the typical example of a lay collective association with a reasonable degree of autonomy. In such a vast territory, the apparatus of religion was decentralized and weakened and, following the tradition of medieval Iberian Catholicism — full of feasts, devotions and sanctuaries — Brazil became home to a whole range of religious practices carried out by lay people. Here, countless brotherhoods emerged, voluntary associations which afforded the individual not only religious worship, but access to leisure, social life, and, above all, a variety of services such as health care, old age and burial assistance, masses for the souls of the departed and aid for their families, prison aid, etc. The most famous and important — active to this day and symbolizing the philanthropic institution in Brazil — is the Brotherhood of Mercy, which was founded in Portugal in the late fifteenth century on the initiative of Dona Leonor, wife of Dom João II, and then brought to Brazil. The Brotherhood of Mercy — yet another of the usual "first lady" models of charitable initiative — built countless hospitals, asylums, and teaching establishments around the country. It was supported chiefly by private donations and bequests. It was the Brotherhood of Mercy that, in 1739 in Rio de Janeiro, founded the first lay institution for the reclusion of women, which was maintained by private donations. Its purpose was to shelter orphans and it was devoted to retreats and the transmission of Christian values and education for marriage. With the labor of a large contingent of nuns, this Brotherhood carried out social work on a large scale under the protection of the Portuguese Crown. From the nineteenth century onwards, these became settings for volunteer work by ladies from local high society, thus contributing to building up and consolidating a model for charitable voluntary work by women in Brazil.

As a general rule, however, the brotherhoods that sprang up across the country were small, locally colored associations, many of a corporatist nature, formed by specific social sectors. These brotherhoods have been identified as one of the main channels through which women acted together and socialized during the colonial period. Their participation in these organizations varied in form and direction, however, according to the social position occupied by the women. Although, for white women, they constituted one place where they were permitted to engage in activities outside the home, they found reproduced there the same barriers encountered in society. Only married women were admitted, at their husbands' discretion — which followed from the outset, since they were unable to pay the contribution due — and even these were forbidden from participating as directors. Recent research regarding the brotherhoods of mulattos or blacks shows the importance of women's participation, a mass phenomenon in some regions of Brazil. "For black and mulatta women, religious participation in the brotherhoods reflected the role they played in the social life of communities in Minas Gerais. The poor conditions to which they were submitted — and the consequent need to avail themselves of the social assistance offered — constituted an important motivation for their entering these corporations. There, they also sought social contact with their color peers" (Figueiredo, 1993, 161). Above all, the "popular" brotherhoods — unlike those for whites — often had statutes that provided for women to participate in their hierarchies and allowed them to pay their own annuities, like any brother.

It remains, finally, to mention the role played by women engaged in small-scale trade in social interaction in the poorer classes of colonial society. Their little stalls scattered along roadways and in the smaller towns were meeting places for passing the time of day, for parties, and for the sessions of drumming, singing, and dancing (*batuques*) characteristic of celebrations in the African religions that have always coexisted with Catholicism, as one aspect of the multifaceted, hidden face of this slave society. Identified with the mass of slaves and the "socially disqualified" — where prostitution also found its place[11] — and associated with consumption and pleasure, these dangerous women were frequently persecuted by the civil and religious authorities in a context where "leisure and entertainment were seen as perilous and harmful to the existing order" (Melo and Souza, 1993, 13). Some interesting approaches are now highlighting the fact that they "contributed decisively to consolidating primary associative bonds among (the poorer classes), where these rarely existed. Thus, by creating and participating in the elementary conditions for spreading solidarity and cohesion, they counteracted the fluidity and dispersion that characterize social groups under domination..." (Figueiredo, 1993, 33). Inside the booths, at the Sunday gatherings, Portuguese and African traditions were mingled with original syncretic forms. "Many poor individuals momentarily forgot their misfortune to the sound of the drums and little Portuguese guitars, but several social gatherings served to facilitate encounters among people of similar condition and to seal bonds of solidarity" (Melo and Souza, 1993, 14).

Although this minor, woman-dominated commerce was for-profit, it nonetheless took on an associative and cultural nature — albeit informally — and came to constitute a kind of "popular salon" centered on female figures.

Some Conclusions

In the early centuries, as Brazilian society was first forming, the only context in which the great majority of white women were permitted activities outside the home were certain "voluntary organizations," if one can so consider the institutions with varying degrees of autonomy generated by the Catholic Church. These activities grew up at frontiers between the secular and confessional spheres and were permeated by ideas of personalized Christian charity.

Covents, retreats, and brotherhoods, as is to be expected in a patriarchal, slave-owning society, took on a normalizing role, reproducing the social pattern of exclusion, subordination, and prohibition from work, all taken to represent women and their position in society.

It should not be overlooked, however, that these institutions, in one way or another, brought women out of the closed world of the home and broke into or interrupted the direct, day-to-day dominion of fathers and husbands. More refined study of sentiments, gestures, and symbols leads us to consider possible ways in which a specifically feminine kind of sociability — or even the seeds of resistance — may have developed behind the (more or less extreme) silences, dramas, and isolation of these women's cloistered existences. Here, we should mention the countless, single, mystical, and devoutly religious women who, in isolation — in their homes or through the religious third orders and brotherhoods — gained social recognition for holiness and were responsible for founding convents and untold charitable works. Acting at the limits of what was considered socially acceptable and at times persecuted as heretics or witches, these women are figures emblematic of a specifically female power gestating in "individualist" philanthropic initiatives which were undertaken on the basis of symbolic not economic capital.

As we have seen, it was chiefly through the brotherhoods — the closest approximation to a lay voluntary association in colonial society — that women could partake in public affairs and play some role there in the social work of these organizations.

As opportunities for sociability, for participation in public matters, and above all for the creation of "parallel powers" (cf. McCarthy, op. cit.), the brotherhoods were most significant for poor women, who were often permitted to pay their own contributions and assume posts in the organizations' hierarchies. Nonetheless, these women from the under-privileged classes — the "disqualified" inhabitants of the first towns — enjoyed greater freedom and participation in the colony's public life through their economic activities, with significant consequences for culture and leisure. As happened throughout most of Brazil's history in the dominated sectors of society, however, this presence — permanent and influential, although lacking in visibility — maintained in the backyard of society, was informal in nature and rarely found expression as civil organizations structured according to the society's dominant legal and cultural codes.

In summary, the endeavor to identify the part played by voluntary organizations as channels through which white women maintained a presence in colonial society is an exercise in following hints — the first signs, the primitive forms of women's action in public matters — a journey through ambiguous terrain. These fields of opportunity were small and contradictory, but they were practically the only ones available to these "idle, recluse women." For that reason, they are significant.

It is important to analyze these practices and this period, which covers the greater part of Brazil's history, because it is there that features and models of women's participation in philanthropy are revealed and shaped. There, action through religion and the church (this institution which hierarchy is totally male) became generalized and consolidated, in a situation where the legitimate motivations for these "homebound" women were the values of religious personalized charity. The women's history in public life, in social assistance, in association building, in organizations involved in social reforms, will refer strongly, by opposition or adhesion, to this "model" — and later to others — in play in activities of the Catholic Church.

In Brazil, as in other Latin American countries, change in the direction of modernity did not occur by a linear process of evolution, but permitted traditional and modern social relations to coexist patently and in complex mixtures. These colonial women — the heretic and the saint, from the home and the street — and the primary sources of their voluntary action coexist in the social imagination with other practices and representations of the female that, in contemporary times, have (perhaps) become dominant.

WOMEN'S VOLUNTARY ACTIVITIES
AT THE ONSET OF MODERNIZATION
FROM THE MID-NINETEENTH CENTURY TO THE 1920S

In Brazil, civil organizations played no leading part in the processes of independence, the abolition of slavery, and the proclamation of the Republic. There was no lack of local revolts, regional conflicts, and popular campaigns or uprisings as these changes were consolidated and a national identity constructed in the second half of the nineteenth century, but none of this depended on nor produced a consolidated field of strong, durable civil organizations.

This fact reflects a feature of this society where political, institutional, and economic changes occur by way of "undertakings at the top" among the dominant sectors, without revolutions and with relatively little participation by organized civil society. Industrialization — culminating in the consolidation of power by the industrial classes from 1930 onwards — was to occur by a process of "conservative modernization," in which the agrarian structure and authoritarianism would be perpetuated and the state would play a pivotal role. Sociological literature, which is silent on voluntary organizations during this period, makes an exception — stemming from its interest in politics — for only two groups of organizations: the ephemeral abolitionist associations and the workers' mutual societies (the seeds of trade unionism) which flourished at the end of the century.

The literature on women in Brazil that has been produced in the last twenty years, however, takes the period beginning in the mid-nineteenth century as a significant time for analysis. These studies are marked by the question of women's emancipation and are interested in reinstating and giving visibility to the political character of women's voluntary actions, groups, and organizations that emerged during this period with their focus on social reform and changing women's traditional identities, images, and roles.

The backdrop to this upsurge was the gradual development of certain urban centers toward the end of the century, with the beginnings of industrialization. Fleeing from the Napoleonic Wars, the Portuguese Court had moved to Brazil in 1808 and made Rio de Janeiro the seat of the monarchy, which also served to introduce European patterns of behavior among women of the upper classes.[12] Ideas of women's emancipation that had been growing in Europe and the United States also began to find their way, little by little and with difficulty, into Brazil.

Certain isolated examples of female intellectualism contributed to this process at the beginning of the century. One mythical example is Nísia

Floresta Brasileira Augusta (pseudonym of Dionísia Gonçalves Pinto), born in 1809, who separated from her first husband at fifteen, took up with another man, and then was widowed at twenty-four with two children. She then devoted herself to teaching and to defending women's interests — especially the right to education — and founded a school. She was a defender of the interests of indigenous groups, an abolitionist, and republican. In 1832 she published in Brazil her free translation, adapted from the original to the Brazilian context, of the pioneering work by Mary Wollstonecraft, *Vindication of the Rights of Women,* which ran through three editions (Duarte, 1989).[13] Nísia, perhaps unable to adapt to the situation in which she was living, finally moved to Europe.

The English traveler, John Luccock, was dismayed in 1813 at Brazilian women's "lack of education and instruction," a situation socially produced: "it was considered that, for them, knowing how to read should not go beyond the prayer book, since it would be useless to them, neither was it wished that they should write, so that — as was wisely observed — they should not misuse this art." The writings of Nísia Floresta, and others that will be mentioned below, certainly justified this concern.

Women's Newspapers:
Recipes for Cakes and Emancipation

There was a great lack of formal education for Brazilian women until nearly the end of the nineteenth century. In 1872, 11.5 percent of women were literate (in urban centers like Rio de Janeiro the figure rose to 29.3 percent). At this time, for a total population of 10,112,061, there were only 5,077 public and private schools, attended by 114,014 male and 46,246 female pupils. The daughters of wealthy families were often educated at home, by nuns or foreigners, from whom they received basic literacy training, "domestic skills," and, at the best of times, French and piano to be used in the salons.

It is in this context that one has to understand, in all its dimensions, the appearance in the second half of the nineteenth century of newspapers founded, directed, and written by women. Their principal emancipation battle-cry was the right to education. This press was established thanks to voluntary efforts and donations of personal funds by a minority of educated women. It is only very recently that these efforts have received due attention from feminist-inspired studies and are being salvaged from the oblivion to which they were consigned by the Brazilian press (Hahner, 1981; Barroso, 1982).

Close reading of these newspapers reveals, contrary to first impressions, publications directed toward modifying women's social expectations by talking about emancipation, rights, and equality. Between 1840 and 1890, eight newspapers were produced with significant continuity by women in Brazilian state capitals. Behind names like "O Jornal das Senhoras" (*The Ladies' Newspaper*), "A Família" (*The Family*), "Bello Sexo" (*Fair Sex*), "A Mulher" (*Woman*), "O Sexo Feminino" (*The Female Sex*), and "Miosotis" — and alongside articles on fashion, cookery, dances, or carnival — were numerous texts claiming rights for women or even containing proposals for concrete action (cf. Crescenti Bernardes, 1983).[14]

Editorial lines varied, depending greatly on the founder and leading light of the newspaper. For example, the first one worthy of note, "The Ladies' Newspaper," was set up in 1852 by the Argentinian Joana Manso, who separated from her Portuguese husband and lived in Rio de Janeiro. Her frame of reference was given by progressive, enlightenment ideas brought from Europe and the United States, which she had visited. In the introductory editorial, she states her intention to work "for women's social improvement and moral emancipation," which presupposed "the fair enjoyment of their rights, of which the brutal egoism of men robs them." The stress is on demonstrating how men are to blame for women's situation and urging change in men's consciousness and conduct. Men have to understand that "an angel will be of more use to them than a doll." While not exactly libertarian, the "angel" option does make sense in this case because it counters the scorn and disparagement with which women were treated in the home and affords them a position of respect and value. The need for women to be educated is also upheld, inevitably invoking the image of Jesus and Mary, "women's natural religious sentiment," and their functions as mothers, who should be enlightened in order better to remove "this dire prejudice from their sons' spirit: this idea of unjust superiority."

Most of the later newspapers went further. Instead of appealing to male consciousness or invoking the image of the Virgin Mary, they incited women to rebel against the legal and social injustices and inequalities of which they were the victims. They advocated job training and economic independence,[15] the right to vote, equal property rights, and some — in defiance of the church — even divorce. Brazilian society would regenerate only when women were educated completely. In a country where women were not granted access to university until 1879, the tactic of advocating greater opportunities and the right to instruction was central and demonstrated not only that the sexes were intellectually equal but even that women were superior, since they possessed more of the "precious patience for higher studies; that is, physics, pharmacy and medicine," while men should devote themselves to labors calling for physical strength (*The Female Sex*). The approach was certainly to highlight women's particular worth in the realm of morality and duty, although even the more libertarian publications would not break with the central values of family, motherly love, and religion. As in the above example of "patience," the familiar manipulation of "feminine attributes" was used to argue that women should be trained professionally in certain areas or even, as in one coherent argument in *The Fair Sex,* that the woman (and not the man) should be the head of the family.

These newspapers served above all as places for the women who published them to meet and form groups. When they appealed for articles to be sent in, the response was good. The many women who initially asked to remain anonymous steadily gave way to others prepared to expose themselves and sign their contributions. The newspapers were a way of breaking out of their isolation, engaging in intellectual exchanges and taking positions in public debate.

The proportion of literate women in Rio de Janeiro rose from 29.3 percent in 1872 to 43.8 percent in 1890. Nonetheless, subscriptions were insufficient to cover the newspapers' costs, perhaps because of their progressive message or the competition they faced from other for-profit entertainment newspapers for women, produced by men. They relied basically on the funds of their pioneering founders, who did not possess great fortunes. They were often in crisis and had to suspend publication for lack of resources.

As we have shown, however, by giving their own time and, generally scarce, resources, groups of women from the middle classes were able to clear a space in society for a rare kind of initiative — organized, autonomous, and secular — in a context that was materially and ideologically averse to their pursuing professional activities. In a society where the public space was itself in a precarious state of construction, these women decided to expose themselves and make their presence felt by voluntary work (in turn helping to build that public arena) and to propose changes in attitudes, laws, and services.

Activists in Social Reforms

As has been said, there is a reasonable body of literature on Brazilian women's participation in struggles for social rights or reforms, especially in the case of suffragism, between the end of the nineteenth century and the 1930s. Here, we encounter types of discourse and action which are quite familiar, given that they took their inspiration from European and, particularly, North American movements of the same kind. This is not the place to explore this subject, but I shall merely outline, in general terms, the features and specific role that these pioneering women's voluntary organizations took on in Brazilian society.

Women played a role in the abolitionist movement which, around

1860, became a legitimate issue for broad sections of the middle and dominant classes. Women's abolitionist associations were set up, like the Sociedade de Libertação (Liberation Society) founded in Rio de Janeiro in 1870 and the Sociedade Redentora (Redemption Society), founded the same year in São Paulo. Women also participated in the movement through fund raising activities, such as producing sweets and flowers or presenting musical gatherings at home. Women also took part in male abolitionist associations. Here, however, in line with the predominant social attitudes, they were not especially visible. Besides the articles written in the newspapers mentioned above, only one activist, Maria Amélia de Queiroz, is known to have made public speeches (Hahner, 1981). In terms of empowerment for their sex, though, women's voluntary participation can be said to have taken conservative forms, although it did contribute to abolition. In supporting the anti-slavery cause, they took a secondary position and contributed basically by way of traditional female activities, reflecting their subordinate position in society. Moreover, there was always some celebrated father or husband, or even a male organization like the Masons, behind the founding of women's abolitionist organizations. Also, the values invoked in granting recognition for this (semi) public activity by women were always charity and love, rather than any associated with citizenship and social equality.

The struggle for the vote — which developed later and culminated in victory in 1932 — was more drawn-out, at times radical, and led to the creation of important voluntary organizations for women. It began with a few isolated voices in the 1880s, went through a frustrated attempt to include the new law in the first republican constitution of 1891, and grew most significantly from the 1920s onwards.

The suffragist movement was led by women, both traveled and of intellectual stature, some of whom — already in the 1920s — occupied government posts of some importance. One outstanding figure was Bertha Lutz, a biologist who had graduated from the Sorbonne and then, by public examination, secured a place on the directorate of the National Museum in Rio de Janeiro. In 1919, she was one of Brazil's representatives on the International Women's Council of the International Labor Organization and, on her return, founded the Liga para a Emancipação Intelectual da Mulher (League for Women's Intellectual Emancipation), which in 1922 produced the Federação Brasileira para o Progresso Feminino (Brazilian Federation for Women's Progress), affiliated to the International Alliance for Women's Vote. Like many of the other organizations that spread through the country — Leagues for Women's Progress in the states, Liga Nacional das Mulheres Eleitoras (National League of Women Electors), Aliança Brasileira pelo Sufrágio

Feminino (Brazilian Alliance for Female Suffrage), etc. — in 1910 it also set up a short-lived political party drawn largely from the ranks of the civil service, the Partido Republicano Feminino (Women's Republican Party).

Certain features can be highlighted in order to describe this women's movement, its role in Brazilian society and in the process of women's emancipation. In the first place, it established the first communications between networks of women and organizations in Brazil and those abroad. In Brazil, the development of suffragist movement was marked by congresses and journeys by leaders, especially to the United States, as well as by visits by suffragists from North America, an exchange which nurtured discourses, action, and legitimacy.[16] These links certainly went beyond just the fight for the vote and reinforced the presence of modern western values and cultural horizons in Brazilian society.

The suffragist movement also served to involve women from a broader range of social origins in emancipation issues. By 1922, emancipation organizations were composed mostly of working women, like civil servants, typists, teachers, engineers, lawyers, pharmacists, etc. (Hahner, 1983).

Finally, in order to set Brazilian women's struggle for the vote in its rightful place, we have to consider the significance of the vote itself, in this 1920s or '30s society. Given that the electoral college was tiny, largely controlled by local oligarchies, and subject to all kinds of political manipulation, no great hopes for social change could be settled in the mere right to vote or the exercise of that right. There was no expectation, as there might have been in other countries, that the movement's success would bring about radical changes in women's share in power — and that is one of the reasons that women's spirits were not particularly raised once they had won the vote (and, on the other hand, their activism in civil society continued).[17] For the women of the time, the suffragist movement most clearly constituted an episode in a multifaceted process of emancipation, where there was even talk of fighting for human rights. In Brazil, it was also allied with broader reform movements against the power of the local oligarchies. This may be one of the reasons why, as of the 1920s, it was so widely accepted by elite political and intellectual circles and gained admittance as a subject for salon debate. What also contributed greatly, in a context where the international frame of reference was important, was the fact that in other countries the women's vote had not led to a breakdown of family structure or the established order.

After years of campaigns and congresses, of setting up organizations and lobbying the legislature, women finally got the vote as a result of the electoral reform undertaken by Getúlio Vargas in 1932.[18] In 1931, the government sanctioned a provisional code granting the vote to only certain segments of women, like self-supporting single women or widows, and married women with their husbands' permission. Led by Bertha Lutz, a commission of leaders from the suffrage movement managed to get an audience with the president, who accepted full suffrage for women, under the same conditions as laid down for men by the new code. The suffragist movement was not to escape a characteristic of so many processes of social change in Brazil: gains granted from above by some authority which, with rare exceptions, was always male. In this case, it was a president known popularly as the "father of the poor."

Conclusions

Like several peripheral societies to which industrialization came late, Brazilian society changed rapidly between the end of the nineteenth century and the 1930s and, with it, so did women's situation change as they entered the labor market and came to share in the egalitarian ideas of more developed western societies. This change, of course, applied to a noisy minority of women from the middle or intellectualized classes of urban society — plus some participants in the nascent workers' movement — whose cosmopolitan habits came to coexist with the traditional attitudes and habits of a large part of the population, permeated by Iberian values of hierarchy and honor, where individualism and the idea of equality have difficulty taking root.

But the conclusions are obvious. There is no doubt that it was through the channels created in the form of nongovernment organizations and with the giving of great quantities of what they had (their time and labor) that women were able to play a role in public matters, even influencing legislative reforms and contributing to the building of citizenship (although they did not bring about a revolution in their position in society). There were certainly fewer expectations that they would be "storming the citadels of power" by participating in government legislative and decision-making circles than there might have been in other societies with consolidated liberal democratic traditions. Borrowing from Gramscian thinking the concept of the "war of positions," we can rediscover the positive significance of women's and feminist movements of this period, as part of a longer process of cultural and ideological change arising from a diversity of organizations and initiatives in society. Note that this is a context where democratic institutions in Brazil were far from consolidated and where civil society was embryonic.

As always, one must highlight the contradictions and ambiguities present in these movements and initiatives, where the traditional female roles of mother, wife, bearer of virtue and religious spirit were reproduced, at the same time as changes in women's position in society were being proposed and accomplished. Various initiatives mingled religious charity and social activism; a detailed research study on the trajectory of these women would certainly find a trail leading more frequently than might be supposed from social assistance work to struggles in the public arena for civil rights, which forged ambiguous female identities (a matter to which we shall return later).[19] Despite the fact that religion was an almost universal frame of reference, it is as well to remember that the women's organizations mentioned in this section were set up in a manner without precedent: outside of church structures.

STATE, CHURCH, AND
WOMEN'S SOCIAL ASSISTANCE WORK AFTER 1930

Omnipresent State and Philanthropic Organizations

Any study concerning itself with the subject will discover a proliferation of voluntary associations in Brazil's cities in the closing years of the nineteenth century and the first two decades of the twentieth century (Conniff, 1975; Landim, 1993). The women's and feminist organizations mentioned above were to coexist with brotherhoods and religious organizations, as well as mutual, professional, and class associations which multiplied in the context of worsening urban problems. Trade union groups were the target of constant repressive action by the state and, in the 1920s, one president declared that "social problems are a case for the police."

This situation of repressive laissez-faire was to change only after state intervention to create a social policy with social security and labor legislation. The 1930s, with Vargas' rise to power, ushered in a period of centralized, nationalist developmentism reinforced by political authoritarianism (tinged with paternalism) and broad state intervention in the economy and society.

As to state regulation of social relations in consolidating industrial society, Brazil took a path analogous to that of more advanced countries. Nonetheless, social policy was developed within certain specific parameters that are incomprehensible if we take the welfare state as the analytical model. This policy was fundamentally corporatist, fragmented, selective, and ineffective. Trade unions and social security institutes were state-controlled and became instruments for communication and the exchange of favors between government and professional categories. Privileges were thus consolidated and, most importantly, since access was conditional upon the individual's or group's position in the labor market, the majority of the population continued to be excluded. A situation of "regulated citizenship" was thus instituted in Brazil, rooted in a system of occupational stratification and not in a code of political values. "Citizens" were those who happened to be located in some occupation recognized by law; citizenship was expanded through recognition of new professions, not by "expanding the values inherent to the concept of belonging of the community" (Santos, 1979). This left its mark on Brazilian civic culture and broadened the notion of marginality. Those sectors whose occupation was ignored by law were "pre-citizens."

As to the relationship between state and church, the symbiotic bond between them was progressively broken in the course of the nineteenth century, until legal separation came with the proclamation of the Republic in 1889. The liberal constitution of 1891 established freedom of religion, prohibited government subventions in temples or in religious education, recognized only civil marriages as valid, etc. From this point on, no longer protected or hampered by the state, the church reformed and reconstituted itself as a strong body of clergy closely attuned to Rome. New contingents of priests and nuns and new congregations arrived in Brazil, convents were built, parishes and lay associations were set up. Fundamental to church plans to forge closer links with the population was the establishment of schools, hospitals, assistance and charity works, which continued to receive the traditional donations of goods and money from the dominant classes of society, and donations of voluntary work, above all from women (nuns and lay women).

Reformed internally, in control of its lay bases, the church was the strongest institution in civil society around the 1930s, when church and state entered into a new period of solid political alliance. The former consolidated its plans for ideological hegemony over the Brazilian people, collaborating in turn with the state to maintain social order, although a sharp distinction was maintained between spiritual and temporal orders. The 1934 constitution was to grant the church a series of privileges. The nonprofit organizations founded by religious bodies played an important part in this collaboration and received large government subsidies (Serbin, 1992).

Mission and Profession: The Place of Women's Social Action in a Centralizing Context

As seen above, the centralist project and strong state presence in Brazilian society from the 1930s onward preserved a place for philanthropic organizations. It is chiefly by way of these organizations that assistance was to reach the broad masses of the population marginalized by corporatist social policies. Private schools and universities, for the most part legally registered as nonprofit organizations and set up chiefly by the Catholic Church, were also to play a role in providing education to the middle classes and elites.

In this model, female volunteers finally found a position with recognition and visibility in Brazilian society. Women's social identity, abilities, and dispositions, built up through centuries of philanthropic work under church protection — in terrain at once public and private, secular and confessional — were now to permit these women to become recognized elements in the execution of government policies, in this Brazilian style "welfare state." Women left the protected, semi-private sphere of personalized charity and entered the public arena, via new, "rationalized" forms of social assistance sponsored by business sectors and the state — with all the ambiguities and contradictions in terms of social and political power that this entailed.

One basic factor in this conversion was to be the granting, in the 1930s and '40s, of professional qualifications in social work, following suitable technical and university curricula. The practices of these specialists in social assistance work were to be recognized in law, opening a new job market. This official recognition was thus especially important in Brazil as a source of full citizenship. Once again, "natural" feminine attributes were manipulated, this time to afford women a monopoly in this kind of training. "There are evidently specifically female careers; those which require aptitudes, tendencies and a set of intellectual and moral qualities that belong, principally, to women. The complex, delicate tasks involved in Social Work are a case in point." This text introduced regulations of the first Federal Public Faculty of Social Work, officially recognized in 1944 in Rio de Janeiro, and justifying the fact that only women students would be admitted (Pinheiro, 1985). The feminine nature of the new profession became clear at the Pan American Congress of Social Work in 1949: of the fifteen social work schools opened in Brazil, thirteen admitted only female students. One more feature of the new professional formation was revealed on this occasion: of the fifteen schools, twelve were set up under the auspices of the Catholic Church, and three by the government (Iamamoto and Carvalho, 1988).

This field of social work and the training of female personnel is a prime example of the alliance between church and state. Social work originated in nongovernment institutions and via initiatives set up by the Catholic Church, where the ideological and confessional influence was strongly European (only after World War II would North American influences be felt in Brazil), and was then appropriated by the state.

As we have seen, philanthropy in Brazil, and female voluntary work, was set up through church channels and organizations. These were differentiated, however, since one of the characteristics of the Catholic Church is its internal diversity. The Catholic initiatives that would result, in the 1930s, in the institution of social work in Brazil drew their inspiration from doctrines of social Catholicism designed to encourage lay participation in missionary action directed to the issues of social inequality and injustice, in response to the materialist, class theories that were spreading, especially among the workers. A channel for direct exchanges was established between these initiatives and the Catholic University of Louvain which produced social work professors — like Adèle de Loneux, a specialist in the working class, sent for the first Initiation to Social Action course in 1932 — and trained Brazilian pioneers on the subject, such as Maria Kiehl and Albertina Ramos, who would become the founders of the first Social Work School in São Paulo in 1936.

As a result of the course in Social Action, autonomous organizations began to be set up for the purpose of founding Social Work schools. Active in this process was Ação Católica (Catholic Action), a lay movement developing at the time and made up of various organizations with strong international ties, such as Juventude Feminina Católica (Catholic Women's Youth), Juventude Operária Católica (Catholic Workers' Youth), and Juventude Universitária Católica (Catholic University Youth). Personnel from these movements would set up civil institutions like the Grupo de Ação Social (organized by a professor-priest from the Faculty of Philosophy of Louvain), the Centro de Estudos e Ação Social (CEAS, whose directorate was exclusively female),[20] the Instituto de Educação Familiar (Institute for Family Education), "Social Formation" circles, and "Social Action" organizations in several states. That is to say, important elements in the Catholic Church were to devote their efforts to implementing social work discourse and practices in Brazil according to church doctrine — rationalizing, modernizing, and establishing a methodology for social assistance work (Lima, 1987; Iamamoto and Carvalho, 1988).

This development occurred at an ideal moment for the populist state to absorb this work, which specialized in dealing not only with particularly vulnerable sectors of the population, but also with the working class. The successive Social Action Weeks held during this period reveal, in their composition, an alliance between the Catholic voluntary organizations that convened them and the Vargas government, which gave these encounters a semi-official nature. For example, the first of them, in 1936, would bring together not only the more active elements of the Catholic lay movement, but also distinguished figures representing the executive, legislative, judiciary, and the military — as well as a group of high-society ladies. The first meeting's Commission of Honor was chaired by an "official" female figure, the first lady, Darcy Vargas. This event, and others of its kind, was dominated by discourse critical of charity which, despite the "beauty" of its work, was "of little social effect": it was necessary to "professionalize the social apostolate" so as to provide women "collaborators" for private projects and "permanent personnel" for employers and government institutions (Iamamoto and Carvalho, 1988).

As we have said, women were the prime executors of this project, and they decidedly claimed this position for themselves. As Stella de Faro, founder of the Associação de Senhoras Brasileiras (Brazilian Ladies' Association, an assistance organization that also took part in the suffrage movement), declared during one of the Social Action Weeks: "The need is beginning to make itself felt among us for this female career in which no-one will dispute women's entitlement to these posts, which even though positions of command, are above all positions of service." These first social workers came from the urban elites and it was only later that social work, above all in public schools, was to become a far more secular, middle-class profession.

As part of Vargas' populist project, recognition for women's status in social work was symbolized by the place given to the president's wife. As in other populist regimes (such as in Argentina, although not quite as effectively and spectacularly as Eva Peron), the first lady was made president of the agency responsible for attending to the most vulnerable sectors of the population, the Legião Brasileira de Assistência (Brazilian Assistance Legion). Created in 1942 to act under agreements with philanthropic organizations, it was financed by public and private funds and, in each state of the Federation, presided over by the governor's wife. The LBA, which always relied on volunteers as well as professionals, spread throughout 90 percent of the municipalities in Brazil, constituting the domain par excellence of "social charity" by first ladies and society ladies. It has entered history as one of the instruments of government clientist policies. It was not until January 1995 that it was dissolved by presidential decree. The negative image of the woman-wife and society lady, associated with a kind of assistance care that bordered on corruption was also projected, along with the other images, into the Brazilian collective unconscious.

Conclusions

Traditional voluntary work by women in the field of philanthropy was to give rise in the 1930s to a women's profession, marking a break between personalized charity and institutionalized public assistance care.[21] In the case of Brazil, however, certain traits were to persist in these activities permeated by religion and marked by the images of self-sacrifice and sensitivity, chiefly because the Catholic Church continued to be fundamental to building up social assistance action, although now brought up to date. While women dedicated to social work came to be called to a labor market, this occupation continued the ambiguity between "apostolate" and "profession," "command" and "service," as attested above and in a number of other statements by pioneers from this period (see the interviews conducted by Lima, 1987) that emphasize the option for social work as a "mission" and reflect the prevailing prejudice against women's earning wages. The fact that the first social work schools were open only to women certainly also had to do with traditional conceptions of morality and decorum.

Nonetheless, the state's appropriation of the new profession was not to be without its consequences. The growing presence of women social workers in state secretariats, government agencies dealing with juveniles, education, and health (where they often held decision-making positions), as well as the creation of more and more public courses in social work, steadily secularized the profession and offered opportunities in Brazilian public life for a segment of the female population. Some of these women, from their positions in the state apparatus, gained access to the media and were able to bring pressure to bear on the formulation of government policies for maternity and infant care.[22] It is important that we add, so as not to stray from out subject of nongovernment organizations, how much these positions owed to action which was built up socially in voluntary organizations.[23] Above all, it is important to remember how much state approval — official recognition for a profession — meant in terms of acknowledgment of citizenship in the 1930s and 40s.

Any deeper understanding of the gains, losses, and ambiguities of women's participation in Brazilian public affairs in this period, through the field of social assistance, depends on a fuller understanding of the biographies and trajectories of these pioneers who, by way of "scientific" social assistance, founded a profession and cut a path through to the realm of public affairs. There are no systematic data on this subject, which is being neglected by feminist-inspired studies (despite the fact that the history of social work is one written basically by women). This is perhaps because, despite what was brought to light above, women's participation in government agencies via social work was almost always in subordinate positions and did not generate radical changes in women's power in Brazilian society. It could not have been otherwise. It should not be forgotten that this professionalization and participation in public life, whether through private or government agencies, was framed by the social project of an authoritarian government, which afforded almost no place for egalitarian, emancipatory ideologies.

Between 1937 and 1945, election-related policies came to an end — not just for women but for all citizens — and opportunities for women to participate in government agencies became even more restricted. The traditional fields for women's participation in private assistance care, which continued to flourish, deserve further study — to include the development of participation by other religions such as the Evangelist churches and Kardecist spiritualist groups. Nonetheless, women's volunteer organizations based on liberal, democratic ideals lost their vigor under the Vargas dictatorship. With the restoration of democracy, especially in the 1950s, there occurred a resurgence of women's organizations participating in the struggle for social reforms.[24] Nonetheless, the 1964 military takeover was to radically destroy the structures of all that had been built up in Brazil in terms of organized civil society.

SEVERAL FACES OF WOMEN'S VOLUNTARY ACTION IN BUILDING CIVIL SOCIETY FROM THE 1970S TO THE PRESENT

Two Decades of Change: Very Little, but Too Much

As in several other parts of the world, so in Brazil the figures point to a situation of inequality and to women's exclusion from public life, the labor market, decision-making mechanisms, and so on. Statistics show that, for example, the average working woman in Brazil earns 43 percent less than the working man. They show that only 7 percent of women who complete higher education earn more than minimum wages, as against 34 percent of men in the same situation. While women make up 35.5 percent of the economically active population, they account for only 2 percent of executive positions. Despite their growing participation in professional organizations, they have little part in executive positions: for example, 52 percent of the members of the Associação Brasileira de Advogados (Brazilian Bar Association), 40 percent of the Associação de Imprensa (Brazilian Press Association), and 31.5 percent of the Conselho Federal de Medicina (Federal Medical Council) are women, although there is not one woman on the boards of these three organizations. And so it goes.

However, against the backdrop of the historical and cultural situation described here, other figures, as to the speed of recent changes, are more encouraging. In 1970, 20.9 percent of Brazil's economically active population was composed of women. In twenty years (1990), this proportion had grown to 35.5 percent (a 70 percent increase). In 1990, there were

23 million women working (not counting informal work, which occupies five women for every man); that is, 39.2 percent of women were in employment. That is a small number and indicates a situation of considerable marginality — above all if we compare these numbers with those for Sweden (81.7 percent) or the United States (66.5 percent). Nonetheless, this contingent is growing under historically adverse conditions (suffice it to say, for instance, that until 1969 women were not admitted to important state financial organizations like the Banco do Brasil — Bank of Brazil). In 1993, 22 percent of Brazilian families had a woman as "head of the family."

Given that it was only in 1879 that the first woman was legally permitted to attend university, and that the first Brazilian woman graduated in medicine in 1887, it is interesting to note that, one hundred years later, women account for 52 percent of the Brazil's university graduates (42 percent of graduates in Law, 62 percent in Medicine, and 19 percent in Engineering) and 57 percent of those who complete secondary school. Once again, the last twenty years have been decisive: women increased their participation in medicine, law, and engineering by 365 percent, 430 percent, and 1,084 percent, respectively. Only 3.4 percent of Brazil's municipal authorities are commanded by women, and women form only 5.8 percent of the Chamber of Deputies (the lower house of the legislature). This, however, is the result of a recent, rapid rise: in 1988, 107 women were elected to mayorships in Brazil; in 1992, the figure had risen to 171. In the 1992 elections, the number of women federal deputies rose from 8 to 26, standing as of this writing at 29. These advances may be ambivalent, but they are undeniable and, as is the case the world over, are due to a complex set of factors. In order to understand the scope of these changes and their characteristics in Brazilian society, they must be placed in context.

As for what interests us here — the role of voluntary associations or nonprofit organizations in the way women's position in Brazilian society has changed recently — the last twenty years are particularly revealing. The 1964 military coup broke with a long-standing populist regime, cut corporatist bonds between state and society, and left trade unions, associations, and universities in disarray. Besides the change in regime, a set of factors — such as galloping modernization and urbanization, the presence of new international actors in nongovernment cooperation, the strained relations between state and church — were to contribute to the appearance, at the height of the military dictatorship, of new fields of nonprofit activity and types of nonprofit organizations. This heralded the beginning of a period, particularly the 1970s, in which civil society organized slowly through the proliferation of autonomous organizations, frequently in opposition to the state and linked to trade union movements and a wide range of interest groups. In the 1980s, geometric growth by a plural sector of voluntary, nonprofit civil organizations represented the more dynamic side of the democracy-building process in Brazil.

In this context of building civil society in Brazil, women's presence was to leave its mark. On the one hand, especially through a variety of separatist organizations inspired by feminist ideas, they managed to bring their specific interests to the table of public debate and to create new identities and exercise pressure on legislative reform and government policies. On the other hand, in "assimilationist" situations, women were a massive presence in important social movements that developed in this period, such as trade unions, professional associations, neighborhood associations, etc. Lately, they have also come to take their place in the institutions and foundations responsible for "business philanthropy" that are now emerging in Brazil. By activism, voluntary work and even professionalization within nongovernment organizations, women have had the opportunity to bring considerable pressure to bear on public affairs in Brazil over the last twenty years. As occurred in the 1930s, so in this recent period, voluntary organizations have constituted important bridges to professionalization and to women's participation in government institutions — except that, in the current democratic and cultural context, there are greater opportunities to place their interests on the political agenda and to influence social reforms, either by transferring personnel trained in private organizations to the state, by partnering between these organizations and government agencies, or by proposing government policies and lobbying.

The Female Bases of Associationism

In the vast terrain of associationism that has steadily developed in Brazil since the 1970s, when civil society was synonymous with opposition to the military regime, women have played an important part, although it is rarely acknowledged or duly researched.

Alongside the autonomous trade unionism that grew up in the same period, the neighborhood and community associations which spread and organized nationwide were responsible for all that was most dynamic in terms of social movements in Brazil. Although these were clearly not women's or feminist organizations, women formed a massive presence in the formation and ongoing activities of these associations that spread chiefly through peripheral neighborhoods. Movements relating to neighborhood, home, or family — such as daycare centers or community schools, informal groups for buying and selling food, or committees to address problems like refuse disposal, sanitation, children's safety, etc. — mobilized women precisely on the basis of their "traditional" functions as mothers and housewives. Women spend more time in the neighborhood and at home than the men and thus establish links and networks of relations with the neighbors. They get to know local people and problems intimately and become emotionally involved with them.

Once again we return to the Catholic Church, which is an important actor in these events. Despite having supported the 1964 military takeover, the church hierarchy came out in open conflict with the government from the end of the 1960s, particularly over the issue of human rights. Not only was repression by the military regime mounting, but priests and nuns were beginning to be targets for prison and torture. The church was the only institution of civil society that had maintained its structure intact after the coup — a structure that comprised capillary connections with Brazilian society by way of its parishes, organizations, and community work. Inspired by Liberation Theology and by the Conferences of Medellín and Puebla (which enunciated a "preferential option for the poor"), new or renewed religious and lay actors began to proliferate, encouraging and providing opportunities for the formation of secular movements and organizations of workers, rural laborers, diverse professionals, etc. These movements took shape autonomously within church structures and were to produce important trade union and political leaders.

To return to women, those traditional volunteers of religious social action, much of their participation in these movements was linked to church initiatives, new or old. Noteworthy here are the hundreds (or thousands?) of Mothers Clubs set up by parishes,[25] the women's cooperatives (sponsored by religious bodies, for producing craft work, clothing, food), and the youth groups. Besides these "separatist" initiatives, we should also mention the Comunidades Eclesiais de Base (Church Base Communities or CEBs), which are small groups organized around parishes or chapels and formed on the initiative of lay people, priests, and bishops. These came to constitute veritable cells, meeting places for educating and mobilizing the local people (in 1980, there were said to be eighty thousand CEBs around the country). Despite the marked predominance of men in the church hierarchy, several studies point to the predominantly female composition of the CEBs — both nuns and lay women — although no clear figure is given.

Women were the prime movers in the emergence of important social movements in Brazil, such as those formed by neighborhood associations, most of which grew out of small, informal community groups that then spread locally. The Movimento do Custo da Vida (Cost of Living Movement, against increases in basic product prices), which grew out of the Mothers' Clubs and was notable for the role women played in it, was one of the first mass movements of the dictatorship years and brought people out onto the streets. With the exception of this movement, however, although women formed the grassroots of many organizations, their presence on the predominantly male steering committees was discrete, an absence that grew more marked as the movements became more formal, politicized, and socially visible.

This women's presence in important movements for social change was not necessarily guided by orthodox feminist ideas of emancipation. The disagreements between feminists and the Catholic Church are well known and made (make) themselves felt in a particular manner in the context described here. On the one hand, in those years, the progressive sectors of the church were important allies in any fight for greater democracy, social justice, and equality in Brazil. They were, however, unyielding on certain basic points of doctrine, such as prohibiting divorce and criminalizing abortion — issues dear to women's emancipation movements.[26] The church upholds broad participation by women in public life, providing they do not neglect their maternal and matrimonial obligations, but shies away from questioning their traditional functions and positions in the family.

The feminist organizations that were to grow in Brazil from the late 1980s onwards found it difficult to work with associations marked by origins in the Catholic Church, even though they might have a broad representation of women. It has become a major challenge to bring together these two currents: women's associationism at the grassroots level and feminist activist participation in Brazilian society. What is at stake here is not just, or not so much, the question of religious following, but rather a deeper cultural issue: the *ethos* that separates the great mass of Brazilian women of popular origins from those who make up a part of the intellectually and professionally equipped middle classes. In practice, over the last two decades, these bridges have been built chiefly in those regions of civil society where voluntary associations play a decisive role.

Feminist Organizations

As had happened with the suffrage movement, so international relations were to be highly significant in building the feminist movement in Brazil. As elsewhere in the world, International Women's Year, called by the United Nations in 1975, yielded linking and initiatives that were to prove fundamental for the Brazilian women's movement, above all by providing forums for discussion in a situation marked by a total lack of democratic freedoms. From here, women's encounters and nongovernment organizations began to emerge with agendas directed to analysis of the situation of women in Brazil and the formulation of strategies against gender discrimination, at the same time as they engaged in the fight for greater democracy and civil rights (for example, the Women's Pro-Amnesty Movement).[27]

In the years that followed 1975, the feminists organized into groups and voluntary associations and devoted their efforts to extending their activities in the direction described above, seeking bridges to church-related women's associations and to trade unions which, generally dominated by class ideology, also had trouble assimilating the specific nature of women's issues. In 1978, the first Congresso da Mulher Metalúrgica (Congress of Women Metalworkers) was held, closely followed by congresses of bank workers and journalists in which women participated.[28] Through newspapers and meetings, they took their ideas into the Mothers' Clubs; they dialogued with the older women's associations, such as the Associação de Donas de Casa (Housewives Association) and the Associação de Empregadas Domésticas (Housemaids' Association), both founded in the 1960s (Barroso, 1982). They tabled relations with assistance care organizations, as used to be the case with the Serviço de Orientação Familiar (Family Guidance Service), today an important organization in defense of women's rights.[29]

One of the basic features of the way the women's movement has developed in Brazil is the role played by so-called nongovernment organizations or NGOs (a feature, by the way, that has raised a great deal of discussion as to what advantages and disadvantages it represents for the development of the movement as a whole). In Brazilian society, the designation NGO has been given socially to those nonprofit organizations that grew out of the authoritarian years and whose efforts were devoted to grassroots community development or advisory services for a variety of popular movements. Comprising agents drawn from universities, churches, and social movements, these organizations are funded by international cooperation agencies, chiefly from Europe and Canada, and also nongovernmental for the most part (see Smith, 1990). They relied only partly on volunteers — on the contrary, there was a growing demand for professionalization in this field. In the 1980s, these organizations broadened their range of subject matters. Women, blacks, street children, physical handicaps, AIDS, the environment, and so on, became the NGOs' fields of action. In their activities, besides the provision of a variety of services, they have in common the promotion of civil rights and, after democracy was restored, proposing and lobbying for public policy.

The feminist movement in Brazil has been carried forward largely by

NGOs founded by and comprised of increasingly professionally trained women, where international contacts are wide-ranging and constitutive. There are no systematic statistical data on Brazilian women's NGOs, and it is hard to know how many exist. The latest catalogue available on these organizations dates from 1989 and was prepared by the Conselho Nacional de Direitos da Mulher (National Council on Women's Rights), a government agency set up in 1982 and made up mostly of women from the feminist movement. That year, the Council recorded 444 non-government organizations acting "in favor of women's rights." What is impressive is how recent this field is. Looking at the founding dates of these organizations — the earliest is 1915 — 78 percent of them were founded between 1980 and 1988, 53 percent in the period between 1985 and 1988 alone. A study I carried out in the Rio de Janeiro Metropolitan Region revealed how rapid this recent growth had been: between 1987 and 1991, the total number of women's NGOs rose from 28 to 93.

These organizations share the familiar ideas and debates of the international feminist movement. In recent years — it was out of the question during the military regime — they have become specialists in acting in the public policy field in Brazil, specifically in seeking to work through partnerships with the state, chiefly in relation to educating and creating public awareness on women's rights, in campaigns to combat violence against women (one product has been the creation in several parts of the country of police stations specially prepared to attend to women), health programs, programs on reproductive rights, etc. They were particularly active in lobbying during the elaboration of the Constitution of 1988. There is a reasonable amount of literature on this field of activities carried out by feminist nongovernment organizations. Although certain women's sectors — in the public eye and with access to the media, universities, and international networks — have been overly partisan and propagandist on behalf of these activities, there is no doubt that the NGOs have been of fundamental importance in Brazilian society in terms both of opening up opportunities for women in the public sphere and in bringing cultural changes toward women's emancipation.

CONCLUSIONS

Despite the scarcity of data, the evidence indicates that women are a majority presence either in the universe of nonprofit charity/assistance organizations, or in the "male" field of politicized, social reform organizations — and, consequently, among contemporary social movements and organizations seeking to break with the assistance/politics dichotomy, which is so marked in the Brazilian context. The field of voluntary organizations thus seems to be one field, or the field, in which women have cleared the most room for their social action.[30]

Some quantitative examples can be given to illustrate the presence of women in different fields of voluntary organizations. Ongoing research into philanthropic action through organizations connected with a variety of religious networks reveals that women form a majority not only in Catholic terrain. For example, in 56 Spiritist Centers studied in the Rio de Janeiro Metropolitan Region, there are 676 women volunteers and 53 women wage-earners involved in the work, compared to only 222 male volunteers and 18 male wage-earners.[31] Thus, not only is the ratio of volunteers to wage-earners slightly higher in the case of women, but also there are nearly three times as many women as men engaged in this kind of activity. If one takes, on the other hand, the more politicized sector of secular organizations belonging to the Associação Brasileira de ONGs (Brazilian Association of NGOs), most directed to promoting citizenship and development and highly active in the public policy sphere, their employees and/or volunteers, too, are mostly women (55 percent). A study of the recent Campaign Against Hunger — a successful nationwide movement based on the mobilization of society around thousands of autonomous local committees on the basis of a discourse linking social assistance with citizenship — shows that 61 percent of the participants in Rio de Janeiro are women.[32]

Returning to the initial question posed by this paper: what does this mean in terms of openings for women to be present and participate in public life? There are some reservations to be considered here, before any conclusion can be drawn.

In the first place, and raising a familiar issue, there is nothing to indicate that, by virtue of their forming a majority among the members, employees, volunteers, or militants of these organizations, women participate in their steering councils. Consider the data for the Brazilian Association of NGOs mentioned above, which is supposed to be a body guided by the values of equality and permeated by the values of feminism: women account for 33 percent of council seats, against, as we have seen, 55 percent of the membership.[33] This is only one example of what is certainly reproduced in other organizations corresponding to "assimilationist" initiatives. Nonetheless, it is worth asking here whether these data regarding voluntary organizations are not relatively favorable to women, especially when compared to those for other sectors (business, for instance, where only 2 percent of upper management is female). Moreover, it is also worth asking ourselves whether there is not also greater scope for further change in this type of voluntary organization, whose discourse upholds the values of egalitarianism and citizenship (as has been seen in the rapid changes in the trade union movement mentioned above).

Besides all this, however, it may be argued that these organizations in which women are a predominant presence are secondary and socially undervalued in the Brazilian context. As it is this subordinate area that is reserved to women, it would reproduce and perpetuate their subordination (the argument is generally directed particularly toward charity and assistance organizations). Put more radically: it is because women "choose" for themselves this field of action that they will remain socially subordinated. There are certainly grounds for comparing the positions in society of philanthropic organizations and of women (the same reasoning applies to women's professions).

Instead of thinking of voluntary organizations as a cause of domination, however, I prefer a more complex and richer interpretation of the facts, which acknowledges their value as one of the possible strategic options — at times the only one — available for Brazilian women to leave the home and take up positions on public ground. As we have also seen, the routing through Christian charity and social assistance was, or is, very often included in the trajectory of women or organizations that became significant leaders of movements for social reform, public policy lobbying, the creation of new professions, and for equality. It has also been through their giving of time and (scarce) money that groups of women have been able to develop creative initiatives which, in adversity, placed them in the public space, as was the example of women's publications at the end of the nineteenth century. By means of voluntary organizations, within either separatist or assimilationist strategies, women have been contributing not only to their own advancement but have as well been performing an important role on the national political stage, as could be seen, for instance, in the struggle for democracy during the military régime. With their participation in these processes of strenghtening of civil society, women accumulate power in society at the same time, so that we can also use, in the Brazilian case, the idea of creation of parallel power structures, as is being used in the United States in a very different context (cf. McCarthy, op cit.). I believe that this paper has contributed data and a perspective that support thinking in that direction.

Over the past fifteen or twenty years, a number of new feminist NGOs has had a clearly visible role in formulating public policies involving the question of gender and the implementation of civil rights for women. These are NGOs which came into being during the years of dictatorship and which, as mentioned, had as a common feature an interest in gender and class issues. In this case, as in other historical situations, the relationship with international cooperation agencies has been crucial for financing their activity and especially to allow the circulation of persons and ideas

Finally, one should emphasize the importance of religion and especially, for historical reasons, the role of the Catholic Church, in the voluntary associationism of Brazilian women. It has been in church spaces — parishes, brotherhoods, religious orders, not-for-profit Catholic organizations devoted to social assistance, education, and medical care — that middle- and upper-class women for many centuries could perform with some regularity and some frequency activities out of their home, in a manner allowed by the prevailing moral standards. Even when it comes to women of the poorer classes, mostly negro or mulatto, who had always performed some sort of economic activity out of their home, the lay Catholic spaces of the brotherhoods had their importance as places of association, protection, and even performance of a form of power.

The values associated with philanthropy in Brazilian society, where women had a place of distinction, bore the deep stamp of Catholic religiosity, in its Iberic, Counter-Reform version, as established in Brazil. Even in the initiatives aimed at social reforms, as inspired by Western and internationalized equalitarian ideals — such as the "women's newspapers" or suffragism — still present is the continuation and affirmation of the ideal models for Catholic women, devoted basically to family, where the Virgin Mary remains an inspiration.

The inner diversity of Catholicism was also reproduced in the women's forms of social organization and participation. As we have seen, the creation of social work colleges and the social work career is linked to voluntary organizations involved with social Catholicism, which competed for the control of union-like movements from the thirties and forties. Then, in the seventies, the leftist Catholic tendencies linked to Liberation Theology played an important role in the organization of civil society, especially through associationism at the grassroots level, where women's presence has always prevailed. No extensive investigation on women and philanthropy in Brazil can be carried out without taking into account the conspicuous presence of the Catholic Church, with all its contradictions and ambiguities.

Thinking into the future, one can imagine that, if the idea of a "third sector" and the practices that define it come to be assigned greater value in Brazil, then women, as a result of their history in the voluntary field, will see new areas opened to them — including new opportunities in the politicized, internationalized NGOs — and their experiences revisited and appreciated. It thus seems that new horizons can be glimpsed for the major challenge facing Brazilian women — combining the attitudes of the great popular masses of women with the values of feminism, so as to fuel changes toward democracy and equality that have yet to take place in Brazilian society.

NOTES

1. In common-sense Brazilian terminology, "filantropia" (philanthropy) is synonymous with "caridade" (charity). But the term is used here in the more generic sense given above (Salamon, 1992,) and it is used interchangeably with "non-governmental," "non-profit" or "voluntary" organization or sector, as well as "third sector." In order to delimit the universe of these very diversified organizations, I use the criteria adopted by Salamon and Anheier (1994, 14).

2. At the University of São Paulo alone, between 1990 and 1991, 98 masters and doctorate theses were submitted on women (Veja, 1994).

3. One important point of reference for this study are the questions being examined by Professor Kathleen McCarthy (McCarthy, 1991; 1994 and others). It forms part of a comparative project on Women and Philanthropy coordinated by her at City University of New York's Center for the Study of Philanthropy.

4. The North American June Hahner, commenting on the relative isolation of Brazilian feminists in their struggles, points out cultural differences: "unlike the United States, Brazil never served as a center for important egalitarian, non-hierarchical religious groups like the Quakers (...), or evangelical protestant groups, with their prefectionist aspirations and activist creed" (Hahner, 1981, 50).

5. These are "separatist," "assimilationist," and "individualistic" initiatives and, for women's access to public affairs and power, "each of them provided a discrete set of drawbacks and gains" (McCarthy, no date).

6. Except where otherwise stated, texts by foreign visitors to Brazil were taken from a collection organized by Miriam Moreira Leite (Leite, 1993). All quotations are retranslated from Portuguese translations.

7. Women were perpetual minors under the law (an extension of the 1603 Philippine Code) until the 1916 Civil Code was passed.

8. For example, the Englishman, the Reverend Robert Walsh, describes a woman going down the road, preceded by a slave: "She was wearing riding clothes, nankeen jacket and a large hat. . . . She rode in long strides, mounted like a man and, at her waist, carried a pair of pistols. . . . Although not a muscular person, she appeared large and careless — she dismounted like a man, in front of us, without the slightest embarrassment — she drank a glass of cane spirit at the bar, to fortify herself. . . . When plantation owners' wives are widowed, they frequently administer the plantations and slaves single-handed, taking on, in full, all their former husbands' responsibilities" (Walsh, 1828). This description, while serving as evidence of women's capacity to take on masculine social roles, also masculinizes the character described, demonstrating the lack of leeway in this society to reconcile the female identity with the entrepreneurial function.

9. This dual stereotype of women as rebels or victims which, as pointed out by Agranti, is present in the literature, is also noted by European and North American students. See Perrot, 1988.

10. Given the lack of white women to people the Colony — which led to social disorder and concubinage — state and church sought to prevent the founding of convents for exclusively devotional purposes, but rather encouraged the creation of retreats which would prepare women for marriage.

11. Prostitution, the unequivocal expression of the sexual repression of women, is approached in some studies from its other perspective, where the pleasure and social interaction for the poor population that were generated around prostitution constituted threats to the established order.

12. Some dates: Brazil became the seat of the Portuguese Kingdom in 1808 when "the ports were opened to friendly nations," to the benefit of British economic interests. In 1822, the Portuguese prince himself declared the Independence of Brazil, which came to be a monarchy governed by him. In 1888, slavery was abolished. In 1889, the Republic was proclaimed.

13. The title of the free Brazilian translation was "Direitos da Mulher e Injustiças dos Homens" (Women's Rights and Men's Injustices).

14. This author, in a study of "educated" women in Brazil between 1840 and 1890, found 99 writers, translators, authors of teaching texts, and essayists. (Crescenti, op. cit.).

15. There were advances in the law, like the 1850 Codigo Commercial (Trade Code), which allowed women who owned businesses to marry without disturbing their rights and married women to enter trade with their husbands' permission. This law was certainly directed to the "tradeswoman" situation common among the poorer classes.

16. In addition to the ILO conference mentioned above, Brazilian suffragists' participation in the First Pan American Conference of Women, held in Baltimore in 1922, was also particularly important, since it yielded close links between Bertha Lutz and the North American leader, Carrie Chapman Catt, who later visited Brazil, thus contributing to bolstering and legitimizing the movement there.

17. Carrie Chapman Catt's foreigner's eye saw the specifics more clearly. On her return from Latin America, she commented that there elections are "almost meaningless" and that there were other legal changes in society that, for women, were more important than the vote. She insisted that Latin American suffrage movements should not be judged by North American standards and that there women "needed to take their own road" (Catt, 1924, apud Hahner, 1981).

18. Vargas represented the coming to power of the industrial class and the dawn of an era of state intervention in the economy, in the creation of heavy industry, of corporatist trade unionism tied to the state, and of social security (in a process known in Latin America as "populism"). He governed Brazil from 1930 to 1945 (from 1937 as a dictator).

19. Bertha Lutz, for instance, had participated in the directorate of a social assistance organization, the Legião da Mulher Brasileira (Brazilian Women's Legion), before founding the Women's Emancipation League, dedicated to the fight for civil rights. And in 1921, at the height of the suffragist struggle, she never ceased to assert the central position of the family in women's identity and social practice: women should acquire the right to vote without relinquishing their natural place, which is the home. Except that the home was redefined as extending

to offices and legislative departments which "are no more than dependencies of the home." There were few suffragist leaders like the famous Maria Lacerda de Moura, opponent of the church, capitalism, and militarism, who affirmed that "while the patrician woman continues under the tutelage of the priest — emancipation is impossible" (Moura, 1920, apud Hahner, 1981; see Leite, 1983).

20. The organizations linked to Ação Católica were to play an important part in social reform movements of the '50s and '60s. Harboring left-wing Catholics (see De Kadt, 1970), they were weakened by the 1964 military coup. As of the 1970s, CEAS was to become a center of reference in the development of "Liberation Theology" and in Catholic anti-dictatorship activities.

21. Evidently, a number of other women's professions were also consolidating around this time, such as those of teacher or nurse. In the same way, women's independence was obtained progressively by professions of prestige like medicine, law, etc. Social Service is singled out here merely because it is particularly linked — by its origins and functioning — to philanthropic organizations based on voluntary work by women. In addition, it opened up what at the time were unprecedented opportunities for women to participate in government agencies.

22. One example is Maria Esolina Pinheiro who, in 1944, founded what today is Rio de Janeiro Federal University's Social Service Faculty, which she directed for more than fifteen years, in addition to occupying important positions in the Federal government administration (Pinheiro, 1985).

23. The CEAS, for instance, a civil organization mentioned earlier, formulated mother and child protection policies and pressured government agencies in that regard. The suffragist leader, Carlota Pereira de Queiroz, the first woman to be elected to Congress in Brazil, in 1934, had been a member of Catholic Action.

24. Of particular note here are the Comitê das Mulheres para a Anistia (Women's Pro-Amnesty Committee), the Ligas Femininas (Women's Leagues), and the Federação das Mulheres do Brasil (Brazil Women's Federation). To the right of the political spectrum and supporting the 1964 military coup, were women's organizations in defense of religion and the family, supposedly threatened by the forces of the left, including the Movimento de Arregimentação Feminina (Women's Regimentation Movement), the União Cívica Feminina (Women's Civic Union) and the Campanha da Mulher pela Democracia (Women's Campaign for Democracy). (Barroso, 1982).

25. Mothers Clubs are small groups of women, generally housewives, who meet in the local church once a week to produce sewing or craftwork while they discuss day-to-day problems or listen to talks, usually given by nuns.

26. In Brazil, "moderate" divorce is accepted — one may divorce and remarry only once. Abortion is illegal.

27. Some female researchers have observed a specific feature of Latin American feminism, namely, to be intrinsically movements of political opposition. Founded during the worst years of military dictatorships, "many Latin American feminists not only would defy patriarchalism... but would also join forces with other streams of the opposition when denouncing exploitation and social, economic and political oppression. Political repression and the struggle of classes have specifically moulded feminism in Latin America" (Sternbach et al., 1994).

28. Feminist political culture was quick to develop in trade union circles in

Brazil. Proof of this is that, in 1993, the Central Unica dos Trabalhadores (Sole Workers' Federation) adopted an obligatory quota of 30 percent for women in steering positions — against male resistance and despite controversy among the women themselves (indicating the existence of a lively debate).

29. At the end of the decade, the vitality of these interactions was demonstrated at the 2º Congress da Mulher Paulista (2d São Paulo Women's Congress) in 1980, organized by fifty-two groups (of which nine were decidedly feminist), which brought together four thousand women from different classes and social situations; students, workers, housewives, housemaids, residents of peripheral areas, etc., organized into a number of associations.

30. This paper has not dealt with the emerging field of corporate foundations or institutes. No data are available on women's presence in these organizations, which are innovating in terms of Brazilian culture and philanthropic activities.

31. The Kardecist Spiritist religion is extremely widespread in Brazil among the urban popular and middle classes. The notion of charity is central to its doctrine and it boasts an extensive network of social welfare organizations providing health and educational care (see Giumbelli, 1995). The study in question is part of the project "Philanthropy and citizenship in Brazil" carried out by ISER with the support of the Inter-American Foundation, under my coordination.

32. These studies form part of the project mentioned above. As concerns NGOs, see Landim, 1996. The data on the campaign come from another study (cf. Landim, 1998).

33. If we set aside from this universe the seventeen "separatist" feminist organizations whose councils are 96 percent female, the statistics worsen: in the other 128 NGOs, only 27 percent of council members are women.

BIBLIOGRAPHICAL REFERENCES

Algranti, Leila Mezan. *Honradas e Devotas: Mulheres na Colônia.* (Honorable and Devout: Women in the Colony). Rio de Janeiro: José Olympio Editora, 1993.

Barroso, Carmen. Mulher, *Sociedade e Estado no Brasil.* (Woman, Society and State in Brazil). São Paulo: Brasiliense, 1982.

Duarte, Constancia Lima. "Introdução e Posfácio," in *Direitos das Mulheres e Injustiça dos Homens.* (Introduction and Postface, in Women's Rights and Men's Injustice), de Nísia Floresta Brasileira Augusta. São Paulo: Cortez, 1989.

Figueiredo, Luciano. *O Avesso da Memória — Cotidiano e trabalho da mulher em Minas Gerais no Século XVIII.* (The Other Side of Remembrance — Women's work and daily life in Minas Gerais in the 18th century). Rio de Janeiro: José Olympio Editora, 1993.

Freyre, Gilberto. *Sobrados e Mucambos — decadência do patrimonio rural e desenvolvimento do urbano.* (Townhouses and Cabins — decadence of rural and development of urban patrimony), Rio de Janeiro: José Olympio Editora, 1961.

Gilligan, G. A. *Une si grande différence.* (Such a great difference). Paris: Flammarion, 1986.

Giumbelli, Emerson. *Instituições Espíritas no Estado do Rio de Janeiro: a caridade em números*. (Spiritist institutions in Rio de Janeiro State: charity in numbers). Mimeograph, 1985.

Hahner, June E. *A mulher brasileira e suas lutas políticas: 1850–1937*. (Brazilian women and their political struggles: 1850–1937). São Paulo: Brasiliense, 1981.

Iamamoto, M. and R. Carvalho. *Protoformas do Serviço Social, in Relações Sociais e Serviço Social no Brasil*. (First Forms of Social Work, in Social Relations and Social Work in Brasil) São Paulo: Cortez/lima, 1988.

Landim, Leilah. *Para Além do Mercado e do Estado? Filantropia e Cidadania no Brasil*. (Beyond Market and State? Philanthropy and Citizenship in Brazil). Rio de Janeiro: ISER, 1993 a.

———. *Defining the Nonprofit Sector: Brazil*. Working Papers of the Johns Hopkins Comparative Nonprofit Sector Project no. 9. Baltimore: Johns Hopkins Institute for Policy Studies, 1993 b.

———. "Notas sobre a Campanha do Betinho: ação cidadã e diversidades brasileiras" ("Notes on Betinho's Campaign: Citizen's Action and Brazilian Diversities"), in Leilah Landim, ed., *Ações em Sociedade — Militância, Caridade, Assistência, etc. (Actions in Society — Activism, Charity, Assistance, etc.)*

———, and Letícia Cotrim. *Notas para um perfil das ONGs, em ONGs, um perfil: Cadastro das Associadas à Associação Brasileira de ONGs* (Notes for an NGO Profile, in NGOs, a Profile: Directory of the Associaties to the Brazilian Association of NGOs). São Paulo: ABONG/ISER, 1996.

Lima, Arlette Alves. *Serviço Social no Brasil*. (Social Work in Brazil). São Paulo: Cortez, 1987.

McCarthy, Kathleen D. *Women's Culture: American Philanthropy and Art, 1830–1930*. Chicago: The University of Chicago Press, 1991.

———. "Women and Philanthropy in the United States." Manuscript, 1994.

———. "Women and Philanthropy: Three Strategies in an Historical Perspective." New York: City University of New York, Center for the Study of Philanthropy, n.d.

Mello e Souza, Laura. *O outro lado do ouro mineiro* (Gold from Minas: the other side of the story), in Luciano Figueiredo, *O Aveso da Memoria*. Rio de Janeiro: José Olympio Editora, 1993.

Moreira Leite, Míriam (org.). *A condição feminina no Rio de Janeiro, século XVIII*. (Female condition in Rio de Janeiro, XVIII century). São Paulo: Hucitec, 1981.

Perrot, Michelle. *Os excluídos da historia, operários, mulheres, prisioneiros*. (The excluded from History: workers, women and prison inmates). Rio de Janeiro: Paz e Terra, 1988.

Pinheiro, Maria Esolina. *Serviço Social: uma interpretação do pioneirismo no Rio de Janeiro*. (Social Work: an interpretation of pioneering work in Rio de Janeiro). Rio de Janeiro: UERJ, 1985.

Russel-Wood, A. J. R. *Fidalgos and Philanthropists: the Santa Casa da Misericórdia da Bahia*. London: Macmillan, 1968.

Salamon, Lester M. *America's Nonprofit Sector: A Primer*. New York: The Foundation Center, 1992.

Salamon, Lester M., and Helmut K. Anheier. *The Emerging Sector: an Overview*. Baltimore: Johns Hopkins University, Institute for Policy Studies, 1994.

Santos, Wanderley Guilherme dos. *Cidadania e Justiça; a Política Social na Ordem Brasileira.* (Citizenship and Justice: Social Policy in the Brazilian Order). Rio de Janeiro: Campus, 1979.

Serbin, Kenneth P. *State Subsidization of Catholic Institutions in Brazil, 1930–1964.* Working Paper 181. The Hellen Kellog Institute for International Studies. University of Notre Dame, U.S.A., 1992.

Smith, Brian H. *More Than Altruism: The Politics of Private Foreign Aid.* New Jersey: Princeton Press, 1990.

Sternbach, Nancy, Marysa Navarro-Aranguren, Patricia Chuchryk, and Sonia Alvarez. *Feminismo na América Latina: de Bogotá a São Bernardo* (Feminism in Latin America: From Bogota to San Bernardo), in *Estudos Feministas* (Feminist Studies), no. 2, 1994.

Vieira, Balbina Ottoni. *Perfil inicial e fatores de evolução do Serviço Social no Brasil.* (Profile and evolutionary factors of Social Work in Brazil). Rio de Janeiro: Agir, 1978.

(Translator's Note: English translations for information purposes only.)

– 4 –

The Norwegian Voluntary Sector and Civil Society in Transition

Women as a Catalyst of Deep-Seated Change

PER SELLE

INTRODUCTION[1]

Local voluntary organizations are relatively easy to start up in Norway, but often they do not live long. A good number of people, at any given time, both join and leave such organizations, as either new organizations crop up, others become defunct, or people leave or join existing organizations. In this respect, the society of local voluntary organizations is an extremely *open* and *dynamic* sector in continual change (Brandal and Selle 1983; Selle and Øymyr 1992). These changes always reflect (and influence) more wide-spread and general social change. For that reason, changes in the society of organizations are one of the best indicators of more general social change in densely organized societies like the Norwegian. The position of women in voluntary organizations at different points in time is an important expression of both women's social role and of "society's" view of this role.[2]

Since the early days of the growth of voluntary organizations in the latter half of the last century, women have played an important role in the voluntary sector of Norwegian society. In certain types of organizations, such as the laymen's movement (missionary societies), the teetotal movement, and in social and humanitarian organizations, women have dominated, although more so at the grass-roots level than at higher levels. *In other words, women have played a decisive role in some of the, historically speaking, largest and, politically speaking, most influential types of*

Reprinted by permission of M. E. Sharpe, Inc., from *Participation and Democracy: East and West*, edited by Dietrich Ruesschemeyer, 1998.

organizations — i.e., those linked to great mass movements. In organizing activities for children and young people, women have also been more involved than men. However, men have by no means been absent where women have been most visible, and they were dominant in the labor movement and in more production-related organizational activity in general, as well as in political parties. Men have also dominated in the organized areas of culture and leisure activities, particularly in that which was to become the largest mass movement in the country, organized sports.

To a certain extent, men and women have always fulfilled complementary roles within our organizational society, as they do in society at large. We cannot claim, however, that there has been a high degree of sex segregation in our organizational society. This is due to the fact that in a number of organization types, where female members were dominant, male members have had considerable significance higher up in the organizational hierarchy. In certain types of organizations, such as within parts of the laymen's movement, for example, sex segregation has been very prevalent at the local level, while it was less obvious for the organization as a whole. In general, women have had a stronger position locally than at regional or central levels.

This essay is concerned with the historical role of women in the voluntary sector and with the ongoing transformation of this role resulting from far-reaching changes in organized social life and the decline of the complementary conception of the woman's role. The idea of a complementary role implies that women are fundamentally different from men (Gordon 1990; Hernes 1982). We shall take a closer look at the processes which alter the position of women in the voluntary sector and thus in civil society. The transformation of women's role is a development which has implications for the state of democracy in our country at the most fundamental level (Selle and Øymyr 1995). So, even if this chapter is on "women," it is at the same time about deep changes in Norwegian civil society, in which women are the main catalyst of a comprehensive organizational transformation.

In what follows we will distinguish between organizations which are only for women (closed),[3] and organizations which are dominated by women. We classify an organization as female-dominated if two-thirds of the members are women. The organizations which are *pure women's organizations* are a visible sign of what society perceives as a purely woman's role at any given time, while *female-dominated organizations* may serve as an indication of a more general gender segregation in the voluntary sector, its existence and its degree.

Our first concern is with changes in the composition of the voluntary sector in the post-war period, in particular with shifts in the gender composition. Subsequently, we will take a closer look at *organizational dynamics in the 1980s,* and compare characteristics of organizations which have "died" with those which were "born" or which had "survived" in the period. An important question is the degree to which the older, female-dominated organizations still have the ideological and organizational strength to meet the challenges of the 1990s, and the degree to which there exist ideological and/or organizational (cultural) barriers which prevent women from participating to the same extent as men in the emerging organizations which constitute an ever increasing portion of the organizational society.[4]

PERSPECTIVES: WOMEN, CIVIL SOCIETY, AND DEMOCRACY

If we analyze the transformation of the role of women in the society of local voluntary organizations, we are at the same time studying changes in women's roles in the general society and thus in a democracy. In *"state-friendly" and "thoroughly organized"* societies like those of Scandinavia, where there is a high degree of *proximity* between the voluntary and public sectors as regards communication and contact (Kuhnle and Selle 1990; 1992), there is an unusually large *overlap* between what we define as the organizational society and the civil society (Allardt 1994; Selle 1994a; Selle and Øymyr 1995). They are virtually two halves of a whole.[5]

Whether we conceive of voluntary local organizations as mostly linked to the *family sphere,* or as an important part of the *public space,* has a great influence on the role we assign women in social and political life, both historically and currently. We believe that "civil society" must primarily be understood in political terms,[6] and not only in sociological and psychological terms, as an expression of the search for social and psychological security. A *political conception* necessitates an analysis of the links to other sectors of society, such as the personal and family sphere and not least the public sector and the market. It is such a *relational understanding* of society that must be developed, transcending a static conception in which civil society a priori caters to particular interests which are not catered for by the public sector or the market (Henriksen 1994; Selle and Øymyr 1995, ch. 4).[7] In a relational perspective such as this, the political role is unavoidable.

A political understanding implies that women have been an important part of the public space and thus of the political process of opinion formation ever since the organizational society and modern democracy began to emerge in Norway at the end of the last century. We believe that research on women's issues, and much of social science research in general, has overlooked women's influence by starting from a general marginalization or disempowerment perspective. The focus has been on studying the family sphere, central elite positions, and the lack of female representation in corporative bodies.[8] With the exception of the family sphere, where it is generally agreed that women are "overrepresented," all of these are places where women and women's organizations have been clearly underrepresented, though they have been far from invisible (Hernes 1982). The everyday activity in civil society, where much public debate and opinion formation takes place, is to a large degree disregarded or not taken seriously. The focus has been on the concrete and purely instrumental part of politics at the highest level. At the same time, there has been a reluctance to relinquish the deceptive distinction between soft and hard sectors of society, a distinction which causes some to believe that influence in matters concerning public construction of roads, water works, or national defense is more important than influence on health and social services or educational policy.[9] There is no social group which stands to gain more from a revaluation and more political understanding of civil society than women.

A reorientation of this type does not imply that women have had as great an influence as men on the development of society. On the contrary, they have not enjoyed such influence in all areas of society. But if we are to take the study of the society of voluntary organizations seriously, then such a change of perspective opens a view of far greater involvement on the part of women, and thus far less powerlessness than the dominant conception implies.[10]

By defining women's organizations as those which are closely linked to the family sphere, and thus the intimate sphere, indeed as being only care-providing organizations in one way or another, scholars in the social sciences have made women invisible in a very important part of the public space in which women have played a crucial role. This is particularly true at the local level. In fact, women have been of vital importance in movements which have enjoyed decisive cultural and political significance at both local and central levels.

It is not only the electoral channel and the ad-hoc channel of less permanent and more narrow grassroots organizations (which are parts of the civil society) that have been open for women since the introduction of general suffrage in 1913. Women have had an impact on specific policy decisions, and also on the more general understanding of public responsibility, through politically significant organizations. Thus we believe that women have been involved in the setting of political priorities; they have put new issues on the public agenda; they have influenced public opinion and had a watchdog function vis-à-vis the public sector.

All of these are actions which the pluralistically inspired democracy theory considers the exercising of influence. Researchers in women's issues, on the other hand, believe that women have been excluded from these areas. This is the more surprising because of the unique political position, in comparative perspective, of Norwegian (Nordic) women since the late 1970s.[11]

But real involvement is clearly more than mere influence and the ability to exert pressure; it is also reflected in corporative representation, the status of the organizations on public committees and councils, and inclusion at the hearing stage of the legislative process. The corporative approach has, since the publication of *The Power Project* (Maktutredningen) in the late 1970s, dominated our understanding of the relationship between the state and the organizational society, and it is a perspective which also characterizes the position of women's research (Hernes 1982; 1987). It is, however, necessary to relinquish this perspective if we are to understand the impact of voluntary organizations, at least in areas where the business community is not a primary actor (Selle 1994a). This paradigm, whether we refer to it as "the segmented state" (Olsen 1978) or "mixed administration" (Hernes 1978), results in one specific understanding of organizational roles and participation, and consequently also of the relationship between voluntary organizations and the public sector. This perspective cannot account for the power of organizations or for the essence of the relationship between the public sector and the voluntary sector in general.

Participation in government councils and committees does not necessarily have to be a good indicator of public-voluntary integration. Even though the growth of corporative bodies may indicate a common ground for organizational interests, business interests, and the state, and consequently increased integration and balancing of interests, it at the same time indicates *distance*. It is a meeting place where knowledge is gained about *the other* actors' positions. Interests are balanced against each other, and an attempt is made to develop a common conceptualization to serve as a basis for discussion. But there is no presumption of a symmetrical power relationship. If the main actors really were deeply integrated and interlocked, the formation of such councils and committees would be largely unnecessary.

Corporative representation thus indicates the coexistence of integration and distance. Within other sectors of society it may be that the integration is so comprehensive, or that the interests and conceptualizations are shared to such a degree, that more informal and personal networks overlap, and a common conceptualization serves the same purpose as the more formalized networks which we understand as corporative. Within the health and social services sector (where there is a relatively high number of councils and committees, and where women's organizations and organizations in which women members are in the majority are highly represented) — and in the culture/leisure sector, including the child/youth sector (particularly sports) — we witness a type of proximity which is not found in the relationship among labor organizations, the business community, and the state (Selle 1994a).

In "state-friendly" societies (Kuhnle and Selle 1990; 1992; Hernes 1987; Lafferty 1986), in which the relationship between the public and the voluntary sector is particularly close and friendly, political decision-making is to an unusual degree open to pressure from below, making it quite problematic to distinguish the voluntary from the public sector in the majority of societal fields, perhaps most particularly those which are the most thoroughly organized. In a conceptualization of women's involvement, this has not been taken into consideration, and the result has been that women's involvement has been made less visible. Leaving the corporatism paradigm, though not abandoning the idea that the organizational society has had, and still has, a real impact on public policy, will make women's power visible.

There is also a specific organizational reason why women's power cannot be excluded. In contrast to most other countries, local and national voluntary organizations are not only to an *unusually high degree member-based and democratically structured.* It is also true that most of the organizations were founded *on local initiatives,* so that the individual local organization, and more particularly the regional organization, has had considerable organizational influence. The regional level often has a considerable degree of autonomy relative to the central organization (Selle and Hestetun 1990).[12] At the same time, the same organizations are found, to an unusually high degree, both centrally and locally — i.e., the local organization is a branch of a national organization. Thus, in contrast to most other countries outside Scandinavia, we do not have a *divided organizational society,* consisting of separate local and central organizations.

Our hierarchically structured organizational society has functioned as a significant *integrating force* throughout the process of nation-building by linking work in local organizations to the national effort, and thus to the overall society at large. In this way Norwegian voluntary organizations are important mechanisms for both horizontal and vertical integration (Putnam 1993). They are community-based organizations of great importance in building local identity and civic connectedness, but have at the same time been very important nation-builders through their organizational links to the national level, making them main political actors both at the local and central level. They have promoted political, social, and cultural identity not only at the local level, but have been decisive in integrating people of different social classes and regions into an overall national context (Rokkan 1970; Selle and Øymyr 1995).[13] These structural features make it far less appropriate to claim that women, or other main social categories for that matter, have been excluded from civil society and from political influence. That is not the least so because we deal with a densely organized society in which so-called low status groups historically have built very strong organizations supporting them, really moderating the sociological "law" of the decisive importance of education and social status in advancing political participation (e.g., Rokkan and Campbell 1960; Hernes and Martinussen 1980).[14] The uniqueness of the voluntary sector in Norway (and Scandinavia) has to do with the way in which this sector historically grew out of and was part of broad and politically important social movements — in several of which women have played a crucial role — while at the same time became close to and an integrated part of the development of the welfare state, making the Scandinavian countries the *prototypical* "state-friendly" societies (e.g., Kuhnle and Selle 1992; Lafferty 1986; Hernes 1987; Allardt 1994; Rothstein 1992; Klausen and Selle 1996). The structure in Norway's society of voluntary organizations links the individual organization member to the local community and the society at large at the same time.

In this essay, we cannot pursue in detail all these issues of women, civil society, and democracy. However, we wish to consider quite a few of them by clarifying the processes involved in the changing of the nature of the voluntary sector and thereby the civil society. These are profound changes which are directly linked to changes in the role of women in society and thus in a democracy.

GROWTH AND TRANSFORMATION 1940–1990

Organization Types Come and Go

Changes in the population of voluntary organizations have a direct effect on the gender composition of the organizational society. Naturally, complete information on the gender composition of all of the organizations which have existed throughout the years does not exist, and we do not have a complete set of figures for the historical development of today's organizations.[15] What we do know is the gender composition in 1980 of the organizations existing in 1980 (see footnote 4), and information regarding the organizations' founding year. Furthermore, for the period 1980–88, we know the gender composition of the organizations in 1988.

Figure 1 shows the gender composition of organizations established in different time periods. In the period prior to 1880, when *pure women's organizations* have the highest founding rate, there is also an extensive growth in missionary organizations. The first significant growth period of more *mixed organizations* corresponds to the first important founding period of organizations for children and youth, i.e., from 1890 to 1920. After 1920, the percentage of such mixed organizations declines slightly, but this trend is reversed around 1960, when these organizations show new growth. Mixed organizations constitute an increasing share of all organizations from the 1960s, which results in a decrease in gender segregation. This is a period of considerable growth in choir and music organizations as well as cultural and leisure organizations. Figure 1 shows quite clearly that mixed organizations comprise the largest group of organizations founded in the years between 1980 and 1988. It is also clear from the figure that far more male-dominated organizations than female-dominated organizations were founded in this period.

It is interesting to note that during the 1980s there is a considerable increase in the founding rate of voluntary organizations which are open to both genders but which so far have only male members. Such organizations are primarily found among the typical leisure organizations. This is a new and interesting feature of Norwegian voluntary society.[16] Whether or not this trend will continue, or whether it is just a matter of time before women also join these organizations, remains to be seen. However, as this argument proceeds we shall see signs pointing in the direction of increased women's participation also in these types of organizations.

In order to take a closer look at changes in the population of organizations since World War II, we shall analyze the differences in gender composition between the various types of organizations. Table 1 shows the composition of organizations in Hordaland (excluding Bergen) in the period from 1940 to 1990. The number of organizations has increased greatly, from approximately 3,000 in 1940 to nearly 6,000 in 1990. The same trend is visible in organizational density. Around 1940 there was one organization for every 49 inhabitants, while 50 years later the figure was one to 33.

The change in the relative positions of different types of organizations is also interesting. Two main groups of organizations show a dramatic decline, and both of these are strongly dominated by women: missionary organizations and teetotal organizations. Their decline continues throughout the 1980s. These organizations represent a type which has, historically speaking, played an important role in the local community and has had considerable influence on both local and national culture

Figure1: Gender Composition and Year of Founding

The gender composition of organizations founded in different time periods.

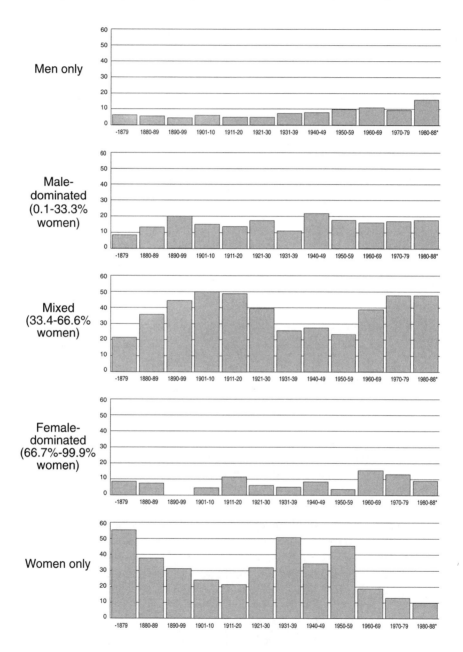

* The figures for 1980-88 are from the 1988-registration, while the rest are from the 1980 survey.
The cases for 1980-88 have been weighted.

Table 1. Changes in the Population of VOs
in a Norwegian Province (Hordaland) 1940–90

	1941		1980		1988		1941–80		1980–88		1941–88	
	N	%	N	%	N	%	N	%	N	%	N	%
Economic	401	13.3	604	11.0	670	11.4	203	-2.3	66	0.4	269	-1.9
Political*	1	0.0	291	5.3	289	4.9	290	5.3	-2	-0.4	288	4.9
Sport	115	3.8	349	6.4	390	6.7	234	2.6	41	0.3	275	2.9
Language	19	0.6	32	0.6	38	0.6	13	0.0	6	0.0	19	0.0
Teetotal	207	6.9	122	2.2	106	1.8	-85	-4.7	-16	-0.4	-101	-5.1
Missionary	1,327	44.1	902	16.5	837	14.3	-425	-27.6	-65	-2.2	-490	-29.8
Youth	631	21.0	1,268	23.2	1,316	22.4	637	2.2	48	-0.8	685	1.4
Song/music	45	1.5	619	11.3	678	11.6	574	9.8	59	0.3	633	10.1
Humanitarian	237	7.9	586	10.7	596	10.2	349	2.8	10	-0.5	359	2.3
Culture/ leisure	25	0.8	698	12.8	943	16.1	673	12.0	245	3.3	918	15.3
N =	3,008	100	5,471	100	5,863	100	2,463	—	392	—	2,855	—
Women	657	21.8	846	15.5	773	13.2	189	-6.3	-73	-2.3	116	-8.6
Youth	697	23.2	1,654	30.2	1,708	29.1	957	7.0	54	-1.1	1,011	5.9
Christian	1,745	58.0	2,109	38.6	2,037	34.7	364	-19.4	-72	-3.9	292	-23.3

*Political organizations were banned by the Nazis in 1941.

and politics. They are organizations which have demonstrated features of a *mass movement.* In addition to *extensive membership,* these organizations have been constructed around an *explicit ideology.* At the same time, they have been *outward looking in their activities* and interested in changing the culture and way of life at both local and central levels. They have also been *highly socializing* through their emphasis on influencing and integrating their own members (Selle 1994b).

As the organizational society has become increasingly centralized, specialized, and oriented towards its own members (self-oriented), the number of organization types exhibiting features of mass movements has declined (Selle 1991; Selle and Øymyr 1995). The organization types which are increasing in number are those which are to a far lesser degree ideological; they are more inward-oriented in their activities, and show far less emphasis on organizational socialization. Traditional women's organizations thus demonstrate some of the features typical of those organization types which have been in decline within the organizational population, and these are not only organization types which are female-dominated. This is thus a general tendency which affects both genders, though a greater impact is witnessed in the female-dominated sector of the organizational society.

Ever since the institutionalization of Norway's modern popular democracy at the end of the last century, organizations with characteristics of mass movements have been core institutions in Norwegian society. Types of organizations with such features have constituted a large and significant portion of organizational society up until the present, although they have gradually evolved through adaptation to changing surroundings. In the current transformation process such organizations are becoming less and less significant, and more *invisible.* This development has consequences for the rest of civil society, and thus for the role of the organizations in the democracy. It weakens their role as real intermediate institutions linking the individual to the society at large.[17]

In turning to religious organizations (including missionary organizations), it becomes clear that these accounted for an impressive 58 percent of the total around 1940, but have decreased to a "mere" 34 percent of all organizations 50 years later, which is a very substantial decline. However, this decline has not prevented religious organizations from playing an important role in the local organizational society, particularly in their work for children and young people.[18] More important here is the fact that the relative importance of organizations that are only for women is in decline, and during the 1980s we even find a substantial decline in the real number of such organizations. This development is partly explained by the decrease in missionary organizations, as organizations for women dominate within this category. But as we shall see, also other typical women's organizations are suffering considerably.

There has been a dramatic increase in the group of culture/leisure organizations and in song and music organizations. Around 1940 these groups constituted less than three percent of the organizational population while their percentage around 1990 is close to 30. While the growth in song and music organizations came to an end during the 1980s, the culture and leisure type organizations continue their dramatic growth, both in real numbers and relative to the entire organizational society. The increase slows, however, at the end of the 1980s. It is also clear that the number of sports organizations has increased substantially. This area represents the most comprehensive and most organized leisure activity in the country. Activity continues to increase throughout the 1980s, but levels off toward the end of the decade.[19]

The growth of the "leisure society," which is an expression of fundamental changes in the relationship between work and leisure, has, in other words, been rapidly and to a large degree reflected in Norway's organizational society. As Figure 1 indicates, the greatest growth has been in organizational types dominated by "mixed" organizations and by men. The combination of male dominance in "modern" and expanding organizations and the erosion of an organizational society for women alone is an illustration of the fundamental transformation of women's role within the voluntary sector. One of the most important characteristics of the local organizational society, historically speaking — the existence of complementary organizations for men and women, and consequently the existence of complementary roles for men and women — is becoming less apparent.

The Changing Gender Composition of the Voluntary Society[20]

Even though the traditional women's organizations are in a process of decline, surveys on participation in voluntary organizations show that there is no general decline in female membership in the voluntary sector. Women must thus be on their way from one position to another. Furthermore, women's overall membership rate is *as high* as that of men (NOU 1988, 17). However, recent surveys, such as the Citizens Survey (Medborgerundersøkelsen) of 1990, clearly show that women under the age of 30 have the lowest rate of organizational participation (Raaum 1995b; see also Table 3 on p. 126). Regardless of whether this is an indication of a lasting or temporary trend, it is necessary to determine what types of organizations women are turning to when their own organizational society is no longer attractive.

The descriptive organizational typology used in Table 1 consisted of 10 main categories. To study change in more detail, we have divided these categories into new subcategories: social/humanitarian, missionary, teetotal, self-help, pensioners, Christian youth, song/music, other social/humanitarian, culture, other youth, unions, youth associations, Red Cross, leisure, political, economic other, sports, language.

Of the social and humanitarian organization types and the missionary organization types, close to 90 percent are dominated by women. Furthermore, the extinction rate of these organizations is much higher than their founding rate. Seven of these 19 organization types have to some degree become less gender-segregated in the 1980s, which means that the share of mixed organization types has increased. These organization types are either stable or growing, and with the exception of political organizations and certain types of youth organizations, a majority of the organizations within these categories were founded within the last 20 years. Among the organization types showing less gender segregation are organizations for children and young people, self-help groups, political parties, culture/neighborhood organizations, and to some degree labor unions.

On the other hand, seven of the organization types have become more sex-segregated during the 1980s: self-help, Christian youth, song/music, other youth, youth associations, leisure, and sports. This development is evident primarily within older types of organizations in which women now represent a larger share than ever before. These are all organization types in decline. *Thus women seem to be the last to desert organization types in decline — i.e., organization types which have had a historical importance for women — while they at the same time are the most reluctant to join "modern" expanding types of organizations.*

However, it is not only within declining organizational types that increasing gender segregation is found. Increasing female dominance is also evident within some expanding organization subtypes, such as in the sphere of leisure (for example in certain organized sports), and within certain subtypes of song and music and hobby organizations, where female dominance is on the rise. However, as main categories of organization, these have thus far shown a clear male dominance. There is also an increase in female-dominated organizations within the growing or stable types of organizations like pensioners' associations, the Norwegian Red Cross, and labor unions. These last tendencies, even if they so far are rather weak, may be an indication of a *lag* in women's organizational participation as compared to men, which may suggest that it is only a matter of time before women participate equally in the "modern" organizational society. In order to test this lag hypothesis, the next section presents an analysis of the differences in organizational participation between women of different age groups.

ARE YOUNG WOMEN MORE LIKE MEN?

In a period of transformation where the "complementary" role of women is becoming less significant, it may be that important differences across generations can be found. To what extent does age seem to influence the type of organization women choose? In considering this question it was necessary to use data showing the mean age of the organizational leadership as an equivalent to the age of members, because the exact age of the members was not available. The age of the leaders does not necessarily reflect the age composition of the members. Nevertheless, we hold that in general the age composition of the leadership gives an indication of the age of the members in most organizational types, even if the average member in most cases will be somewhat younger. At any rate,

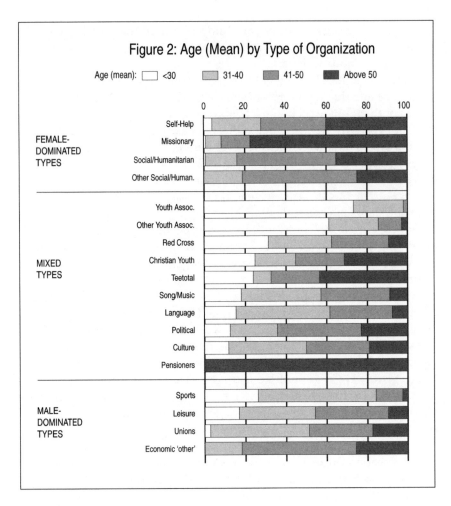

Figure 2: Age (Mean) by Type of Organization

any discrepancy in the exact ages should not lead to serious distortions of the relations between the organization types.

In Figure 2 we categorize the average age of the leadership and consequently the members into four groups. The figure shows the percentage of organizations with an average age of leaders and members aged 30 or less, 31–40, 41–50, and 50 and above. There is a clear difference visible between the female-dominated organization types and the others. With the exception of the female leisure organizations (a group which consists of only eight organizations) the majority of the leaders and members within the female-dominated organizational types are more than 40 years of age, and, furthermore, if we exclude the group of social and humanitarian organizations, the leaders are 50 years of age or older. In general,

Table 2. Gender Composition by Age (percentage)

	30	31–40	41–50	51+
Male dominated	36.2	46.9	38.6	22.2
Mixed	39.9	28.0	21.8	16.6
Female dominated	23.9	25.1	39.6	61.2
Total	100.0	100.0	100.0	100.0
N =	401	586	624	613

organizations related to sports, leisure, and youth associations have the youngest leaders and members, while missionary organizations, teetotal organizations, and traditional social welfare organizations have the oldest leaders and members. All of these represent organizational types in which women dominate.

Table 2 systematizes the relationship between age and gender composition. There is an obvious difference between organization types dominated by different age groups. Close to two-thirds of the organization types with an average age of leaders and members above 50 are dominated by women, while only roughly a quarter of the organization types with leaders and members below 30 are female-dominated organization types. The structural picture is quite clear: the proportion of female-dominated organization types increases with age, the proportion of mixed organization types decreases with age, while the proportion of male-dominated organization types is largest when the average leader and member are between 30 and 50 years of age. *Thus female-dominated organization types are clearly in the most difficult position structurally,* particularly if the members are primarily older women who joined the organizations when they were younger. On the other hand, if there is actually a large-scale recruitment of older women, the picture is more positive.[21]

In order to take a closer look at long-term changes, we have also compared two Norwegian surveys on participation in voluntary organizations, one from 1957, the other from 1986.[22] The aim of this analysis is to go beyond the organizational data to gain a more detailed picture of changes over time in the types of organizations to which different age groups belong.[23]

Figure 3 shows considerable differences over time.[24] The most dramatic change is found within the religious and social and humanitarian organizations, and within other typical women's organizations. Within these categories we find a strong overall decline in membership. However, there is one important difference. For those above 50 years of age, membership

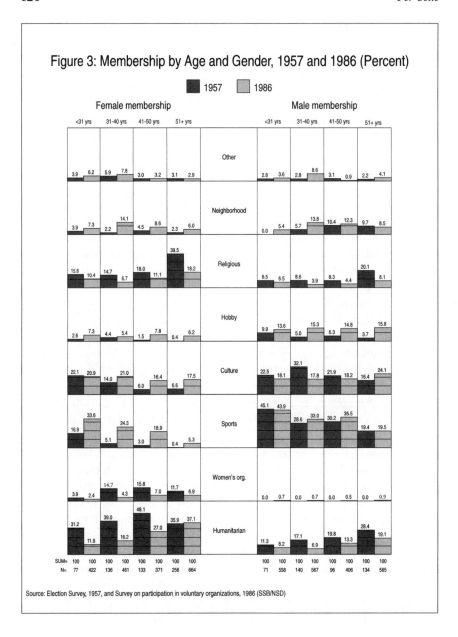

Figure 3: Membership by Age and Gender, 1957 and 1986 (Percent)

■ 1957   □ 1986

Source: Election Survey, 1957, and Survey on participation in voluntary organizations, 1986 (SSB/NSD)

in religious organizations was more than halved between 1957 and 1986, both for men and women. But, within this age group there is no such decrease in women's participation in social and humanitarian organizations. In other words, younger women have left both types of organization.

Older women have to an increasing degree left missionary organizations, but to a far less extent social and humanitarian organizations.[25]

The survey data reveal considerable growth in female membership in sports organizations, and it is noteworthy also that women over 30 are involved in such organizations to an increasing degree. It is interesting that women, young people, and children have to such a degree joined organized athletics since the 1960s. This development is also an expression of a deep reorientation with regard to what kinds of activity are suitable for women (and for young people and children). Just as in politics, the legitimation of women at the highest levels of athletics, and the growing participation of women in Norway's National Athletics Association, have been vital expressions of profound changes in social attitudes about what women can and should do (Selle 1995).[26] Up until the mid- to late-1970s, exhausted female athletes were often considered offensive. They represented a lack of femininity and the violation of an aesthetic. In a very short time, there has been a transformation in our conceptualization which has had enormous consequences for "the life space" of modern women.

There has also been an increase in female membership in certain types of neighborhood associations,[27] various types of leisure organizations, and hobby and cultural organizations, all of which are types of organizations which are far less outward-oriented, at least in terms of orientation outside the most narrow local community. They are also far less political/ideological than was the case for typical women's organizations in their heyday. The largest growth in male membership is to be found within hobby clubs. *Both men and women are thus to an increasing degree moving towards apolitical types of organizations*[28] *with limited goals and often little interest for events outside the organizational boundaries.*

Two more important observations are clear from Figure 3. The changes *in membership patterns seem to be less dramatic for men than for women,* although this does not imply that male membership has not changed. Men were the impetus behind the explosive growth of cultural and leisure organizations which started in the mid-1960s. This is perhaps not surprising, as growth has primarily taken place in organization types to which men have belonged all along, although up until 1960 only to a limited extent. To simplify greatly, when the relationship between work and leisure changes, it seems that men are given the opportunity to participate in things for which they have been ready for a long time. For women, who up until 1960 were virtually invisible in the same organization types, the shift in self-conception and social role is far more profound. It partially explains why it takes time for women to participate on a large scale. There must first be a gradual cognitive/ideological maturation process which fosters a *new* type of participation. Once the process has started,

Table 3. Membership and Participation by Age,
1980 and 1991 (percentage)

		Members				Nonactive members			
		> 30	31–50	Over 50	Total	> 30	31–50	Over 50	Total
Trade Unions									
Men	1980	30.6	50.9	44.6	43.0	73.9	61.6	70.4	67.6
	1991	26.6	52.4	27.8	42.7	79.9	71.4	79.2	75.5
Women	1980	23.9	25.3	18.1	22.2	79.6	75.3	72.3	75.7
	1991	26.7	47.9	27.8	35.3	77.4	75.5	82.1	77.6
Professional, branch associations									
Men	1980	14.6	32.2	24.5	24.3	71.4	51.8	62.9	59.5
	1991	9.4	27.1	24.6	21.4	78.3	61.3	61.4	63.4
Women	1980	7.2	11.4	6.8	8.4	71.8	66.7	74.0	70.3
	1991	8.2	15.4	7.3	10.7	75.6	69.8	64.3	69.8
Political parties									
Men	1980	12.3	19.9	28.0	20.8	54.7	51.6	66.7	59.7
	1991	7.6	13.8	21.1	14.4	70.3	58.0	69.2	65.0
Women	1980	6.5	13.2	16.8	12.7	56.8	64.6	70.2	66.4
	1991	5.6	8.3	11.4	8.5	75.0	69.0	72.1	71.4
Religious associations									
Men	1980	6.3	4.5	7.2	6.0	25.8	14.8	32.7	33.6
	1991	6.6	4.6	5.4	5.4	21.2	24.2	23.3	22.9
Women	1980	8.1	8.0	19.7	12.6	17.0	16.0	14.7	15.4
	1991	6.5	6.0	13.5	8.6	12.1	9.5	16.2	13.5
Sports									
Men	1980	47.2	43.0	21.8	36.2	29.7	35.7	68.8	40.7
	1991	44.8	42.5	25.2	37.6	23.3	36.4	64.8	38.1
Women	1980	25.8	29.1	7.6	19.6	32.7	57.5	73.7	50.3
	1991	32.9	29.8	10.1	24.2	30.1	46.9	66.1	43.1
Women's associations									
Women	1980	3.9	11.3	10.7	8.9	31.8	39.1	51.9	44.1
	1991	1.0	7.3	7.9	5.7	75.0	39.2	38.6	40.4

the change is relatively rapid, and it is this growth which has most dramatically changed the *composition* and thus the *nature* of the organizational society. Furthermore, it is obvious that in the second half of the 1980s the membership pattern for young women (below 40 years of age) is closer to the overall male membership pattern than to the membership patterns for women over 50. This means that today there is *more of a generation gap than a gender gap in social participation. Young women seem to be in the process of changing their self-conception to the extent that they are ready for what has so far been the male dominated part of the organizational society.*

Furthermore, missionary organizations, which had their peak early in this century, are not only in a process of decline, but the membership rates are declining within all age groups. Humanitarian organizations, the

Table 3. Membership and Participation by Age,
1980 and 1991 (percentage), continued

		Members				Nonactive members			
		>30	31–50	Over 50	Total	>30	31–50	Over 50	Total
Health clubs, etc.									
Men	1980	4.9	9.2	19.8	12.0	61.5	81.0	88.0	82.9
	1991	3.4	8.0	18.3	10.0	35.3	84.7	77.9	76.1
Women	1980	7.2	21.8	34.2	22.4	64.3	69.6	66.2	64.7
	1991	5.0	15.3	32.6	18.1	52.0	61.3	63.3	61.8
Associations for youths/parents/pensioners									
Men	1980	14.8	9.9	9.7	11.0	34.2	43.5	41.9	39.5
	1991	7.6	8.7	13.1	9.8	40.5	45.2	40.0	42.0
Women	1980	8.5	13.9	12.0	11.6	30.4	29.1	50.5	38.1
	1991	4.8	9.5	15.8	10.2	21.7	30.3	41.3	38.7
Music and theater									
Men	1980	9.9	10.2	6.9	7.0	0.0	15.6	23.4	13.0
	1991	8.0	8.9	7.3	8.1	17.5	13.6	12.8	14.5
Women	1980	8.2	8.6	4.8	7.5	2.1	9.6	23.7	10.9
	1991	11.6	8.3	5.3	8.2	15.5	7.0	10.0	11.0
Neighborhood associations									
Men	1980	4.7	16.6	13.5	12.0	68.0	64.4	69.9	67.1
	1991	7.2	28.8	19.1	19.4	61.8	61.4	74.1	65.4
Women	1980	5.8	14.2	9.2	9.8	68.8	72.4	88.6	77.8
	1991	6.3	23.6	13.6	15.5	59.4	63.4	77.3	66.8
Environmental, actions groups, etc.									
Men	1980	5.5	5.1	4.0	4.8	24.1	41.4	33.3	32.9
	1991	3.6	5.7	5.2	4.9	33.3	26.2	26.7	27.8
Women	1980	2.7	4.0	3.3	3.3	6.2	28.0	37.5	26.2
	1991	3.6	2.6	2.0	2.7	33.3	17.6	25.0	25.5

Note: The figures are uncertain regarding types of organizations having few members. The questions asked: "Are you a member of any of the following organizations?" Those who answered yes were also asked: "Would you describe yourself as a very active, active, or rather passive member?"

Source: Data from the Levekårsundersøkelsen 1980 and 1991, carried out by Statistics Norway, made available through the Norwegian Social Science Data Services.

majority of which were founded between 1945 and 1960, are becoming less important within all age groups, except for women over 50 years of age. In this respect, the survey data reinforce the impression gained from the organization data. Organizations in the most important subcategories do actually have real difficulty in recruiting new members. This could imply that these organizations will continue to decline as the members gradually grow old and pass away (Selle and Øymyr 1992; 1995).

The long-term changes discussed above are supported by the data presented in *Survey on Life Conditions* (Levekårsdata).[29] Table 3 shows quite clearly that younger women in particular vary only slightly from men and that the differences have become smaller in the years between 1980 and 1991. The only significant distinction is within the category of song and music organizations, where younger women are now participating to a larger degree, while men show the opposite tendency. Moreover, it is clear that very few young women and men are involved in humanitarian organizations, and that the numbers are falling. Among those young people who are organizationally active, there is a considerable male majority, which some may find surprising.[30] It is also clear that for those over 30 years of age there is still an obvious difference in membership in humanitarian organizations and that women are the most active. The drop in the 1980s female membership in the 31–50 age group has, nevertheless, been dramatic, and much stronger than within the group of women over 50. As for membership in religious organizations, there is no difference between younger women and men, and while female membership has fallen, membership figures for younger men have actually shown a slight increase. Women are somewhat more active in the organizations. For those over 30, there is still a clear difference in membership, and women are also the most active. However, the decline in women's participation has been great, not least for those over 50. Nevertheless, these organizations still represent an important meeting place for older women.

The figures also show a clear increase in female membership in labor unions and various business organizations (see footnote 12), while male membership in both shows a slight decline. Both genders are less involved in political parties in 1991 than they were in 1980, and it is still more common for men to belong than women.[31] Table 3 also indicates the increase in female participation in sports, and it is obvious that this increase is most noticeable for those under 30.

The data from the *Life Conditions Survey* support the claims presented regarding the decline of typical women's organizations. Interestingly enough, it also appears that membership in neighborhood organizations (i.e., of the residential type) is growing rapidly for both genders — neighborhood organizations of the new and more narrow type (see footnote 29) — and that there has been a decline in membership in action groups and environment-related organizations in the 1980s. The latter is particularly true for women, though not for those under 30. Furthermore, it is clear that in the types of organization which are enjoying membership growth, the members are *normally passive*. It is also clear that organizations such as labor unions, business associations, political parties, and social and humanitarian organizations all have members who primarily describe themselves as passive. It is within organized song and music, sports, local action groups, and religion that members are most active.

In the interpretation of the developmental trends in the organizational society more generally, we have emphasized that the level of activity seems to be receding, and that people seem to be joining voluntary organizations more for instrumental reasons: there is decreasing interest in idea-based organizations or even in the participation aspect of membership (Selle and Øymyr 1995, chapters 10 and 11). The *Life Conditions Survey* data support this view. This is not a good sign for our democracy, and points towards a deteriorating culture of participation, at least if we look outside of the most narrow residential areas. There seems to be a decline in activity, though the same is not true to the same degree for membership.[32]

In order to take a closer look at this process of transformation, we shall return to the organization data and analyze the organization dynamics of the 1980s. We shall consider both *speed* and *form*.

ORGANIZATIONAL DYNAMICS OF THE 1980S

Extinct Versus Surviving Organizations

To dig deeper into the transformation process, we compare those organizations that disappeared during the 1980s with those that survived.[33] The starting point in this comparison is the individual organization (see note 21). The figures show the sex composition of the membership: male-dominated indicates 0–33.3 percent female members; "mixed" means 33.3–66.6 percent female members; female-dominated organizations have 66.7–100 percent female members.

Including the year of founding adds important new information about the organizational transformation, primarily because research in the field in general assumes that there is a strong tendency toward higher mortality figures for newer organizations. This is the premise of the so-called *"liability of newness"* hypothesis, which is a central hypothesis in organization theory.[34] Within the extinct male-dominated and mixed organizations we find a higher proportion of newly formed organizations (organizations established in the periods after 1974), compared to the surviving organizations. Almost half of the extinct mixed organizations were established between 1975 and 1980, and more than 25 percent of the male-dominated organizations that have disappeared were established in the same period. This shows that older organizations within these categories seem to be the most stable, as the above hypothesis predicts.

For female-dominated organizations the situation is the exact reverse. Here there is a higher proportion of old organizations among the extinct organizations as compared to the surviving ones. As many as 35 percent of the extinct female organizations were established before the turn of the century, and as high a proportion as 56 percent were established before 1920. These figures cannot illustrate more clearly that the historically powerful mass movements, in which women played such an important role, are in decline. Even though the figures may not be completely precise, they still provide a clear picture of the transformation process which in such a fundamental way affects the role of women in voluntary organizations. Furthermore, this is an important finding, as it implies that the "liability of newness" hypothesis being valid for the male-dominated and mixed organizations but not for the female-dominated organizations, requires a more specific reformulation.

Historical factors, such as the structural position of the various types of organizations, must be taken into consideration. Generally accepted theoretical assumptions lose the challenge posed by history; or more specifically, by the social mass movements and their decline (Selle and Øymyr 1992).

Table 4 also shows quite clearly that a larger proportion of female-dominated organizations are small in size compared to male-dominated and mixed organizations. However, the extinct organizations are in general smaller than the surviving ones. More than three out of four female organizations that ceased to exist during the 1980s had fewer than 20 members. When it comes to the male-dominated organizations, close to six out of ten organizations had such low membership figures, while only every fourth mixed organization that ceased to exist had fewer than 20 members.

There are considerable differences between the male-dominated, mixed, and female-dominated organizations when it comes to the frequency of membership meetings,[35] but it is only within the male-dominated category that we find significant differences between the extinct and surviving organizations. In fact, meeting frequency is highest among the extinct organizations. This is probably a result of the fact that a considerable majority of the stable organizations are sports organizations, where training activities are only included in the data to a very small degree. Far more interesting are the dramatic differences in meeting activity between male- and female-dominated organizations. The female-dominated organizations show a far higher level of meeting frequency than the male-dominated and mixed organizations. About two-thirds of the female-dominated organizations have meetings at least once a month, while the same may be said only of four out of ten mixed organizations. Female-dominated organizations seem to disappear independently of the frequency of meetings.

Table 4. Characteristics of the Surviving and Extinct Organizations, 1980–88

	Male dominated		Mixed		Female dominated	
	Surv.	Ext.	Surv.	Ext.	Surv.	Ext.
Problems						
Economy	11.1	2.4	8.4	ɟ.0	2.7	1.4
Recruitment of members	7.3	6.1	7.4	10.9	11.8	13.0
Recruitment of leaders	7.5	8.1	8.7	6.4	4.5	4.3
Activity level	8.4	6.2	8.8	10.3	3.7	2.0
N =	359	33	502	51	549	92
Year of founding						
1847–90	3.9	2.4	4.3	0.0	7.4	35.0
1891–1900	2.3	0.0	3.5	5.7	1.5	0.4
1901–20	7.0	4.8	13.5	1.4	9.1	20.6
1921–44	14.4	4.7	13.0	4.8	18.0	13.6
1945–60	22.3	27.6	12.9	9.2	23.7	8.8
1961–74	31.3	34.4	24.2	32.3	26.5	10.4
1975–80	18.8	26.1	28.5	46.7	13.9	11.1
N =	336	29	465	51	515	84
Membership figures						
20 or less	19.3	59.3	16.4	25.9	62.3	78.3
21 to 50	40.6	27.5	42.7	39.1	25.5	14.1
51 to 100	22.4	11.2	23.5	16.5	6.6	4.6
101 to 200	8.9	0.0	8.7	17.2	3.6	0.0
More than 200	8.8	2.1	8.7	1.4	2.1	3.0
N =	342	30	468	48	501	82
Economy						
Budget 10,000 NOK (1980)	38.2	13.4	32.8	15.1	11.6	22.2
Satisfactory economy	72.5	53.7	77.3	79.9	82.7	80.1
Public finance	57.6	58.4	81.6	86.1	55.9	49.8
Internal activity						
Meetings at least once a month	25.5	34.7	39.5	39.7	66.5	63.2
Members participating:						
33%	24.3	9.5	18.1	22.1	5.7	2.4
33–50%	30.9	26.5	27.3	29.7	12.8	5.0
50%	44.8	64.0	54.6	48.2	81.5	92.6
N =	339	29	449	47	508	77
Extrovert activity index						
Zero	37.9	37.9	59.7	67.1	73.2	89.4
Low	22.3	17.2	18.2	2.9	15.2	6.0
Medium	23.9	33.0	10.7	8.7	7.1	3.4
High	15.9	10.1	11.4	21.3	4.4	1.2
N =	359	33	502	51	549	92
Geographical space						
Village	42.9	56.8	76.5	69.5	76.8	70.7
Municipality	40.8	43.2	20.9	26.9	21.1	29.3
Larger areas	16.3	0.0	2.6	3.6	2.1	0.0
N =	357	33	502	51	549	92
Org. networks						
Hold subgroups	6.8	4.2	8.1	10.1	3.9	3.4
Regional motherorg.	74.1	58.1	64.5	53.9	55.4	49.6
National motherorg.	83.5	65.6	65.1	61.4	58.5	50.5
Coop. council	25.7	13.9	18.4	17.8	11.6	7.8
N =	336	31	453	44	464	79

When it comes to the extent to which members take part in such meetings (attendance), a very interesting picture appears. It seems that those organizations which disappeared during the 1980s had a larger proportion of their members participating back in 1980. This is so both within the group of male-dominated and the group of female-dominated organizations. We do not find this tendency among mixed organizations. It is important to note that in general the female-dominated organizations, whether they survive or not, have a higher attendance rate compared to the male-dominated and mixed organizations, while at the same time they have a higher turnover-rate. Foundings of new organizations are very rare, and an increasing number of organizations die. Many of these organizations recruit virtually no new members at all, although as long as there are enough members left to run the organization, they manage to maintain a certain level of organizational activity, and meeting attendance is very high for the remaining members. The decisive stroke is often the resignation of the leader; when that happens, the organization disappears over night. This explains in part why organization types with considerable internal activity can have such a high turnover rate.

The fact that the female-dominated organizations in general have a higher level of membership participation than mixed and male-dominated organizations might be partly explained by size, but it also has to do with organizational culture. Small membership-based organizations require that a high proportion of members take part in order to keep a certain level of activity going. But it might also be that members of old and traditional organizations feel more obliged to take part: they are part of a "participation culture." Such a culture is not only a feature of a more general female culture: it is more widespread and related to more traditional concepts of civic duty, which seem to be less pervasive today. These ideas of civic duty have played a central role in the most typical women's organizations. Furthermore, since not all organizational mortality is a result of the aging or death of the members, it is surprising that *social and cultural density do not prevent organizational extinction.*

If we consider the index showing the degree of public involvement,[36] we find that among the male-dominated and mixed categories a higher proportion of the extinct, compared to the surviving, organizations have a low score on this index. Being extroverted increases the chances of survival. Furthermore, it is important that the female-dominated organizations generally are less engaged in extrovert activities than the mixed and male-dominated organizations, both for surviving and extinct organizations. Of the female-dominated and mixed organizations, very few which had a high level of extroverted activity disappeared. Consequently, *extrovert activity seems to be much more important for organizational survival than introvert activity.*

If we consider organizational networks, the general picture is that the extinct organizations to a lesser degree maintain subgroups, are part of national organizational networks, or participate in co-operating councils with their local governments. We also see that male-dominated organizations seem to be the most integrated into extensive organizational networks, while the female-dominated organizations are the least so. This is the case for religious organizations, but also, somewhat surprisingly, for the social and humanitarian organizations. *Linkages to other groups and to public institutions tend to sustain organizations.* Both features are of great theoretical interest. Linkages to the outside environment increase the chances of organizational survival, of which linkage to the public sector is one of the crucial ones. To be related to the welfare state increases organizational survival and not the other way around.[37] These are all characteristics which are *atypical* for the typical women's organization of today, though this was not the case in the heyday of such organizations. In those days these organizations played a decisive role in the civil society, had large memberships, were extroverted, and wanted to influence everyone.[38] Such organizations have since become far more invisible for those of us who do not belong. Their political role have been greatly impaired and their linkages out of the local community has been greatly weakened.

Are the New Organizations Different?

So far we have compared the organizations that have disappeared with those that have survived, but we have not given any information about main characteristics of the new and emerging organizations of the 1980s. Information on these organizations is, of course, essential if we are to develop a more complete picture of the transformation process. This is particularly important since it is these new organizations which are the impetus for the "modernization" of the voluntary sector; it is they who are concerned with new issues, organizational forms, and "ideologies." Even though we do not have comprehensive survey data to add to our 1988 registration, we do have some important *structural* information about the organizations founded during the 1980s. We are able to compare them with the extinct and the surviving ones on such important variables as geographical space, membership figures, and gender composition.

Table 5[39] on the following page shows large and very crucial differences. Both within male-dominated and mixed organizations, we find that the surviving organizations are larger than both the new and the

Table 5. The New Organizations of the 1980s
Compared with the Extinct and Surviving Organizations

	Male dominated			Mixed			Female dominated		
	Surv.	Ext.	New	Surv.	Ext.	New	Surv.	Ext.	New
Membership figures									
> 20	23.8	57.8	49.4	14.7	26.2	23.9	56.9	81.8	47.4
21 to 50	36.7	31.8	39.2	37.5	47.2	45.1	27.8	12.3	34.2
51 to 100	21.6	7.8	5.1	24.5	13.5	22.5	8.0	3.0	15.8
More than 100	18.0	2.5	6.3	23.2	13.1	8.5	7.3	2.9	2.6
N =	370	28	79	707	80	71	557	83	38
Geographical area									
Village	60.2	45.9	52.6	71.3	62.1	63.4	87.7	80.1	50.0
Municipality	27.9	54.1	35.9	25.5	34.5	23.9	11.2	19.9	44.4
Larger areas	11.9	0.0	11.5	3.2	3.5	12.7	1.1	0.0	5.6
N =	413	34	78	797	89	71	598	98	36

Note: Surviving and extinct organizations,
data from 1980; new organizations: data from 1988.

extinct ones. There are no major differences in size between the extinct and the new organizations. New organizations are already as big as those going out of existence.

The figures for female-dominated organizations are quite different. In this category, *organizations born in the 1980s are not only bigger than those which disappeared, they also have a larger membership on average than those which survived.* Furthermore, the size of the extinct female-dominated organizations clearly differs, with eight of ten organizations of less than 20 members.[40] It is the old, small neighborhood organizations that are really disappearing. These are the organizational types in which women historically have dominated, but in the centralization and professionalization process of today these organizational types have increasingly become perceived as old fashioned, partly because the neighborhoods (i.e., school districts) themselves have lost most of their old functions (see note 29) (Selle 1991; Selle and Øymyr 1995). This is an indication that the organizational society is decreasingly related to the local level, in spite of the growth in certain types of neighborhood organizations (of the residential type) as well as other local organizations. At least this is so if we by "neighborhood" mean something geographically wider than a residential area.[41]

Looking into the geographical area from which the organizations recruit their members, we find a complex, but very interesting picture. A new tendency seems to be that new organizations more often try to recruit members from larger geographical areas as compared to the extinct and surviving ones. However, this characteristic does not seem to apply for male- and female-dominated organizations alike. New male-dominated organizations do not cover larger areas than the extinct and surviving organizations, and there are only small differences within the group of mixed organizations. On the other hand, there is a rather strong tendency in this direction within the female-dominated organizations. Here only half of the new organizations are organized as neighborhood organizations, while between 80 and 90 percent of the surviving and extinct organizations are organized in this way. *Women are in the process of breaking out of neighborhood organizations,* and are no longer visible in only the most local organizational networks, even if we at the same time find a move toward the most narrow neighborhoods — i.e., residential areas. This represents a break with one of the most *typical* characteristics of our organizational society. Thus what we are witnessing is a truly profound transformation of the civil society. To an increasing degree women participate in organizations which direct their activities toward the entire city or municipality, or towards the society at large; these are often organizations which may be clearly instrumental and in which most members are passive.

It may be, however, that women to an increasing degree maintain important social functions (which resemble those functions previously being the domain of voluntary organizations) through more *informal networks.*[42] There is not sufficient empirical material to determine whether such networks have shown real growth in the period, but if this is the case (we believe so), then it lessens the large-scale decline in female activity directed towards others — it makes the transition from working for others to working for oneself less drastic (see Selle and Øymyr 1995, chapters 10–11).

Such a growth in more informal network organization would also imply a weakening of the *organization syndrome,* the belief that all important matters must be formalized and organized. But this would not necessarily be an indication of a dramatic change in women's responsibilities in the civil society. Rather it would just be part of a more general change increasing the separation between voluntary organizations and voluntary work. The result would be that more and more voluntary work will be done outside what we normally understand as voluntary organizations. That would be a comprehensive change since voluntary organizations and voluntary work so far have been two sides of the same coin in Norway (Selle and Øymyr 1995). Furthermore, this implies that there will be less of an overlap between the organizational society and the civil society. Consequently, the political role of the civil society, and its link to the society at large may deteriorate.[43]

Both in terms of size and geographical space, new female-dominated organizations are highly *prototypically modern;* they have rather large memberships and they cover at least a whole local authority area. This points in the direction of supporting the lag hypothesis that the barriers between the genders when it comes to organizational participation are gradually breaking down even further and that women are on their way into organizational types that have so far been male dominated. However, the extent to which this will happen is too early to tell: we cannot know whether gender differences are vanishing. The majority of the female-dominated organizations which are disappearing, on the other hand, are as previously mentioned of the *old* and *traditional* type, small and neighborhood-based. These organizational types were the bearer of a comprehensive "participation culture" that is now in decline. This is a decline that may have a profound influence upon the political role of civil society. Now, the participation is much more instrumental and at the same time less idea-based.

Traditional women's organizations have lost much of their contact with the "modern" surroundings in which they must function, and in which they must, to a certain degree, take part. They have not become more inward-looking out of choice, but because they have been forced to direct their energy toward their internal activities as membership and external support have dwindled. They have thus lost much of their power, and as a consequence, also their ability to influence those of us who are not part of the movement, either cognitively or when it comes to the ability to act. This implies that these organizations are in a far more *marginal position in the civil society, and thus in the democracy* than they were only a generation ago. Their goals were more suited to an earlier historical context.

These developments seem to indicate that the ongoing, deep-seated transformation of the voluntary sector is most clearly *visible* in the female-dominated part of the organizational society. While women as a group or social category seem to hold a weaker position in the organizational society, it may be that the individual woman has strengthened her position. These are changes that not only have an influence upon women, but on the condition on which our democracy rests.

DISCUSSION AND CONCLUSION

Traditional Women's Organizations Crumble

We are in the midst of a profound transformation of women's role in the voluntary organizational society, and consequently in the society at large. At the same time, the entire voluntary organizational society is changing. Mass movements which were historically important, such as the layman's movement, and particularly the teetotal movement, have shown a gradual decline in the period after World War II, but their decline gained real momentum from the mid-1960s. The demise of the large traditional humanitarian organizations, which had enjoyed considerable growth in the early post-war years, also began in the early 1970s.

All of the above are organizations which were greatly influenced by women,[44] and these organization types played a very central role both politically and culturally. They were engaged in public affairs and were strong enough to have an effect on their surroundings, both in terms of thoughts and actions. At the same time as the number of organizations has fallen, many of the remaining organizations have become more introverted, so that we might say that the weakening of their political and cultural power is far greater than their decrease in number. The traditional women's organizations have become increasingly peripheral in the public's general understanding, and they have gradually lost their identity as social mass movements (Selle 1994a).[45] The organizations showing highest growth are those which are *not primarily ideology-based,* which are more *introverted in their activities,* and which *do not to such a degree emphasize organizational socialization.* Even the so-called *modern mass movements,* such as the feminist women's movement or the environmental movement, have not at all had a great organizational effect, although they have had considerable influence over government policy.[46]

Furthermore, we see an increased pressure upon the prototypical way of organizing. The membership-based and democratically built local organization is not the only option any longer, and we do see tendencies in the direction of a growth of a dual organizational society, one in which important organizations do not build out local branches at all. An overall centralization and bureaucratization of the voluntary sector at the same time as we at the local level see a move (or a retreat) toward the most narrow neighborhoods, means a weakening of the organizational links between the local and central level. The result of a local organizational society decreasingly interested in and connected to the society at large may be that particularly low status groups loose their strong connections with the national level and weaken their position in the "large democracy." Such groups' historically unique position vis-à-vis the society at large, and thereby one of the most distinctive characteristics of Norwegian (Scandinavian) society, may be gradually impaired. We may now be in the middle of a process in which both the locally based and democratically built voluntary society, and thereby the civil society, take on a more marginal position within Norwegian democracy. *Voluntary organizations are to an ever decreasing extent real (empirical) intermediate structures* linking the individual to the society at large. However, that does not necessarily mean that voluntary organizations have lost impact upon public policies. What it means is that organizational strength understood in part as membership strength is not at all as important as before; at the same time as it has become less obvious whom the organizations influencing public policies and public opinion really represent. Both features are problematic from a democratic point of view.

Women are losing the organizational society which was their own, which both culturally and politically was much more important than the conventional wisdom would have it. This was a society which partially reflected the complementary woman's role of the "old" society, with distinct areas of responsibility and social and cultural environments for women and men. Nevertheless, there has never been a state of pure segregation; this has been prevented particularly by the hierarchical organizational model linking the local and the central level — i.e., by the coexistence of the same organizations at local and central levels. Thus, to a certain extent, historically there has been a *functional specialization* by gender. In some cases such specialization may be seen as a division into *complementary* but *"equal"* organizations and responsibilities, while in other cases it may represent a hierarchical ordering which allowed men to maintain power over women.[47] However, even then there has been political space open to women.

Women Are So Far Not Represented in the "Modern" Organizational Society to the Same Degree as Men

Starting in the mid-1960s, and more definitely after 1980, the tendency has been toward a less gender-segregated organizational society. Small, neighborhood-based organizations, most often dominated by women, are in serious decline, and the founding rate for organizations of this type is far lower than the mortality rate. Furthermore, the dynamics of the organizational society in the 1980s (and probably also the 1990s) do not provide strong signs of a new type of a comprehensive organizational society solely for women, or highly dominated by women. This is a significant indication of a general cognitive and ideological move away from understanding women primarily as complements to men, as fundamentally different from men, in the direction of understanding them as equals. Such a development indicates a shift toward believing that women and men can and should be concerned with the same things.[48] This is not automatically the same as real involvement, but it does indicate increased space for women, both socially, culturally, and politically.

Men dominate the vast majority of the new types of organizations, those which emerged starting in the mid-1960s and are primarily involved in "leisure" activities in the broadest sense of the term. Women, consequently, are in the process of losing their own organizational society, while they thus far do not constitute an equal part of the new, "modern" organizational society. It may then be that women as a separate social category are losing influence in civil society as they become more diversified in terms of interests and participation. *"Women" as a category is becoming less relevant in the description of the typical features of the organizational society.*

All of this is well and good, if our belief is that the genders should be as similar as possible. However, in spite of explosive growth and differentiation in female employment and participation in activities and fora which were previously considered typically male (sports, for example) the new female role in the labor market or in athletics has not been fully extended to the organizational society. Even though organizations are open to women, and women do participate, they are still dominated by men. It is at present too early to say the extent to which this indicates that the modern woman is less interested in the new, dominant "leisure and market ideology" of many of these organizations (Selle and Svåsand 1991), and that many of these organizations primarily express typically male value systems, or whether the lack of female participation is best explained by internal organizational characteristics (organizational culture) which make it difficult to be a woman inside the organization (Kanter 1977). The only certain thing is that in the large-scale transformation process which is now in progress, the organizational society has been increasingly dominated by men. Women have become *less visible* in the organizational society as gender has become a less pertinent social category.

The question of whether the above will become a permanent feature of a less gender-segregated organizational society, or whether it is only a matter of time before women become fully integrated into the modern, emerging organizational society, is an extremely important social issue, and a vital one for future research. The developments of the 1980s seem to indicate that there is some support for the lag hypothesis, and that the tendency is towards integration of women into the modern organizational society. Young women participate more like men; female-dominated organizations, even if they are not really a large group of organizations, have a highly modern organizational structure. We now find more differentiated participation of women in the voluntary sector than ever before, but the differences among women of different ages have increased.

Influence in Organizations versus Influence in Society

In order to broaden our understanding of women's position and involvement in the organizational society, it is *necessary to distinguish between women's position inside various organization types and the position and involvement of these organization types in society.* Power inside organizations and social power are two different things. Types of organizations with predominantly female members, but predominantly male leaders, where women have been "marginalized" at the higher levels, may have enjoyed considerable social influence. In spite of women's subordinate position in the *internal* organizational hierarchy, it is still legitimate to consider their role here as female influence or involvement, although of course not solely that. *Women may exercise social power through organization types in which they play a subordinate role internally.*[49]

Our understanding of influence and involvement is also linked to the level concerned; the direct and specific politics of interests, or higher level (cognitive/ideological) conceptualizations of "normal" versus "abnormal," "right" versus "wrong." An example of an interesting question in this respect, in which researchers have shown little interest, is: how important have women, women's organizations, and organizations with large female memberships been for the formation of an understanding of what a welfare state is, or what a welfare society is? In other words, what influence have women had on recently developing higher level welfare ideology — for example, the principle of universality, which was extremely important in the organization of the modern Norwegian welfare state. Other questions might be: how important were women in the teetotal movement (often in alliances with [female] missionaries); how important were they for the Norwegian people's views on alcohol, or on the actual alcohol policies introduced in Norway?

We have just started to look into such research questions, but we are convinced that if the significance of the civil society is taken seriously, then the political influence and involvement of women must be reevaluated. Our task is to clarify the areas in which women have made an impact, and the extent and nature of their influence. A dynamic civil society with a large space for women and a political system which is to an unusual degree open to pressure from below, and consequently closely linked to the same civil society (Morken and Selle 1994), have made women's organization and participation far more than a free space for the release of psychological tensions created in the family sphere.[50] To figure out how much more is not the least important now when the political status of men and women is more equal than ever and the political gender gap is closing down (Karvonen and Selle 1995; Raaum 1995a).

Men have been the main impetus behind much of the current "modernization" of the voluntary sector. *Men are the most important agents of modernization.* Women hold back, but their resistance is weakening constantly, and neither alternative values nor internal organizational barriers seem to be sufficient to stop women's integration into the modern organizational society. Women are apparently heading full speed into the organizational society, as they are into the society at large.

APPENDIX: Typology

Main Categories	Typology used in most of this paper	Subgroups
ECONOMIC	Unions	Unions
	Other	Cooperative org. Farmers assoc. Landowners' assoc. Fishermens' assoc. Breeding assoc. Other
POLITICAL	Political	All political parties
SPORTS	Sports	Sports Workers assoc. Shooters assoc. Other
LANGUAGE	Language	New Norwegian org. [Mållag] Other
TEETOTAL	Teetotal	All teetotal organizations
MISSIONARY	Missionary	All missionary org. except Christian org. for children and youth
CHILDREN/YOUTH	Christian Children/Youth	Sunday schools Christian youth org.
	Youth assoc. [Frilynde UL]	Youth assoc.
	Other	Scouts Youth clubs 4-H Other
SONG, MUSIC, THEATRE	Song, Music, Theatre	Music assoc. School orchestra (janitsjar) Choirs Dance/Theatre Jazz/Pop Folk dance (Leikarring) Other
SOCIAL AND HUMANITARIAN	Social and Humanitarian	Housewives orgs. [Helselag] [Sanitetslag] [NSSR] [Fisker/Bondekvinnelag]
	Red Cross	Red Cross/[N. Folkehjelp]
	Handicap/Self help	Handikap/Self help
	Other	Other
CULTURE AND LEISURE	Culture/Neighbourhood	Culture/Education Neighbourhood assoc.
	Pensioners assoc.	Pensioners assoc.
	Leisure	Leisure
	Other	[Nærradio/TV] [Innvandrerlag] [Forsamlingshus] Other

NOTES

1. This is a considerably expanded, far more theoretical version of the article, "The changing role of women within local voluntary organizations: sex segregation in the voluntary sector," which was published in Karvonen and Selle (1995). Many thanks to Nina Raaum and Dietrich Rueschemeyer, for very helpful comments.

2. Selle and Øymyr (1995) provides a more comprehensive discussion of our view of how the organizational society reflects the general society at various points in time — i.e., the degree to which the organizations reflect social change, promote social development (are an autonomous force), or are able to impede such change.

3. By closed we mean organizations which by formal or mostly formal means are closed to men. However, we also include some types of organization which, due to normative or structural factors, are virtually impossible for men to join. For example, missionary women's organizations are for women only: they are closed to men. Housewives' organizations, on the other hand, were for quite some time purely women's organizations in practice, though they were formally open to men. This was a result of the fact that there were few male "housewives," and participation in a "housewives" organization was a virtually impossible and highly unlikely venture for the few there were. There are also examples of organizations which are formally purely women's organizations, such as Women's public health associations, which nevertheless sometimes have male members at the local level. These organizations, too, are classified as women's organizations here. For a detailed survey of our classification of pure women's organizations, see Leipart and Selle 1984, and Selle and Øymyr 1995.

4. The data has been taken from "Prosjektet Organisasjonane i Hordaland" (POH), which covers not only a complete register of all local voluntary organizations in the region of Hordaland, but also in the regions of Buskerud and Finnmark as well. As the developmental data are best for Hordaland, we have taken this region as the object of study for the present chapter. The composition of the organizational society varies somewhat from region to region, but there is far less variation today than 50 years ago. Furthermore, developments are parallel, so that the trends we reveal for one county are largely representative for the country as a whole. We have data sets for 1941, 1980, and 1988. The registration in 1941 was carried out by the Norwegian Nazis, and as far as we have been able to ascertain, represents the only such registration. In Hordaland, in addition to the registration of organizations, in 1980 we carried out a comprehensive survey for all organizations, using questionnaires. This survey provided us with information regarding the age of the organization, their catchment areas, organizational networks, contact with the public sector, membership and leadership structures, scope and type of activity, finances, etc. For more information on the project and on methodological problems, see Leipart and Selle 1984, and Selle and Øymyr 1989. The main study using these data is Selle and Øymyr 1995.

5. Selle and Øymyr (1995) discusses the relationship among organization, society, and democracy in much greater detail.

6. Skov Henriksen (1994) presents an interesting survey of how the civil so-

ciety is perceived in the literature. Henriksen himself argues for a political role. See also Rueschemeyer 1992; Cohen and Arato 1992, and Turner 1992.

7. A good deal of current research in the social sciences (for example, Habermas-inspired research and more economically oriented models) incorporates a concept of sectors as the bearers of a priori qualities or functions.

8. As the literature on corporatism has shown (e.g., Olsen 1981; Katzenstein 1985; Schmitter 1983), Norway scores high. This implies a process of institutional co-optation into public decision making that is quite comprehensive. The most important study showing the limited participation and integration of Norwegian women's organizations in this system of policy making is Hernes 1982.

9. This is also true of as important and undogmatic a researcher in women's issues as Helga Hernes (1982; 1987). For a discussion of why we should break with the marginalization perspective and the corporative approach in the study of organizational influence, see Selle 1994a.

10. Selle (1994a) presents a more in-depth discussion of the possible consequences of such a switch in perspective for women's roles as citizens.

11. See, e.g., Hernes 1982; 1987. For a critique of this view see Selle 1994a. Also Norwegian female historians open up for such organizational impact, however, without trying to separate the particular role of women (Blom 1994; Seip 1994). Two very important American books that are really changing the interpretations of the historical role of women in the voluntary sector and in society at large are McCarthy 1992, and Skocpol 1992. Three new books that are also breaking with the a priori marginalization of women, while at the same time giving a very broad and detailed overview of changes in the political position of women in the Nordic countries, and in Norway especially, are Karvonen and Selle 1995; Raaum 1995a, and Nagel 1997. They all show the tremendous improvements of the political position of women in the Nordic countries since the 1970s, emphasizing the unique political role of Nordic women in which *the gender gap is closing down*. In Norway, for instance, women today participate in mass politics to the same extent as men, and concerning political leadership the increase in women's leadership has been extensive and fast. However, when it comes to women's leadership in business or even in trade unions, there is still quite clearly a gender gap, even if there has been a considerable improvement. The weaker role of women within this sector is in part explained by the extensive part-time work of Norwegian women. Research on the role of women in business' and trade unions are still rather undeveloped research areas (e.g., Karvonen 1995; Raaum 1995a; Wright, Baxter, and Birkelund 1995; Skjeie 1991; Kjelstad and Lyngstad 1993).

12. There have been considerable changes in this since the late 1970s, and in a number of organizational types there has been an overwhelming centralization of power. See Heitmann and Selle 1993.

13. As research on women's issues in Norway is now increasingly changing its view of the state, from a patriarchal, oppressive state to a women-friendly state (see, e.g., Hernes 1987; Skjeie 1992; Raaum 1995a), it is perhaps time to re-evaluate women's role in the organizational society and thus in the civil society, both in historical terms and at present. For further discussion of this question, see Selle 1994a.

14. In understanding the specific role of the voluntary sector and of civil soci-

ety in Norway (Scandinavia), the focus must be on the democratic associational tradition rather than the Anglo-American tradition of paying attention to these voluntary associations as NGOs and their role as service-producing nonprofit and non-governmental organizations (Powell 1987; Gidron, Kramer, and Salamon 1992). In doing so one must focus on the interconnection between such associations and social movements — i.e., the five large enduring social movements: the peasant movement, the labor movement, the laymen's movement, the teetotal movement, and the sports movement (e.g., Rokkan 1970; Klausen and Selle 1996).

15. For possible implications, see Selle and Øymyr 1992.

16. There have also previously been organizations which were exclusively open to men, such as men's choirs, and "lodges" of various sorts. But the percentage of the total represented by these organizations is decreasing in contrast to new foundations.

17. For a comprehensive discussion of the evolution of various types of mass movements and of changes in the role of voluntary organizations in society at large, see Selle and Øymyr 1995, Chapters 10 and 11. In those chapters, we argue that the local organizational society and thus the civil society are becoming less significant within the democracy. This development is seen as a consequence of, among other things, the weakening of the links between the local organizational society and the society at large, and the tendency toward a dual organizational society — i.e., one at the local and one at the central level. We also argue that there is now a pressure on the *core* of the Norwegian voluntary society, the local membership based and democratically built organizations, while there is a growth in organizations of the NGO-type, organizations that are not necessarily membership based and democratically built, organizations set up to implement public policies. To a lesser degree we see modern voluntary organizations as real intermediate structures. See also Klausen and Selle 1996.

18. In recent years the press has reported on the difficulties of involving children and young people in organizations. Several of the traditional organizations for children and young people are showing signs of stagnation or decline. This is also true of significant numbers of Christian organizations for the above groups. Selle and Øymyr 1995, Chapter 11, argue that the traditional children's organizations have passed their prime. The introduction of longer school days, among other things, has had a decisive effect on the conditions under which these organizations work.

19. Selle and Øymyr 1995, Chapters 6–9, provides a detailed survey of the relative positions of the various types of organizations after 1940.

20. Throughout this paper we have utilized different typologies to show the gender composition of different organizational types. In this section, we use a typology based on the dominant gender composition within each subtype of organizations. Thus we refer to a male-dominated or female-dominated *organization type*. In the section dealing with characteristics of the "surviving" and "dead" organizations in the period 1980–88, we use the *gender composition of the individual organization*.

21. The "turnover rate" refers to the proportion of new and defunct organizations within a given time span.

22. Our data here are not particularly good. However, considerable experience suggests that such types of organization in general are currently suffering severe recruitment difficulties, and most are unable to recruit young members at all.

23. Valgundersøkelsen, 1957 [Election Survey] (Leipart and Sande 1980) and Undersøkelse om deltaking i frivillige organisasjoner [Survey on participation in voluntary organizations, 1986] (Bregnballe 1987).

24. The respondents may belong to a varying number of organizations, with a maximum of 15 different memberships. Each membership is registered as one case. In Figure 3, the unit is membership.

25. The categories in Figure 3 have been defined and coded by Statistisk Sentralbyrå (Central Bureau of Statistics), and are not fully comparable with our categories. Economic and political organizations were not included in these surveys.

26. It would be interesting to find out whether this group consists primarily of women who do not participate in the labor market, or whether this also includes working women over 50.

27. There can be little doubt that Norway's Prime Minister, Gro Harlem Brundtland, and the internationally known marathon runner Grete Waitz have been important figures with both actual and symbolic effect.

28. It may be important to notice that the concept "neighborhood organizations" covers two rather different ways of organizing. When we talk about modern neighborhood organizations, we most often talk about an organization recruiting members from the most narrow residential area. However, neighborhood organizations of the traditional type were recruiting members from a wider geographical area, most often a school district. Furthermore, the organizations of the older type were much less self-oriented than the new ones and were to quite another extent interested in what was going on outside of the organizational borders. This has implications for the role of the different types of neighborhood organizations in civil society, in democracy.

29. Describing these organizations as apolitical does not imply that they are without a system of values. In several publications we have argued that a considerable number of modern organizations which are linked to leisure activities in a broad sense are both ideologically and organizationally close to market-oriented thinking. See Selle and Svåsand 1991.

30. Teigum (1992) documents and provides frequencies for the data collected in the Survey on Life Conditions. In Table 3 we use data only from 1980 and 1991, as the data for the intervening surveys only indicate tendencies which become even clearer with time. The above survey asked people, subjectively, to evaluate whether or not they are active, and does not ask in the same way as the Election Survey or the Citizens Survey for a specified response as regards participation. This results in a slight variation between the figures, though the main tendencies are the same. Furthermore, it may be that women and men, or the young and the old, have a somewhat different perceptions as to what it means to be active.

31. These findings were supported by the results of the *Citizens Survey* of 1990 (Medborgerundersøkelsen), which showed that women under 30 constitute the group which participated least in voluntary organizations of all kinds. For a

more comprehensive analysis of women's participation in organizational society based on the data from the *Citizens Survey*, see Raaum 1995b.

32. For a comprehensive analysis of changes in the gender composition of Norwegian political parties, see Heidar and Raaum 1995a, and Sundberg 1995.

33. These findings seem to correspond to developments in Sweden and Denmark. See Micheletti 1994, and Andersen et. al. 1993. See also Klausen and Selle 1996.

34. In the 1988 registration the organizations that had ceased to exist during the 1980–88 period were registered. Thus we have traced these organizations back to the 1980 survey. We found that 255 of the extinct organizations had answered the survey back in 1980. However, not all of these organizations answered all the questions, and the tables represent those organizations that did answer the relevant questions. There is no major skewness between the main categories of organizations answering the survey in 1980 (Selle and Øymyr 1992). Still, there is some skewness concerning subgroups within main categories. We know, for instance, that among the traditional missionary organizations the reply percentage is low. To correct for this the organizations have been weighted.

35. See, e.g., Stinchcombe 1965; Freeman, Carroll and Hannan 1984; Hannan and Freeman 1989, and Aldrich and Marsden 1988. See also Selle and Øymyr 1992 for a more thorough analysis of the "liability of newness" hypothesis based on the same data as are used here.

36. We have to emphasize that these figures do not necessarily contain information on all the internal activities. Organizational types having membership meetings as their main activity (e.g., missionary organizations) will necessarily have a higher score on this question than sports organizations, where members often meet to practice sports, but only have membership meetings a few times a year.

37. The index shows the degree of engagement in public affairs. It is based on the following variables: the number of engagements in the course of one year, whether the organizations have arranged meetings about public matters, whether they have sent notes/letters to the authorities or made personal contact with officials.

38. How the welfare state influences civil society is an important discourse in modern social theory. We argue that in "state-friendly" societies like the Norwegian in which the boundaries between what is the public and what is the voluntary sector is really blurred, governmental contact and governmental funding are important as factors of organizational legitimation (Kuhnle and Selle 1992). It promotes organizational survival or may even promote organizational "birth." It is our general understanding that governmental contact and support and the policies of comprehensive social provision by the state do not primarily smother civic engagement in a country like Norway, but on the contrary, are in general supportive — it has kept or even expanded the scope of the voluntary sector. However, it has also affected in more complex ways the density, forms, and direction of the voluntary sector and social participation more in general (e.g., Selle and Øymyr 1992; 1995). However, how and to what extent are still a somewhat open and extremely difficult question to answer (e.g., Kuhnle and Selle 1992; Rothstein 1992; Klausen and Selle 1996).

39. Our historical data here are not adequate, and the extent to which the individual local organization was extroverted in its activity may be somewhat unclear. It was probably primarily the "municipality" organization, or a local confederation of organizations (umbrella organization) which was responsible for much of the extrovert activity, particularly vis-à-vis the authorities (e.g. Selle and Øymyr 1995). However, in spite of the fact that there is some doubt as to whether the individual organization engaged in extrovert activities as a general rule, the organization was part of and highly influential for the local culture. It may often be reasonable to consider such organizations as reflections of the typical features of a local culture where there are no clear boundaries between the organization and its surroundings. This is not at all the case today, in itself implying crucial changes in the role of voluntary organizations in civil society.

40. The figures are somewhat uncertain, partly since N is low and there is some statistical skewness on these variables. Still we argue that the extensive differences express real differences. See Selle and Øymyr 1995, Chapter 9.

41. Still, there are more surviving organizations with more than 100 members as compared to new ones.

42. For a discussion of possible consequences of a less local based organizational society, which coincides with a strong position for decentralization and proximity as political ideas, see Selle 1991.

43. This can be seen as part of the same tendency as the "retreat" towards the the most narrow neighborhood. It should be understood as a certain type of privatization, a lack of interest in the society at large (Wuthnow 1991; Selle and Øymyr 1995).

44. For a more in-depth discussion, see Selle and Øymyr 1995, Chapter 11. In that chapter we discuss how what we refer to as *the organization syndrome*, the belief that all important matters must be formalized and organized, has reached a saturation point. It may be that women are the catalysts behind the establishment of alternative networks which are not formalized in a way that allows for their designation as voluntary organizations. At the same time there has been a comprehensive growth in voluntary work growing out of public or semi-public institutions like schools, kindergartens, museums, stadiums, and churches weakening the historically very intimate relationship between voluntary organizations and voluntary work, while at the same time making the boundaries between what is public and what is voluntary even more blurred than they already are.

45. In this context it is interesting to note that the Norwegian Red Cross, which has emphasized mixed organizations, has done much better than the two other large organizations, Norwegian National Health Association, and the Norwegian Women's Public Health Associations.

46. In Selle and Øymyr 1995, Chapters 10 and 11, we provide a much more detailed discussion of these changes and the consequences they have for the nature of the civil society and our democracy. We also discuss whether the voluntary organizational society is gradually weakened and whether it consequently will assume a more limited role in the democracy.

47. For a discussion of the reason for this, and the implications for the influence of the voluntary sector on governmental policy, and on politics more

generally, see Selle 1994a, and Selle and Øymyr 1995. Voluntary organizations probably play a less important role in the formation of public opinion than was earlier the case, and there seems to be weaker correlation between organization strength and political influence than there used to be. The new role of the media is an important factor in this respect. Morken and Selle (1994) argue that in a comparative context, it is extremely difficult for alternative movements such as the women's movement and the environmental movement, to maintain a position as an alternative movement in systems such as the Norwegian. This is a result of the fact that the mechanisms of coopting are unusually strong, which in turn is a result of, among other things, the ease with which organizations are able to influence — i.e., the access structure is in a comparative perspective unusually open. At the same time, the "distance" between the voluntary and public sectors is, compared to countries outside of Scandinavia, very small. That is not the least so concerning ideology (e.g. Selle and Kuhnle 1992; Klausen and Selle 1996). In Klausen and Selle (1996) we argue that the Norwegian (Scandinavian) voluntary sector historically is characterized by seven distinct features of which several of them — as this article shows — are under severe pressure. These are: historical rootedness in social movements; membership-based and democratically built organizations within a hierarchical organizational structure linking the local and national organizational level; a strong voluntary tradition and a rather weak NGO-tradition (even if several social and humanitarian organizations also are great institution builders); pragmatism and consensus orientation with widely shared values crossing sectoral borders; close contact and integrated cooperation with public authorities (not a colonization of the voluntary sector by the state), institutionalized co-optation into public decision making, and a noninterference tradition in organizational matters (organizational autonomy). For a much more detailed overview of the changes within the voluntary sector and possible consequences for Norwegian democracy, see especially Selle and Øymyr 1995.

48. New and more detailed studies are necessary in order to determine when either of these situations exists, i.e., it is not at all an a priori question. It is also necessary to study further the conditions under which organizations which are about to make an entrance into the society at large are best served by utilizing exclusive or inclusive strategies.

49. If there is a shift in the direction of new sex differences in the organizational society, it is, as mentioned, in the increase in organizations which are open to both sexes, but which have only male members.

50. There are some who would consider women's participation in such organizations an extreme example of false consciousness, an example of women being without responsibility for their own lives. In that case, the implication is that women have joined organizations which for generations have not catered for their interests. For such a view in Norwegian women's studies, see Gulli 1982. Neither modern women's studies nor others have shown particular interest in such traditional women's organizations. To the extent that these organizations have been the object of study (Gulli 1982; Hernes 1982; 1987), the marginalization perspective has dominated. In other words, it has been the organizational powerlessness of women that has been in focus. Furthermore, the overall pic-

ture has not been presented in any detail. Historians have been more concerned with female influence and involvement than political scientists or sociologists (see e.g. Blom 1994, Ibsen 1989; Martinsen 1989; Melby 1990, and Seip 1994). But these studies do not provide a systematic discussion of the degree and nature of the influence of women's organizations on final results. For a discussion of how and why modern feminist women's studies marginalize older women's organizations, see Selle 1994a.

LITERATURE

Aldrich, Howard E., and Marsden, Peter V. 1988. "Environment and Organizations." In *Handbook of Sociology*, ed. Neil J. Smelser. Newbury Park: Sage.

Allardt, Erik. 1994. "Makrosociala forandringar och politik i dagens Europa." *Sosiologia* no. 1:1–10.

Andersen, Johannes, et al. 1993. *Medborgerskap. Demokrati og politisk deltagelse*. Herning: Systime.

Blom, Ida 1994. *Det er forskjell på folk — nå som før*. Oslo: Universitetsforlaget.

Brandal, Trygve, and Selle, Per. 1983. "Endringar i Organisasjonsmønsteret i Hordaland 1940–1980." *Heimen* no. 4:259–270.

Bregnballe, Anne 1987. *Sluttrapport. Undersøkelse om deltaking i frivillige organisasjoner. Interne notater*. Oslo: Statistisk Sentralbyrå, Report 87/13.

Cohen, Jean, and Arato, Andrew. 1992. *Civil Society and Political Theory*. Cambridge: MIT Press.

Freeman, John; Carrol, Glenn R.; and Hannan, Michael T. 1983. "The Liability of Newness: Age Dependence in Organizational Death Rates." *Sociological Review* 48:692–710.

Gidron, Benjamin; Kramer, Ralph M.; and Salamon, Lester M. 1992. *Government and the Third Sector. Emerging Relationships in Welfare States*. San Francisco: Jossey-Bass.

Gordon, Linda, ed. 1990. *Women, the State, and Welfare*. Madison: University of Wisconsin Press.

Gulli, Brita 1982. "Likeverd, likestilling, frigjøring. En analyse av de eldre kvinneorganisasjonene." In *Kvinner i fellesskap*, ed. Harriet Holter. Oslo: Universitetsforlaget.

Hannan, Michael T., and Freeman, John. 1989. *Organizational Ecology*. Cambridge: Harvard University Press.

Heidar, Knut, and Raaum, Nina. 1995. "Partidemokrati i endring." In Raaum 1995a.

Heitmann, Jan H., and Selle, Per. 1993. "Styrets rolle i frivillige organisasjonar." In *Styrets rolle*, ed. Torger Reve and Tore Grønlie. Oslo: Tano.

Henriksen, Lars S. 1994. "Det civile samfunn: tilbage til politisk filosofi." *Norsk Statsvitenskapelig Tidsskrift* no. 4:357–374.

Hernes, Gudmund. 1978. *Forhandlingsøkonomi og blandingsadministrasjon*. Oslo: Universitetsforlaget.

Hernes, Gudmund, and Martinussen, Willy 1980. *Demokrati og politiske ressurser*. Oslo: NOU 1980:7.

Hernes, Helga. 1982. "Norske kvinneorganisasjoner: Kvinner som maktgrunnlag eller kvinners maktgrunnlag." In *Staten — Kvinner ingen adgang?* Helga Hernes. Oslo: Universitetsforlaget.

———. 1987. *Welfare State and Women Power: Essays in State Feminism.* Oslo: Universitetsforlaget.

Ibsen, Hilde 1989. *Med kunnskap mot kreft. Norsk forening til kreftens bekjempelse, 1938–1988.* Oslo: Den norske kreftforening.

Kanter, Rosabeth M. 1977. *Men and Women in the Corporation.* New York: Basic Books.

Karvonen, Lauri. 1995. "Trade unions and the feminization of the labour market in Scandinavia." In Karvonen and Selle 1995.

Karvonen, Lauri, and Selle, Per, eds. 1995. *Women in Nordic Politics: Closing the Gap.* Aldershot: Dartmouth.

Katzenstein, Peter 1985. *Small States in World Market: Industrial Policy in Europe.* Ithaca: Cornell University Press.

Kjellstad, Randi, and Lyngstad, Jan 1993. *Arbeid, lønn og likestilling.* Oslo: Universitetsforlaget.

Klausen, Kurt Klaudi, and Selle, Per. 1996. "The Third Sector in Scandinavia." *Voluntas* no 2:99–122.

Kuhnle, Stein, and Selle, Per. 1990. "Autonomi eller underordning: Frivillige organisasjoner og det offentlige." In *Frivillig organisert velferd. Alternativ til offentlig?* ed. Stein Kuhnle and Per Selle. Bergen: Alma Mater.

———. 1992. "The Historical Precedent for Government-Nonprofit Cooperation in Norway." In Gidron, Kramer, and Salamon 1992.

Lafferty, William M. 1986. "Den sosialdemokratiske stat." *Nytt Norsk Tidsskrift* no. 3:23–37.

Leipart, Jørn Y., and Sande, Terje 1980. *Valgundersøkelsen 1957.* Bergen: Norsk Samfunnsvitenskapelige Datatjeneste, University of Bergen, Report 47.

Leipart, Jørn Y., and Selle, Per. 1984. *Organisasjonane i Hordaland 1980. Ei vurdering av representativitet, svarprosent og spørjeskjema.* Bergen: Hordaland Fylkeskommune.

Martinsen, Kari 1989. *Omsorg, sykepleie og medisin. Historisk-filosofisk essays.* Oslo: Tano.

McCarthy, Kathleen D. 1993. *Women's Culture: American Philantrophy and Art, 1830–1930.* Chicago: University of Chicago Press.

Melby, Kari 1990. *Kall til kamp. Norsk Sykepleierforbunds historie.* Oslo: Cappelen.

Micheletti, Michele 1994. *Det civila samhället och staten.* Stockholm: Fritzes.

Morken, Kristin, and Selle, Per. 1994. "The Women's Shelter Movement." In *Women and Social Change,* ed. Feliece Perlmutter. Washington, D.C.: NASW Press.

Nagel, Anne Hilde, ed. 1997. *Kjønn og velferdsstat.* Bergen: Alma Mater.

Olsen, Johan P. 1978. *Politisk organisering.* Oslo: Universitetsforlaget.

———. 1981. "Integrated Organizational Participation in Government." In *Handbook of Organizational Design, 2,* ed. Paul C. Nystrom and William H. Starbuck. Oxford: Oxford University Press.

Powell, William W., ed. 1987. *The Nonprofit Sector.* New Haven: Yale University Press.

Putnam, Robert D. 1993. *Making Democracy Work. Civic Traditions in Modern Italy.* Princeton: Princeton University Press.

Raaum, Nina C., ed. 1995a. *Kjønn og politikk.* Oslo: Tano.

———. 1995b: "Politisk medborgerskap." In Raaum 1995a.

Rokkan, Stein. 1970. *Citizens, Elections, Parties.* Oslo: Universitetsforlaget.

Rokkan, Stein, and Campbell, Angus. 1960. "Citizen participation in political life: Norway and the United States of America." *International Social Science Journal* no. 1:66–99.

Rothstein, Bo. 1992. *Den korporative staten. Interesseorganisationer och statsforvaltning i svensk politik.* Stockholm: Norstedts.

Rueschemeyer, Dietrich. 1992. "The Development of Civil Society after Authoritarian Rule." Bergen: LOS-senter notat 92/47.

Schmitter, Philippe C. 1983. "Interest intermediation and regime governability in contemporary Western Europe and North America." In *Organizing Interests in Western Europe,* ed. Suzanne Berger. Cambridge: Cambridge University Press.

Seip, Anne Lise 1984. *Sosialhjelpstaten blir til. Norsk sosialpolitikk 1740–1920.* Oslo: Gyldendal.

———. 1994. *Veiene til velferdsstaten. Norsk sosialpolitikk 1920–1975.* Oslo: Gyldendal.

Selle, Per. 1991. "Det frivillige organisasjonssamfunnet under gjennomgripande endring." In *Organisasjonssamfunnet i ei brytningstid,* ed. Per Selle. Bergen: Alma Mater.

———. 1994a. "Marginalisering eller kvinnemakt." *Syn og Segn* no. 3:202–211.

———. 1994b. "Er tiden for de kollektive bevegelsene over? En kommentar til Knut Kjeldstadli." *Tilbake til framtiden.* Oslo: Alternativ Framtid.

———. 1995. "Idretten og det offentlege: Ein familie?" In *Frivillig organisering i Norden,* ed. Kurt Klaudi Klausen and Per Selle. Oslo: Tano/Jurist og Økonomiforbundets Forlag.

Selle, Per, and Hestetun, Per Arne. 1990. *Fylkesnivået i Organisasjonssamfunnet.* Oslo: Tano.

Selle, Per, and Svåsand, Lars. 1991. "Kulturpolitikk, fritid og frivillige organisasjonar." In *Politisk Kultur. Misjon og Revolusjon frå Bremnes til Buenos Aires,* Per Selle and Einar Berntzen. Oslo: Tano.

Selle, Per, and Øymyr, Bjarne. 1989. "Organisasjonane i Hordaland 1987/88." Bergen: LOS-Report 89/1.

———. 1992. "Explaining Changes in the Population of Voluntary Organizations: The Role of Aggregate and Individual Level Data." *Nonprofit and Voluntary Sector Quarterly* no. 2:147–179.

———. 1995. *Frivillig organisering og demokrati. Det frivillige organisasjonssamfunnet endrar seg 1940–1990.* Oslo: Samlaget.

Skjeie, Hege 1991. "The Uneven Advance of Norwegian Women." *New Left Review* 187:79– 102.

———. 1992. *Den politiske betydningen av kjønn. En studie av norsk topp-politikk.* Oslo: ISF Report no. 11.

Skocpol, Theda. 1992. *Protecting Soldiers and Mothers. The Political Origins of Social Policy in the United States.* Cambridge: Harvard University Press.

Stinchcombe, Arthur L. 1965. "Social Structure and Organization." In *Handbook of Organizations*, ed. James G. March. Chicago: Rand McNally.

Sundberg, Jan. 1995. "Women in Scandinavian party organizations." In Karvonen and Selle 1995.

Teigum, Hanne 1992. *Levekårsundersøkelsene 1980, 1983, 1987 og 1991. Dokumentasjon og frekvenser.* Bergen: Norsk Samfunnsvitenskapelig Datatjeneste, University of Bergen. Report no. 97.

Turner, Charles 1992. "Organicism, pluralism and civil associations; some neglected political thinkers." *History of the Human Sciences* no. 3:175–184.

Wright, Erik O.; Baxter, Janeen; and Birkelund, Gunn 1995. "The Gender Gap in Workplace Authority: A Cross-National Study." *American Sociological Review* 60:405–435.

Wuthnow, Robert 1991. "The Voluntary Sector: Legacy of the Past, Hope for the Future?" In *Between States and Markets. The Voluntary Sector in Comparative Perspective*, ed. Robert Wuthnow. Princeton University Press.

– 5 –

Women and Philanthropy
in Colonial and Post-Colonial Australia

SHURLEE SWAIN

> Ladies of Toorak and elsewhere who give your balls, and At Homes, and get your elegant costumes described in the society papers, do you know that your sisters and their children are starving.... It is not the spending of all that money that is wrong; it is the spending of it in the wrong way, and on the wrong persons.... Stop your dances, and take better exercise by ministering to the poor.
>
> (*Melbourne Spectator*, July 21, 1893).

This admonition delivered to the women of Australia's then largest city in the midst of their deepest economic depression might wrongly suggest that English patterns of philanthropy had not taken hold in the colonies. In the century following European settlement, the women of Australia did establish a distinctive pattern of philanthropy built upon inherited traditions and adapted to the unique colonial situation.* However, in the twentieth century, women's philanthropy was marginalized and provided limited access to power. The contemporary Australian welfare state was constructed in response to the perceived failure of a government-funded voluntary system. It was never broad enough to remove the need for women's philanthropy, but its domination discredited their efforts and limited their ability to bring about change. In the last

This is a revised and extended version of a paper originally published in *Voluntas* (vol. 7, no. 4), the International Journal of Voluntary and Nonprofit Organizations and the official journal of the International Society for Third-Sector Research (ISTR). The authors gratefully acknowledge *Voluntas* and ISTR for their permission to reproduce this paper.

*The Aboriginal society which Europeans had dispossessed had no concept of, or need for, philanthropy. Although women continue to play an important role within surviving Aboriginal communities, they would see their activity not as philanthropic but as simply a sharing of resources and expertise. Their experience therefore is not the subject of this article.

twenty years, the state has withdrawn and women's philanthropy has revived, offering a legitimate platform from which women can contest state policy and practice for groups in need.

COLONIAL CONTEXT

The concept of philanthropy transported to Australia was a British one, born out of a class-divided society and justified by religious injunctions to care for the less fortunate. British philanthropy was at its peak when the Australian colonies were being formed. This brand of philanthropy was individualistic: the rich were expected to reach out to the poor, giving money and time to alleviate immediate need. Its emergence in New South Wales was celebrated as evidence of the truly British character of the settlement. Only twenty-five years after the arrival of the First Fleet, the Society for the Promotion of Christian Knowledge reported

> that even in this distant and obscure corner of the world, the British character does not degenerate; but that Englishmen, in every clime and on every shore, cease not to remember the characteristic benevolence of their native land; and which benevolence is not the least cause of her present exalted greatness (quoted in Berreen, 1994).

Six coastal settlements served as administrative centers for the colonies that became states when the Commonwealth of Australia was established in 1901. These colonies were creations of free-trade capitalism; this showed in their attitudes to poor relief, rejecting the British Poor Law in favor of (primarily) voluntary charity (Dickey, 1980, 31). The mix of state and voluntary effort in each colony in part reflected their origins. The governments of the ex-convict colonies (New South Wales, Tasmania, Western Australia and Queensland) inherited an extensive institutional structure that could be put to benevolent purposes and a continuing responsibility for those transported to the colonies, while the predominantly free settlements of Victoria and South Australia had no such inheritance. But this explanation alone is insufficient. Victoria relied strongly on government-subsidized voluntary effort, South Australia developed the most centralized government relief system. New South Wales developed a strong voluntary sector; Tasmania relied on former penal institutions (see Brown, 1972).

Size is a more important factor: Victoria and New South Wales had larger, wealthier populations than other colonies. Both governments encouraged the emerging bourgeoisie to be involved in philanthropy: they would support charity work, but citizens had to form voluntary organizations to get funding. However, New South Wales retained the stratified society of its convict period and developed a philanthropic network dominated by centralized organizations. Victoria, populated through gold rush immigration, developed a more level society and favored a local approach with small specialized societies (Lyons, 1994, 77).

Despite such regional differences, voluntary activity in all areas showed strong similarities. Where a need was identified, a public society was established with membership through annual subscription. Members elected the committee of management and had the right to nominate "suitable objects for relief. Government assisted with capital and maintenance, initial grants of land, and legal incorporation. By relating funding to donations, it was hoped that government support would encourage charitable habits among the general population. So successful was this approach that in most colonies the state was left with responsibility only for prisons, mental hospitals and, increasingly, a residual child welfare system (Dickey, 1980, 36–37).

The government-funded voluntary system was neither more economical nor more humane than the English system it replaced. The decision of governments to channel relief through voluntary societies removed their opportunity to have a significant say in how that relief was delivered. Yet with no alternatives to offer, colonial governments were left with little choice but to underwrite such organizations when voluntarism failed. However, although it was often the major subscriber, the government had no direct representation on the governing bodies which decided how such relief would be distributed. Philanthropy thus became more central in the Australian colonies than in the countries from which they were settled, but this philanthropy often replicated the very attitudes for which the Poor Law was condemned.

A GENDERED ACTIVITY

Much of the analysis of the origins and pattern of Australian philanthropy has been non-gendered. Yet once the extreme gender imbalance of the early colonial period was overcome, patterns already observed in Britain and the United States were apparent (see Windschuttle, 1982). Philanthropy "was one of the few public and highly visible activities allowed women" in the developing settlements, just as it was in other European societies (Godden, 1982, 91). As the numbers of bourgeois women sufficiently free of domestic and child care responsibilities grew, so too did women's philanthropic activity. Philanthropy in the nineteenth century was thus largely confined to married women, generally beyond their child-rearing years.

Involvement in philanthropic work was distinctly gendered. Of the 240 people who between them occupied 628 positions on 70 Melbourne charities during the 1890s, for example, 102 were men concentrated in the high-status organizations, while the 138 women were spread throughout the system (Swain, 1985b, 104). Men dominated public giving and sat on the committees controlling high-status charities such as general hospitals. It was a privilege they guarded jealously. Replying to a proposal in 1882 to allow women to sit on the Melbourne Benevolent Asylum Board, the honorary treasurer replied "that he was totally opposed, as he considered the ladies were better in their own homes than in public institutions" (Argus, January 20, 1882). Men were managers and patrons offering name, wealth and social prestige, but rarely any great commitment of time.

Although no nineteenth-century charities had large endowments, male-controlled institutions were able to set annual subscriptions rates high and, using business and political networks, quickly build up a large subscription list. The large mercantile and shipping firms that controlled much of the colonial economy were generous contributors, which established their status as good corporate citizens and also ensured support for any of their employees who had fallen on hard times. The local branch of Dennistoun & Co for example contributed £194 over and above regular subscriptions to Melbourne charities over the period 1855–61. Of these charities only one had a female committee: the Lying-in Hospital, which received £50 towards its building fund in 1860 (*Victorian Reports*). Male committee members avoided direct contact with the clientele. Organizations that could not afford paid employees had little chance of attracting other than clergymen to their management committees.

The bulk of the poor, however, were female and most had needs which were not met by male-dominated institutions (Godden, 1982, 88). Colonial economies presumed a male breadwinner, and single women lived a precarious existence which became desperate if they had dependants. In most colonies it was left to philanthropic women to fill the gaps. Very few had control of substantial fortunes, but many were willing to contribute their labor and connections to establish and maintain alternative organizations. An exception is Tasmania, where Brown's (1972) study identifies no distinctive female contribution. Certainly, the major outdoor relief functions which fell to women in the major mainland settlements were controlled by men in Tasmania. It could be that the predominance of convicts and ex-convicts in the colonial population limited women's enthusiasm to be involved in philanthropy without male protection.

There were only 28 women of more than 250 "exceptional" donors (who contributed more than twice the required annual subscription) identified in a survey of early Victorian charities compiled from the annual reports of 52 charitable organizations in the *Victoria Reports.* Fourteen were widowed or single and gave predominantly to the more prestigious organizations managed by men; fourteen were married women who gave to women's charities with which they were associated. Their monetary contributions were small when compared with donations their husbands had made. The most generous donor gave £195 to women's charities over an eight-year period, while her merchant husband gave £1185, all but £175 to organizations managed by men. It was in the giving of time that women eclipsed men. Through the three strategies identified by McCarthy (1994) — assimilation, separatism, and individualism — women used the skills and power they acquired through such activities to extend their role in the public sphere locally and nationally.

In the early voluntary charities, women sat alongside men on planning committees. As the number of bourgeois women in the colonies increased, they were more likely to act alone as it became apparent that only through separatism could women gain power. Of the fifteen major public charities in Melbourne in 1887, eight excluded women from their management committee, but many of these had a ladies committee to which they could delegate "housekeeping tasks." Women, however, had founded and/or controlled the other seven, including two hospitals and the city's major outdoor relief society, although several of these retained "Gentlemen's" Committees which they could consult over financial or property matters.

There were also smaller organizations founded and administered by individual women, perhaps drawing financial support from their husbands but in all other respects acting independently in a world which allowed few women such a place. The leader of Melbourne's licensed child rescuers, Selina Sutherland, fell out with two church-based supervisory committees and decided, in 1893, that the cause would be best served if she worked alone. Establishing her non-denominational Victorian Neglected Children's Aid Society, she became the prime authority on child rescue in the colony, dealing with more children annually than all the other denominationally based organizations combined. She focused hostility on the "men of wealth . . . [the] legislators and so called leaders of society" believing them to be the real sinners. Fallen women and illegitimate children were their innocent victims, who should be effectively and compassionately relieved (Swain, 1985a).

Evangelical Christianity strongly influenced most of these women which encouraged such activity. Like Christ, charitable women were "seeking and saving the lost." By couching their activity in religious terms, women extended the boundaries of their accepted sphere without ever publicly challenging their accepted and subordinate role.

Although many women came to philanthropy via religion, the organizations they founded moved across Protestant denominational boundaries and mobilized women for whom religious identity was not central. The major denominations focused on building schools, and the responsibility for establishing charities was left largely to colonial elites motivated but not bound by their religious beliefs. The Protestant/Catholic boundary was harder to cross. Catholics were concentrated in the lower socio-economic classes and hence were less likely to have the resources for philanthropy. Yet their presence was essential if a charity was to escape accusations of proselytism.

Compromise was possible in elite charities where a male committee could include the local priest. It was less practical in the smaller organizations where most of the women were involved. Here the few eligible Catholic women were seldom acceptable to the Protestant majority and were left with no alternative but to develop their own organizations. The strength of the Protestant/Catholic divide in charity reflects the strength of this division in the community. Prominent women in the small Jewish community, for example, were welcomed to committees before the small number of wealthy Catholic women. While Catholic women supported schools and charities, these were staffed and controlled by religious orders imported into the colonies, and offered few opportunities beyond fundraising for lay women.

In part this divide persisted because neither Catholic nor Protestant organizations were able to transcend class boundaries. While socially prominent supporters took on the roles of patroness and president, attendance records suggest that for many it was the position rather than the work which was important. Lady Janet Clarke is a typical example. She embarked on a career as a philanthropist after marrying her wealthy employer in 1873. Her biographer lists fourteen organizations on which she held office but an examination of attendance records suggests it was her name rather than her presence which such committees valued (Morrissey, 1969, 415; Swain, 1977, 295). The bulk of the work was done by women of somewhat lower social status, who had sufficient leisure for such demanding work and who were excluded from the demanding social round that occupied the time of their social superiors. Where upper-class women gained status from giving their name and money to philanthropic organizations, middle-class women were content with the prestige their association with such women brought.

While most "ladies" had a narrow definition of philanthropy, a significant minority used their experience in charity work as a base from which to agitate for social reform or as a base for a public career. Most notable of these was South Australia's Catherine Helen Spence (see Margarey, 1985). Born in Scotland, she migrated, with her family, to Australia, where she was obliged to earn an income working as a governess and later through writing. In the new colony, Spence abandoned her Presbyterian faith and joined the Unitarian church. The small South Australian branch of the church was little involved in social reform, but on a visit to England in 1865–6 Spence carried introductions to key Unitarian reformers and quickly became interested in their work, particularly because of the opportunities it offered for women to "trespass" into the world of men (Margarey, 1985, 92).

Spence found an outlet for her interest through government, establishing a committee to manage the boarding-out system for the Destitute Board. In response to criticism from this committee, the government removed all children from the Destitute Board's control and established a State Children's Council with a majority of women members. Spence was the Council's chief publicist, writing its official history (Spence, 1907) and travelling widely to speak of its success. In 1897 she was appointed to the Destitute Board where she argued for programs to prevent rather than simply relieve destitution. For Spence, philanthropy provided access to the public sphere where she could work for such causes as federation, suffrage and marriage reform.

Other women who led the various colonial suffrage movements followed a similar path but spent far less time in the "charitable phase" before turning their attention to political solutions (see Allen, 1994; Bomford, 1993). Many women concentrated on social reform, particularly between 1880 and 1920, when "women of the bourgeois philanthropic or charity network" formed an alliance with "the technical experts of the professional middle class" to rationalize the domestic world, "reconstructing housewifery, motherhood, childrearing and sexuality" (Reiger, 1993). Campaigns for better housing, safer childbirth, reduced infant mortality, and sex education drew their strength from this uneasy alliance, and many of their leaders made careers from what was initially a philanthropic interest.

In the absence of a Poor Law, philanthropic women were central to the maintenance of an established order, even though they were effectively excluded from its economy (Harris, 1992, 291). They staked their claim to full citizenship on their contribution of time rather than taxes. Where other European societies were developing a welfare bureaucracy, in the Australian colonies critical decisions as to whom should be relieved and how were made by philanthropic women who appear to have felt no necessity to justify the way they worked.

It has become a commonplace to assert that women achieved this position at the expense of the people they claimed to be helping, participating in the extension of bourgeois regulation of proletarian domestic life, thus buttressing the prevailing patriarchal structure. Yet, as Spence's biographer argues, it is unduly reductionist to dismiss these women so hastily (Margarey, 1985, 91). Nineteenth-century philanthropy could be alleviatory and oppressive at the same time. Where Kennedy (1982, 65) sees "a ritual of stigmatization and humiliation in the process of inquiry," others see a more discerning process in which the ability of the donor to identify with the recipient was critical to the way in which aid was dispensed (see, for example, Dickey, 1980, 92; Swain, 1985b, 110–11). Nineteenth-century philanthropists were, like their clients, caught in a trap

> bound by the limitations of an ideological moral framework which allocated them very meager sums to distribute on a weekly basis … [W]itnessing misery of such a degree on such a scale must have caused them to become judgmental and hardened over time (O'Brien, 1988, 35).

Even this judgement is overly harsh. No charity worker would admit to helping the "undeserving," but case records disclose that all except those in the most exclusive charities did so because practical experience forced them to see that need and merit were not always related (Swain, 1985b, 111). This apparent contradiction did not distress them as their object was to relieve poverty, not to eliminate it. Nor indeed were working-class women and children silent victims in this interaction. There is considerable evidence that they courted such philanthropic intrusion into their lives, actively negotiating with those offering assistance in order to ensure the best for their families (Van Krieken, 1991, 137–38).

Such woman-to-woman interactions existed at the junction of two discourses, one based on a common sisterhood and the other intent on preserving the distinctions of class. Yet the notion of shared sisterhood was flawed because bourgeois women sought to re-create their working-class "sisters" in their own image, constructing a notion of the good woman in opposition to the "viciousness" of the unreformed (Stansell, 1982, 219). The poor woman could be transformed into a good mother through lessons in thrift and economy, and provision of the means to augment her income, but the "fallen" women was always at risk of "failing again." While girls in orphanages or foster homes were prepared for domestic service, their fallen sisters were trained for laundry work, a position that enabled them to earn a living without coming in direct contact with the families of their employers (Windschuttle, 1982). For women, the primary attraction of philanthropy was that it confirmed their gentility.

The pathway to power philanthropy offered to Australian women was flawed. Patricia Harris argues that women's exercise of power was restricted to their own sphere. They worked only with those seen as social subordinates and this seldom included white males. Philanthropy gave women power but only in areas men saw as an extension of their domestic role. Harris (1992, 293, drawing on Godden, 1982, 92ff) argues that women never had authority over white males, but this was not always true. In Victoria, ladies benevolent societies administered outdoor relief. Although meant to be confined to women and children, the societies also assisted families where male wage earners were ill or unemployed. Within this area they exercised almost complete autonomy but were limited by lack of resources.

Both radicals and conservatives accepted that men should be breadwinners and believed that taking charity was a sign of weakness. Where conservatives condemned the man who begged, radicals condemned the society that drove him to beg (Scates, 1993, 46). They also condemned the women who administered relief, classing them with the men whose interests philanthropy upheld. The relief of suffering was conflated with the maintenance of the system that produced such suffering and seen as something which a just society would not support.

Stephen Garton argues that the movement of some women away from charity into social reform was indicative of a growing disillusionment with the efficacy of ameliorative relief as a solution. More telling, however, was the rise of a labor critique which argued that poverty arose from structural rather than personal failings and hence that relief was a right and should not be so grudgingly administered (Garton, 1994, 30–31). Although charity survived this ordeal, it did so with its image tarnished and was left far more vulnerable to attack. Because movements for social reform were constructed in opposition to charitable solutions, it became more difficult for women's philanthropy to encompass both endeavors.

PHILANTHROPY AND THE WELFARE STATE

The federation of Australian colonies in 1901 gave greater political power to the male-based labor movement, and its ideas dominated social policy formation in the new nation. The notion of Australia as a social laboratory was a masculinist, egalitarian one that gave primacy to the state's role in ensuring an adequate life for the working man. If the worker could provide for his family, it was assumed there would be no need for philanthropy. The constitutional powers necessary to bring this about were delegated to the new federal legislature, but those more relevant to women (education, health, housing and child welfare) were left with the increasingly poor states. Reformist women were forced to fragment their activities between the six state legislatures, leaving the federal jurisdiction to the men (Harris, 1992, 294).

Not surprisingly, the rudimentary welfare state that emerged was highly gendered. Although means-tested old age and invalid pensions were available for both men and women, in other areas women were assumed to have male providers. Means and morals testing implicit in these new provisions are evidence of the survival of a charitable ideology into the area of state provision. Protective labor legislation served to restrict women in the workforce, while minimum wages were established sufficient to allow a man to support a wife and three children. Working women, whether or not they had dependants, received only 54 per cent of the male wage. While later legislation introduced pensions for widows and deserted wives with dependent children, these were essentially a recognition of the failure of their breadwinners to provide rather than of the status of these women as breadwinners in their own right.

It is ironic that when women achieved political citizenship, these policies dislodged them from social citizenship (Roe, 1988). They were to be the mothers of the nation their husbands and brothers would defend (Garton, 1994, 34). Unemployment relief introduced during the 1930s Depression preserved this distinction, restricting women's eligibility on the assumption they would have a man to support them. In the Australian welfare state, Wendy Weeks argues, "Women have been wives not individual citizens... not cared for, but assigned to do the caring work for family and local community" (1993, 68).

The gendered Australian welfare state preserved a space for philanthropy, but it was no longer central; nor is it central to histories of the period which concentrate on the growth of state provision, ignoring the survival of older philanthropic forms (see Dickey, 1980, ch. 5). Women continued to dominate philanthropy, but philanthropy itself was marginalized as backward and judgmental compared with the progressive, benevolent, supposedly universalist state. Philanthropists were generally in the vanguard of opposition to social change; men effectively took that opposition into the political sphere, but women, still basically atheoretical and preoccupied with keeping services operating, were ineffective in self-defense. As fundraisers and direct service providers, they were involved in identifying needs and filling the gaps in state provision arguably on a larger scale than ever before. Indeed, the continuing success of voluntary charity explains why the early state provision, which in retrospect appears so meager, was so widely acclaimed (O'Brien, 1988 188).

Yet such activity was increasingly dismissed as residual. When women gained access to previously all-male committees, they still found themselves confined to subordinate roles. However, their success at integration made women-exclusive organizations anachronistic. Godden (1982, 96) relates this to the irrelevance of the separate spheres concept. Beginning in hospitals, and moving through the charitable sector, committees were forced to cede power to their professional employees. In smaller, locally based organizations, the ability of philanthropy to give access to power was diminished by isolation, loss of status and the increasing impossibility of the task. Outside welfare bureaucracies, women aiding women claimants "came face to face with their respective subordinations" (Roe, 1988, 17).

At an even more isolated level, larger numbers of wives and mothers were drawn into raising funds that underwrote the activities of charities, churches and schools. Smaller families and labor-reducing technology provided leisure time, while such small-scale organizations ensured that women were harnessed to ensure the social good without disturbing the status quo. The "benevolent" state provided all that was necessary for family life, with the women's efforts marginalized as providing the extras (Lyons, 1993). This characterization is quite clear in state education, where the government provided funds based on enrollment, while mothers' clubs funded the canteens, teaching aids, furnishings and "treats" which distinguished schools in middle-class areas from those in poorer regions.

The inter-war period did see the development of some trusts and foundations, but few were in female hands and those that were usually commemorated husbands and fathers with grants to high-prestige projects rather than services in what was seen as the women's sphere. There was little of the flowering of trusts and foundations that occurred in America as families consolidated their wealth. Although the Australian middle class embraced American progressivism, they were not economically or ideologically equipped to transform their ideas into action. Neither the large fortunes nor the deep suspicion of the state that motivated US philanthropists ever developed in Australia.

CONCLUDING DISCUSSION

This survey confirms the importance of religion as a motivating factor, but while religious systems validated such activity they did not control or constrain it. Women were involved in philanthropy both within and across denominational boundaries, sometimes working under clerical authority but far more commonly not. In establishing non-denominational organizations, class overshadowed gender as a unifying factor, opening such organizations to upper-class Jewish women while leaving the far more numerous Catholic women constrained within church organizations which they did not control. The preeminence of evangelical Christianity is still evident: volunteering and volunteerism are predominantly an Anglo-Saxon enterprise in which women of other ethnicities, have not yet found a place.

Women's organizations have made their greatest impact on public policy-making agendas through "maternalist" programs for women and children, although this is more a feature of the twentieth century. In the colonial period, men funded and controlled the major institutions but women took responsibility for the bulk of the outdoor relief. This brought some men, as well as large numbers of women and children, within their control, but few women used this position to claim a voice in the development of public policy. The issues which they considered to be their concern included campaigns for infant life protection, pure milk, raising of the age of consent, reduction in maternal mortality, protective labor legislation and the like, all issues which were common to other Western democracies.

Australian non-profit organizations have always been dependent on government funding. Although the nature of this dependence has changed over time, it appears that the 70 to 80 per cent funding which was common among the major organizations; in the nineteenth century remains the standard today. Smaller organizations, though able to survive on private donations in the past, have been drawn into government funding. However, these figures measure only monetary contributions and take no account of the contributions of time which characterized the smaller organizations women controlled. It was the willingness of women to perform unpaid labor that allowed for the survival of such organizations during the expansion of the welfare state, but the invisibility of this labor increased their marginalization. Because the invaluable work they were performing did not have to be paid for, it was easy to deny the existence of the needs it addressed.

Such invisibility limited the degree to which philanthropy led to the development of power structures that paralleled the political and commercial structures available to men. In the nineteenth century, when philanthropy was central to service provision, participation did give women access to power. However, this was power over the lives of their social inferiors rather than power over their own. Where organizations were developed to co-ordinate such activity, they remained within male control and it was men who represented their causes to government. While there were women beginning to explore this path towards the end of the century, their early success in winning the vote tended to divert their energies into political networks. Where women were able to exercise power, it was more likely to be through interest or industrial groups — such as the Country Women's Association, War Widows' Guilds and women's trade unions — than through those with a philanthropic base.

There is little evidence that, through their philanthropy, women were able to exercise power which they were denied in the political, legal or business spheres at the time. Most women-exclusive organizations apparently turned to male supporters to deal with business matters. Apart from a few organizations like the Queen Victoria Hospital for Women, there is little evidence of women using their position to create employment for women. Most organizations women controlled ran on small budgets, encouraging any staff they did employ to see their work primarily as an act of charity. Only male-controlled organizations had the funding to develop a hierarchical career structure for their employees. Participation in non-profit organizations continues to be highly gendered as a survey of Western Australia clearly demonstrates: "Where 75.4 per cent of the volunteers and 72.9 per cent of the paid staff involved in direct service provision were women, they represented only 42 per cent of committee members and 49.2 per cent of administrators" (Vellekoop-Baldock, 1990).

The absence of a parallel power structure may perhaps be explained by the early supremacy of a blend of the assimilationist and subsidiary models of women's philanthropy. While in the nineteenth century there was considerable exploration of the separatist model and space too for individualism to develop, the marginalization of women's philanthropy in the early years of the welfare state saw a move back towards an accommodation with men. Women fought to be accepted in male-dominated organizations where they were inevitably confined to "domestic" roles. Simultaneously they developed women-only organizations allied to masculine centers of power like political parties and trade unions. In order to maintain access to such sources of power, women-controlled organizations invited prominent men to join their committees. In the inter-war years, when class became the major source of social division, organizations that sought allegiance on the basis of gender were regarded with suspicion while those that brought men and women together attracted the support they needed to survive. Survival, however, extinguished the distinctiveness of women's philanthropy and left such organizations as a focus for class antagonism when ideology changed.

The pattern of Australian women's philanthropy was established by the first European bourgeois women, most of whom were of English or Scottish origin, and reinforced by continuing close contact between the province and the center over the intervening period. The first goal of any group seeking to establish a philanthropic organization was to gain access to government funding under the conditions of the time. Although these conditions have changed dramatically over time, the expectation that government would fund voluntary effort is constant. The success which feminists within the bureaucracy have had in Australia can perhaps be explained within this context. As government had supported services managed by women in the past, there was an expectation that it would also subsidize the domestic violence, rape crisis and child care agencies which "second-wave" feminists were seeking to establish in the 1970s. This is not to suggest that the relationship between feminist organizations and government has been trouble-free, or that women's services have not been underfunded when compared with those managed by and for men, but the differences have clearly not been as great as those in countries where the notion of such shared responsibility is not so well established.

It is in accessing private funding that Australian women's organizations find themselves more markedly disadvantaged. In a nation without a strong tradition of individual giving, the bulk of such funding is collected through business and professional networks in which women continue to be underrepresented. Only when women's marginal position in the workforce is reduced will they be able to enter such networks in equal numbers and perhaps to direct their resources to women's philanthropic organizations more equally than today.

REFERENCES

Allen, J. 1994. *Rose Scott: Vision and Revision in Feminism.*, Oxford University Press, Melbourne.

Berreen, R. 1994. "And Thereby to Discountenance Mendicity": Practices of charity in early nineteenth century Australia, in M. Wearing and R. Berreen, eds. *Welfare and Social Policy in Australia.* Sydney: Harcourt Brace Jovanovich.

Bomford, J. 1993. *That Dangerous and Persuasive Woman: Vida Goldstein.* Melbourne: Melbourne University Press.

Brown, J. 1972. *"Poverty is not a Crime": The Development of Social Services in Tasmania 1803–1900,* Hobart: Tasmanian Historical Research Association.

Dickey, B. 1980. *No Charity There: A Short History of Social Welfare in Australia.* Melbourne: Thomas Nelson Australia.

Garton, S. 1994. "Rights and Duties: Arguing Charity and Welfare 1880–1920," in M. Wearing and R. Berreen, eds. *Welfare and Social Policy in Australia*. Sydney: Harcourt Brace Jovanovich.

Godden, J. 1982. "The Work for Them and the Glory for Us!': Sydney Women's Philanthropy, 1870–1900, in R. Kennedy, ed., *Australian Welfare History: Critical Essays*. Melbourne: Macmillan.

Harris, P. 1992. "Pennypinching Activities: Managing Poverty Under the Eye of Welfare," in K. Saunders and R. Evans, eds., *Gender Relations in Australia: Domination and Negotiation*. Sydney: Harcourt Brace Jovanovich.

Kennedy, R., ed. 1982. *Australian Welfare History: Critical Essays*. Melbourne: Macmillan.

Lyons, M. 1993. "Can the Modern Foundation Ever Flourish Outside the United States — Or, Why Not in Australia?" Unpublished paper presented at "Foundations: An International Research Symposium," Paris.

———. 1994. *Australia's Charitable Organizations*. Melbourne.

Margarey, S. 1985. *Unbridling the Tongues of Women: A Biography of Catherine Helen Spence*. Sydney: Hale and Iremonger.

McCarthy, K. D. 1994. *Women and Philanthropy: Three Strategies in an Historical Perspective*. New York: The Center for the Study of Philanthropy, Graduate School and University Center, City University of New York.

Morrissey, S. 1969. "Clarke, Lady Janet Marion," in *Australian Dictionary of Biography*. Vol. 3. Melbourne: Melbourne University Press.

O'Brien, A. 1988. *Poverty's Prison: The Poor in New South Wales 1880–1918*. Melbourne: Melbourne University Press.

Reiger, K. 1993. *The Disenchantment of the Home: Modernizing the Australian Family 1880–1940*. Melbourne: Oxford University Press.

Roe, J. 1988. "The End Is Where We Start From: Women and Welfare since 1901," in C. Baldock and B. Cass, eds., *Women, Social Welfare and the State*. London: Allen and Unwin.

Scates, B. 1993. "Knocking Out a Living: Survival Strategies and Popular Protest in the 1890s Depression," in S. Margarey, S. Rowley and S. Sheridan, eds., *Debutante Nation: Feminism Contests the 1890s*. St. Leonards: Allen and Unwin.

Spence, C. H. 1907. *State Children in Adelaide*. Adelaide: South Australia Government Printer.

Stansell, C. 1982. *City of Women*. New York: Knopf.

Swain, S. 1977. "The Victorian Charity Network in the 1890s," Ph.D. thesis, University of Melbourne.

Swain, S. 1985a. "Selina Sutherland: Licensed Child Rescuer," in M. Lake and F. Kelly, eds., *Double Time: Women in Victoria — 150 Years*. Melbourne: Penguin.

Swain, S. 1985b. "The Poor People of Melbourne," in G. Davison, D. Dunstan and C. McConville, eds., *The Outcasts of Melbourne*. Sydney: Allen and Unwin.

Van Krieken, R. 1991. *Children and the State: Social Control and the Formation of Australian Child Welfare*. Sydney: Allen and Unwin.

Vellekoop-Baldock, C. 1990. *Volunteers in Welfare*. Sydney: Allen and Unwin.

Victorian Reports: Religious and Benevolent. State Library of Victoria, 22 vols.

Weeks, W. 1993. "Women's Contribution to Community Services," in J. Inglis and L. Rogan, eds., *Beyond Swings and Roundabouts: Shaping the Future of Community Services in Australia.* Sydney: Pluto Press.

Windschuttle, E. 1982. "Feeding the Poor and Sapping Their Strength: The Public Role of Ruling-Class Women in Eastern Australia, 1788–1850," in R. Kennedy, ed., *Australian Welfare History: Critical Essays.* Melbourne: Macmillan.

– 6 –

Parallel Power Structures, Invisible Careers, and the Changing Nature of American Jewish Women's Philanthropy

SUSAN M. CHAMBRÉ

INTRODUCTION

One of my most vivid childhood memories is the turquoise and white *pushke, or tzedaka* (charity) box for the Jewish National Fund (JNF) in my grandmother's apartment. Many people share this memory; Jewish homes all over the world had JNF boxes to collect money to purchase land in Palestine and later in Israel. Today, public and private places — homes, synagogues, restaurants, stores, and ritual baths — have *pushkes* for specific organizations or metal containers simply labeled *tzedaka*. Researchers interested in understanding charitable giving have found that many of the Jews they interviewed specifically mentioned that they learned about the importance of philanthropy from *pushkes*: they serve as an icon and a reminder of the central place of *tzedaka* in daily life (Odendahl, 1990; Ostrower, 1995; Havens and Schervish, 1998).

Other than her family, the focus of my grandmother's life was her societies. The most important was the United Wilner Ladies Relief, the women's auxiliary of a *landsmanschaftn, or* hometown society. Both the *pushke* and the society have had an important place in the lives of Jewish American women. But their importance has changed as the result of a number of cultural and social forces that have created both continuities and discontinuities in the nature of Jewish women's voluntary and philanthropic work.

An earlier version of this paper was published in the *Journal of Jewish Communal Service*. The author acknowledges partial financial support from the Center of the Study of Philanthropy of the City University of New York. Carol Poll, Rela Geffen, Susan Weidman Schneider, Deborah Levi Mayerfeld, Georgette Eden, and Danijela Milic provided invaluable assistance at various stages of this project.

WOMEN'S PHILANTHROPY AND
THE CONSTRUCTION OF CIVIL SOCIETY

Current interest in civil society, combined with a decline in the number of American women available to commit significant blocks of time to volunteering, is an important backdrop for understanding the changing nature of Jewish women's philanthropy (Putnam, 1995; Skocpol, 1997; Ladd, 1999). Much of the scholarly work on women's philanthropy in the U.S. has been historical and it has focused on white, middle-class Protestant women whose organizations began to expand in the early nineteenth century. These women played a major role in various events and social movements during the nineteenth and twentieth centuries including the Sanitary Commission, where women raised money and nursed soldiers during the Civil War and in the development of "scientific charity" in the latter half of the nineteenth century. Toward the end of the nineteenth century, women's organizations became involved in advocacy and social reform. Much of this work was "maternalist" and was concerned about improving the well-being of women and children (Ginsburg, 1990; Scott, 1992; Skocpol, 1992). Women's organizations developed innovative fundraising methods like the charity fair and distinctive organizational forms like the women's exchange selling homemade handicrafts to promote women's self-employment (Sander, 1998; Gordon, 1998).

A small but significant amount of published work focuses on the philanthropic work of various subgroups including women of color, members of various ethnic groups, immigrants, and Catholic and Jewish women (Oates, 1995; Hewitt, 1990; Hine, 1990). Since grass-roots and community-based efforts, particularly churches and synagogues, are key building blocks in creating social capital (Verba, Schlozman, and Brady, 1995; Cnaan and Milofsky, 1997), our understanding of the role of women in building civil society is incomplete without close examination of the past contributions of women in various subgroups in the U.S., especially religious groups, and their present role in a multicultural society where the redefinition of gender roles has meant that women are less committed to working in single sex organizations.

This article describes the evolution of American Jewish women's philanthropy. It focuses on several questions. The first and central question is: How was Jewish women's philanthropy similar to the activities of other types of women in the U.S. and in what ways has it been different? In addition, it addresses two broader theoretical questions: What role did Jewish women's volunteering, fundraising, organization-building, and advocacy — efforts subsumed under the term "philanthropy" — play in building American Jewish communities over the last century? What is likely to be the future role of Jewish women's organizations?

Although it has strong parallels to trends in American philanthropy, reflecting the impact of acculturation, Jewish women's philanthropy has also been distinctively Jewish. It has been influenced by perspectives on philanthropy derived from Jewish tradition and has included institutional forms that are mainly found within Jewish communities. Two traditional functions of women's philanthropy — serving as parallel power structures and as a context for invisible careers — need to be redefined in light of changing gender roles. This discussion suggests that the past and current roles of Jewish women's philanthropy provide an important key to defining its future. Serving as an important cornerstone of Jewish civil society, women's organizations can continue to be sources of innovation that promote the continued existence of the American Jewish community.

FUNCTIONS OF PHILANTHROPY

Philanthropic organizations perform several functions; women's organizations have two additional and distinctive functions. First, they are benevolent. They enhance the well-being of members of a community or a society through actions that are charitable, provide self-help or mutual benefit. A second purpose is that they are key elements in the creation of communities by serving a broad constituency, not just people who are in need. A third function is advocacy or reform. Voluntary associations and community organizations investigate social issues, recommend policies, and design programs. Often, this involves establishing new organizations and lobbying public officials to support, create, or modify social institutions. A fourth, and latent function of philanthropic activities is sociability and social support. Closely allied to community building but nonetheless distinct, philanthropic organizations bring together people with common concerns. At the same time, participation fulfills expressive needs. Philanthropic activities are important mechanisms in maintaining social networks particularly those related to social class (Ostrower, 1995; McPherson, and Smith-Lovin, 1982) and in maintaining the social networks that are central in creating social capital.

Women's organizations have several additional functions. Kathleen D. McCarthy (1990) observes that they engage in a distinctive type of advocacy since they are parallel power structures in designing social policies and stimulating social and political reform. This was particularly evident when married women were unable to own property or to vote. Women's organizations actively promoted social change in the latter half of the nineteenth century. Members of large national women's organizations and volunteers in settlement houses helped shape reforms during the Progressive Era and the New Deal (Skocpol, 1992; Ginsburg, 1990; Scott, 1992). Some of this work focused on maternalist social policies like Mother's Pensions and the Sheppard-Towner Act which "transformed motherhood from women's primary *private* responsibility into public policy" (Koven and Michel, 1993: 2). Rather than being grounded in social science research or the exigencies of party politics, women reformers defined their work as "municipal housekeeping" based on expertise garnered from managing their households (Scott, 1992). Arlene Kaplan Daniels (1988) outlines a second distinctive feature of women's philanthropic work: it provides a context for the development of "invisible careers." In contrast to the conventional career consisting of a progression of paid jobs, the invisible career involves a series of volunteer jobs. Invisible careers are harder to trace and are shaped by different contingencies than paid careers. Clearly, there is no direct financial benefit. Women with invisible careers emphasized how their work benefited their community rather than themselves. The number of women involved in "invisible careers" expanded during the late nineteenth century and for the first half of the twentieth century. Several changes contributed to this rise including a growing number of middle class women with large blocks of free time because they had fewer children, smaller households and domestic servants. Labor saving devices and mass-produced consumer products also allowed women to spend less time on domestic chores (Cowan, 1983).

GENDER AND PHILANTHROPY IN JEWISH TRADITION

Jewish tradition outlines two types of actions that correspond to the American notion of philanthropy. They are *gemulat chasadim* (*chesed* or acts of loving kindness) and *tzedaka*, a term often translated as charity which also means acts of righteousness or social justice. Rabbi Israel Meir HaKohen, the *Chafetz Chaim* (1997), a late nineteenth, and early twentieth century Rabbi, codified laws pertaining to acts of loving kindness. He pointed out that *chesed* is superior to *tzedaka* as it involves actions, not just giving money like *tzedaka*, and is directed toward the dead as well as the living: the preparation of a dead person for burial is the highest act of *chesed* since there is no possibility of reciprocity. *Tzedaka* is limited in scope whereas *gemulat chasadim* are unlimited. Ten percent of a person's earnings are to be devoted to *tzedaka* and it is desirable but not required to give an additional ten percent. In contrast, there are no upper limits on the time devoted to *gemulat chasadim*.

Men and women are equally obligated to perform acts of loving kindness and to give *tzedaka:* they are expected to tithe, to visit the sick, prepare the dead for burial, comfort the mourner, give to the poor and the needy, support widows and orphans, offer hospitality, provide dowries for brides, and support community institutions. There are, however, qualitative differences in the ways that men and women have fulfilled these requirements at different times and in different contexts. Under strict interpretation of Jewish law, which governed most communities until this century, women were not held to the same standards of ritual performance or expected to devote significant amounts of time to learning Torah as men. Women are not obligated to do positive commandments that must be performed at a specific time but they may perform time-bound religious actions voluntarily (Meiselman, 1978). Traditionally, Jewish men were far better educated than women. This disparity began to narrow toward the end of the nineteenth century when more Jewish women began to receive a secular education and religious leaders recognized the importance of having formal religious training. First in Europe and later in the U.S., religious education expanded for Jewish women during the twentieth century (Zolty, 1997).

Because of different religious expectations for men and women in the past, philanthropy has been a principal vehicle for religious expression for Jewish women, giving them a separate sphere for contributing to community life and sometimes operating as a parallel power structure to channel concerns and influence communal life. Our knowledge of Jewish women's philanthropy is fragmentary until the nineteenth century. Glückl of Hamlen (or as Natalie Zemon Davis calls her, Glickl Bas Yehudah Leib), the seventeenth-century German Jewish woman, described many aspects of her life in great detail: her business transactions, caring for her numerous children, and arranging their marriages. Glückl tells us little about her acts of *chesed* and *tzedaka* perhaps because her memoirs were written as a record for her children and such actions required little comment by such a pious woman (Lowenthal, 1973; Davis, 1995). Probably in response to urbanization, German Jews began to develop burial, and sick care associations during the sixteenth century. They were originally organized by men and women who were members because they were needed to prepare other women for burial. Later, during the seventeenth century, German women organized their own burial societies. In contrast to Christian women, who had a central place in caring for the sick, Jewish women restricted their activities to caring for other women because Jewish law restricts the amount of physical contact between men and women who are not close relatives (Marcus, 1947).

Scholars have devoted far more attention to Jewish women's philanthropy starting in the nineteenth century. Before then, Jewish communities in the U.S. were small and philanthropy was highly informal. In the first quarter of the nineteenth century, ladies' benevolent societies were founded in the handful of existing communities. The first one was established in Philadelphia in 1819 (Kohut, 1931). Some feminist historians point out that they were modeled after the benevolent societies that Christian women were establishing (Kuzmack, 1990). Rudolph Glanz (1976) has a different view. He points out that they were transplanted from Germany. Female benevolent societies were major charitable organizations before centralized Hebrew charities were formed in cities with large Jewish populations during the final third of the century. They had a parallel existence to men's benevolent societies. The Atlanta Hebrew Ladies' Benevolent Society, for example, was established by members of the city's major Reform congregation in 1870. Members provided immigrants with food, coal, clothing, financial assistance, temporary housing, and cash (Wenger, 1987). Over time, some benevolent societies altered their functions and called themselves "Sisterhoods." The first Jewish sisterhood was established as the *Unabhaegiger Orden Treuer Schwestern* at New York City's Temple Emanu-El in 1846. The name was changed to the United Order of True Sisters five years later to reflect the increasing acculturation of the group's members. The New York group was the first chapter of a national fraternal order of women's groups that had 35 lodges and 12,000 members in 1931 (Kohut, 1931).

With the growth in the Jewish population and in the number of synagogues which operated as community centers, not just houses of prayer and of study (Kaufman, 1999), the number of sisterhoods expanded by the 1920s. Many of them were involved in community service activities like being friendly visitors for the United Hebrew Charities in New York (Joselit, 1987). The Sisterhood of Congregation *Shearith Israel*, the Spanish and Portuguese synagogue on the Upper West Side of Manhattan, formed an "Oriental Committee" to serve the small and relatively impoverished Levantine or Sephardic ("Spanish") immigrants moving to the Lower East Side during the early part of the twentieth century. This committee sponsored a synagogue, a religious school and a settlement house (Angel, 1982). For some organizations, the transition from benevolent society to Sisterhood involved a shift in focus. Jenna Joselit (1987) points out that some Sisterhoods became less involved in charitable work when social workers began to do friendly visiting. Sisterhoods turned their attention inward and focused on serving congregations rather than the community at large. They raised money for synagogues, organized social events, supported Hebrew schools and established gift shops. Synagogue gift shops had a dual purpose. They raised money but they also had an important latent function. At a time when American culture and public policy encouraged Americanization, synagogue members could conveniently purchase ritual objects and books which might anchor them to their tradition.

By the nineteen twenties, a broad array of local volunteer opportunities existed for American Jewish women. These included participation in synagogue-based sisterhoods, volunteering for institutions like orphanages and old age homes, and working for local chapters of several national and international women's organizations. The New York Hebrew Orphan Asylum's Godmother's Association, founded in 1920 was "a society of clubs led by women who would take on the role of confidant for a small number of children." The women would bring residents to their homes to "give the children a taste of family life." They also took children to concerts, art galleries, parks, the theater and sometimes to their country homes to broaden their horizons (Bogin, 1992: 209). At the Jewish Children's Home in Rochester, neighborhood women formed a mother's club which sponsored collations and luncheons for each child's Bar Mitzvah, obtained clothing for Jewish holidays, and raised money to improve the quality of life. More importantly, however, they were aunts (*tantes* in Yiddish) to the children: "They did what aunties are supposed to do: dote, indulge, provide for, celebrate, honor and preserve ritual and tradition." (Goldstein, 1995: 104).

A second strand of organizational development in the U.S. was large national, and international Jewish women's organizations established after 1890. A similar development took place in the United Kingdom, Germany, and Australia (Kuzmack, 1990; Kaplan, 1979; Cohen, 1987). These organizations played a central role in domestic, and international philanthropy, providing health care, education, vocational training, and social services.

The first one was the National Council of Jewish Women (NCJW) founded in 1893 at the World Congress of Religions of the Columbian Exposition in Chicago. NCJW was modeled on the Protestant woman's club which sponsored social, literary, and cultural activities for middle-class women. Like women's clubs, NCJW's purpose expanded to include service and advocacy for Jewish women and children. Paralleling events in the broader society, where American women established clubs, and became involved in settlement houses and social reform movements, NCJW provided an important mechanism for Jewish women to exercise public roles at a time when relatively few middle-class women were employed and when the inability to vote meant that women had no formal political power. NCJW provided a place where Reform women, mostly of German descent, could express themselves both as Jews and as Americans. Its members collaborated with other women's groups in the international effort to reduce the white slave trade. NCJW sections performed many of the traditional activities of benevolent societies and organized Sabbath schools and study groups. Members of the New York section visited patients in city hospitals. They established a kosher kitchen and a synagogue for patients in public hospitals on New York's Welfare Island and sponsored a settlement house, a therapeutic nursery, and a home for wayward girls ("All Our Yesterdays," n.d.).

NCJW's founding coincided with the beginning of the period of mass immigration of Jews. The organization established programs designed to assist new immigrants, especially young women. Volunteers and paid agents met young women as they disembarked at Ellis Island, particularly those arriving without families, who might become prey to white slavers. Its immigrant work continued through the post-Holocaust period (Welt, 1948). Initially envisioned as an organization for a broad cross section of Jewish women, NCJW was unable to bridge religious differences (Rogow, 1993). Although most of its founders were members of the Reform movement, it initially attracted some members who were more traditional. Many of them left NCJW once the number of synagogue Sisterhoods began to increase (Rogow, 1997). Others were attracted to Zionist women's organizations and groups like the Organization for Rehabilitation, and Training (ORT).

Reform Judaism's initial opposition to Zionism also meant that many women joined other organizations like Hadassah rather than NCJW. Hadassah traces its origins to a Zionist study circle begun in 1898. It was founded by Henrietta Szold in 1912 to raise money to support public health nursing and medical clinics in Palestine. By the nineteen thirties, Hadassah was a major provider of health care and social services. One of its programs, Youth Aliyah, rescued Jewish children from Europe, and resettled them in Palestine (Levin, 1997). Accounts of Hadassah suggest that many of its members were Orthodox or Conservative compared to NCJW's largely Reform membership. Whereas NCJW experienced a great deal of dissension in its early years over the religious standards of its members (Rogow, 1993), a commitment to Zionism overshadowed the religious diversity within Hadassah. Several other women's Zionist organizations with a narrower purpose or ideology were established during the nineteen twenties. These included American Mizrachi Women (now Amit, founded in 1925), Pioneer Women (1925) now called Naamat, and the Women's League for Israel (1928).

The growth of Jewish women's organizations, particularly large national organizations, can be traced to the convergence of a number of social forces. They were able to grow because of the expanding population of Jewish women, both single and married, who were not employed and had time to devote to organizational work. Yet, they also attracted working women. Ewa Moraska (1996) points out that in the Jewish community of Johnstown, Pennsylvania, women worked in family-owned businesses, and had relatively little leisure even when they became more prosperous but nonetheless were actively involved in organizations. The rise of large, autonomous Jewish women's organizations in the early twentieth century occurred at an historical moment when more Jewish women were able to spend time volunteering, when they chose to devote their time to Jewish organizations, and when they were either discouraged or barred from participation in some non-Jewish organizations. The pool of potential volunteers expanded further after World War II as Jewish families achieved greater prosperity and many of them moved to the suburbs where a welter of groups were created.

WAS JEWISH WOMEN'S PHILANTHROPY DISTINCTIVE?

In some respects, there was nothing distinctively Jewish about the form and the content of these activities. Their evolution parallels women's groups in the broader society. During the first third of the nineteenth century, women's voluntary efforts were focused on benevolent associations. Nineteenth- and early twentieth-century Jewish and non-Jewish women channeled domestic skills into philanthropic activities like sewing societies that supplied immigrants, orphans, and soldiers with clothing and blankets. Beginning in the middle of the century, Jewish and non-Jewish women began to establish asylums for dependents like orphanages and old age homes. In the late nineteenth, and early twentieth century, Jewish, and non-Jewish women began to form large national organizations. A great deal of their work was maternalist, focused on women and children, or directed to the adjustment and well-being of immigrants, like settlement house work.

A second similarity is that some women's organizations relied on men's business expertise. Organizations begun by women included men as board members. In some cases, organizations experienced a transition and became dominated by men in order to ensure their financial viability. The Philadelphia Jewish Foster Home, established in 1855, and the Brooklyn Ladies Hebrew Home for the Aged, founded in Williamsburg in 1907 and relocated to Brownsville, were established by women but later recruited male donors and board members (Bodek, 1983; Landesman, 1971). Philadelphia's *Ezrath Nashim*, translated as "women's aid" (which is also the term for the woman's section of a synagogue) was founded in 1873. It was later renamed the Jewish Maternity Home and expanded its activities to include personal visiting, a sewing circle to produce clothing and other items, a Nurses' Training school, a seaside Home for Invalid Women and Children, and a temporary Nursery (Bodek, 1983). The transition from female to male dominance also occurred in organizations founded by Catholic laywomen and by Protestant women in Chicago (Oates, 1995; McCarthy, 1982).

What, then, was distinctively Jewish about Jewish women's philanthropy in the past? A great deal. For the past century, the philanthropy of most American Jews has been guided by Jewish values that stress the obligatory nature of giving both money and time (Woocher, 1986; Chambré, 1998). A strong sense of Jewish identity and a commitment to Jewish survival was palpable in many of these organizations even while they stressed their commitment to Americanization. NCJW's maternalist policies and programs drew upon a wellspring of Jewish tradition including the important philanthropic role of the *Eshet Chayil*, the Woman of Valor extolled in verses from Proverbs that are sung at the Sabbath table in Jewish homes (Rogow, 1993). Although NCJW's work was directed toward Americanizing immigrants, its Sunday Schools and study circles were important early efforts in providing Jewish education to girls and to women.

Jewish women's philanthropic activities also included participation in several types of organizations that were distinctive although not entirely unique to Jewish communities. The first were hometown societies or *landsmanschaftn*. Initially restricted to men, Soyer (1997) suggests that women expanded their participation in direct response to the women's suffrage movement. A small number of the 2,500 *landsmanschaftn* that responded to a survey done in the 1930s were "Ladies' Societies"; 71 were founded by women and 287 were women's auxiliaries. A majority of the women's *landsmanschaftn* had male presidents or secretaries such as the Proskurover Ladies Benevolent Society founded in 1909 and incorporated in 1916 by five women and one man (Kliger, 1992; Milamid, 1986). Women also actively participated in another distinctive type of organization, the free loan society; they either started or were the major donors for free loan societies in several cities. The Ladies' Hebrew Free Loan Society of Providence only lent money to women and groups in Seattle and Chicago assisted men and women. Women are probably even more important in a second type of free loan society, the *gemach*, which lends goods rather than cash. Since histories of Jewish philanthropy fail to mention *gemachim*, it is not possible to assert whether they are a modern development or were so informal as to escape the historical record. The only systematic discussion of contemporary *gemachim* is based on Julia Bernstein's (1993) informal survey in Jerusalem. Bernstein found that most *gemachim* were started by one person and operate on a small scale usually out of the founder's home and sometimes with the assistance of a few friends. They tend to specialize in lending only one or two types of objects, such as bridal gowns, baby formula, ritual objects, and tables and chairs. One *gemach* in Jerusalem, Yad Sarah, has grown into a large charitable organization providing medical supplies and equipment. In the U.S., *gemachim* exist in densely populated Orthodox communities like Boro Park in Brooklyn and Monsey in Rockland County, New York.

For large numbers of American Jews during the first half of the century, the dominant force in their lives was neither religious tradition nor particularistic ties to their hometown. Rather, they viewed themselves as workers, often as Socialists, or Communists. In many cases, they brought these strong ideological commitments with them from Poland or Russia. Jewish women took leadership roles in labor unions, particularly the ILGWU (International Ladies' Garment Workers Union). Beginning with the kosher meat boycott of 1902 and followed by food boycotts and rent strikes, working-class Jewish women engaged in activism that expands our definition of "social housekeeping" (Broadkin, 1998; Baum, Hyman, and Michel, 1975; Blumenfeld, 1982). This important strand of Jewish life was reflected in the Emma Lazarus Federation of Jewish Women's Clubs (ELF). Its founder, Clara Lemlich Shavelson, was instrumental in calling the first massive strike of garment workers in 1909. Founded in the 1940s, later than other national women's groups, it combined social, political, literary, and maternalist welfare activities. It commissioned biographies of notable Jewish women, members participated in the March on Washington in 1963, fought actively against anti-Semitic acts, and generally promoted a progressive, secular Jewish agenda that reflected the working class and European origin of its members. The ELF established the first day care center in Israel for Jewish and Arab children, and supported the Magan David Adam, the Israeli equivalent of the Red Cross. With the demise of both the Jewish working class and the immigrant generation that had formed this group, the federation disbanded in 1989 (Antler, 1995).

While many external similarities appear, then, between the organizational work of Jewish and non-Jewish women, there are important normative and structural differences. The work done by the women who created these organizations was central to the elaborate network of communal social welfare institutions that have provided domestic and international assistance during the last century in response to massive migration and social dislocation, war, and destruction, as well as to personal and family problems associated with death, developmental disabilities, mental health problems, substance abuse, and vocational needs.

For the most part, Jewish communal institutions were, and to a lesser extent still are, highly gendered. Jewish philanthropy in general and Jewish women's organizations in particular are undergoing significant changes as a result of the confluence of several factors.

CONTEMPORARY JEWISH WOMEN'S VOLUNTARISM

Patterns of Jewish women's voluntarism have become greatly altered in the last three decades. One source is a change in gender roles and the socio-economic status of Jewish women (Schneider, 1984; Fishman, 1993; National Commission on American Jewish Women, 1995). Jewish women are better educated and more affluent than they were in the past; fewer are full-time homemakers and many are unwilling to participate in parallel power structures. In the past, Jewish women had circumscribed roles or had token involvement in major national organizations as well as in local federations. Although there were exceptional women who played key roles in male-dominated institutions, like Rebecca Gratz of Philadelphia who started the Jewish Orphan Society in 1815, and the Hebrew Sunday School Society in 1838, and Pauline Perlmutter Steinem, President of the Toledo, Ohio Hebrew Free Loan Society, large Jewish communal institutions have been dominated by men. In addition to autonomous single-sex organizations, many Jewish women were involved in the woman's divisions of large local, or national organizations. Some of them were affiliates of national or international groups such as Bnai Brith Women's, organization and the Women's Divisions of the American Jewish Congress and the United Jewish Appeal. Usually they were auxiliaries, a separate sphere for women within a small local group like a *landsmanschaftn* that served as a vehicle where women carried out charitable and communal work without necessarily being included in the organization's power structure. Frequently, organizations included representatives of women's auxiliaries on their boards but membership did not always lead to authority or influence.

Gender inequality is being reduced but parity has yet to be achieved. Adoption of feminist ideology, higher education and more women with organizational skills led women to challenge the restricted role of women in Jewish communal affairs. Jacqueline Levine first raised the issue nationally in 1972 at the annual General Assembly of the Council of Jewish Federations and Welfare funds (Cohen, Dessel and Pelavin, 1976). Seven years later, Aviva Cantor (1979) pointed out that volunteering served as a "sheltered workshop" for Jewish women: they engaged in tasks that provided them with the sense that they were participating in communal life but in reality they had little influence. These challenges have begun to alter the governance of Jewish communal institutions, particularly Jewish Federations, where the proportion of women on boards and key committees has increased and more women are involved in top leadership roles (Power, and Parity, 1998; Gold, 1997). In 1998, Carole Solomon of Philadelphia was the first woman selected as the National Chairman of UJA (Sofer, 1998). Energy once devoted to women's organizations has been redirected to community-wide organizations. Rather than accept second class citizenship or involvement in parallel organizations, Jewish women have been challenging the male dominance of many communal institutions. In 1975, 17 percent of the board members in Jewish federations in the U.S. were women. By 1993, nearly one in three federation board members were women (Kosmin, 1994). Increased participation is uneven. A major study sponsored by Ma'yan: The Jewish Women's Project found that 25 percent of board members of 45 key national organizations were women. There are significant variations. Less than five percent of the Board members of the national organization of Jewish day schools (*Torah U'Mesorah*), the Orthodox Union and the Zionist Organization of America are women (*Power & Parity,* 1998).

An allied development is that Jewish women's organizations may have lost the backbone of the kinds of volunteers they once relied upon: young and middle aged women who are full-time homemakers. Although widely assumed to have withdrawn from volunteerism, leaving some organizations with an aging pool of active volunteers, the impact of women's employment on volunteering has yet to be systematically studied. Fragmentary data based on the population as a whole suggest that the pattern is more complex than a zero-sum relation between working and volunteering. Among all American women surveyed in 1996, volunteer participation was higher among employed women (56 percent) than unemployed (47 percent) and retired women (46 percent). When asked to estimate about how many hours each week they spent volunteering, the number of hours was higher among working women (4.3) than unemployed (4.0) or retired (3.8) women (Independent Sector, 1996). A slim majority of women serving as lay leaders in Jewish federations are employed. In 1993, 34 percent worked full-time and approximately 20 percent worked part-time (Kosmin, 1994).

The transformation of Jewish women's philanthropy is taking place at the same time that broader changes are taking place in Jewish philanthropy in general and in declining levels of civic engagement in the U.S. For much of the twentieth century, joining organizations and donating money were important ways that many Americans expressed their Jewish identity. Jewish organizations achieved enormous success both in terms of the dollars they raised and the institutions they created. Organizations attracted donors and volunteers exerted peer pressure, relying on an ideology that Woocher calls "Civil Judaism," which draws upon Jewish notions about charity and communal responsibility combined with support for the State of Israel and concern for the survival of the Jewish people. Several trends suggest that this situation is changing and that the "Jewish Civil Religion" that sustained Jewish philanthropy for much of this century will not continue in its present form without conscious changes in the structure of organizations and the techniques they employ to motivate donors and volunteers.

Jews have become more integrated into philanthropic organizations of the broader society. They are less exclusively involved in Jewish organizations and a significant if not growing portion of their donations go to non-Jewish organizations (Wertheimer, 1997; Keysar, n.d.). Declining social barriers combined with an increase in the number of very wealthy and philanthropic Jewish families has meant that Jews are courted as donors and board members for mainstream institutions which excluded them in the past such as non-Jewish hospitals, art museums, orchestras, and public libraries (Ostrower, 1995). Commitment to Jewish philanthropy is declining in each succeeding generation. The 1990 National Jewish Population survey data reveal that seven in ten first and second generation American Jews contributed to Jewish philanthropies. By the third generation, this declined to half and was reduced further to 36 percent in the fourth generation (Tobin, 1995).

Empirical studies reveal much more about women's organizational affiliations than their patterns of giving money or volunteering for Jewish and for non-Jewish organizations. Just as the benevolent association was superceded by the Sisterhood and by national groups like Hadassah, each generation joined different types of organizations. In his study of a small New England City, which he called Yankee City, W. Lloyd Warner (1945) found that immigrant women joined the Jewish Ladies' Aid Society and their daughters joined Hadassah. To continue the analogy further, were Warner to revisit Yankee City he might find some of their granddaughters in Hadassah or on the board of the local Federation but others in the Junior League, an organization once closed to Jewish women. Alice Goldstein (1990) points out that it is misleading to view women's involvement in Jewish and non-Jewish organizations as mutually exclusive. In fact, data derived from a study she conducted suggest that the two types of involvement are positively related and in fact rise in tandem. Jewish organizations need to consider ways that they might attract a different population than in the past, namely, better educated women many of whom have careers. Another pattern of changing participation, noted by Susan Weidman Schneider (1992), is the involvement of younger Jewish women in new philanthropic organizations like the New Israel Fund and the Shefa Fund. These attract women who want to synthesize their commitment to feminism, to social justice, and to Jewish community life.

HAS JEWISH WOMEN'S PHILANTHROPY LOST ITS FUNCTIONS?

Two traditional functions of Jewish women's philanthropy — as parallel power structures and as a context for invisible careers — have taken on a different meaning. At a time when Jewish women are "taking their place at the table," the parallel power structure function might seem to be insignificant. Yet, at the same time, one can make a case for the fact that the traditionally maternalistic concerns of women's organizations continue to have an important place in communal life. Jewish women's organizations are more likely to be sensitive to otherwise unidentified or emerging issues. They can mobilize the expertise of women to do the kind of "domestic housekeeping" done by Jewish women's groups in the past that continues to be meaningful.

The advocacy function of NCJW is well-documented. Less well-known was the important role of women in establishing the largest kosher supervision service which is under the auspices of the, Orthodox Union. Writing in 1931, Rebecca Kohut (1931: 195) pointed out that "Not only are the women exhorted to observe scrupulously the Jewish dietary laws in their own homes, but as an organization they have undertaken to investigate the *Kashruth* of manufactured food products." A more contemporary example pertains to violence against women. The Shalom Task Force in New York City and similar organizations in other areas, have successfully directed attention to the issue of domestic violence in the Jewish community. Notices are discreetly posted in synagogue ladies' rooms and in ritual baths in order to reach out to women otherwise disconnected from the social service system who are unlikely to go to a federation-sponsored agency which may not be culturally sensitive to these women's needs including their need for kosher food. This role has been institutionalized with the creation of Jewish women's foundations, a trend that parallels a development in the broader society. The Jewish Women's Foundation of New York, established in 1995, has a maternalist agenda including support for domestic violence programs (Ain, 1998).

With a larger number of working women, fewer women seek invisible careers in Jewish women's organizations. This poses some important challenges. While there are still some full-time volunteers, like the board members of many of the large national organizations, an overwhelming proportion of younger women are employed and few are likely to choose the unpaid full-time career paths of their mothers and grandmothers. Yet, it is important to recall the organizational involvement of women in Johnstown, Pennsylvania so vividly described by Ewa Moraska. These women combined volunteering and work — as men always have — and yet many of them made significant contributions as volunteers.

This suggests a need to clarify the notion of an invisible career. Arlene Kaplan Daniels (1988) developed this concept in a study of elite women who were not employed. Yet, the idea can apply to a volunteer work life that exists both parallel to and in interaction with a career that consists of paid work. Volunteers are valuable to organizations when they can apply skills from their paid jobs to volunteering. Jewish women's philanthropy needs to adapt to changing social roles and historical conditions in ways that it did in the past by tailoring activities to women with jobs and careers and utilizing the skills of retired women who may not have been actively involved in volunteer work while they were working.

Women's philanthropic organizations can continue to fulfill one important latent function, serving as a context for sociability. Arlene Kaplan Daniels (1988) points out that women are not only attracted by the opportunity to do "good works" but also the ability to have "good times." In an era when many women are engaged in a delicate balance between work and family responsibilities, women's organizations can provide a context for sociability and personal growth: a place for having good times, doing good work and contributing to the Jewish community.

Jewish women's organizations might look to their past role in creating institutions that promoted identity and continuity. Several organizations including Hadassah, Amit, Emunah, and the Women of Reformed Judaism, have made a renewed commitment to promoting serious study of Jewish texts as well as distinctive issues that confront Jewish women like Jewish divorce laws and ethnic stereotyping (Diament, 1997; Bohm, 1997). Participation in youth organizations, like Hadassah's Young Judaea, strengthens Jewish identity and is associated with a lower rate of intermarriage (1998 Young Judea Continuity Study, n.d.). At a time when many are alarmed and concerned about Jewish survival, Jewish women may once again take a leadership role in the kind of "municipal housekeeping" that led to past reforms and innovative programs.

CONCLUSION

Jewish women's philanthropy has played an important role in the development of Jewish communal institutions — encouraging women to engage in acts of *chesed*, initiating new institutions, raising funds, and identifying issues for the broader communal agenda. Over the course of time, the nature of Jewish women's philanthropy has echoed trends and patterns of women's philanthropy in the broader society both in the kinds of organizations women have created and in the nature of their activities. Yet, at the same time, the work has been distinctively Jewish both in terms of its normative quality and its emphasis on building Jewish institutions both domestically and internationally. With major changes in gender roles, many Jewish women are less interested in working in women-only organizations which have traditionally served as parallel power structures. Increasingly, women have taken on leadership roles in previously male-dominated communal institutions.

What, then, might be the future function of Jewish women's philanthropy? The lessons of the past are a key to the future. Jewish women's organizations have served a vital role as a context for sociability but also being incubators for developing new policies and programs. Much of this work has focused on a maternalist agenda, activities directed toward women and children. At a time when the issue of the continued existence of the American Jewish community has a central place in the communal agenda, women's organizations can continue to play an important role in the building of Jewish civil society.

REFERENCES

Ain, S. 1998. "Protecting 'the Underdogs': Jewish Women's Foundation Provides Grants to Help Domestic-violence Victims, Low Income Women." *The Jewish Week* 211, no. 8, 8.

All Our Yesterdays, All Our Tomorrows. (1974). New York: New York Section, National Council of Jewish Women.

Angel, M. D. 1982. *La America: The Sephardic Experience in the United States.* Philadelphia: Jewish Publication Society.

Antler, J. 1995. "Between Culture and Politics: The Emma Lazarus Federation of Jewish Women's Clubs and the Promulgation of Women's History, 1944–1989." In L. Kerber and A. Kessler-Harris, eds., *U.S. History as Women's.* Pp. 267–95. Chapel Hill: University of North Carolina Press.

Baum, C. P. Hyman, and S. Michel. 1975. *The Jewish Woman in America.* New York: Dial Press.

Bernstein, J. March 12, 1993. "The Trend to Lend: Gemachimin Action." *Jerusalem Post*, 12.

Birnbaum, P. 1944. *Mishneh Torah: Maimonides' Code of Law, and Ethics.* New York: Hebrew Publishing Company.

Blumenfeld, H. F. 1982. "Jewish Women Sew the Union Label: A Study of Sexism and Feminism in the Emerging Unionization of the Garment Industry, New York City." *Humanity and Society* 6:33–45.

Bodek, E. 1983. "Making Do': Jewish Women and Philanthropy." In Murray Friedman, ed. *Jewish Life in Philadelphia, 1830–1940.* Pp. 143–62. Philadelphia: Institute for the Study of Human Issues.

Bogin, H. 1992. *The Luckiest Orphans.* Chicago: University of Illinois Press.

Bohm, L. 1997. "Rosh Chodesh Guide: Resources for Sisterhood Study and Celebration." New York: Women of Reform Judaism.

Brodkin, K. 1998. *How Jews Became White Folks and What That Says about Race in America.* New Brunswick, N.J.: Rutgers University Press.

Cantor, A. 1979. "The Sheltered Workshop." *Lilith* (Spring).

Chafetz Chaim (Rabbi Israel Meir Kagan HaKohen). 1997. *Ahavath Chesed.* Trans. Leonard Oshry. Nanuet, N.Y.: Feldheim.

Chambré, S. M. 1993. "Parallel Power Structures, Invisible Careers, Benevolence and Reform: Implications of Women's Philanthropy." *Nonprofit Management and Leadership* 4, 233–39.

———. 1998. "What Is Jewish about Jewish Philanthropy?" Unpublished paper presented at the ARNOVA Meeting, Seattle.

Cnaan, R. and C. Milofsky. 1997. "Small Religious Nonprofits: A Neglected Topic." *Nonprofit and Voluntary Quarterly* 26, S3–S13.

Cohen, L. 1987. *Beginning with Esther: Jewish Women in New South Wales from 1788.* Sydney, Australia: Ayers & James Heritage Books.

Cohen, S. M., S. Dessel and M. Pelavin. 1976. "The Changing (?) Role of Women in Jewish Communal Affairs: A Look into the UJA." In E. Koltun, ed., *The Jewish Woman: New Perspectives.* Pp. 193–201. New York: Schocken.

Cowan, R. S. 1983. *More Work for Mother: The Ironies of Household Technology from the Open Hearth to the Microwave.* New York: Basic Books.

Daniels, A. K. 1988. *Invisible Careers: Women Civic Leaders from the Volunteer World.* Chicago: University of Chicago Press.

Davis, N. Z. 1995. *Women on the Margins: Three Seventeenth-Century Lives.* Cambridge, Mass.: Harvard University Press.

Diament, C., ed. 1997. *Jewish Women Living the Challenge: A Hadassah Compendium.* New York: Hadassah.

Fishman, S. B. 1993. *A Breath of Life: Feminism in the American Jewish Community.* New York: Free Press.

Ginzberg, L. D. 1990. *Women, and the Work of Benevolence.* New Haven: Yale University Press.

Glanz, R. 1976. *The Jewish Woman in America: Two Female Immigrant Generations, 1820–1929.* Volume 2: *The German Jewish Woman.* New York: Ktav and National Council of Jewish Women.

Goldstein, A. 1990. "New Roles, New Commitments: Jewish Women's Involvement in the Community's Organizational Structure." *Contemporary Jewry* 11, 49–76.

Goldstein, H. 1995. *The Home on Gorham Street and the Voices of Its Children.* Tuscaloosa: University of Alabama Press.

Gordon, B. 1998. *Bazaars, and Fair Ladies: The History of the American Fundraising Fair.* Knoxville: University of Tennessee Press.

Havens, J. and P. Schervish. 1998. Personal communication, November 7.

Hewitt, N. A. 1990. "Charity, or Mutual Aid? Two Perspectives on Latin Women in Tampa, Florida." In K. D. McCarthy, *Lady Bountiful Revisited: Women, Philanthropy and Power.* Pp. 55–69. New Brunswick, Rutgers N.J.: Rutgers University Press.

Hine, D. C. 1990. "We Specialize in the Wholly Impossible: The Philanthropic Work of Black Women." In K. D. McCarthy, ed., *Lady Bountiful Revisited: Women, Philanthropy, and Power.* Pp. 70–93. New Brunswick, N.J.: Rutgers University Press.

Independent Sector. 1996. *Giving and Volunteering in the United States.* Washington, D.C.: Author.

Joselit, J. 1987. "The Special Sphere of the Middle-class American Jewish Woman: The Synagogue Sisterhood, 1890–1940." In J. Wertheimer, ed., *The American Synagogue: A Sanctuary Transformed.* Pp. 206–30. New York: Cambridge University Press.

Kaminer, W. 1984. *Women Volunteering: The Pleasure, Pain, and Politics of Unpaid Work from 1830 to the Present.* New York: Anchor.

Kaplan, M. A. 1979. *The Jewish Feminist Movement in Germany: The Campaigns of the Jüdisher Frauenbund, 1904–1938.* Westport, Conn.: Greenwood Press.

Keysar, A. n.d. Patterns of Philanthropy: New York versus Non-New York Jewry in 1990. Working Paper: Center for the Study of Philanthropy, City University of New York.

Kliger, H., ed. 1992. *Jewish Hometown Associations and Family Circles in New York.* Bloomington: Indiana University Press.

Kohut, R. 1931. "Jewish Women's Organizations." *American Jewish Yearbook,* 33, 165–201.

Kosmin, B. A. 1994. *The Status of Women in Lay and Professional Leadership Positions of Federations.* New York: Council of Jewish Federations, and Welfare Funds.

Koven, S. and S. Michel. 1993. "Introduction: 'Mother Worlds.' In S. Koven and S. Michel, eds. *Mothers of a New World: Maternalist Politics, and the Origin of Welfare States.* Pp. 1–42. New York: Routledge.

Kuzmack, L. G. 1990. *Woman's Cause: The Jewish Woman's Movement in England and the United States, 1881–1933.* Columbus: Ohio State University Press.

Ladd, E. C. 1999. *The Ladd Report.* New York: Free Press.

Landesman, A. F. 1971. *Brownsville: The Birth, Development and Passing of a Jewish Community in New York.* New York: Bloch Publishing.

Levin, M. 1997. *It Takes a Dream: The Story of Hadassah.* New York: Gefen Books.

Light, I. 1972. *Ethnic Enterprise in America: Business and Welfare Among Chinese, Japanese, and Blacks.* Berkeley, Calif.: University of California Press.

Lowenthal, M. trans. 1973. *The Memoirs of Glückel of Hameln.* New York: Schocken.

Marcus, J. R. 1947. *Communal Sick-Care in the German Ghetto.* Cincinnati: Hebrew Union College Press.

McCarthy, K. D. 1982. *Nobless Oblige: Charity, and Cultural Philanthropy in Chicago, 1849–1929.* Chicago: University of Chicago Press.

———. 1990. "Parallel Power Structures: Women and the Voluntary Sphere." In K. D. McCarthy, *Lady Bountiful Revisited: Women, Philanthropy, and Power.* Pp. 1–31. New Brunswick, N.J.: Rutgers University Press.

McPherson, J. M. and L. Smith-Lovin. 1982. "Women and Weak Ties: Differences by Sex in the Size of Voluntary Organizations." *American Journal of Sociology* 87, no. 4, 883–904.

Meiselman, M. 1978. *Jewish Women in Jewish Law*. New York: Ktav.

Milamed, S. 1986. "Proskurover Landsmanschaftn: A Case Study in Jewish Communal Development." *American Jewish History* 76:40–55.

Morawska, E. 1996. *Insecure Prosperity: Small-town Jews in Industrial America, 1890–1940*. Princeton: Princeton University Press.

National Commission on American Jewish Women. 1995. *Voices for Change: Future Directions for American Jewish Women*. Waltham, Mass.: Cohen Center, Brandeis University.

Neusner, J. 1997. *Tzedakah: Can Jewish Philanthropy Buy Jewish Survival?* New York: UAHC Press.

Oates, M. J. 1995. *The Catholic Philanthropic Tradition in America*. Bloomington: Indiana University Press.

Odendahl, T. 1990. *Charity Begins at Home*. New York: Basic Books.

Ostrower, F. 1995. *Why the Wealthy Give*. Princeton, N.J.: Princeton University Press.

Power & Parity: Women on the Boards of Major American Jewish, Organizations. 1998. New York: Ma'yan.

Putnam, R. D. 1995. "Bowling Alone: America's Declining Social Capital." *Journal of Democracy* 6, no. 1: 65–78.

———. 1996. "The Strange Disappearance of Civic America." *The American Prospect* (Winter): 34–48.

———. 2000. *Bowling Alone: The Collapse, and Revival of American Community*. New York: Simon and Schuster.

Rogow, F. 1993. *Gone to Another Meeting: The National Council of Jewish Women, 1893–1993*. Tuscaloosa: University of Alabama Press.

———. 1997. "National Council of Jewish Women." In P. E. Hyman and D. D. Moore, eds., *Jewish Women in America: An Historical Encyclopedia*. Vol. 2, Pp. 968–79. New York: Routledge.

Sander, K. W. 1998. *The Business of Charity: The Woman's Exchange Movement, 1832–1900*. Urbana: University of Illinois Press.

Schneider, S. W. 1984. *Jewish and Female*. New York: Simon and Schuster.

Scott, A. F. 1992. *Natural Allies: Women's Associations in American History*. Urbana: University of Illinois Press.

Skocpol, T. 1997. "The Tocqueville Problem: Civic Engagement in American Democracy." *Social Science History* 21:455–79.

———. 1992. *Protecting Soldiers and Mothers: The Political, Origins of Social Policy in the United States*. Cambridge, Mass.: Harvard University Press.

Sochen, J. 1981. *Consecrate Every Day: The Public Lives of Jewish American Women, 1880–1980*. Albany: State University of New York Press.

Sofer, Barbara 1999. "Carole Solomon's Sacred Mission." *Pennsylvania Gazette* (March/April): 36–39.

Soyer, D. 1997. *Jewish Immigrant Associations and American Identity in New York, 1880–1939*. Cambridge, Mass.: Harvard University Press.

———. 1992. Jewish Women's Philanthropy." *Lilith* (Winter): 1–10.

Tennenbaum, S. 1993. *A Credit to Their Community*. Detroit: Wayne State University Press.

Tobin, G. A., and A. Z. Tobin, 1995. *American Jewish Philanthropy in the 1990's*. Waltham, Mass.: Cohen Center for Modern Jewish Studies.

Verba, S., K. L. Schlozman, and H. E. Brady. 1995. *Voice and Equality: Civic Voluntarism in American Politics*. Cambridge, Mass.: Harvard University Press.

Warner, W. L. 1945. *The Social System of American Ethnic Groups*. New Haven: Yale University Press.

Welt, M. G. 1948. "The National Council of Jewish Women." *American Jewish Yearbook*, 46, 55–72.

Wenger, B. S. 1987. "Jewish Women of the Club: The Changing Public Role of Atlanta's Jewish Women, 1870–1930." *American Jewish History* 76, 311–33.

Wertheimer, J. 1997. "Current Trends in American Jewish Philanthropy." *American Jewish Yearbook*, 97:3–92.

Woocher, J. 1986. *Sacred Survival: The Civil Religion of American Jews*. Bloomington: Indiana University Press.

Zolty, S. P. 1997. *And All Your Children Shall Be Learned: Women and the Study of Torah in Jewish Law and History*. Northvale, N.J.: Jason Aronson.

– 7 –

Women and Philanthropy in Egypt

AMANI KANDIL

INTRODUCTION

In all the periods of Egyptian history, what we call the "Women's Question" was, and remains, salient. It is a question that involves the state, the scope and nature of civil society, and Islam as an important place in a variety of fundamentalist and leftist political discourses. The debates on "Women's Issues" fostered by the feminist voluntary organizations (FVOs) in the first and second decades of the twentieth century centered on women's rights in education, work, and politics (including the right to vote). Women's agenda at this early stage focused on the principle of equality and the need to change the personal status law* (as a step toward liberalizing Egyptian women's position in society and relieving them from patriarchal domination). Although many reforms had been introduced by the end of the twentieth century, women's issues continue to be debated, although in different ways, and much of the discourse still concerns women's rights in education, work, political participation, revisions in the personal status law, and the principle of equality.

The struggle for education is no longer aimed at recognizing women's right to education, as at the beginning of the twentieth century, but at affording educational opportunities in poor villages where more than 50 percent of all females are still illiterate. Women's right to work is now recognized in the constitution and the laws, but women's agenda continues to address discriminatory practices. Although the percentage of women in the labor force is continually increasing, conservative Islamic voices are asking women to go back home, giving priority to their roles in the family and the raising of children.

The political rights of women were legally recognized in 1956, but the impact of women's political participation remains slight. Nor has

---

*Personal status law or the family law is under the jurisdiction of Islam, although the state removed all other areas of law from the jurisdiction of Islam; accordingly, different responsibilities and duties are placed in the family.

191

their policy-making role in parliament significantly influenced women's issues on the national level. Feminist struggles to change the personal status law at the beginning of the twentieth century had been partly realized in 1979, but a "retreat" at the state level in 1984 undermined many of these changes.

In conclusion, women's right to work, to be educated, to participate in political life, and to change the personal status laws were the main issues of women's voluntary organizations at the beginning of the twentieth century. These issues remain on the agenda at century's end, but with different components and objectives. Competing discourses and agendas relating to the "Question of Women" in Egypt have had important implications for women's philanthropy, especially in women's voluntary organizations (WVOs). These efforts have been marked by solidarity and collaboration between different voluntary organizations. This paper investigates the historical development of women's contributions to philanthropy and WVOs in Egypt, from the nineteenth century to 1996, focusing on key debates and women's agenda in each period that have shaped women's voluntary organizations.

Before I proceed, three points should be noted, two of them related to the conceptual framework, and the third related to social, religious, and political factors conditioning the "women's question" in Egypt.

1. The project and the title of the paper are centered on "Women and Philanthropy in Egypt." As it is understood and used in Arabic culture and language, the concept of philanthropy is linked to help and assistance of poor people and those who are in need. The idea of giving is connected to religions — Islam and Christianity — and, thus, the concept does not go beyond this "traditional" way of helping the poor. From this point of view, the concept of "philanthropy" is quite limited and does not cover advocacy activities, nor does it include certain modern types of service delivery. Moreover, the concept of "philanthropy," from this point of view, is not related to institutional entities but might cover "individual giving" whether institutional or not. This understanding leads us to define philanthropy as used in this study as: voluntary initiatives to establish non-profit organizations. We call these "voluntary organizations." These voluntary organizations aim to achieve collective benefit and/or sectoral benefits for groups or individuals. They have autonomous or independent structures, are administered by people themselves, and, thus, are by nature nongovernmental, although ruled according to certain laws.

Thus, I am concerned in this paper with organized and institutionalized initiatives active in different areas, such as health, advocacy, education, culture, training and rehabilitation, childhood, etc. These voluntary organizations reflect women's initiatives and visions to change reality.

2. The second observation deals with the special nature of the relationship between WVOs in Egypt and the women's movement. The boundaries between them are not very clear, because historically and in the twentieth century, most of the leaders of these voluntary organizations were involved in the women's movement. In addition, WVOs were the main vehicles and channels for the expression of the demands and opinions of the women's movement before 1952. Therefore, when we address at some points of this paper the issue of women in philanthropy, we have to acknowledge the role played by voluntary organizations in strengthening the women's movement.

3. The third note is related to the understanding of the triangle of state, society, and Islam that has historically shaped the women's question in Egypt and, in part, WVOs. The strong central state characterizes Egypt even in the historical moments of weakness in the country. This central state, which could be described as the "distrustful state," has had an impact on the voluntary sector in general and on WVOs in particular. There have been moments of confrontation and moments of alliance, but tensions between the state and civil society were present at all times. The central state might have adopted at some points socio-economic policies to promote and empower women (educational policies under Nasser are an example). Nevertheless, the same state remained reluctant when it came to introducing amendments in the personal status law, which is governed by Islamic law, *Shari'a* (and, thus, contributed to perpetuating patriarchal relations inside the family, as we shall see later). Consequently, while Islam played a crucial role in motivating women in philanthropy, in addition to recognizing women's identity and economic independence (granting them the right to property ownership, to buy, sell, and sign contracts), some Islamic interpretations tend to withhold complete recognition of Muslim women and impose restrictive interpretations of Islam.[1] The interaction of the state, society, and Islam have had serious implications for the formulation of women's agendas, issues, and priorities since the nineteenth century.

THE BIRTH OF WOMEN'S CONSCIOUSNESS
IN THE NINETEENTH CENTURY

The nineteenth century witnessed the rise of the modern Egyptian state and a fuller incorporation into the European-dominated world market system with its components of secularization, technological innovation, education, and urbanization. As Margot Badran notes in her book,[2] these forces changed the lives of Egyptians across classes and genders. After Egypt won its *de facto* independence from the Ottoman Empire when Muhammad Ali got rid of the Ottoman domination and set himself as a ruler of Egypt, he started the country on an ambitious project of modernization. He intended to build a strong army, develop cotton as a cash crop for exportation, establish industrial projects, establish a printing press, and achieve urban improvements. In this context, crucial educational reforms took place: educational missions were sent for the first time to Europe, public and technical schools were built, and in 1836 a first attempt to create a state system for girls' education occurred. However, the appointed council for public education found it impossible to implement the system of girls' education due to cultural and societal constraints imposed on women at that time.

In his discussion of the "women's question" Abdel Malik[3] believes that at this time "there were no women in men's society, and no men in women's society.... There is no society in a complete sense.... The status of Coptic women did not differ qualitatively. The question was not the status of women in Islamic countries; would it be different in any other traditional country?" Confining women to the home, rendering them invisible for urban upper and middle classes, are concepts linked to the "harim" culture. The Arabic word "harim" is applied to women and to the quarters where women live in the house. Neither domestic confinement nor veiling the face was ordered by Islam, although both had been imposed on women in the name of religion. These practices were reinforced by deeply rooted sexual and moral beliefs, which were likewise associated with religion. Domestic seclusion and veiling in Egypt were not practiced solely by Muslims but by Jews and Christians as well.[4]

Restricting women to their homes and camouflaging them if they went out were deemed necessary to the preservation of their purity and the honor of their men and families. In all classes, girls were commonly married without their free consent (which contradicts the precepts of Islam) around the age of thirteen.

About the end of the century, the patriarch of the Coptic Church set sixteen as the minimum age of marriage for Coptic women. Nevertheless, the marriage age for females remained generally low until the 1920s. As Islam allows men under certain conditions to marry four wives at the same time, polygamy was widespread in the nineteenth century in the upper and middle classes. By the turn of the century, polygamy began to diminish but did not disappear totally.[5] Setting a minimum marriage age, restricting polygamy and the right of men to repudiate their wives outside the courts, are part of the demands of the women's movement in the twentieth century to amend the personal status law.

By the end of the nineteenth century, girls' education had begun to emerge, despite the initial resistance of families and conservative intellectuals at the beginning of the century. The School for Hakimats (Medical Nurses) was established in 1832. At first, Egyptian families refused to send their daughters to this school. However, very soon after it had proven its success, Egyptian women from modest families joined it. Although Muhammad Ali was unable to launch a state school system for girls, he set an example followed by the elite when he hired European women to teach his daughters at home. In 1830, religious associations established schools, and in 1853 a Coptic school for girls was founded.[6]

In the second half of the century, when the state renewed its efforts to promote female education, some intellectuals helped to create a favorable environment for girls' education. Ali Mubarak, a technocrat, and Sheikh Rifa'I al-Tahtawi, a religious scholar and the first to be sent abroad on an educational mission, advocated for girls' education. For al-Tahtawi, educating girls was considered important "to prepare them to be wives and to be capable of participating with men in opinions and talks." However, he did not recommend women's political rights.[7]

In 1873, the first state school for girls — El Siyufiyah School — was established; the wife of Khedive Ismail became its patron. Then, the Qirabiya School was established under the leadership of the Minister of Awqaf, Ali Mubarak, followed by the Bent al-Ashraf School (Daughters of the Nobles) in 1878. In 1889, the Saniyah School expanded educational opportunity to middle-class women. Around the turn of the twentieth century, girls from the upper class began for the first time to attend schools, after having previously been restricted to home education by European teachers.

It is worth mentioning that having the right to allocate money or real estate for charitable purposes through *Waqfs* or endowments, some women, and men, allocated *Waqfs* to support and encourage girls' education in the last two decades of the nineteenth and at the beginning of the twentieth century. The salient example is Samiha El Selehdar's *Waqf*, which allocated 1794 feddans (1 feddan = 4200 square meters) for the education of poor girls. Another example is that of Princess Fatima, the daughter of Ismail, who devoted a *Waqf* in 1910 to the education of girls in Mansoura, one of the governing districts of the Delta. Some other important contributions through the channel of *Waqfs* were made by women in upper Egypt in 1919, and before that in 1909 by Aisha Sidiqa, to send educational missions to Europe (two Muslim students every year).[8]

Women's contributions through *Waqfs* to support education and culture in Egypt reflect the birth of a feminist consciousness of females' right to education. It is also an indication of women's economic independence and the recognition of this right by Islam, despite the strong patriarchal practices based on conservative interpretations of Islam. Estimates of the total number of students, according to historical writings, differ. In his important book, "Egypt's Renaissance," Anwar Abdel Malik indicates that among a total of 89,893 students in Egypt in 1873, 3,018 were girls.[9]Some early feminists, such as Maryam al-Nahas (1856–86) and Zaynab Fawwaz (1860–94), emigrated to Egypt from Lebanon. They presented in their writings models of women that were radical at that time. The first women to show a new awareness of gender were born in the middle decades of the nineteenth century. They published books, articles, and poetry in the 1870s and 1880s, and succeeded for the first time in expanding women's voices to the public and in communicating with each other.

Writer Aisha al-Taymuriyah (1840–1902) tackled the issue of women's domestic seclusion. She wrote about her life, revealing her early yearnings to become literate. She learned Arabic, Turkish, and Persian and succeeded in becoming a writer and a poet through her determination and with the help of a supportive father. Aisha al-Taymuriyah published in 1873 two collections of poems in which she expresses her isolation as a woman.[10]

In 1892, Hind Noufal published the magazine *Al-Fatah* (Young Women); *El-Hawanem* (Ladies) magazine was published in 1900; and *Women in Islam* magazine in 1901. In 1892, Zaynab El Fawwaz expressed her protest in *Al Nile* magazine with these words: "We have not seen any of the divinely ordered systems of law, or any law from among the corpus of [Islamic] religious law ruling that woman is to be prohibited from involvement in the occupations of men."[11] When Hind Noufal founded *Al-Fatah* inaugurating a women's press in Egypt, women found a new forum for discussing and spreading their opinions and ideas related to women's issues. This emergent feminism was grounded and legitimized in the framework of Islamic modernism that was expounded toward the end of the century by Sheikh Muhammad Abdu, a distinguished teacher and scholar from Al-Azhar. (Al-Azhar as a religious establishment interprets religious commandments. These advisories are "Fatawi" in Islam and have the force of orders. Al-Azhar is also the biggest Islamic university.) According to Abdu, through *ijtihad* (independent inquiry into sources of religion), one could be both Muslim and modern. Not all traditional practice was in accordance with Islam. In dealing with gender issues, Abdu confronted the problem of patriarchal excesses committed in the name of Islam, including males' abuse of the institutions of divorce and polygamy.[12]

Before the early twentieth century, a few voices of liberal men advocated for women's rights. As women had already begun to manifest their discontent and had undertaken steps to liberate themselves from patriarchal practices, men began in a more abstract way to criticize the backwardness of their country in terms of the situation and status of women. These highly educated men had also been legally trained and exposed to European thought. One of them, Morqus Fahmi, argued that the country was retarded because women were oppressed by males in the family. He wrote and published in 1894 a four-act play about women in the East.[13] It did not raise much debate in Egypt because, as a Copt, he was not able to challenge the main Islamic religious practices, such as veiling the face, repudiation, and polygamy.

Qasim Amin, a Muslim judge, published his first book in 1894. He used to attend Princess Nazli Fazil's salon to debate and discuss with other intellectuals progressive issues in Egypt. In 1899, Qasim Amin published his book *Tahrir al-Mar'ah* (*Liberation of Women*) asking for gender reform. Like Fahmi, Amin depicted patriarchal oppression and called for the abolition of female seclusion which, as he demonstrated, has nothing to do with Islam.[14] He also adopted the claims of women feminists, such as the right to work and to education and the elimination of repudiation and polygamy. He called for an end to face veiling and argued that this practice had nothing to do with Islam. The opinions he preached were attacked by conservative voices and writings. In 1900, Amin published his book *al-Mar'ah al-Jjadida* (*The New Woman*), in which he uses secular arguments in favor of women's emancipation, and hence national liberation. Since that time, Amin's book has been considered a touchstone for feminist writings in Egypt (although, as Badran indicates in her book, Hoda Sha'rawi and Bahithat al Badiya argued that uncovering the face was a premature fight because society was not ready yet to accept it and that it was only a matter of time before the veil would disappear).[15]

In conclusion, different variables contributed to the rise of feminist consciousness in the last two decades of the nineteenth century, the most important being feminist newspapers and writings advocating for women's liberation. This rise of feminist consciousness helped to create an enabling environment for the establishment of women's organizations in the twentieth century.

THE INTERACTION BETWEEN THE WOMEN'S MOVEMENT AND WOMEN'S VOLUNTARY ORGANIZATIONS (1900–23)

The period 1900–23 witnessed the birth of women's voluntary organizations, which represented more than an institutional framework to enable women's participation in public life. These WVOs were fora where women had the opportunity to express their claims to the right to education, work, participation in political life, and amendments in the personal status law. In addition, they constituted vehicles for women's empowerment and channels to achieve solidarity. Thus, interaction was established between WVOs and the women's movement. Another interaction existed between the participation of Egyptian women in the national struggle for independence from the British occupation and their role in voluntary organizations. In the context of interaction between the women's movement and WVOs, upper-class women, like Hoda Sha'rawi, and to a lesser extent middle-class women, like Nabawiyah Musa, operated within and beyond their classes.

By the early twentieth century, Egyptian women in the upper class tried to initiate their own independent voluntary organizations. Four main attempts were made to organize women's groups, culminating in the establishment of the Women's Union in 1923. The first was made under the initiative of Princess Ain Al Hiat, who invited in 1904 a group of women to establish the Mabarat Muhammad Ali Hospital. Hoda Sha'rawi, who later became the president of the Women's Union (1923), was a member of this pioneer group. The second effort came in 1906, when Hoda Sha'rawi established a Ladies' Club in Alexandria, which was considered by conservatives a breaking of tradition and culture. Actually, Sha'rawi aimed to create a forum to bring women together rather than establish a sports' club, as Doreya Shafik noted in her book on Egyptian women: "the club was a way to bring women together towards solidarity."[16] This organization also provided care for mothers and their children.

The New Woman organization was established in 1919 by a group of distinguished upper-class women at a meeting in the house of one of the country's most famous and wealthy families (Hussein Sabet). (There are historical references to two different dates for the establishment of the New Woman Association, 1919 and 1909; however, most historians favor 1919.) A few weeks later, Hoda Sha'rawi was elected honorary president; she subsequently supported the organization out of her own pocket. The New Woman, which was directly operated by Sherifa Riadh, was active in culture, education, training girls in certain fields (making carpets, nursing), and in philanthropy. One of its most remarkable economic contributions was the establishment of workshops for girls in poor areas to produce carpets using modern equipment. The New Woman's pathbreaking contribution was recognized in newspapers and by official figures.[17]

The women's agenda gradually formulated at that time included advocacy for participation in public life, care services for poor women and children, and the right to education and work. Face veiling was not included in their priorities, as these women were aware that they should, for practical reasons, adopt a more conservative strategy regarding the process of unveiling women. Nabawiya Musa asserted in a public lecture the right of women to work and to be educated, arguing that "maternal duties did not imply that women should be imprisoned in houses...people can decide for themselves." Bahithat al-Badiyah and Hoda Sha'rawi pleaded that women should keep the veil until men were ready for change. Men needed to be re-socialized in order to look at women not only as sexual objects. Women also needed to know how to conduct themselves when unveiled.[18] Thus, the process of unveiling women was not on women's agenda nor a priority. They gave priority to the right of education, of work, of participation in public life, and in changing the personal status law. They believed that by gaining these rights, women would tend to unveil.

During the struggle against British occupation in 1919, and while negotiations between England and the Wafd Committee were of primary political concern, women participated in politics for the first time. They organized demonstrations against occupation; and some of them were killed. In 1920, a group of women linked to the Wafd gathered at St. Mark's Cathedral and created the Wafdist Women's Central Committee (WWCC). Hoda Sha'rawi was elected president of the WWCC, whose initial members included Ulfat Ratib, Regina Habib, Mrs. Wissa Wassef, Sharifa Riyad, and others. Several were married to Wafdist leaders; most of them came from important landowning families. However, a few of them were from middle-class families of Cairo.[19] Safiya Zaghlul, the wife of the Wafdist leader Saad Zaghlul, was not a member of this group. She kept strong ties with it, however, and came to be considered as the "Mother of Egyptians."

The WWCC organized demonstrations, led women in the political struggle, helped and supported the families of prisoners and those who died in demonstrations. One of the important contributions of the WWCC was establishing ties and bridges with women in governing disctricts through women's associations. The Committee also assisted in the process of establishing women's unions in the Delta and in Upper Egypt.[20] and led a campaign for the boycott of British banks, shops, and goods in Egypt.

Women's organizations were not limited to the capital nor to providing care services for mothers and children. Among associations established in Alexandria, the Association for the Promotion of Egyptian Girls was concerned with girls' education and awareness. In the city of Tanta an organization was established in 1919 under the name of The

Union for the Promotion of Women's Training and Empowering Poor Egyptian Women. In the same year, another voluntary organization, the Egyptian Ladies Renaissance, was created under the chairmanship of Labiba Ahmed. This organization was partly characterized by its adoption of Islamic principles. Because the number of women's organizations is not documented, it is not clear how many of them existed.

The establishment of Cairo University in 1906 constituted a historic event in Egypt's history.[21] The university was established as a result of public initiatives through voluntary activities and donations, partly with funds allocated by Islamic *Waqfs*. Wealthy women, such as Princess Ain Al-Hiat, allocated agricultural land as *Waqf* to fund the University. A few years after the University's opening, calls were raised to open its doors to women; a few lectures were eventually organized for Egyptian and foreign women intellectuals to give presentations. However, the branch for girls was closed in 1912–13 following conservative protests. Later, due to a decision by Ahmed Lotfi El-Sayed, Rector of the University and one of the intellectuals most supportive of women's rights, the University again opened its doors to women in 1929.

Some of the major characteristics of the birth and development of women's voluntary organizations in Egypt can be summarized as follows.

1. The women's movement was first labeled feminist in 1923 by women activists using the French form of the word, since the Arabic translation was somehow different. The development of the women's movement to obtain their liberation, mainly the right to education and waged labor, was institutionalized in the twentieth century through women's voluntary organizations. The struggle against veiling the face (*Hijab*) in the late nineteenth century was raised and led by liberal intellectual men such as Qasim Amin. Female leaders, like Hoda Sha'rawi and Malak Hefni Nassef (known under the name Bahithat al-Badiya), preferred to focus on advocating for women's rights to work and to education, and on requesting amendments in the personal status law. The question of the veil was not the major priority in women's agendas it became in the next period (1923–52).

2. Cultural, socio-economic, and political variables shaped Egyptian women's philanthropy. Religion has always been an important feature in motivating women's giving, through the recognition of their economic independence and their active roles in *Waqfs*, and later in the twentieth century through wealthy women's funding of voluntary organizations. Socio-economic factors also characterized the roles and responsibilities of women's philanthropy. Women activists in the beginning of the twentieth century were mainly advocating the right to education and work,

at a time when the conservative culture was denying these rights, limiting females' roles to being wives and rearing children. Thus, women in voluntary organizations established schools and training centers to enable poor women to have access to some professions (sewing, nursing, and producing carpets).

This movement could not have been a reality without the existence of educated, intellectual women and without consciousness of the woman's question. Nor would it have occurred without the support of liberal men who believed in the emancipation of Egyptian women, as well as that provided by a few religious writings, such as those of Muhammad Abdu, which legitimized women's rights according to Islam and emphasized that there is no antagonism between women's rights (in education and work) and the Muslim faith.

The national struggle against British occupation (1882–1923) also had an impact on formulating the roles and responsibilities of women in philanthropy. Women participated in the national struggle, whether directly or indirectly, since social work was a mixture of advocacy and politics.

3. Women activists who had led the women's movement and established voluntary organizations were mainly members of the upper class; few of them belonged to the middle class. The involvement of middle-class women characterizes the next stage (1923–52). Upper-class women were capable of leading the first steps of the women's movement because they were educated and wealthy enough to initiate organizations and volunteer their time and efforts. These women were involved not only in advocating women's rights, but also in social services addressed to poor women. Some of the voluntary organizations that opened schools and training centers for women in poor areas sought to meet women's daily demands and needs.

4. Women activists gave both money and time to support women's voluntary organizations. Some invested their own money in support of their non-profit organizations. But as a general rule, women granted support to their voluntary organizations by giving both time and money and tended to adopt the strategy of separatism by creating single-sex organizations, alhough we should remember that the cultural framework favored this type or organization in the first stage of the women's liberation movement.

5. Until 1922, the fields of interest of these organizations were mixed since they were active in advocacy, social work, and politics. It is difficult to typify women's philanthropic concerns as solely focused on motherhood and childhood, although this interest was developed in the next stages and ultimately became one of the characteristics of women's philanthropy in Egypt.

6. Liberal women who believed in equality and advocated for their rights in education and work were the only activists challenging conservative culture. Female Islamic activists were not active before 1922; their voice was nearly absent in the struggles between liberal women and conservative Islamic men. Leftists were also absent up to 1922. The main discourse belonged either to liberal women or to Islamic conservative men.

THE DEVELOPMENT OF WOMEN'S PHILANTHROPY:
COMPETING DISCOURSES, 1923–52

Now we reach what we call in Egypt the "Liberal Era." This period witnessed the development and diversification of the voluntary sector in general and women's voluntary organizations in particular. Progressive women, or feminists, became openly militant, while most men who had been pro-feminist nationalists shifted their attention toward their new political careers following conditional independence from Britain in 1922. This era also witnessed the rise of Islamic activism, part of which — such as Zaynab Al-Ghazali — would move from feminism to Islamic fundamentalism, beginning an Islamic women's political movement, accompanied by organized Islamic voluntary organizations. The 1923–52 period, therefore, had an impact on the nature of women's voluntary organizations. One of the most important developments in women's philanthropy in Egypt between 1923 and 1952 was the involvement of middle-class professional women in addressing and motivating popular bases in different areas of Egypt. Cultural and class conflicts were salient in some instances, solidarity and cooperation were clear at other points, particularly concerning the national struggle and selected confrontations with the state. This era witnessed the emergence of both compatible and conflicting discourses, raised by feminists, radical Islamists, leftists, and the state.

With formal independence (British troops remained on Egyptian soil until 1956), nationalist men became part of the new state. At first the official discourse articulated in the new constitution of 1923 seemed to fulfill their promises to women, when it declared: "All Egyptians are equal before the law. They enjoy equally civil and political rights and equally have public responsibilities without distinction of race, language, or religion." However, the principle of gender equality was soon abrogated when an electoral law restricted suffrage to males only. At this point feminism became explicit — the word "feminist" began to be used — and tied to an organized political movement led by the Egyptian Feminist Union (EFU) created in 1923 and headed by Hoda Sha'rawi.

Egyptian feminism crystallized around this new organization, providing a clear agenda for women's claims to political, social, economic, and legal rights. However, priority was given to education followed by work opportunities, and reforms in the personal status law (see endnote 1). The profile of the EFU program also included demands to protect the family, health, security, and unions, recognize professional groups, establish national banks, provide more attention to improving the farmers' conditions and those of the unemployed, and decrease foreign authority in Egypt.

On June 26, 1923, the secretary general of the EFU clarified the main objective of the organization by these words: "We have seen the spread of ignorance which is responsible for the backward condition of women, half the society, we have witnessed declining health conditions and rising death rates. We have seen the bad relations between men and wives, the increase in divorces and multiple marriages. It is clear that we are aiming at promoting the social status of women, and building a strong base to liberalize her condition."[22] In its first years, the EFU settled in a popular poor area, Al Sayeda Zeinab, to educate, train, and inform women. Then the EFU established the Woman Home (*Dar El Mara'a*) as a large central training center. "Egyptian and foreign newspapers have pointed to it as an open university for women in all classes."[23]

The EFU dealt with the family and with women's and children's security (included in the personal status law) in two ways, both moderate if not conservative, keeping in mind that the issues are the concern of Islamic religious establishment (Al Azhar). In the 1920s the EFU concentrated on reforming the family's legal structure, calling mainly for controls of male excess and abuses. They employed Islamic reformist arguments in a discourse of persuasion aimed at influencing the politically empowered male to enact changes in the Muslim personal status code. After the 1920s, they understood that chances for success were minimal. The EFU in the 1930s tried a different approach to dealing with family issues, addressing women themselves to protect and enhance their lives in the family through improved performance of their family roles.[24] In their campaign to change the Muslim laws of personal status, they have addressed four issues:

The establishment of minimum marriage age, which was achieved in 1923;

The extension of the mother's legal custody (*hadanah*) over her children, which was achieved in 1929;

The regulation of men's ability to divorce;

The restriction of men's practice of polygamy.

The last two demands are related to the patriarchal relations between men and women, explained and understood by men as primary rights in Islam. None of these demands were met. Only some minor changes occurred in the personal status laws that were abolished in 1983. What feminists saw as "patriarchal excesses" men regarded as "patriarchal privileges."[25]

The EFU was active in health service, training, economic activities, philanthropy, and advocacy; the women involved in the organization were addressing social needs, and also policy makers through sub-professional committees. Their effort on the level of fund raising was remarkable. Due to the broadened areas of activities, donations from wealthy women were not sufficient to cope with all of the organization's work, so the EFU organized special parties where distinguished artists contributed to supporting the organization. The products of the women who benefited from the training inside the EFU's workshops were also sold, constituting another source of funds. The queen, princess, and ministers' wives also supported the EFU. On the other hand, there is little evidence of public funding.

The EFU was not the only actor in the field of women's voluntary organizations. Others were established in the same era, focusing on different activities. The Sisters of the EFU, established in 1924 and headed by Hawa Edris, was mainly active in supporting orphan girls. Working for Egypt was another women's organization, created in 1924 and headed by Ister Fahmi Wisa, an intellectual activist who collaborated with 140 women in health services, advocacy for children and women's rights, and opposition to drugs and alcoholism. Working for Egypt established a branch in Alexandria in 1926 and also in upper Egypt (Assiut, with a total membership of 200 women). It opened a school in 1927 to help the poor in educating their children.

Perhaps the most important role played by the Working for Egypt organization was the advocacy stance it adopted against the drug law. It advocated changes in the law in terms of adding restrictions on individuals to protect the society from the negative effects of alcohol and cocaine, both in widespread use at the time. Members of the Senate were invited to discuss the law with members of this organization, after which the Parliament agreed to change a few items in the legislation.[26] Another, similar example was their successful effort to persuade the minister of education to include the art of taking care of children in the curriculum of girls' schools.

Still another distinguished voluntary organization was established in 1929 under the name Egyptian Young Ladies (*Al Shabat Al Masriate*). Headed by a twenty-two-year-old woman, Young Ladies focused on providing cultural services for girls. It created a library, artists' workshop, sports programs, and a classroom to study languages; it also published a weekly magazine aimed at the middle and poorer classes.

Women also began to get involved in maternalist campaigns at this point. One example is the Association of Motherhood and Childhood, which was established by businessmen's wives; another is the Promoting Health Association, which was funded by princes and the upper class; and others include the Committee of Red Cross Ladies, Developing Health Associations, and other groups focusing on health in general, and childhood and motherhood in particular. Christian women's voluntary organizations were also established, such as the Association of Christian Women, which had much in common with Muslim organizations, most importantly in working against drugs and alcoholism.

1932 marked a historical turning point, as the first committee for Muslim sisters was established in Ismailia City under the name Teams of Muslim Sisters. Another committee was established in Cairo, through the support of the Muslim Brothers, which had been established in Cairo in 1927, headed by Hassan El-Bana. Before that, the same year, they had announced the group in Ismailia; Cairo then became the head office. These Muslim Sisters, who were mainly the wives, daughters, and sisters of members of the Muslim Brothers, presented an Islamic discourse addressed to the middle and lower classes, emphasizing the differences between themselves and the Western feminist discourse. However, this Islamic popular movement was the product of tensions and confrontations between themselves and the upper-class women who had adopted elements of Western manners expressed in dress, in everyday life, and in the use of the French language (the language of the EFU journal founded in 1924 was French). The Islamic Sisters movement achieved substantial successes in terms of mobilizing members, efforts, and funds throughout Egypt, and by 1948, fifty branches had been founded in different places, totaling five thousand members, most of whom were women from the middle and lower classes.[27]

Due to the confrontation between the Islamic political movement and the government, the Muslim Brothers and Sisters were dissolved and their activities disbanded. However, Muslim Sisters were active in taking care of Muslim prisoners, and afterwards, when they began to work again, they established the head office of Muslim Sisters in Cairo. Their program was promulgated in 1947 under the name The Muslim Women; it included:

"Fighting against the ongoing system and ideologies, and correcting the present status of the woman, identifying all her rights, and recognizing her with respect";

Mobilizing women to lead the "correct" and "right women" promotion, and preparing them for this leadership;

Announcing women's right on the basis of the Qura'n and Islam,
including "her right to freedom, her natural and private rights,
[and] recognizing her equality with men in human rights which
do not contradict with her special function to society."[28]

Another part of the Muslim Sisters program clearly indicated the importance of the role of the Muslim woman in philanthropic action, and
promoted her role in social activities as part of her mission.

The sub-law of the Muslim Sisters organization expressed the previous principles and objectives, emphasizing the teaching of Islam to
women, educating them in the methods of "Islamic Socialization,"
women's rights and duties, and also "contributing to social projects such
as schools, hospitals, and taking care of orphans and children." So the
main activities of the Muslim Sisters were teaching Islam, developing
health information and awareness, advancing education, and fostering
women's training centers and philanthropy.[29]

In one of their most important publications, they identified the right
of woman to work; "but if there is a necessity for this," she also has the
right to birth control due to health or economic conditions; and there is
a need to recognize her political rights. The tensions between feminism
and cultural authenticity were deepened after Zaynab Al-Ghazali, who
was a member of the EFU, embraced the Islamic discourse after accepting
the notion of secularism. In 1936 she established the Muslim Women's
Association, which was depicted in their writings as the women's wing
of Muslim Brothers. Al-Ghazali, in her book *Days of My Life* (1984), mentioned that she had known Hassan El Bana since 1937. He invited her
to become the head of Muslim Sisters, stating that "this means that the
new baby who I am proud of will be part of the Muslim Brothers movement."[30] El-Ghazali refused the suggestion, but supported the idea of
cooperation between both groups.

The Muslim Women's Association (MWA) was disbanded twice before 1952 — first in 1940, and then in 1950 — resuming its activities after
being granted a court decree in both instances. The MWA, headed by Al-
Ghazali, led the call to respect Islamic traditions, and to teach women
"the proper principles of Islam." Intensive activities were initiated in
poor areas, addressing poor and uneducated women who had adopted
ideas and practices far from the real Islam. Al-Ghazali and her group
adopted Islamic dress, prayed in mosques, and wore veils for newspaper
photographs, to provide models for Egyptian women.[31]

In the 1940s, the younger generation of female university students and graduates moved in a new direction, as socialists and communists. For them the liberation of women was tied to the liberation of the masses, and both necessitated the end of imperialism and class oppression in Egypt. Inji Aflaton discovered Marxism, and after her graduation from Fouad University (later Cairo University), she founded the League of University and Institutes for Young Women, which Latifa Zayyat, a student leader, soon joined. The League sent Aflaton and others to the first conference of the International Democratic Federation of Women. But the League was closed in 1946 in the drive to suppress communists. Socialist feminists established another association, the National Feminist Association. Aflaton linked class and gender oppression in her published books, being careful to argue that women's liberation was compatible with Islam.[32]

Popular aspects of the feminist movement were added in the 1940s, not only by Islamic trends but also by liberal trends. New voluntary organizations were established in the 1940s, headed by middle-class professional women who had lacked popular bases before, including the National Feminist Party (NFP) (1942). Fatma Rashed, the head of the organization, gradually gained popularity after she announced her program, emphasizing equality between men and women, and recognizing women's national, political, and social rights.

The other example of a women's voluntary organization established in the 1940s was the Daughter of the Nile Union (DNU) (1949), headed by Doria Shafik. Both the NFP and the DNU mounted literacy and hygienic campaigns among the poor. They also sustained the concern with family law reform. Doria Shafik was very distinguished in the advocacy fields. As Aflaton mentioned in her book, "she was the most active in advocating women's political rights."[33]

During this period, 1923–52, the official religious establishment supported some of the demands adopted by women's voluntary organizations, such as their campaigns against drugs and alcoholism. But they opposed others, including efforts to change the personal status law. When religious scholars held a conference to examine all aspects of women's status within the context of Islamic law in 1952, they openly attacked the feminist movement, claiming it was influenced and supported by British imperialists. The reactionary conclusions of the conference seemed to be in part a response to the growing numbers of women in the work force.[34] By the early 1950s, women were found in shops, factories, the professions, and the social services in sufficient numbers to alarm the patriarchal sensibilities of male fundamentalists.

The period of the liberal experiment in Egypt was a time when a capitalist economy with ties of dependency to a dominant Europe still operated largely within a neo-imperialistic framework. The feminist or the pro-feminist ideology that served the nationalist cause was no longer useful or desirable during the period after the revolution (1952). In response, women began to crystallize their concerns around the concept of development, which was subsequently adopted by the state. Although women's voluntary organizations in the Liberal Era gained only limited success in political terms, their efforts constituted the wealthiest and most active chapter in the history of women's philanthropy in Egypt. In this context some conclusions are important:

1. As we have seen in the previous analysis, a host of differing ideologies were put forward through women's voluntary organizations in this period: feminism, Islam, the left. Moreover, cultural and class conflicts within the women's movement had a strong impact on the nature of women's voluntary organizations, and their agendas, their tactics.

2. Although there were differences between women's discourses, a coalition was created among the different wings of the movement in opposing occupation and laying claim to national liberation. The most important example was the establishment of the Women's Committee for Popular Struggle in 1951, which included all the wings involved in women's issues.

3. Women's participation in voluntary organizations provided an efficient mechanism for building parallel power structures. These organizations enabled women to gain political power, although their political rights were denied. These parallel power structures were channels for obtaining legal rights and recognition. In the case of Egypt, women had a modicum of economic independence, as they had the right to acquire and hold property and to sign contracts. For them, voluntary associations were mainly channels for advocating their political and social rights, and gaining political power. Women's economic independence, recognized in Islam, enabled upper-class women to establish and fund their own organizations and create opportunities for other women to work or to be involved in economic projects created by them.

4. Although the type of strategy that most of women's groups adopted was separatism (working in gender-segregated women's groups), some individual males and some other male voluntary organizations gave them support. This was clear whether in the case of the feminists or the Islamists. Thus, the common pattern between 1923 and 1952 was separatism, which proved suitable in that social and

cultural framework, and efficient in attracting members and funds due to women's control over their own property. Since the Muslim Sisters were the other wing of Muslim Brothers, it is difficult to conclude that they were independent.

5. Women's nonprofit organizations did not depend on public funds (from the government), but instead used private donations to fund their organizations. Economic activities, such as selling the products of their organizations, were another source of funds. This diversified funding mix enabled women's voluntary associations to enjoy great independence in the Liberal Era (1923–52), allowing them to engage in advocacy and to shape their own agendas and priorities.

6. There was a growing tendency, particularly in the 1940s, to focus on maternalist campaigns, as a series of women's voluntary organizations became active in providing health services for mothers and children. This might have been partly a result of some women's preference not to be involved in advocacy, or it might have been a result of the low priority given by the state to maternalist issues. The most important maternalist organization was the Association of Mothers and Children.

Women's philanthropy had an impact in drawing women's attention into the public sphere through voluntary activities. Islam encouraged and supported women's voluntarism through *Zakat, Sadakat,* and *Waqf,* and through the recognition of their legal rights to own their own property. This recognition played an essential role in facilitating the creation of women's voluntary associations, not only to give support to the poor but also to advocate women's rights. Conversely, the only sources sustaining women's organizations at that time were the time, money, and income-generating activities they developed for themselves.

SOCIALIST POLICIES AND INTEGRATING VOLUNTARY ORGANIZATIONS INTO THE STATE, 1952–70

The military-led revolution of 1952 marked a historic turning point in Egypt's policies. Socialism was adopted, the one-party system dominated political life, civil society was quashed, and the Muslim Brothers, leftists, and liberal forces were suppressed as being dangerous to the state. This was also a time of contradictions because, although independent feminist voices were silenced, women gained political rights and expanded educational and labor prerogatives. State feminism had an active role in the political economy,[35] with genuine accomplishments during the 1950s and 1960s in the areas of education, employment, and political rights. Women's access to education and to public employment rose dramatically at all levels during this period.

Social attitudes toward women's education and employment also changed, while the extension of suffrage to women in 1956 successfully crowned the struggles of the older generation. On the whole, these public achievements presented a progressive picture in which women were integrated into the public arena; discrimination on the basis of gender was outlawed by the constitutions of 1956 and 1964, as well as by political discourse. At the same time, no changes occurred on the level of the personal status law, as the state under Nasser maintained the old patriarchal rules and relationships within the family.[36]

Although state policies accomplished a great deal on the level of women's rights, state authorities were distrustful of civil society. When feminist leaders tried to continue their political struggles, the government blocked their public activities. In 1956, the same year that the state granted women the right to vote, it paradoxically started to ban feminist organizations and to suppress the public expression of feminist views. The Egyptian Feminist Union (EFU), under pressure from the government, purged the alleged communist, Seiza Nabarawi, from its membership. The state dismantled the old EFU, but allowed selected members to reconstitute it as a social welfare association under the name Hoda Sha'rawi Association.

The authorities also closed down the Women's Committee for Electoral Awareness within a year of its establishment. Around the same time, when a coalition of women came together representing different political tendencies (under the name of the National Feminist Union [NFU]), the authorities did not permit them to work and finally shut them down in 1959. The leftist activist Aflaton was sent to prison in the same year, and Shafik, who had struggled to obtain women's political rights, was under house arrest. The Muslim Sisters were disbanded in 1964, and their leader Al Ghazali was sent to prison. This suppression of women's voluntary organizations and feminist leaders should be seen as part of the suppression of civil society in general, and also within the context of state policies toward the voluntary sector in particular.

Before the 1952 revolution, voluntary associations were subject to the civic code which recognized the freedom of the people to establish or to initiate voluntary organizations. The only restrictions were related to political actions and underground organizations. Articles 54–80 in the civic code recognized the legal status of the association as soon as it was established, so the state had no control over the people's initiatives.

Closing down an association could only be done with a decree from the court (article 63).

In 1956, a new law was issued (No. 348 for the year 1956) "to establish a new relation between the state and the voluntary associations..." with many restrictions on the establishment process and the members of the organization, denying the right of participation to people designated as "enemies of the revolution." One of the main conditions included in Law No. 348 was the government's right to recognize voluntary organizations. Under this law, all the active associations had to receive government permission to work. Thus, many active women's voluntary organizations (and others), were prohibited by the government. Beginning in this period many voluntary organizations were functionally integrated into the state, funded mainly by the public budget to carry out socialist policies in the field of social welfare. Eight years later, Law No. 32 for the year 1964 (which is still in operation) was issued, imposing numerous constraints on both the establishment and the activities of voluntary associations and foundations. Restrictions on the creation of new groups were imposed for four broad reasons: "national security," preservation of the nation's political system, support for social morality, and opposition to the revival of previously active associations. This last justification was used — and is still used — against the reestablishment of the outlawed Muslim Brothers (and Muslim Sisters). These restrictions allow the government wide latitude both in preventing associations from developing (Article 12), and in dissolving those already in existence (Article 57). Concerning associational activities, the government exercises control through several key provisions, such as checking the documents and records of the organization "to make sure of their conformity to laws." State authorities may, therefore, terminate "the material and legal entity" of associations.[37] This last power was used in many cases of women's voluntary organizations. In this context, it should be mentioned that Law 32 recognizes thirteen activities of associations, including efforts focusing on childhood and motherhood, so the majority of women's organizations have tended to act in this field. The public funds allocated to support this type of activity contributed to the increasing number of associations in this area. It is also important to note the absence of women's advocacy organizations, partly because Law 32 does not recognize this type of activity, and because of the oppressive political climate.

Considering the impact of different socio-economic and political frameworks, if we compare women's philanthropic roles in the period 1952–70 with those of the liberal era (1923–52), a few comments might be useful:

1. Women's Voluntary associations in the Liberal Era were the main channels of the feminist movement, and also the main channels for anti-feminists. Comparable discourses were taking place, and each was mobilizing supporters through advocacy action and social work. On the other hand, in Nasser's era (1952–70) there was only socialist discourse, and women's voluntary organizations were not able to challenge the state. Oppositional tendencies were either suppressed or forced underground. The women's movement — what remained of it — was integrated into the state.

2. Due to the cultural and the socio-economic context, women's voluntary organizations — as a general trend in the liberal era — were primarily separatist groups. On the other hand women's voluntary organizations in the Nasser era played an auxiliary role, implementing the socialist objectives adopted by the state.

3. Women's voluntary organizations in the Liberal Era (1923–52) were mainly funded and established by wealthy upper-class and middle-class women. In Nasser's era, women's voluntary organizations were mainly funded by the state, a factor which deeply affected their independence.

4. The involvement of lower middle-class and grassroots groups was one of the characteristics of voluntary action in Nasser's era, compared with the liberal era. This was partly an outcome of state policies on education and work opportunities, which contributed to the process of social mobility. It was also related to the government's commitment to developing rural areas in Egypt.

5. Women's issues, or gender issues, were not part of the agenda of women's organizations under Nasser, as "state feminism" seemed to take care of these issues.

6. The intensive involvement of women's voluntary organizations in maternalist agendas, which characterized Nasser's era, was due mainly to the family planning policies adopted by the state in the 1960s. Thus the state encouraged, and occasionally created, voluntary organizations to implement its policies (such as the Egyptian Association for Family Planning, founded in 1964), indicating the functional integration of voluntary associations into the state.

In conclusion, although Nasser's government technically increased women's rights and educational and work opportunities, it simultaneously suppressed feminism and subsumed women's voluntary organizations under the state, stifling their independence.

ECONOMIC LIBERALIZATION POLICIES, DEMOCRATIZATION, AND ISLAM: COMPETING AGENDAS FOR WOMEN'S PHILANTHROPY, 1970–96

This period witnessed the re-emergence of a more hospitable climate for women's philanthropy. As feminism became public once more, Islamic fundamentalists also found new scope for expression and for mobilizing supporters.

Under Sadat (1970–81), the state became an agent in the promotion of new forms of feminist and Islamist discourses. This role decreased under the Mubarak regime (1981–96), particularly concerning Islamists, as controls were imposed on civil society institutions to reduce their domination of civil society institutions, particularly professional groups (i.e., Law No. 100 concerning professional groups). The 1980s and the 1990s also witnessed a reformulation of the role of voluntary organizations in light of new political and economic variables (e.g., economic liberalization, a controlled multiple party system, and freedom of expression).

Egypt witnessed a dramatic shift from socialism to an economic open-door policy under Sadat, with the private sector taking a leading role in order to strengthen the market system and capitalism. On the political level there was a shift from the one-party system toward a multiple party system (with some controls) beginning in 1975, accompanied by a marginal space for freedoms of expression. These political and economic shifts were more pronounced under Mubarak (1981–96). The number of political parties had increased from four to fourteen by 1996, the arena of freedom of expression had been broadened, and the open-door economic policy became an economic liberalization policy accompanied by privatization related to the economic structural adjustment. (Privatization is a policy that leads to the strengthening of the private sector and to the liquidation of the public sector.)

In the 1970s, Sadat capitalized on the popular religious resurgence that followed the war with Israel (1973) and encouraged these groups, partly to create counter forces to Nasser's Arab socialism, and to control leftist forces. That was the beginning of strengthening Islamic forces again in Egypt, which gradually succeeded in creating a popular base in the society, and an effective role in some civil society institutions (e.g., political parties, professional groups, and voluntary organizations).

The advocacy of women's causes was espoused by Jihan Al Sadat and inspired by the UN decade of women (1975–85). As the wife of the president, Sadat styled herself as the supreme advocate of women in Egypt, pushing for fundamental changes in the personal status laws for the first time in fifty years. Excessive patriarchal privileges were curtailed in an unprecedented manner with the expansion of women's ability to initiate divorce, added protections for women in divorce, and controls placed on polygamy. The president's wife actively lobbied for the 1979 decree, which was issued when parliament was in recess.[38] These gains constituted an important if still inadequate step, although portions of the new legislation were rescinded in the 1980s, following public attacks on the changes of the personal status law (1985).

The 1980s and the 1990s witnessed the renewed visibility and organization of independent feminist and Islamist groups, a period of acquiring supporters, and a period of testing the new political and economic climate. Thus, although no distinguished women's voluntary organizations were active, individual activists from different political tendencies (e.g., the famous feminist Nawal El Sa'dawi and the Islamist Zaynab El Ghazali after her release from prison) assumed an increasingly prominent public role. The 1970s were years of preparation for all political discourses within civil society. The 1980s witnessed the "explosion" of these discourses, revealing the strength of several often-competing forces.

It is worth mentioning the new constitution adopted in 1971 (and still operating with some changes), which reveals the state's contribution in spelling out a dichotomy between woman as "public" citizen and as "private" family member governed by the Shari'a. Article 40 guarantees that "citizens are equal before the law, they are equal in public rights and duties, with no discrimination made on the basis of race, sex, language, ideology or belief." The explicit declaration against discrimination on the basis of sex would seem at first glance to represent a step forward. However, according to some observers, the 1971 language "equal in public rights and duties," was weaker than that of the 1923 constitution, which read: "they enjoy equally civil and political rights and equally have public responsibilities." Moreover, the clauses in the 1971 constitution, mentioning state guarantees to balance between women's duties toward their families on one hand and toward their work on the other, ultimately underscored the dichotomy between women's roles as citizens and family members.[39]

When we reach the 1980s and the present, we realize the serious impact of these contradictory socio-economic and cultural pressures. The retreat of the state sector as a result of economic liberalization policies and privatization made many women increasingly vulnerable to low-income levels and the loss of employment opportunities, particularly after the state rescinded its obligation to employ graduates in the state apparatus. Women also suffered from the government's retreat from its former role in subsidizing goods and services, as retrenchment policies dovetailed with those of economic structural adjustment. At the same time, conservatives began encouraging women to go back home, in order to open more employment opportunities for men, on one hand, and to respect the Islamic explanations, understood in a very rigid way, on the other hand.

At this point, Islamist factions began to strengthen their voluntary organizations and to dominate the council boards of some professional groups (including doctors, engineers, pharmacists, and lawyers). In the process, they became an increasingly visible factor in public life. The economic crisis and the success of Islamists in reaching public opinion and penetrating the most important civil society institutions, as well as their efficiency in delivering services, raised a competing model which attracted both men and women. Islamists' views of women's education and employment may have a serious impact on the coming generation. A study by Zaynab Radwan of veiled college women recently found that most embraced the new conservative perspectives. While they supported women's education, they saw it primarily as a means of preparing good wives. One third of the sample supported the unqualified right of women to work, while another third stated that women should only work if there is an economic need.[40] All of these economic, political, and social variables have had an impact on the country's voluntary organizations in general, and on women's groups in particular.

The Islamist activist Zaynab Al Ghazali assumed prominence as the president of the Association of Young Muslim Women. Other new organizations were also established to advocate Islamic discourse. On the other hand, the feminist Nawal El Sa'dawi has struggled to establish the Arab Women's Solidarity Association (AWSA), created in 1985. The AWSA holds that the liberation of the people as a whole cannot take place without the liberation of women. The AWSA owned a publishing house, held conferences and seminars, built their own network, and attracted international contacts and communications, all of which advocated women's rights. But her organization was dissolved by the ministry of social welfare in the 1990s, under Law 32 (of 1964), which gives government the right to do so if the association has broken the law, which was the officially announced reason for disbanding El Sa'dawi's group.

Feminists were deeply disturbed by the growing conservatism in Egyptian public life. This concern increased when the state capitulated to growing opposition to the 1979 revisions of the personal status law in 1985. However, within two months new legislation was passed, restoring most of the benefits to women provided under the 1979 law.

In this context, and in response to the withdrawal of the state from the recognition of women's rights, an informal group of professional women, including those concerned with women's rights, published *Legal Rights and the Work Law.* They considered this book "a vital document to support every Egyptian woman who is struggling to achieve a better life for herself and her family."[41]

A number of women's voluntary organizations were established in the 1980s and the 1990s in Cairo and the provinces, some of which were related to the competing political discourses that surfaced during the Sadat and Mubarak regimes. Others were related to economic crises, particularly those focusing on the promotion of increased opportunities for earned income for Egyptian women. Still other organizations acted in traditional fields to support the poor.

At this point, it is important to analyze the profile of women's voluntary organizations in the 1990s, patterns intimately linked to socio-economic and political factors:

Size and Development

It should be noted in this context that there is a dearth of official data concerning voluntary organizations in general, and women's organizations in particular, as official data do not recognize women's organizations as a separate and independent category. The following analysis is based on the results of surveys conducted by the author and on partial official data.

The total number of voluntary organizations registered in Egypt in 1994 was 13,526, according to the report of the Ministry of Social Affairs. There is an imbalance in the geographical distribution of these groups, with Cairo and Alexandria accounting for the highest numbers.[42]

In trying to discern the total number of women's organizations, the writer conducted a survey (1993) which identified 123 organizations. These institutions identified themselves as women's organizations, most of which were separatist groups (membership for women only). This number — according to an official announcement — increased in the last three years, particularly before the Women's Conference in Beijing in 1995 (estimated about 200). This tendency to increase is in accordance with the general tendency of voluntary organizations to increase over the last few years, due to government tolerance and willingness to accept the registration of voluntary organizations which are perceived as mechanisms for mitigating the negative effects of structural adjustment. The tendency to proliferate in the last few years can also be explained in light of the development of civil society, which has increased the level of citizen participation in public life. Table 1 underscores the trend among Egypt's voluntary organizations:[43]

Table 1

Year	Number
1976	7,593
1978	8,402
1985	11,471
1987	12,013
1990	12,832
1992	13,526
1995	15,000

Strategic Types Adopted by Women's Voluntary Organizations

Although separatist strategies were adopted by women's groups in the liberal era (1923–52), they are no longer dominant, even in traditional areas of women's interests such as maternalist and social assistance programs. The number of closed women's organizations only increased from 123 in 1993 to 200 in 1996. The indicators of membership in voluntary organizations in general reveal that there is a growing tendency among women to work in male-dominated organizations.

In some female organizations, the members play an auxiliary role to the government, or to the main donor (as in the case of some development organizations). The second model of subsidiarity in women's organizations can be found among some religious (Islamic and Christian) voluntary associations, where they integrate themselves into a male-dominated religious body (the Muslim Brothers as an example).

Membership and Decision Making Positions

The official data do not indicate the total scope of nonprofit membership, or the distribution according to sex, but a general figure announced by the Minister of Social Affairs in 1993 placed the number of all members of voluntary organizations at approximately three million.

To reach a better understanding of the scope of women's membership in voluntary organizations, this paper depends on some partial indicators, including official data on 1084 voluntary organizations, which indicate that women constituted less than a quarter (22.4 percent) of all members. Women account for about 18.8 percent of all board members. But these general data can hide or ignore important discrepancies because women's membership in voluntary organizations tends to decrease in rural areas. Also women's roles as decision makers on the board tended to increase in certain areas of activity, such as motherhood and childhood associations (and maternalist activities in general), and in organizations located in Cairo and other large cities. Table 2

Table 2

Field	Number of	Members		Board Members	
Activity	Associations	Males	Females	Males	Females
Motherhood and Childhood (maternalist)	174	26,831	9,627	1,126	620
Family planning	108	11,576	8,044	787	438
Philanthropy (social assistance)	259	62,168	14,044	2,581	305
Disability	72	4,303	1,111	538	130
Cultural and scientific services	230	50,040	11,439	2,278	174
Mixed activities	241	75,993	22,568	1,989	488

highlights women's membership and board membership within 1084 Egyptian associations.

Table 2 reveals the gap between male and female membership. It also indicates the small contribution of women in the decision-making process. The only exceptions are family planning and maternalist associations. The situation is more promising in advocacy, a key conclusion drawn from a field study of 137 advocacy organizations in Egypt conducted by the writer in 1995.[44] According to this study, women's membership in groups that deal with these types of issues is about 30 percent, increasing to 60 percent in some fields of activity such as environmental concerns. Also the percentage of women on boards of directors was about 34 percent of the total, indicating a positive trend toward women's increased participation in public life which was previously absent.

Fields of Activity

If we classify the activities of women in voluntary associations, four main fields emerge:

(a) **Motherhood, Childhood, and Family Planning,** or maternalist activities, represent the main focus of women's philanthropy, particularly since the 1980s. These types of voluntary organizations are funded primarily by the state, although family planning in particular also receives foreign and international funds. This type of activity is "state oriented" and functionally integrated into the state.

(b) **Social assistance** is a second main area of activity for women in philanthropy. In this context it is important to note the high percentage of Islamic and Christian voluntary organizations active in this field. A survey conducted by the writer in 1993 revealed that 34 percent of the total number of voluntary organizations were Islamic, and about 7 percent Christian. Most of these organizations were active in social assistance (traditional philanthropic activities). Thus about 40 percent of the contemporary women's organizations were religiously oriented.

(c) **Development activities** represent a growing arena for women's involvement in voluntary organizations in significant numbers. This type of activity is strongly supported by the government and foreign donors, including projects to change women's roles in society and raise their income levels.

(d) **Advocacy** is the fourth type of activity in which women participate in voluntary organizations. In this context in a developing country like Egypt, advocacy is not limited to lobbying and influencing policy-making, but also includes influencing public opinion to shed light on important issues such as women's political participation and their legal rights.

Some of these advocacy organizations are not registered under Law 32, but rather according to the civic code as civil companies, a device employed in order to free themselves from the bureaucratic controls of the Ministry of Social Affairs. Most of the advocacy organizations in Egypt are funded primarily by foreign donations, in part because the traditions of collective action in Egypt do not favor this type of activity. Also, the concept of advocacy — to the government — is often understood as opposition, so advocacy organizations which are active in human rights and women's rights do not receive support from the public budget.

There is also a clear lack of solidarity among contemporary women's organizations. There is no union, no single institutional body to advocate the rights of women, to push towards influencing the policy making process, and/or to lobby to change laws, in particular the personal status law. But there have been some positive initiatives in recent years. The national committee for Egyptian NGOs, which was established to prepare for the International conference of population and development held in Cairo 1994, convened a women's task force to address women's main issues in Egypt. They focused on justice and equality in educational opportunities, since there are still gaps between males and females according to economic status, and between rural and urban areas, the Delta and Upper Egypt. The ratio of female enrollments to those of males in preparatory schools is 44.2 percent, a ratio which declines for higher education. The aforementioned document also indicates equality in employment: in agriculture woman's contribution is 50.7 percent, in the economic formal sector it is 35.4 percent; and 22 percent of Egyptian families are headed by women. "[B]ut there are still calls asking for women to go back to their homes due to high national unemployment levels."[45]

The NGO document presented to the international conference on population and development (1994), in addressing questions of legal equity, raised a debatable issue (although one in accordance with the Share): the conditions under which stipulations might be included in the marriage contract to protect women's interests. Another important issue adopted by the NGO document concerns women's equality in the nationality law. Under current law, an Egyptian woman married to a foreigner, even an Arab Muslim, cannot automatically guarantee that her sons will have Egyptian citizenship. On the contrary, if the man is married to a foreigner, his sons enjoy Egyptian citizenship, a reality which runs against the grain of principles of equality in the constitution.

The International Population and Development Conference provided an opportunity for voluntary organizations to work together, to build solidarity, and to explore women's issues. The preparations for NGO participation in the "International Conference for Women" in Beijing afforded another occasion for women's voluntary organizations to build their networks and announce their demands. The Arab Alliance of Women, an Egyptian organization headed by Hoda Badran, made a substantial effort to bring women's grassroots organizations in the provinces together with elitist organizations in Cairo, to jointly prepare the document for Beijing. But most of these efforts to build solidarity among women's organizations are related to specific occasions and international events, more than an ongoing campaign to recreate the "women's movement" of the Liberal Era (1923–52).

The contradictory socio-economic pressures of the last two decades negatively affected the creation of a national women's movement in Egypt. Islamists contributed to these contradictory pressures, as did feminist organizations, which ignored grassroots issues for a long time. The state, although adopting a pluralistic system, where civil society institutions enjoy a modicum of marginal freedoms, is not yet ready to accept the institutionalization of a women's movement.

Pressures from Islamists and conservative voices partially explain this situation. As an alternative, the government created the National Committee for Women, headed by the president's wife, which included women leaders, professional women, voluntary organization representatives, and some official figures. This semi-governmental body prioritized women's issues, influenced public policy making, and made some serious efforts to build a database related to women's issues, which have been broadly discussed in the Women National Conferences.

CONCLUSION

1. **From the nineteenth century to 1996, religion has been a primary factor in the birth and the development of women's philanthropy.** Islamic teachings and traditions, in particular *Zakat* and *Sadakat*, traditionally motivated Muslims to give and to volunteer. Also the Islamic practice, *Al Waqf* seems to be another organized tradition that has encouraged women's philanthropy. These teachings and practices were present before the nineteenth century, when philanthropy began to be institutionalized. What helped Muslim women to become active was Islam's recognition of their rights as a legal entity and recognition of women's economic independence. Other factors, such as the struggle against their seclusion and rigid explanations of Islam, the national struggle against the British occupation, the presence of foreign minorities in Egypt, education and communication with western culture also played a role.

   The role of religion was not always accompanied by positive results. Islamists contributed mainly to developing an Islamic discourse on women's issues, in particular concerning the contradiction between "public roles" and "private roles." These competing discourses about gender relations have often been rooted in efforts to sustain sexual hegemony and mixed with issues of political power.

   The state was another partner in shaping women's philanthropic role, and the "woman question" in general. Different positions were adopted in different eras, according to the state's vision concerning social and political stability.

   In brief the state, society, and Islam presented the three angles which contributed to the formulation and development of women's philanthropy.

2. **Secular feminists created the only discourse that insists upon the need for radical changes in gender relations.** Since the beginning of the twentieth century, they have used voluntary organizations as the main channels for building parallel power structures, particularly in the 1930s and the 1940s, when they lacked political rights.

3. **Although women's organizations, adopting "maternalist" programs,** constitute a high proportion of voluntary organizations in general, and although other indicators suggest substantial contributions — as members and on boards — in this field of activity, it wouldn't be wise in the case of Egypt to conclude that women made their greatest impact on policy-making agendas through maternalist campaigns. The state integrated the maternalist programs of voluntary organizations into its plans, and the state is the main

funding resource for these activities. Thus, the public policies in this field are in accordance with the "maternalist programs" of voluntary organizations.

Equally important is the recent establishment of independent advocacy organizations which are designed to influence the policy making process concerning reproductive rights of women, children's rights, the issue of street children, and the quality of health services, but it is too early to evaluate their impact.

4. **Women's organizations had a greater impact on policy making before independence** (1952) and the centralized Nasser regime. This study reveals that in the liberal era (1923–52), women made a substantial imprint on policy making. Their leaders participated on official committees addressing some of the main issues facing the nation at this time (i.e., drugs, women's education, privileges and exceptions enjoyed by foreign minorities, health services, etc.), and they succeeded in implementing part of their agenda.

   If we compare what women's organizations gained in this stage of the nation building, with what they gained in the 1970s and 1980s, we find that the strong "centralized" state introduced under Nasser offered women only marginal opportunities to influence state policies. The changes in the personal status law (in 1979) were mainly pushed by the president's wife, while the retreat of the state (in 1985) through passage of a new law according only minor benefits to women, was influenced by conservative opposition.

5. Another conclusion concerns **independence and the source of funds.** Women's organizations between 1923 and 1952 generally enjoyed greater independence, forming the Egyptian Women's Union, and engaging in advocacy as well as social welfare, trends due mainly to their economic independence. Thus, rich upper-class women established and/or funded their organizations, and they adopted other types of fundraising, such as income-generating activities and charity events. The public budget and/or foreign donations did not represent a substantial portion of their funds. In the 1980s and the 1990s, the main source of support shifted to public funding and/or foreign donations, an important factor influencing women's voluntary organizations agenda.

   Ironically, Egyptian women's organizations were not historically under-funded, receiving *Waqf, Zakat,* and *Sadakat* donations. This enabled them to pursue a mix of advocacy and social welfare activities. By the 1980s and the 1990s, donations tended to decrease after a long historical experience of depending on the state (1952–70). When

Egypt began to suffer an economic crisis, most of the voluntary organizations — including women's groups — became under-funded. The flow of foreign donations from international organizations and institutions seemed to be an open option to depend on. This foreign funding, particularly in the last few years, has placed a high priority to women's organizations and women's projects.

Now the challenge facing the non-profit sector in general and women's organizations in particular is related to the country's funding crisis and independence. Promoting the development of local funds is a critical task for women's organizations, as is the need to forge new types of collaboration within the private sector, and to motivate the upper classes to support women's organizations as they used to. Meeting these challenges will not be possible without increased solidarity among women's groups.

NOTES

1. Harb Al-Ghazali, "Esteqlal Al Mar'a Fi Al Islam" (The Independence of Women in Islam) (Cairo: Dar Al Mostaqbal, n.d.), 36–38.

2. Margo Badran, *Feminists, Islam and Nation* (Princeton, N.J.: Princeton University Press, 1995), 4.

3. Anwar Abdel Malik, "Nahedet Miser" (Egypt Renaissance) (Cairo: The Egyptian Public Organization for Books, 1983), 171.

4. Badran, *Feminists, Islam and Nation*, 5.

5. Ibid., 6.

6. Abdel Malik, "Nahedet Miser," 329.

7. Ibid., 335.

8. Al-Bayumi Ghanem, Ibrahim, "Al Awqaf Wa Al Siassa" (Al Waqf and Politics; Ph.D. thesis, Cairo University, 1997), 213–31.

9. Abdel Malik, "Nahedet Miser," 171.

10. Badran, *Feminists, Islam and Nation*, 14–15.

11. Margo Badran, "Competing Agendas: Feminists, Islam and the State in Nineteenth and Twentieth Century in Egypt," in Woman Deniz Kandiyoti, ed., *Islam and the State* (Philadelphia: Temple University Press, 1995), 204.

12. Ibid.

13. Badran, *Feminists, Islam, and Nation*, 17.

14. Ibid., 19.

15. Ibid., 23.

16. Doria Shafik, "Al Mar'a Al Masria" (Egyptian Woman) (Cairo: Dar El Ma'ref, 1995), 143.

17. Latifa Salem, "Al Mar'a Al Masria Wa Al Tahrir Al Egtema'ai" (Egyptian Women and Social Change 1919–1945) (Cairo: Egyptian Public Organization for Books, 1984), 52–53.

18. Badran, *Feminists, Islam and Nation*, 67.

19. Ibid., 80.

20. Badran, *Feminists, Islam and Nation,* 80–82.

21. Abdel Moneim Dessouki, "Al Game'a Al Masria Wa Al Mogtameh" (The Egyptian University and Society) (Cairo: Center for Political and Strategic Studies, 1982), 19.

22. Badran, "Competing Agendas," 208.

23. Salem, "Al Mar'a," 54.

24. Badran, *Feminists, Islam and Nation,* 125.

25. Ibid., 126.

26. Salem, "Al Mar'a," 55.

27. Ibid., 56–58.

28. Mohamed Shawki Zaki, "Al Ekhouan Al Moslimin Wa Al Mogatmeh Al Masri" (Muslim Brothers and Egyptian Society) (Cairo, 1952), 185.

29. Ibid., 188–89.

30. Zaynab Al Ghazali, "Ayam Fi Hayati" (Days in My Life) (Cairo: Dar El Sherouk, 1981), 25.

31. Ibid., 27.

32. Badran, "Competing Agendas," 212–13.

33. Inji Aflaton, "Nahno El Nesa'a Al Masriate" (We the Egyptian Women) (Cairo, 1949), 112.

34. Badran, "Competing Agendas," 214.

35. Mervat Hatem, "Egypt's Economic and Political Crisis and the Decline of State Feminism," *International Journal of Middle East Studies* (1995): 4.

36. Ibid. 5.

37. Amani Kandil, "Defining the Non-Profit Sector in Egypt," Working Paper No. 10 (Baltimore: Johns Hopkins Comparative Non-Profit Sector, Johns Hopkins University, 1993).

38. Badran, "Competing Agendas," 222–24.

39. Ibid., 222.

40. Radwan, Zaynab, *Zaherate Al Hijab Bain Banat Al Game'at* (The Phenomenon of Hijab Among University Students) (Cairo: National Center for Social Research, 1982), 15–16.

41. "Al Hokouk al Kanounia Lil Mar'a Al Masria" (The Legal Rights of Egyptian Women in Theory and practice) (Cairo: Communication Group for the Enhancement of the Status of Women in Egypt, 1992), 2.

42. Statistical Indicators in the Field of Social Care and Development, Cairo: Ministry of Social Affairs, 1996, 173–74.

43. Amani Kandil and Sarah Ben Nafis, "Al Gamiat Al Ahliya Fi Mist" (Voluntary Associations in Egypt) (Cairo: Center for Political and Strategic Studies, 1995), 60–61.

44. Amani Kandil, Advocacy Organizations in Egypt, Cairo: USAID Cairo Office, 1996.

45. Population and Development in Egypt, Cairo: The National Committee for Egyptian NGOs, 1994.

– 8 –

An Islamic Activist in Interwar Egypt

BETH BARON

Islamism has generally been presented as a male movement, with women only recently becoming adherents. Observers point to the proliferation of head scarves and attempts to offer new readings of religious texts as evidence of women's growing commitment to the Islamist cause. Some have even identified a trend of "Islamic feminism," although it clearly has roots much earlier in the century. Since Hasan al-Banna (1906–49) founded the Muslim Brothers in 1928, most Islamist writers and speakers have been men. Yet one of the central figures in the movement in its infancy — from the early 1920s until the Second World War — was an elite woman. Senior to al-Banna in years and sometimes his associate, Labiba Ahmad (1870s–1951) played a critical role in nurturing the younger generation that made the transformation from Islamic reform (Salafiyya) to Islamic radicalism (Islamism). The former was mostly a literary movement that claimed to be seeking a return to the practices of the early Muslims and had a limited circle of followers; the latter became a political movement with broad appeal.

Philanthropist, writer, traveller, and speaker, Labiba Ahmad used a variety of strategies to further the Islamic revival at the local, national, and international levels. She founded the Society of Egyptian Ladies' Awakening a year or so after the 1919 Egyptian Revolution to provide welfare services to the poor and to propagate a blend of Islam and nationalism or Islamic nationalism.[1] Shortly thereafter, she started the Arabic monthly *al-Nahda al-Nisa'iyya* (the Women's Awakening) to disseminate the views of the society. She made the pilgrimage to Mecca many times to build a network of contacts.

Labiba argued that the path to women's and national progress was through a return to Islam, not (as many argued) through copying West-

Reprinted by permission of Mazda Press from *Iran and Beyond: Essays in Middle Eastern History in Honor of Nikki R. Keddie,* edited by Rudi Matthee and Beth Baron (Costa Mesa, Calif.: Mazda Publishers, 2000).

ern ways. In this, she presents a distinct contrast to secular feminists in Egypt, who came from similar elite backgrounds but were oriented toward Paris and not Mecca. Hers would seem the minority voice with few echoes at the time. Yet Labiba had a wide following among professional classes; she struck a deep chord among male and female Egyptians identifying with Islam rather than the West and yearning for the re-Islamicization of society. This article examines her philanthropy, literary output, travels, and Islamist connections. Her story shows that women were not just objects of the Islamist discourse, but thinkers and activists in their own right, and critical participants during the formative years of the movement.

A PIONEER AND HER PHILANTHROPIC WORK

Labiba Ahmad was born in Cairo in the 1870s. Her father, Ahmad 'Abd al-Nabi Bey, was a doctor, and her two brothers followed in his footsteps. Her son and a daughter later chose the medical profession as well.[2] Yet the profession was closed to elite women in her lifetime. In the late nineteenth century, a well-to-do doctor may have had an al-Azhar shaykh tutor his children at home. Labiba had an excellent command of Arabic and a good knowledge of Islamic subjects; she also learned to play the piano.[3] Her husband, 'Uthman Pasha Murtadi (d. 1935), rose through the judiciary to the post of judge in the Mixed Court of Appeals in Alexandria and for a short time became master of ceremonies for Khedive 'Abbas Hilmi II (r. 1892–1914), to whom he was closely tied.[4]

Labiba had a son and five daughters.[5] Her son, Dr. Isma'il Bey, occasionally contributed pieces to her journal or was featured there. One daughter married 'Abd al-Sattar Bey al-Basil, a tribal *shaykh* from al-Fayyum (and husband of the late writer Malak Hifni Nasif). This unnamed daughter died in the "spring of youth" in 1929, much to her mother's grief, and her orphaned children were subsequently raised alongside those of Labiba's second daughter, Hayat Murtadi.[6] A third daughter, Malak, was noted for her Sufi attributes: nighttime praying and daytime fasts.[7] The last two daughters, Zaynab and Qamar, were the twin "babies" of the family. They probably both attended the Saniya Girls' School, a state institution popular with nationalists because its curriculum included Arabic and Islamic instruction. Together they joined a group of female students who in 1925 were sent by the Egyptian government to England. After three years of study, Zaynab was awarded a teacher-artist certificate by the Royal Drawing Society. While Zaynab "nurtured the spirit," Qamar "treated the body" and studied medicine. (Teaching and medicine were among those professions that Labiba approved for women.)[8] By the time she founded her society and launched its journal, Labiba Ahmad had already passed through the childbearing and rearing years. In pictures published in the 1920s, she appears to be in her forties or so. She wears glasses and has a serious, intellectual demeanor, a look enhanced by her black head covering and the dark robe she wears over her clothes. She has the air of a woman of strong commitment and determination.[9]

In the period before the First World War, Labiba had participated in women's associations, given speeches, and written in newspapers and journals.[10] A strong nationalist, she supported Mustafa Kamil's Watani (Nationalist) Party, founded in 1907 to work for the liberation of Egypt from de facto British control.[11] In 1919 she marched in the "ladies' demonstrations" and affixed her signature to the petitions submitted to foreign legations protesting British actions.[12] In the next few years, she worked to mobilize women and girls from working-class neighborhoods against the British occupation.[13] She presided over memorial services for Mustafa Kamil and spoke at the funeral of his brother, 'Ali Fahmi Kamil, also a Watani leader. At the same time, she had close ties to Safiya Zaghlul ("Mother of the Egyptians") and Sa'd Zaghlul, head of the Wafd (Delegation) founded in 1918 to negotiate with the British for Egypt's independence.[14]

Yet Labiba consciously chose not to join other female notables who after the 1919 Revolution formed the Women's Wafd Central Committee, an auxiliary of the Wafd Party.[15] Instead, she committed herself to philanthropy and education through the Society of Egyptian Ladies' Awakening. Organizations with similar names had been established in previous decades, and members often spoke of their work as a contribution to the national cause. These associations, in turn, opened new outlets for the talents of affluent women. After the war, the two best known philanthropies run by women — Mabarrat Muhammad 'Ali (the Muhammad 'Ali Charity) and Jam'iyyat al-Mar'a al-Jadida (the New Woman's Society) — focused on health care and training for the poor.[16]

Labiba wrote that in founding her society she had been "inspired by God" and motivated by the "desire to help the nation." Her philanthropic work and Islamic nationalist impulse were clearly linked. The goal of the society was "to raise girls and to teach them the commandments of their religion." She had a broad mission of inculcating young girls with Islamic values and a specific project for the society: she gathered together 170 girls who had been orphaned or abandoned by their parents and vowed to raise, protect, and provide for them.[17] Labiba presided over the society; other officers included a deputy, a secretary, and a secretary's assistant. Little is known about the officers or about the composition or size of the group.[18] Labiba headed delegations that visited schools, hosted graduation celebrations, and called on ministers. She proved to be the driving force behind the group: administering its affairs, raising funds, and taking responsibility for the girls in her care.

"The [Society of] Egyptian Ladies' Awakening saw that uplifting nations is by uplifting the mothers in it," Labiba wrote when announcing the founding of a workshop in July 1921 in which poor girls would be taught sewing and other skills so that they might later support themselves. She emphasized that the large workshop was in a healthy, well-lit, and airy space. The doors were opened to other girls to come to learn household management, embroidery, and handiwork; the society set a sliding fee scale.[19] Labiba appealed for donations of clothes and money for the girls she had promised to raise, twenty of whom were shown in a photograph appearing in the journal. The office of the workshop stood ready, she wrote, to accept volunteers willing to render "holy national service" by lecturing on morality and teaching the principles of housekeeping and handiwork. Support came in different forms: physicians (among them Labiba's son) examined poor women and children connected to the society free of charge; an administrator at a nearby girls' school offered to waive tuition for orphans from the society.[20]

In 1923 in the wake of the discovery of an Egyptian gang that apparently "debauched" young native girls — kidnapping, raping, and locking them in brothels in Cairo — Labiba resolved to broaden her educational program. "We all felt sorrow in our souls, a wound in our hearts, and pain in our core from that distressing affair," wrote Labiba. "It made an impression on me as it made an impression on many others. I resolved to dedicate what remained of my life in service to Egypt, and to sacrifice every valuable and dear thing for the sake of rescuing the Egyptian girl from the hands of those devils who abuse her." She decided to open a public institute and workshop together to train girls so that they could make an honorable living.[21] After searching for an appropriate site for the institute, Labiba reported that "God gave us success." The Society rented the palace of the late 'Abd al-Qadir Pasha Hilmi in the working-class neighborhood of Sayyida Zaynab and had it outfitted with the necessary equipment. Labiba prepared to receive up to one hundred girls from the age of nine. A picture taken on opening day in late 1923 shows approximately forty-two students gathered around the bench where Labiba, the director of the institute, sat in the midst of three other veiled women. The bareheaded girls appear a bit ragged, clustered together so that the faces of some do not even show. A photo taken a few months later in the same setting shows the girls arranged in straight rows, dressed in white uniforms, and now wearing white head scarves. (Similar white head scarves would become a symbol of the Islamist movement.) A new sign was painted for the occasion: The Institute and Workshop of the Women's Awakening.[22]

Labiba's actions won the praise of observers. "She does not limit herself to literary activity alone," noted Rose Haddad, a fellow journalist, announcing the opening of the institute, "but she also endeavors to promote social welfare in the country."[23] Labiba thanked the readers of *al-Nahda al-Nisa'iyya* profusely for supporting her effort to educate young girls. Earlier she had made an emotional appeal to "the sons of my country" to support the school in whatever way possible. To raise funds for the workshop, she offered a book for sale — a collection of pieces of wisdom, religious exhortation, and extracts from history as well as practical advice in health, housekeeping, and sport — which school inspectors helped her to distribute. Other students visited her school, a poet wrote a new song for the girls, and owners of businesses gave generously. In addition, the new Wafdist interior minister announced that his ministry would donate the proceeds of a special lottery toward the education of the girls of the institute and the workshop.[24]

The Society of Ladies' Awakening not only established its own private education ventures; it pressed for reforms in state education as well. Labiba headed a delegation that met with the minister of education to demand that religious education be made compulsory and that fees for girls be equivalent to those for boys. The society reiterated its call after the 1924 elections, pressuring the new Wafdist minister to comply. The latter decided to place the new primary school proposed by the governing body of the Institute and Workshop of the Women's Awakening under the supervision of his ministry. Labiba pressed for greater attention to religious education in state schools, emphasizing memorization of the Quran and the teaching of morality.[25] Her social welfare work inspired other Islamist initiatives, which proved to be important vehicles for winning adherents as well as supplying essential services.

DISSEMINATING THE MESSAGE

The Society of Egyptian Ladies' Awakening operated the orphanage, workshop, and institute on one track, a track of philanthropic enterprises dedicated to poor women and children. On a second track, the society sought to encourage Islamic revival in other layers of society. In the fall of 1921, Labiba approached the administrators of Cairo University for permission to hold meetings on their campus. They turned her down, but officials at the American University in Cairo offered her space. A large assembly of women gathered in the main hall for the first session in late November 1921. Readings from religious texts opened the meeting, followed by remarks by the founder-president, piano playing, poetry, and finally a lecture by Dr. 'Abd al-'Aziz Bey Nizami, author of many books on family health.[26] Members of the society planned to convene weekly to hear in-depth lectures on scientific and religious topics.

The society continued to meet throughout the interwar years in order to spread its message about morality. Labiba held that the state should take the lead in curbing vices such as drinking, narcotics, and dancing. When the head of the Cairo City Police issued regulations limiting dancing and preventing dancers from sitting with the crowds in large halls, the group sent him a letter of commendation.[27] The Society issued a call for new members in the mid-1930s with a promise of new guidelines "propagating moral virtue." As they prepared for "a war against innovation, immorality, and corruption," they asked other women to embark with them in this bold step "in service of religion and humanity."[28]

The society won accolades from observers, even those who condemned other women's groups in Egypt for pursuing Egyptian women's interests abroad rather than at home (a lightly veiled attack on Huda Sha'rawi and her Egyptian Feminist Union).[29] The EFU was founded some two years after the Society of Egyptian Ladies' Awakening and had a secular orientation. Although Labiba, an honorary member of the union, occasionally praised Huda, her goals and that of the EFU clearly diverged.[30] The society's oath emphasized its moral values: "I swear that modesty will be my crown, and virtue my light, and I will live purely: a useful and devout wife, whose hand in childraising is superior. I will fulfill my rightful and correct duty, toward God, the homeland, the family...."[31] According to the society, every Egyptian girl and woman had to follow a special code of behavior: (1) to strive for the happiness of her household; (2) to maintain proper modesty in the street; (3) to wear traditional Egyptian dress and to cover her face, hands, and other body parts as stipulated by Islamic law; (4) to avoid theaters and comedy houses; and (5) to leave behind corrupt ancient customs.[32]

This cluster of suggestions was hardly new. The Society for Women's Progress, founded in 1908, and contributors to the conservative press had issued similar calls in the first two decades of the century.[33] These calls constituted an integral part of the program of Islamic reformers (Salafis), who ostensibly sought a return to the ways of the early Muslims while modernizing Islam. The reformers opposed folk customs that deviated from Islamic injunctions as well as the infiltration of Western practices into Egyptian society. But Labiba Ahmad injected a new element into this battle. She balanced words with actions, organizing and spreading the message to wider circles of Egyptians through the activities of her association and through her journal.

Labiba published the first issue of *al-Nahda al-Nisa'iyya* in July 1921. A monthly founded to publicize the society's positions, it ran for nearly two decades, the first journal founded by an Egyptian Muslim woman to enjoy such longevity. This record alone presents strong evidence of its positive reception. For the title, Labiba chose the phrase "the Women's Awakening," which had come to stand for the sense of dramatic trans-formation in Egyptian women's lives.[34] The mottos that appeared on the front page summarized her political philosophy that women's awaken-ing and national revival went hand-in-hand: "A people will not die so long as both sexes work together energetically toward a goal." And on the top and sides, in smaller type, the sayings, "If your women awaken, then your homelands will thrive"; and, "Men make nations; women make men."

No subject received more attention in Labiba's opening essays than that of education and the need for reform. As higher education for Egyptian women expanded during the interwar years, Labiba argued that women should enter fields such as medicine and teaching rather than law or lit-erature. "When will the people understand that the duty of a girl is to be a mother?"[35] She valued the role of teachers highly, commending some by name, and called for the opening of a school like Dar al-'Ulum (a male teacher-training college) for women. In general, she rallied for more reli-gious education: studying of the Quran more deeply, strengthening Arabic instruction, and boycotting foreign schools. She also appealed for more schools for the poor. Yet she critiqued a curriculum that trained boys and girls identically, preparing them for the same exams, when she saw them destined for different roles in life. Women lacked preparation for childrais-ing, their true vocation, and needed greater religious instruction to guide the family. She referred to the "influence of the virtuous in shaping the nation — and what is the nation if not a collection of families?"[36]

Labiba's essays also often attacked the presence of "un-Islamic" practices and Western influences in Egypt. She vehemently opposed le-galized prostitution, alcohol consumption, narcotics use, theater going, and gambling in Egypt. That the British occupation made it difficult or impossible to eliminate some of these practices only strengthened her na-tionalist convictions. She also condemned recreational activities such as mixed bathing at the beach and called on "morals police" to enforce sep-arate swimming hours for men and women. In opposition to the building of a sports complex for girls, she asked, "Isn't the woman capable of ex-ercising while she is at home . . . for in prayer and its movements are the greatest exercise."[37]

Labiba opened the pages of the journal to male and female authors, providing an outlet for others to express their views on Islamic revival at a time when few such forums existed. *Al-Nahda al-Nisa'iyya* enjoyed regular contributions from such figures as Muhammad Farid Wajdi, a prominent Salafi writer whose wife had earlier founded the Society of Women's Progress and who later edited al-Azhar's journal *Nur al-Islam* (Light of Islam, 1930), and 'Aisha 'Abd al-Rahman, who under the pen-name Bint al-Shati' (Daughter of the Coast) later became famous for her biographies of the early women of Islam and her Quranic exegesis.[38] The names of quite a few of those whose articles were published in Labiba's journal, particularly in the first decade, later appeared in the context of the Islamist movement and in particular in connection with the Muslim Brothers.

In a development that virtually guaranteed the financial security of the journal, Labiba received the backing of various Arab governments. The Egyptian and Sudanese Ministries of Education and Awqafs (Trusts) as well as the Egyptian Provincial Councils officially authorized the distribution of *al-Nahda al-Nisa'iyya* in their schools; the Iraqi Ministry of Education assigned the journal as a text; the Syrian government purchased block subscriptions; and the Saudis subscribed to a "large number" at the instructions of King 'Abd al-'Aziz Ibn Sa'ud.[39] Additionally, the journal received support from royal and wealthy donors, among them the kings of Egypt, Saudi Arabia, and Iraq.[40] Such support was unprecedented for an Egyptian women's journal and, indeed, rare for any periodical. It showed that Labiba had the backing of powerful personalities and politicians in high places. Yet it also showed that they did not find her message in any way threatening. To the contrary, her influential supporters may have seen this Islamic journal as a good antidote to the secular feminist literature of the day. The journal also had a circle of loyal readers who sent in letters of support.

Labiba Ahmad's activism took a new form when in the summer of 1933 she took to the airwaves. Once a week she went to the recording studio to deliver a regularly scheduled address on Royal Egyptian Radio. Readers, "who loved her and showered her with their affection and their encouragement," could tune in to listen. Radios were new to Egypt and probably existed mostly in the homes of the urban well-to-do and in coffee shops. Yet as they increasingly spread into towns and villages, they became a popular form of entertainment and instruction. Labiba's talks resembled her monthly column, treating moral, religious, and social themes.[41] 'Aisha 'Abd al-Rahman described Labiba during this period: "She barely stops or rests! She is all movement and activity and sanctifies work, dedicating her life to it. She does not understand the meaning of living if it is not for the sake of work. These long years that have passed with sorrow and suffering [a daughter had died in 1929] were unable to harm her love for work or to cause in her any amount of despair or resignation."[42]

VISITING HOLY CITIES

Through her social welfare work and writings, Labiba disseminated a brand of Islamic nationalism that countered the secular variety. But the combination of directing a complex of philanthropic operations and running a journal apparently exhausted Labiba, who fell ill in the fall of 1924. She suspended publication of *al-Nahda al-Nisa'iyya* after the October 1924 issue and did not resume production until March 1926.[43] After her recovery, she resolved to go on *hajj* making her sixth pilgrimage to the holy city of Mecca. Two years later, Labiba travelled to the Hijaz on a seventh *hajj* and thereafter went almost every year. By 1938, she had made sixteen pilgrimages, equaling the number of years she had published her journal.[44] These trips reinforced her Islamic outlook and enhanced her international reputation.

A journey incumbent upon Muslims once in their lifetime became an annual ritual for Labiba, who was drawn repeatedly to Arabia, she wrote, in an "attempt to satisfy the spirit."[45] Combining official business with her spiritual quest, her pilgrimages took on a familiar pattern over the years as the readers of her journal and her supporters vicariously undertook the journey with her. Prior to her departure, she announced her intention to travel and called on others to share the experience. Friends bid her farewell at home or at the train station, and *al-Nahda al-Nisa'iyya* published her photograph in celebration of her trip. She travelled with her daughter Malak or with other family members and friends.[46] After completing her duties in Mecca, she proceeded to Medina to visit the tomb of the Prophet Muhammad, and then took the opportunity to enjoy a summer or two in the mountain resort of Ta'if.[47] The Egyptian press reported her successful completion of the *hajj* upon her return, and Labiba received telegrams and letters congratulating her from numerous friends in Egypt, Syria, the Hijaz, Iraq, and as far away as Singapore. She thanked those who had assisted her during her travels — consuls, doctors, boat captains, engineers, and especially King Ibn Sa'ud, who had solidified his rule over Arabia in the 1920s and safeguarded the route.[48]

Labiba's pilgrimages gave her an opportunity to expand her circle of contacts. She nurtured ties with the Saudi King, who extended his hospitality to her and gave her journal a generous subvention. She met with shaykhs, government officials, professionals, and other pilgrims in a search for religious knowledge and political information. Others sought her out, giving receptions in her honor. She mingled with Muslims from different countries as she solicited essays and advertisers for her journal. She accomplished this in spite of the fact that Egypt had no official state relations with Saudi Arabia until 1936, when after the signing of the Anglo-Egyptian Treaty, they concluded a much celebrated agreement.[49]

Labiba's annual *hajj* enhanced her prestige, as Egyptians praised "al-Hajja" in poems and letters. But at the same time, they urged her "to return to your homeland to shine your light on the Nile Valley, which awaits your guiding hand, and to your children, who await your sympathy and affection."[50] While abroad or after returning, she wrote essays on the trip, sent her new acquaintances copies of the journal, and received letters and essays in return. She had a wide circle of correspondents that spread beyond the Arab world to India and East Asia.

Labiba also made a visitation to the third sacred city of Islam — Jerusalem — in the fall of 1930 in the company of al-Hajja Maryam al-Kabiyya, whom Labiba saw as the model of a determined mother and patriot and praised for her "strength of purpose." Maryam had apparently arrived in Egypt from her sub-Saharan home five years earlier so that her sons could be educated at al-Azhar. After they had completed their studies and before they returned home, their mother decided to take them on the *hajj* to Mecca and a visit to Jerusalem. A camera captured the group — Labiba, Maryam, and her three sons in ceremonial dress standing alongside two guards — at the Mosque of 'Umar (Dome of the Rock) in Jerusalem. Labiba also met such religious dignitaries as al-Sayyid Muhammad Amin al-Ansari, custodian of the Mosques of 'Umar and al-Aqsa, as well as the director of the Khalidiyya Library. After her return, the journal printed on its cover a picture of al-Sayyid Amin al-Husayni, the Mufti of Jerusalem and president of the Supreme Muslim Council, who had recently visited Cairo.[51] Throughout the 1930s, and in particular in the midst of the Arab Revolt of 1936, the journal showed sympathy to the cause of the Arabs of Palestine.

ISLAMIST CIRCLES

During her travels and at home, Labiba forged personal contacts with the other leading Islamic personalities of the day. She had reached that stage in her life in which she could hold discussions with unrelated men without raising eyebrows. She had particularly close ties to the leadership of the Society of Muslim Youth, founded in 1927 "to teach Islamic morals and ethics; to spread that knowledge best suited to the modern way of life; to discourage dissensions and abuses amongst the Muslims; and to make use of the best of Eastern and Western cultures and to reject all that is bad in them."[52] Many members were "alumni" of the Watani Party, to which Labiba was linked. These included Dr. 'Abd al-Hamid Bey Sa'id (first president), Shaykh 'Abd al-'Aziz Shawish (vice president), and the Syrian émigré Muhibb al-Din al-Khatib (secretary-general), whom Labiba called "my son" (he later edited *al-Nahda al-Nisa'iyya* and periodicals of the Muslim Brothers). Labiba reported on speeches given at the club, sometimes to female audiences, and covered a congress on education held in their hall in 1936 that was attended by over four thousand participants. When Labiba was invited to speak, she picked a male delegate to deliver her address. She also published the communiqué drafted by the assembled Islamic groups calling on the government to institute various reforms.[53]

By the 1930s, more of these Islamic organizations were open to men and women. Fatima Amin guided one such group, the Society for Memorizing the Noble Quran. At the opening of a charity bazaar to raise funds for their school for orphans and the poor, Fatima thanked journalists, especially "al-Hajja Labiba Ahmad," for supporting religious associations.[54] Labiba had a direct role in the blossoming of Islamic organizations in the late 1920s and 1930s, and she herself saw the rise of societies — Islamic Guidance, Noble Islamic Characteristics, and Memorizing the Noble Quran, as well as the Society of Muslim Youth — as the "results of our cries on the pages (of *al-Nahda*)."[55] In her journal, she had encouraged a new generation of religious thinkers and activists. She also had various links with different organizations and was instrumental in starting a few. In the mid-1930s, she founded the League of Islamic Awakening (*Rabitat al-Nahda al-Islamiyya*), inviting men and women to join in a venture that strove for moral revival. Notices in the press announced that the league gathered every Friday evening to hear lectures on a variety of topics. A delegation from the league met with Hasan al-Banna, who spoke at the opening session. There he delivered Labiba Ahmad's recommendations, urging listeners to develop noble traits of character, virtuous actions, and devotion to the true religion, Islam.[56]

Al-Banna is credited with launching the Islamist movement, yet it is often presumed that this was done on his own and against great odds. Placed in a line of earlier reformers like Labiba Ahmad, he can better be seen as adding youthful vigor and energy to a revival already underway. He was only sixteen when he moved in 1923 from a small town in the Delta to Cairo to commence a three-year course of study at Dar al-'Ulum. Increasingly concerned about the gap between Muslims and their faith, he sought the counsels of elders. These included Labiba's associates Muhammad Farid Wajdi, whose house was a center for Muslim scholars and intellectuals, and Muhibb al-Din al-Khatib, director of the Salafiyya book store that al-Banna frequented. He also met with another Syrian, Rashid Rida (editor of *al-Manar*), although the latter probably had cool relations with Labiba due to his earlier fight with the Egyptian nationalist Mustafa Kamil.[57]

Al-Banna took up a teaching post in the Suez Canal town of Isma'il-iyya in 1927 and in March of the following year founded the Society of the Muslim Brothers.[58] The Salafi thinkers he so admired were of an older generation and had focused on disseminating their views prin-ciply through their writings. Al-Banna preferred direct contact and preached to groups of Muslims in a variety of venues, including cof-fee shops, homes, mosques, and the streets. Fueled by young men who were motivated like al-Banna, the new organization aimed to counter the secularizing trends dominating Egyptian society and to spread Is-lamic teaching in their stead. In this it shared goals with the Society for Ladies' Awakening and the Society of Muslim Youth. Yet the Mus-lim Brothers quickly became distinguished from other Islamic groups by its ability to recruit large numbers of followers. Hasan al-Banna built a base in Isma'iliyya and branches in other provincial towns and cities. Transferred to Cairo in 1932, he merged his group with one started by a younger brother and continued to organize from the capital.[59]

In May 1932, a small photo of a young man wearing a fez, suit, and tie (the proper attire of an Egyptian school teacher) appeared in the upper right-hand corner of the picture of the sculpture "Egypt's Awakening" that regularly appeared on the cover of *al-Nahda al-Nisa'iyya*. The man is bearded, a sign of Islamic piety, and his eyes have the piercing look of a man with a mission. The likeness, which appeared several times thereafter, is very possibly than that of Hasan al-Banna, who at the time was only twenty-six. Earlier, a speech of al-Banna's before the Society of Muslim Youth had been reprinted in the journal. The appearance of al-Banna's picture on the cover may suggest that Labiba saw him as a figure capable of guiding Egypt's religious revival and may signal her involvement in his organization. In time, the Muslim Brothers came to rival the Wafd Party in popularity. Their success was due to the com-bination of al-Banna's magnetism, rhetorical skills, and organizational abilities, as well as the readiness of young, urban Egyptians to respond to such a message.[60]

Early on Hasan al-Banna recognized the centrality of women to his movement. In Isma'iliyya he created a school to teach girls — future mothers who would shape their childrens' characters — about religion. The "Institute for Mothers of the Believers" developed around 1932 into the first branch of the Muslim Sisters, which was composed mostly of female relatives of Brothers.[61] A larger branch with the same name was subsequently founded in Cairo, and headed, according to some accounts, by Labiba Ahmad.[62] It was possibly in this context that Labiba printed Hasan al-Banna's photograph on the cover of her journal.

The recruitment of women and building of a women's section, however, met with resistance by male members of the Muslim Brothers in spite of support from the highest quarters. Women continued, therefore, to form separate organizations, which were announced on the pages of *al-Nahda al-Nisa'iyya*. One such organization was the Muslim Ladies' Association founded in 1937 by Zaynab al-Ghazali (b. 1917), a young woman who had recently resigned from the Egyptian Feminist Union. Membership lists of the group reveal a preponderance of younger women, such as Widad Sadiq 'Anbar, the group's secretary and a contributor to *al-Nahda al-Nisa'iyya*, and Na'ima Murtadi, Labiba's granddaughter.[63] These women were thus figuratively and sometimes quite literally the descendants of Labiba Ahmad, and the group followed the line she had set. The members sought to familiarize Muslim women with their religion, through which they would find emancipation. Their goal was to "purify society in general and Muslim women in particular from the filth shaking their convictions and to fight passion and disgraceful abominations...."[64] Like Labiba's Society of Ladies' Awakening, the group maintained an orphanage and helped poor families in an effort to disseminate its call.

Zaynab al-Ghazali later became the most important and best-known female Islamist figure in Egypt, but her debt to Labiba Ahmad has rarely been recognized. Some time after Zaynab founded her Muslim Ladies' Association, Hasan al-Banna urged her to fold her association into his, arguing that Muslims must be unified and differences of opinion eradicated. He suggested that she head the centralized women's section of the Muslim Brothers that he was creating. Her group turned down his offer, and she opted for a looser cooperation instead. She changed her mind only in 1948 when the Muslim Brothers came under attack, and she pledged allegiance to al-Banna; at that time, however, he asked her to keep her group separate for strategic reasons.[65] She subsequently became an active member of the Muslim Brothers and was among those arrested in 1965 in the wake of an apparent Islamist conspiracy to assassinate Gamal 'Abd al-Nasir. After her release in 1971, she composed the prison memoir *Ayyam min Hayati* (Days of My Life, 1977), which has been reprinted more than ten times in Arabic and has been translated into English, Persian, and Turkish.[66]

The Muslim Sisters (the group inside the Muslim Brothers) only took off in 1944 when a group of women determined to organize anew. They formed a central leadership made up of twelve members renewed annually and under the directorship of Hasan al-Banna, who named a liaison between his office and the women, and they established a headquarters in Cairo. The Muslim Sisters adopted as their sign a white head scarf like that worn by students in Labiba Ahmad's schools, instead of the black one that had often been associated with grief and mourning. Members taught at special schools for "mothers of the believers," worked in medical facilities, and propagated their message wherever they could. To these Sisters, true emancipation for women would come only with a knowledge of their religion. Branches quickly spread throughout Egypt and within four years they numbered fifty as membership reached five thousand.[67] The Muslim Sisters helped the society develop their ideas about women and the family and played a crucial role in sustaining the families of those Brothers imprisoned from 1948 to 1950 when the society was banned.[68]

The number of female members paled in comparison to the approximately one-half million men enlisted in the Muslim Brothers in 1948, leading one knowledgeable observer of the organization to claim that it failed to capture the imagination of young Egyptian women. A male member suggested that women resisted the call to Islam, for they associated it with a "return to the *harim*" rather than the path to "true female emancipation."[69] Yet considering that the fifty branches and five thousand members reflected less than four years of organizing, and that women simply did not mobilize in mass for any party or organization in the 1940s, the numbers prove significant. Moreover, they should be compared with female membership in secular organizations rather than just male membership in the Muslim Brothers. Adding the number of Muslim Sisters to members of the Muslim Ladies' Association (which Zaynab al-Ghazali claimed had 118 or 119 branches), points to the success of Islamist organizations in mobilizing women in this period.[70] The Egyptian Feminist Union never claimed close to even a thousand members. Indeed, its aging leadership and lack of a general following pushed younger women such as Doria Shafik to found their own feminist associations. Younger women were also attracted to communist organizations in the 1940s, but again not nearly on the scale of those attracted to the Islamist groups.[71]

Labiba Ahmad's own role in the Muslim Sisters remains unclear. When the first branches were founded in the 1930s, she was probably a woman in her late fifties or early sixties. Her presidency of the Cairo branch may have been an honorary position in acknowledgement of her pioneering work throughout the years, her commitment to the Islamic cause, and her seniority. When the Muslim Sisters became more active in the 1940s, she would have been in her seventies. By then, the keeper of the flame, who had stoked the fire in a period when it had grown faint, had passed the torch to a new generation. This new generation of Islamists, which could have been her children or grandchildren, pushed the movement in a more militant direction. They spoke increasingly not only of an Islamic society, but of an Islamic state and the restoration of Islamic law.

CONCLUSION

When Labiba returned from the *hajj* in 1937, she went through her papers and began to prepare her memoirs. "Life is made of memory and hope: memory of the past and hope for the future," she wrote in the introduction. "It was among my greatest hopes to serve my homeland (*watani*), my community (*ummati*), and the daughters of my sex by producing the journal *al-Nahda al-Nisa'iyya*, which I founded sixteen years ago and persisted in publishing all this time without interruption, praise God." As a result of working on the journal, she explained, she had corresponded with kings, ministers, politicians, and clerics; and she arranged this correspondence chronologically and by region in her memoirs. The earliest letters had come from King Ibn Sa'ud, and with these she placed other correspondence from the Hijaz. Next followed a letter from Mustafa Kemal Ataturk, Turkey's nationalist hero and first president (whom she had watched closely before he abolished the caliphate in 1924); notes and telegrams from the staff of the Egyptian royal family; and letters from Sa'd Zaghlul and other Egyptian politicians. Finally, she ended with letters from "the dear ones and people of virtue," religious scholars and thinkers. With her typical modesty, she presented the collection as a testimony of the sympathy of those mentioned for her "small service." She placed and dated the memoirs Cairo 1356, and identified herself as she had throughout the years — as the founder of the Society for Ladies' Awakening. In this way, she created a testament to decades of activism.[72]

The last issue of *al-Nahda al-Nisa'iyya* appeared in 1939.[73] Two other long-running Arabic women's journals (*al-Mar'a al-Misriyya* and *Fatat al-Sharq*) also folded on the eve of the Second World War, signalling the end of an era in the Egyptian women's press. By then Labiba, who had recently undergone surgery, was ready to retire.[74] In her final years she withdrew into ritual and prayer. Perhaps she heard about the detention of Islamists during the war and the troubles of the Muslim Brothers after it: the assassination of Prime Minister Mahmud al-Nuqrashi by a member of the Society in 1948, the subsequent banning of the Brothers, the murder of Hasan al-Banna in 1949 by government agents, and the imprisonment of numerous members. She may even have heard that the Muslim Brothers expected a lifting of the ban after the Wafd swept elections in early January 1951. Labiba died later that month at the age of about eighty. She left behind four children, six grandchildren, and numerous nieces and nephews. The obituary notices in the daily press specified that there would be no public mourning for women or place for them in the funeral procession, practices that Labiba had probably condemned.[75]

Labiba Ahmad's life parallels that of the Islamist Zaynab al-Ghazali in many ways: both founded Muslim women's associations, both started journals, both went on the *hajj* numerous times, and both envisioned women's progress in Islamic terms. Yet their lives also differed in important ways, reflecting their situations, their dispositions, and the times in which they lived. Labiba started her activism after having raised six children, a second career of sorts. Zaynab, who was forty or so years younger, married twice but never had children (considering this "a great blessing"[76]) and became an activist in her youth. Labiba dedicated herself to social welfare and moral reform; Zaynab asserted that she was political "by nature" and her goal was the realization of an Islamic state. Labiba fused religious revivalism with nationalism, struggling against British colonialism and the infiltration of Western practices into Egyptian society; Zaynab rejected territorial nationalism, aligned herself with the Islamic *umma,* and fought the post-1952 military regime in Egypt.[77] Labiba may have disapproved of the militant direction taken by Zaynab and her associates; for Labiba's politics were the politics of female notables, of gentlewomen and a gentler time, when different rules prevailed.

Labiba Ahmad came out of the same context as contemporary female activists of the interwar years, having participated in the women's associations of the prewar years and the 1919 Revolution. Her circles were similar as she had contacts with nationalist leaders, ministers, and kings. Moreover, she shared with other female notables conceptions about her role in society as the daughter of a bey and the wife of a pasha: her right to speak on behalf of Egyptians and her obligation to help improve society. Yet Labiba's vision of society differed from that of many of her contemporaries. Unlike those who eyed Europe for answers, Labiba looked to Islam for solutions to society's ills. She propagated her message widely in Egypt and abroad by founding associations, publishing in Arabic, travelling throughout the region, and speaking on the radio and in front of gatherings. She combined literary activity with philanthropy, bringing her message to the poor through the institutions she sponsored in the working-class quarters of Sayyida Zaynab and elsewhere.

Islamism in Egypt sprang from fertile soil, and Islamic activists such as Labiba Ahmad played an important role in preparing the ground by forming a bridge from Islamic reform to radicalism. Perhaps it is not so surprising that at the roots of Islamism one finds a woman advocating a religious path to women's and national progress. Labiba sought a way that had resonance and meaning in her society. And gender issues — family relations, male-female segregation, sexuality — lay at the heart of Islamist ideology and practice.

NOTES

1. On Islamic nationalism see Israel Gershoni and James P. Jankowski, *Redefining the Egyptian Nation, 1930–1945* (Cambridge: Cambridge University Press, 1995), 79–96. Labiba Ahmad anticipated the nationalists discussed there in propagating this sort of synthesis.

2. Khayr al-Din al-Zirikli, *al-'Alam: Qamus Tarajim* (Beirut, 1986, 7th ed.), 5:240; *al-Ahram* (January 31, 1951): 7.

3. *Al-Nahda al-Nisa'iyya* (henceforth *NN*) 1, no. 6 (January 1922): 159.

4. Maged M. Farag, *1952, The Last Protocol (Royal Albums of Egypt)* (Cairo: Max Group, 1996), 39; *The Memoirs and Diaries of Muhammad Farid, An Egyptian Nationalist Leader (1868–1919)*, trans. Arthur Goldschmidt, Jr. (San Francisco: Edwin Mellen, 1992), 121.

5. *NN* 8, no. 89 (May 1930): 145–46.

6. See eulogy in *al-Mar'a al-Misriyya* 10 (November 1929): 389; *NN* 7, no. 83 (November 1929): 387.

7. *NN* 14, no. 3 (March 1936): 83–85, 96; *NN* 14, no. 4 (April 1936): 111; *NN* 14, no. 9 (September 1936): 390.

8. *NN* 4, no. 42 (May 1926): 187; *NN* 6, no. 62 (February 1928): 56; *NN* 6, no. 9 (September 1928): 308; *NN* 6, no. 11 (November 1928): 390; *NN* 7, no. 78 (June 1929): 181–83; *NN* 16, no. 2 (February 1938): 55.

9. See *NN* 3, no. 12 (July 1924): cover; *NN* 4, no. 43 (June 1926): 227.

10. *NN* 3, no. 11 (June 1924): 386.

11. For background on the party, see Arthur Goldschmidt, Jr. "The Egyptian Nationalist Party: 1892–1919," in *Political and Social Change in Modern Egypt* (London: Oxford University Press, 1968), 308–33.

12. U.S. National Archives, State Department (SD) 883.00/135, Ladies of Egypt to the Diplomatic Agent and Consul-General of the U.S., Cairo, March 20, 1919.

13. Ijlal Khalifa, *al-Haraka al-Nisa'iyya al-Haditha* (Cairo, 1974), 60. Khalifa interviewed Labiba Ahmad's daughter Zaynab 'Abduh as well as some Cairene housewives and students from that period.

14. *Al-Lata'if al-Musawwara* (March 1, 1920): 5; SD 883.00/431, enclosure: "Cairo's Goodbye to Madame Zaghlul: A Monster Demonstration," *Egyptian Mail* (October 9, 1922); *NN* 2, no. 4 (November 1922): 109; *NN* 4, no. 48 (November 1926): 419.

15. On female notables as political actors, see Beth Baron, "The Politics of Female Notables in Postwar Egypt," in *Borderlines: Genders and Identities in War and Peace, 1870–1930,* ed. Billie Melman (New York: Routledge, 1998), 329–50.

16. Beth Baron, *The Women's Awakening in Egypt: Culture, Society, and the Press* (New Haven: Yale University Press, 1994), 169–75; see also Margot Badran, *Feminists, Islam, and Nation: Gender and the Making of Modern Egypt* (Princeton: Princeton University Press, 1995), chap. 6; Afaf Lutfi al-Sayyid Marsot, "The Revolutionary Gentlewomen in Egypt," *Women in the Muslim World,* ed. Lois Beck and Nikki Keddie (Cambridge, Mass.: Harvard University Press, 1978), 261–76.

17. *NN* 1, no. 1 (July 1921): 3; *NN* 1, no. 12 (July 1922): 378.

18. *NN* 1, no. 5 (December 1921): 129.

19. *NN* 1, no. 1 (July 1921): 28.

20. *NN* 1, no. 1 (July 1921): 17; *NN* 1, no. 2 (September 1921): 32, 56; *NN* 1, no. 3 (October 1921): facing p. 68; *NN* 1, no. 5 (December 1921): 129; *NN* 5, no. 50 (February 1927): 67.

21. *NN* 3, no. 6 (January 1924): 209. See Great Britain, Public Records, Foreign Office 141/466/1415–26, Eastern Department to Chancery, London, January 31, 1924; Hughes to Baker, Cairo, March 3, 1924.

22. *NN* 3, no. 5 (December 1923); *NN* 3, no. 7 (February 1924): 252; *NN* 3, no. 9 (April 1924): 316.

23. *Majallat al-Sayyidat wa'l-Rijal* 5, no. 1 (November 15, 1923): 306.

24. *NN* 3, no. 11 (June 1924): 387; *NN* 3, no. 10 (May 1924): 343; *NN* 3, no. 12 (July 1924): 427; *NN* 3, no. 12 (July 1924): 419.

25. *NN* 3, no. 5 (December 1923): 156; *NN* 3, no. 11 (June 1924): 395; *NN* 4, no. 39 (October 1924): 103; *NN* 2, no. 10 (May 1923): 253–54.

26. *NN* 1, no. 2 (September 1921): 55; *NN* 1, no. 5 (December 1921): 135; *NN* 1, no. 6 (January 1922): 159.

27. *NN* 11, no. 12 (December 1933): 386.

28. *NN* 12, no. 2 (February 1934): back page; no. 4 (April 1934): back page.

29. See *NN* 4, no. 48 (November 1926): 399–401.

30. Badran, *Feminists,* 96.

31. *NN* 1, no. 1 (July 1921): 3.

32. *NN* 1, no. 2 (September 1921): 35.

33. Baron, *Women's Awakening,* 28–29, 32–34, 176–79.

34. See Baron, *Women's Awakening.*

35. *NN* 12, no. 10 (October 1934): 326.

36. *NN* 1, no. 10 (May 1922): 260.

37. *NN* 9, no. 77 (August 1931): 255.

38. *NN* 6, no. 10 (October 1928): 347; *NN* 11, no. 3 (March 1933): 95; Joseph T. Zeidan, *Arab Women Novelists: The Formative Years and Beyond* (Albany: State University of New York Press, 1995), 79–80; Issa J. Boullata, "Modern Qur'an Exegesis: A Study of Bint al-Shati's Method," *Muslims World* 64 (1974): 103–13.

39. *NN* 2, no. 5 (December 1922): 136; *NN* 3, no. 2 (September 1923): back page; *NN* 8, no. 92 (August 1930): back page; *NN* 11, no. 8–9 (August 1933): 277; *NN* 12, no. 5 (May 1934): back page.

40. *NN* 6, no. 10 (October 1928): 346; *NN* 8, no. 86 (February 1930): 62; *NN* 8,

no. 86 (February 1930): 63; *NN* 12, no. 3 (March 1934): 101; *NN* 16, no. 1 (January 1938): 2.

41. *NN* 11, no. 8–9 (August 1933): 310.

42. *NN* 11, no. 3 (March 1933): 95.

43. *NN* 4, no. 40 (March 1926): 136.

44. *NN* 4, no. 43 (June 1926): 227; *NN* 6, no. 6 (June 1928): 202; *NN* 8, no. 89 (May 1930): cover; *NN* 10, no. 85 (April 1932): 127; *NN* 11, no. 3 (March 1933): cover; *NN* 12, no. 2 (February 1934): back page; *NN* 12, no. 5 (May 1934): back page; *NN* 14, no. 3 (March 1936): 86.

45. *NN* 16, no. 2 (February 1938): 65.

46. *NN* 8, no. 89 (May 1930): 146.

47. *NN* 12, no. 5 (May 1934): back page; *NN* 12, no. 7 (July 1934): 237; *NN* 14, no. 5 (May 1936): 175.

48. *NN* 6, no. 5 (May 1928): 176; *NN* 6, no. 8 (August 1928): 278; *NN* 6, no. 9 (September 1928): 315; *NN* 6, no. 10 (October 1928): 357; *NN* 8, no. 88 (April 1930): 142; *NN* 8, no. 91 (July 1930): cover; *NN* 8, no. 92 (August 1930): 283–84; *NN* 10, no. 84 (March 1932): 102; *NN* 10, no. 84 (March 1932): 107; *NN* 10, no. 12 (December 1932): 429; *NN* 14, no. 4 (April 1936): 135.

49. *NN* 4, no. 45 (August 1926): 287–90; *NN* 8, no. 91 (July 1930): 15; *NN* 8, no. 92 (August 1930): 259; *NN* 9, no. 75 (June 1931): 206; *NN* 10, no. 11 (November 1932): 365–67; *NN* 14, no. 12 (December 1936): 397–98.

50. *NN* 8, no. 92 (August 1930): 283–84.

51. *NN* 8, no. 94 (October 1930): 353; *NN* 8, no. 95 (November 1930): cover, 361–62, photo, 372, 386.

52. J. Heyworth-Dunne, *Religious and Political Trends in Modern Egypt* (Washington, D.C.: Newr and Middle East Monographs, 1950), 13.

53. Heyworth-Dunne, *Religious and Political Trends*, 11–14; correspondence from Arthur Goldschmidt, Jr. May 23, 1997; *NN* 9, no. 72 (March 1931): 86; *NN* 14, no. 8 (August 1936): 253–55, 262–63, 269–72; *NN* 14, no. 9 (September 1936): 390.

54. *NN* 11, no. 8, 9 (August 1933): 302; *NN* 14, no. 7 (July 1936): 250; *NN* 16, no. 9 (September 1938): 291.

55. *NN* 10, no. 12 (December 1932): 398.

56. *NN* 12, no. 3 (March 1934): 92, 98; no. 4 (April 1934): 114.

57. Hasan al-Banna, *Memoirs of Hasan al Banna Shaheed*, trans. M. N. Shaikh (Karachi: International Islamic Publishers, 1981), 121–22.

58. Richard P. Mitchell, *The Society of the Muslim Brothers* (Oxford: Oxford University Press, 1969; repr. 1993), 1–8.

59. Mitchell, *Muslim Brothers*, 9–11.

60. *NN* 10, no. 86 (May 1932): cover, and in subsequent issues; *NN* 9, no. 74 (May 1931): 148. Compare insert to photo of Banna in *Five Tracts of Hasan Al-Banna (1906–1949)*, trans. Charles Wendell (Berkeley: University of California Press, 1978).

61. Al-Banna, *Memoirs*, 189; Muhammad Shawqi Zaki, *al-Ikhwan al-Muslimun wa'l-Mujtama' al-Misri* (Cairo, 2d ed., 1980), 193; Mitchell, 175.

62. Amal al-Subki, *al-Haraka al-Nisa'iyya fi Misr, 1919–1952* (Cairo, 1986), 118. Subki's notes seem to have been misnumbered. If this is the case, another note may be more instructive: she may have found evidence that Labiba Ahmad

headed the Cairo branch in the legal files compiled for the trial of the assassins of Mahmud al-Nuqrashi dated December 28, 1948. These are stored at the High Court (p. 135, n. 36). Talhami draws almost exclusively on al-Subki for her account of Labiba Ahmad's activities in Ghada Hashem Talhami, *The Mobilization of Muslim Women in Egypt* (Gainesville: University of Florida Press, 1996), 46–49.

63. Zaynab al-Ghazali, *al-Da'iya Zaynab al-Ghazali* (Cairo, 1989), 196–97, 200, 218.

64. Al-Ghazali, *Da'iya,* 196–97; *NN* 16, no. 9 (September 1938): 317.

65. Interview by Ibn al-Hashimi with Zaynab al-Ghazali in *al-Da'iya* (Cairo, 1989), 17–23; Valerie J. Hoffman, "An Islamic Activist: Zaynab al-Ghazali," excerpts from a 1981 interview and translations from Ghazali's *Ayyam min Hayati* in *Women and the Family in the Middle East,* ed. Elizabeth Warnock Fernea (Austin: University of Texas Press, 1985): 234–41; al-Ghazali, *Ayyam min Hayati* (Cairo, 1988, 10th ed.), 23; for a full translation of the book, see Zainab al-Ghazali, *Return of the Pharaoh: Memoir in Nasir's Prison,* trans. Mokrane Guezzou (Leicester: Islamic Foundation, 1994).

66. Al-Ghazali, *Da'iya,* 227–31; Miriam Cooke, "Zaynab al-Ghazali: Saint or Subversive?" in *Die Welt des Islams* 34 (1994): 1–20; and idem, "*Ayyam min Hayati:* The Prison Memoirs of a Muslim Sister," in *Journal of Arabic Literature* 26, nos.1–2 (March–June 1995): 147–64.

67. Muhammad Shawqi Zaki, *al-Ikhwan al-Muslimin wa'l-Mujtami'a al-Misri* (Cairo, 2d ed., 1980), 193–235; al-Subki, *al-Haraka al-Nisa'iyya,* 117–19; Mitchell, *Society of the Muslim Brothers,* 175, 288.

68. Mitchell, *Muslim Brothers,* 175.

69. Mitchell, *Muslim Brothers,* quote p. 175, 328.

70. Al-Ghazali, *al-Da'iya,* 18.

71. Cynthia Nelson, *Doria Shafik, Egyptian Feminist* (Gainesville: University of Florida Press, 1996); Selma Botman, "The Experience of Women in the Egyptian Communist Movement, 1939–1954," *Women's Studies International Forum* 2, no. 5 (1988): 117–26.

72. *NN* 16, no. 2 (February 1938): 65. The memoirs, which I have not seen, are described as a collection of correspondence rather than an autobiography.

73. I have not seen issues of *NN* from that year. In 1938 the Ministry of Education instructed school supervisors that it would no longer purchase blocks of subscriptions and that they should subscribe themselves. This no doubt hurt the circulation of journals that had been used in schools. (*NN* 16, no. 1 (January 1938): notice in front of issue).

74. *NN* 16, no. 11 (November 1938): 361–62.

75. Al-Zirikli, *al-'Alam,* 240; *al-Ahram* (January 31, 1951): 7; *al-Misr* (January 31, 1951): 7.

76. Valerie J. Hoffman, "Muslim Fundamentalists: Psychosocial Profiles," in *The Fundamentalism Project,* vol. 4: *Fundamentalisms Comprehended,* ed. Martin E. Marty and R. Scott Appleby (Chicago: University of Chicago Press, 1995), 5:216.

77. Al-Ghazali, *al-Da'iya,* 19.

– 9 –

Women and Philanthropy
in Palestinian and Egyptian Societies:
The Contributions of Islamic Thought
and the Strategy of National Survival

GHADA HASHEM TALHAMI

Arab societies provide a variety of models for the study of women and philanthropy. Although it has been customary to emphasize the role of religion in shaping women's roles in the Arab Middle East, the most instructive lessons are to be found in secular societies. Islam dominates the culture and social expectations of most people of the Middle East, but Islam was not always the unchallenged philosophy of life. Moreover, the impact of Islam varies greatly from one country to another due to the succession of contrasting political ideologies such as liberalism, authoritarianism, socialism, and Islamic fundamentalism. Often, Islam took a back seat to more popular ideologies, such as Arab nationalism. Indeed, the present-day ascendancy of Islam as the political ideology of mass appeal camouflages recent periods of secular nationalism. Thus, it would be difficult to avoid the conclusion that the primordial influence of Islam was often modified by powerful currents emanating from the quest for a strategy of national survival.

Islamic influences, however, shaped the lives of women more than any other sector in society. Even when challenged by secular currents, the radius of Islamic influence invariably encompassed family and gender relations. There are historical reasons for this observation, such as colonialism, which banished the Shari'a, or canon law, from every area of life except family relations. Fatimah Mernissi, Moroccan feminist and scholar, has concluded that this aspect of the colonial legacy resulted from the cynical neglect of Western colonial powers, which did not hesitate to reform the Islamic penal and commercial laws but stopped short of confronting personal status law.[1] The Islamic patriarchy was, therefore,

245

strengthened by the transforming colonial experience. But in the case of the Palestinians, the patriarchal family institution succumbed to later pressures due to the threat of national annihilation posed by such forces as Zionist settlement in Palestine and the sectarian onslaught against Palestinian refugee camps in Lebanon. The family unit, as the last surviving indigenous institution in Palestinian society, became the target of secular nationalist attention. The transformed family institution was finally able to transcend the inertia imposed upon it by colonial strategies of selective modernization and change.

The Palestinian experience, thus, presents the clearest case of gender mobilization by nationalist and revolutionary forces. This was a case of gender activation in the interest of national survival, a cause which religious forces were incapable of contesting. Egypt's case, on the other hand, illustrates the Islamic capacity for gender mobilization in the interest of a total transformation of society. Ever since the 1930s, Egypt's Islamic forces entered the political arena in order to establish an Islamic state. Islamic attitudes toward gender, economic equity, the family institution, the guardianship and socialization of children, and the state's responsibility for the preservation of the national culture underwent extensive redefinition. Since the greatest Islamic critique of the secular state centered around the absence of economic equality, Islamic mobilization often entailed addressing the community's economic needs. The modern Islamic movement in Egypt, both in the 1930s and the 1970s, sought to alleviate the economic deprivation of males and females as a demonstration of the Islamic commitment to egalitarian principles. Whether or not this mobilization led to the empowerment of women is questionable. Similarly, whether the secular and national gender activation of Palestinian women will ultimately lead to autonomy and empowerment is still debatable.

ISLAM'S TOLERANCE OF WOMEN'S PUBLIC ROLES

Muslim female activists have long concluded that even though reforming the Shari'a may be difficult, a liberal interpretation of the Islamic religious code is possible. Muslims were always able to choose between four schools of Islamic jurisprudence which differed in their interpretation of the Qur'an and *hadith* (statements by the Prophet Muhammad). Moreover, efforts of Muslim male reformers in the past succeeded in disestablishing the restrictive and conservative Hanafi school of law in favor of the more expansive and tolerant Maliki school. This effort, which began in Egypt around the turn of the century, was led by the famed Muslim reformer Muhammad 'Abduh and was later emulated by the personal status laws of other Arab countries. These reforms, which improved women's material compensation in the case of divorce, were the beginning of a long effort stretching to the era of President Anwar Sadat.[2]

This tendency to maneuver within the four Islamic schools of jurisprudence and to rely on interpretive, rather than confrontational strategies, is fully appreciated by Palestinian women today. According to a Palestinian female lawyer, Muslim women often maximize their rights by publicizing specific portions of the religious texts which accord women clear and undeniable rights. Among these, the most important are women's right to own their own businesses, conduct business transactions, and own property in their own name.[3] The extension of specific economic rights to women was a natural consequence of the Qur'anic recognition of women as legal entities and as full members of the new spiritual community of Islam. Not only were women given the right to inherit, though half of the share of a brother, but they were the first among adherents of other religions to enjoy the right of disposal of their own wealth even after marriage.[4] Muhammad's allusion to women as "the sisters of men" was not empty rhetoric. Women's other rights, such as the freedom to choose a husband and to specify certain conditions in the marriage contract as protection against the threat of polygyny or summary divorce were later written in the laws.[5] The inspiration for these rights came from the Qur'an, which stipulated, among other things, that the principle of compatibility should always govern marital unions. The dowry should be paid to the woman, not her father, according to Islamic scholars. But in practice, local cultural customs, particularly where Bedouin customs survived, eroded and restricted women's Islamic rights.

Perhaps the most crucial aspect of the Islamic view of women is the religion's outlook on a woman's right to work and to education. The Islamic view of these crucial but contested rights, however, has often been influenced by the twin necessities of economic need and national survival. For example, Muhammad al-Ghazzali, one of Egypt's most prominent Islamic voices, was the strongest advocate of women's education and their right to leave their homes. In his view, women's education is not only necessitated by their role as the educators of children and the mainstay of the family, but also as the ideological emissaries to other women in the battle for Islamic ascendancy.[6]

The right to work was not an unqualified right in the Islamic view, but was constrained by the concept of *fitrah*, or woman's special nature. Since Islam implied that men and women are not equal but are destined for complementary roles, not all occupations are considered suitable for women. Only genteel occupations which minimized opportunities for mixing of the two sexes are permissible, such as teaching, medicine, nursing, social service, and writing and publishing.[7] Women are also encouraged to work in family-related endeavors, as joint partners with husbands, or in support of children of an absent or deceased father.[8]

Islamic advocates also object to female employment as an assertion of feminine autonomy and independence. The right to work is considered subject to approval by a woman's husband or father. Muslims often assert men's guardianship over women, which they do not consider as an elevated status but a serious male obligation to the family.[9] The concept of male guardianship, however, does not extend to a woman's property rights, seeking an education, or the free choice of a marital partner. But as a corollary to a woman's unequal right of inheritance, she is not obligated to extend financial support to the family.[10] Islam's definition of acceptable public roles for women, therefore, can be restrictive if allowed to go unchallenged. But given the Islamic emphasis on women's economic rights and the desire for educating females, rights could be expanded and roles redefined when powerful historical forces intervene.

Thus, while Islam does not recognize class divisions or gender considerations, it does accord women a certain degree of dignity and respect. The Islamic institution of the *waqf* (charitable religious trusts), for instance, deems it necessary to alleviate poverty when it afflicts families, not individual females. With Islam's strong preference for marriage over celibacy under any conditions, women are expected always to be sheltered by the powerful institution of the family. But when the male headship of the family is weakened or eliminated by political and military forces, women naturally assume the headship role and qualify for religious charitable assistance. This has been the case of Palestinian women who lost their males in large numbers as a result of war, exile, or Israeli and Arab repressive policies. Social welfare institutions in the West Bank and Gaza, a sizeable phenomenon during the period of Israeli occupation, often solicited *zakat* (religious tithing) for their female-directed projects. No one objected to this type of religiously sanctioned charity, even when it was dispensed to females directly.

SOCIAL ACTIVISM OF PALESTINIAN WOMEN

The scholarly but controversial leader of the Islamic regime of the Sudan, Hassan al-Turabi, has condemned the segregation of women as truly un-Islamic. In his view, Islam intended such domestic sequestration of women only as a punishment for adultery.[11] No virtuous woman can be confined to her home as a requirement of the religion, and the Palestinian experience validates that. Men, particularly nationalist leaders and members of the political elite, were the greatest driving force behind the public activism of Palestinian women. The early Executive Committee of the Arab Women's Union in 1929, was dominated by female descendants of some of Palestine's most prominent families.[12] This activism, which accompanied the beginnings of the Zionist enterprise in Palestine following the First World War, nevertheless confined the female leadership to a specific role. With the exception of some memorable all-female demonstrations protesting the Balfour Declaration and its impact on Palestinian national rights, women's early activities were channeled into social welfare projects.[13] Although males provided psychological support, the women provided all the ingenuity, hard labor, and funding activities. The oldest of these women's organizations, the Arab Women's Union of Jerusalem, founded in 1929, began by serving orphaned children and providing literacy and sewing classes for women.[14] Another sports and cultural club for girls founded in 1945 in Nablus was later turned into a center for female literacy classes. In 1952, a girl's orphanage serving daughters of those killed in the 1948 War was opened.[15]

The tempo of women's charitable work accelerated after the loss of the Palestinian homeland to Israel, Jordan, and Egypt in 1948. Charitable societies serving a new generation of war orphans developed in most Palestinian towns such as Tulkarm (1961), al-Bireh (1955), Hebron (1956), and Kalandia refugee camp (1958). Two of these institutions achieved a great deal of renown because of their prominent ministering to women and children. These were Dar al-Tifl al-Arabi (Home of the Arab Child), founded in Jerusalem in 1949 specifically to shelter the orphans of the massacred village of Deir Yassin, and In'ash al-Usrah (Society for the Sustenance of the Family), which devoted itself to economic projects benefiting rural women.[16] The older Arab Women's Union of Nablus, which predated the 1948 War, undertook one of the most ambitious of the women's projects, namely the founding of a women and children's hospital, Al-Ittihad al-Nisa'i Hospital, offering its services free of charge.[17] The hospital opened its doors in 1948 and today maintains a staff of a hundred and fifty.[18] A community-based clinic was later founded by the Birzeit Women's Charitable Society.[19]

During the British Mandate period (1921–48) and the Jordanian period (1948–67), women's organizations and social projects were financed entirely by the activities of members. With the exception of the very few, such as Dar al-Tifl, which managed to tap into private German funding and government and private funding from the Arab oil states, most of these charitable societies relied on community resources. Another restrictive aspect of their operations was the Jordanian Law on Charitable Societies, first promulgated in 1956. The law established strict supervisory procedures which threatened these societies with dissolution if, for instance, executive officers failed to show up at meetings. Other grounds for dismissal included refusal by the societies to permit governmental search of records and sites. Applications for registration were not easy to obtain, and the law permitting appeal before the Jordanian High Court of Justice was finally repealed in 1966.[20] Jordanian hostility toward this national activity was only matched by the later obstructionist policies of the Israeli occupation regime. National need for public health services, educational facilities for orphaned children, and literacy classes for women, however, were critical. The Jordanian regime favored the East Bank (the former Transjordan) with investments and services, and the Israelis later punished Palestinian national resistance with a policy of studied neglect and repression. No area was as badly in need of improvement as natal and maternal care. Women in the West Bank and Gaza gave birth seven times on the average during their lifetime, but public health facilities lagged behind. Most delivered their babies at home with the assistance of ill-trained midwives. Only the health clinics of some refugee camps, operated by the UN Relief and Works Agency (UNRWA) aided pregnant mothers who technically qualified as refugees.[21] The urgency of the health situation was mostly addressed by women's social organizations, providing yet another example of women's self-reliance and autonomous activity.

THE PLO AND THE GENERAL UNION OF PALESTINIAN WOMEN

Women's social activism, in time, produced not only an intensification of national sentiment but also feminist consciousness. Women's organizations proved to be a springboard to the official ranks of the first Palestinian national organization emerging in the 1960s. According to Issam 'Abd al-Hadi, the founder of the General Union of Palestinian Women, an invitation was extended to twelve active women by the Palestine Liberation Organization in 1964 to serve as delegates to the first Palestinian national assembly meeting in East Jerusalem. 'Abd al-Hadi asserts that the women were selected for their national, rather than feminist, credentials. The PLO then encouraged the women to call for a national meeting in order to create a representative organization as an official cadre of the PLO. This group turned out to be the General Union of Palestinian Women, which is officially attached to the PLO as the second oldest cadre following the General Union of Palestinian Students. Around 139 delegates from all over the West Bank elected an administrative council, which in turn chose a nine-member executive committee. The women delegates, however, retained their positions within the charitable institutions, fearing a Jordanian crackdown against the GUPW. The repression against this PLO institution became real when the Israeli army occupied union President 'Abd al-Hadi's hometown, Nablus. The Israeli authorities were quick to sense the nationalist and mobilizational potential of the political and charitable women's institutions. 'Abd al-Hadi was eventually imprisoned and later expelled from the West Bank by the Israelis.[22]

The headquarters of the GUPW moved from Jerusalem to wherever the PLO relocated. As the original PLO, led by Ahmad Shukairy, de-clined and the latter Arafat-led PLO emerged in 1969, the GUPW moved to Amman, Jordan, then to Beirut. As an official arm of the PLO, the women's union flourished economically but lost much of its autonomy. The union was allowed a free hand in recruiting camp women to em-ployment created by the PLO in the Red Crescent Society and SAMED, the organization's major economic cooperative. It was said that the PLO encouraged refugee women in Lebanon to seek employment in order to free the energies of males for fighting duties. The GUPW leadership, on the other hand, was encouraged to become more and more involved in the political institutions of the PLO. The PLO nominated the members of the female leadership to the Palestinian parliament in exile, the Palestine National Council. Some women were even named to the Central Commit-tee of the PLO, and Fateh loyalists in the camps who supported Arafat's faction within the PLO were accorded membership in the military and administrative councils of the camps.[23]

One woman made her way to the inner circle of the PLO leadership by virtue of her membership in the Fateh guerilla organization. This was Intissar al-Wazir (also known as Um Jihad), whose husband, Khalil al-Wazir, was Arafat's second in command. Considered a co-founder of Fateh, Um Jihad headed the guerilla organization in 1966 while the male leadership suffered imprisonment in Syria. She was made the director of Palestinian veterans' affairs and welfare department in Lebanon. Po-litical activists like Um Jihad found their way to prominence through involvement in the national sphere of social work.[24] Later examination of the contribution of the male leadership to the mobilization of women was also particularly critical of the loss of fiscal control within the GUPW upon the standardization of fiscal procedures in Lebanon. Once they lost the power of the purse, the women were forbidden to raise their own funds and were held to a stricter system of accounting by the newly established Palestine National Fund. Until the latter years of the PLO's residency in Lebanon, the GUPW derived their income from the dues of their twenty-five thousand members, private contri-butions, and some grants from European and UN agencies. Once the

PLO established its national treasury, known as the Palestine National Fund, in the mid-1970s, the GUPW began to rely on the Fund to supply teachers' salaries and some operating funds. The PLO finally took over the financial management of all PLO-affiliated unions, including the women's union.[25] Branches of the GUPW outside of Lebanon continued to provide valuable and badly needed services to the Palestinian community in the diaspora, and not only to women. The GUPW President in Kuwait, Salwa al-Khadhra, was able to coordinate a massive effort in 1985 to provide schools for Palestinian children after the Kuwaiti government complained of lack of space in its congested public schools. Her efforts resulted in an arrangement availing Palestinian children, estimated at 120,000, of school space in the afternoon following the dismissal of Kuwaiti children. The cost of this operation was borne by Palestinian families, the Palestine National Fund, and the Kuwaiti government.[26]

WOMEN'S WORK COMMITTEES IN THE WEST BANK AND GAZA

Absence of the PLO from the Israeli-occupied West Bank and Gaza following the 1967 Arab-Israeli War forced the female population to fall back on their own resources. The combined effect of Israeli military repression, economic migration of males, and Israeli confiscation of agricultural lands resulted in a massive shift in the direction of female-headed households. According to UNRWA's statistics for 1983, out of 72,272 Palestinian families registered as refugees in the West Bank, 27,226 were headed by females. In the Gaza Strip, UNRWA's figures showed 75,296 registered families, of whom 14,567 were headed by females. These figures, of course, do not include non-refugee families who may have experienced a similar development. Women were also forced to enter the labor force, but their lack of experience, particularly in the area of unionization, exposed them to considerable exploitation. Women began to enter three types of employment: unskilled wage labor within Israel proper, wage labor in Israeli factories in the West Bank, and self-employed labor within the family structure. Much of female employment in the Occupied Territories was centered around the Israeli-controlled garment industry, where they usually received wages 50 percent lower than compensation for similar work within Israel. Those women employed within the Israeli sector had to contend with long commuting hours, unequal pay, lack of social benefits, and absence of day-care services.[27] Some of these problems were tackled individually by pioneering women who sought a political solution, and some collectively by organizations who ministered to the suffering female population. Some women, like Amal Wahdan, became active in the labor union at her place of employment and worked hard to educate and involve other women. The difficulty was not only in finding a niche for herself in an all-male union, but also in convincing other female workers to invade this male-dominated territory. Amal Wahdan's success in mobilizing and educating other women grew naturally out of her involvement with the women's work committees. These committees organized special sub-sections to deal with labor issues, thereby making it easier for women bound by family traditionalism to broach such topics without any contact with males.[28]

The women's work committees were a new phenomenon in the West Bank and Gaza which sought to address the drastic economic and political pressures resulting from Israel's military occupation. Although an effort directed by and for women which was typical of the Palestinian history of self-help and gender solidarity, the work committees represented a different assessment of the women's question. Whereas the charitable organizations dominating the Palestinian scene from the 1920s until the end of Jordanian period performed purely charitable work, the new committees focused on work-related problems. The committees also instilled a new spirit aimed at nurturing self-help and gender consciousness by sponsoring projects and not merely through acts of charity. The first of these groups, the Federation of Women's Work Committees, emerged in 1978 and spawned 107 subcommittees with a membership of 4,000. The Federation (sometimes translated as the Union of Women's Work Committees) for the first time targeted and organized village women. These were badly in need of services rarely offered by the urban elite women, such as vocational training in heritage crafts and in such basic marketable skills as sewing and weaving. For the first time in the history of social welfare organizations, the federation of work committees began to operate kindergartens as a service to working women and to educate them in the politics of unionization.[29]

The federation did not remain united for long and eventually splintered along ideological lines. The core group within the federation remained loyal to one of the PLO's major leftist groups, namely the Democratic Front for the Liberation of Palestine. Female members of the Communist Party organized their own Union of Palestinian Working Women's Committees in 1980 and emphasized women's economic rights and their role within labor unions. A year later, another group, the Palestinian Women's Committees, was organized with the support of another PLO radical organization, the Popular Front for the Liberation of Palestine. Of all the work committees, this one openly gave precedence to gender issues, elevating these above any national considerations. The women's goal was to empower poorer and peasant women and to help them develop a working-class ethos. Numbering 1,450 women, this group was composed mainly of factory workers and support members. Finally, Fateh, the Arafat-led dominant group within the PLO, organized the Union of Women's Committees for Social Work in 1982. This union established kindergartens and literacy programs for women.[30]

The exciting story of the women's work committees, however, cannot be appreciated through a description of their services and projects. A real appreciation of this radical shift in the direction of women's organizations can only be attained through an understanding of the general philosophy underlying this new social infrastructure. According to Rita Giacaman, a leading member of these committees, an expert on rural health conditions, and a professor at Birzeit University in the West Bank, the work committees were a response to the Israeli occupation. Writing in the twentieth year of the occupation, Giacaman stated that the Palestinians felt compelled to prevent the Israeli destruction of the Palestinian health, educational, and economic infrastructure. Since the occupation regime suppressed all political activity, the occupied population channelled their energies into social welfare activities. Outside assistance from the PLO's steadfastness Arab fund dispensed from Jordan and UNRWA's acts of pure charity were no longer adequate. The most grievously afflicted sector of the occupied population, which suffered the destruction of families, labor exploitation, and general economic deprivation, women finally rose to the occasion. Within this sector of the population, village women and those living in the refugee camps of the West Bank and Gaza suffered the most.[31]

The urban women's movement, now made up largely of younger, university-educated women, in contrast to the older, socially prominent female leadership, initially sought to mobilize village women in order to resist the occupation. This political objective, it was soon realized, could not be achieved in the context of abject rural poverty and social deprivation. According to Giacaman, it was the discovery of the villages which inspired the women's work committees. Not only were the committees now focused on the needs of village women, such as health, education, and economic viability, but the thrust of the new organizations was development and not charity. Moreover, rural branches of these committees were run by village women in an attempt to build grass roots organizations more decentralized than the original urban social welfare groups. Now, the Israeli authorities became incapable of paralyzing an entire operation by imposing a prison sentence or house arrest on a limited number of leaders. By bringing urban and rural women closer together, village women acquired greater gender consciousness as well, which was perceived by the female leadership as a necessary prerequisite for national liberation. Gender consciousness came naturally as a result of economic empowerment when village women experienced a measure of self-control over their lives. This explains the determination to shift emphasis from charity to development. The economic effect of the work committees' activities was intended to evolve into autonomous programs.[32]

TRANSFORMATION OF THE CHARITABLE ORGANIZATIONS

Some of the traditional women's social welfare organizations evolved into a hybrid form of charitable associations, combining elements of the old and the new social welfare structure of the West Bank and Gaza. The most prominent of this model was In'ash al-Usrah, or Sustenance of the Family, an organization dating back to the Jordanian period. Founded in 1965 with a budget of 500 dollars, In'ash began in a two-room apartment with a sewing machine and ten female students.[33] By 1989, the organization had a budget of 180,000 dollars. At the beginning, eight wealthy Palestinians were persuaded to provide scholarships for eight female students, and by 1987, In'ash al-Usrah was able to provide loans and scholarships to 360 students. By the late 1980s, the organization employed 152 teachers and skilled individuals. Having started with a kindergarten serving 25 children, In'ash's services are now offered to 150 children. There is also a boarding school for 132 orphaned children, all girls. A sponsorship program now supports 1,300 needy families with annual stipends of 500 dollars provided by private donors. There are eighty-five doctors who regularly treat the families of In'ash free of charge, and patients are often referred to al-Makased Hospital for free treatment.[34]

In'ash al-Usrah combined charitable works with development projects. Women from nearby villages were offered literacy classes in cooperation with Birzeit University. Women's processed food products and home-made textiles were marketed, the number growing to two thousand women who were encouraged to produce out of their home base. The organization also established its own food-processing plant. The founder of In'ash, Samiha Khalil (Um Khalil), understood that opportunities for income-generating projects eventually lead to empowerment. Although not a feminist in the Western sense, Um Khalil recognized that these opportunities improved women's standing within the family. Men began to allow wives to attend meetings and daughters to seek a university education. Mixing politics and social work also became more acceptable, unlike in previous Palestinian periods when genteel women philanthropists and social workers scorned political activity. Um Khalil, despite her affinity for the pre-1967 generation, viewed her social work as an act of national defiance and steadfastness. She shared this view with the younger generation of the work committees, in the belief that empowering poorer women and keeping them on the land was an objective of national survival. Um Khalil is also credited with initiating the idea of economic boycotts of Israeli production. Indeed, her name symbolizes *sumud* or steadfastness in the face of overwhelming Israeli economic and political oppression.[35]

Often, Um Khalil's nationalist strategy overshadowed her philanthropic work. Helping unskilled women develop their domestic production was intended to prevent their engagement in exploitative and demeaning employment in the Israeli sector. This, it was felt, would only strengthen Palestinian dependence on the occupation regime. Marketing these home-made products also pressured West Bank buyers not to purchase Israeli products. Underprivileged members of the occupied Palestinian society, however, were the most vulnerable to the economic lure of Israeli industries. Um Khalil's In'ash, therefore, attempted to strengthen the national identity of underprivileged women by any means possible. This was accomplished through developing heritage crafts, public commemoration of national culture, a folklore museum, and an anthropological study of Palestinian villages.[36]

In'ash al-Usrah was clearly founded with nationalist ends in mind. The founder's political agitation and defiance of the Israeli authorities earned her a spot on the three-person Palestinian National Guidance Committee, which coordinated peaceful resistance to the occupation regime in the West Bank and Gaza until 1987. It was in that year that a semi-violent movement of national resistance, the *intifada,* erupted and created a serious emergency for the Israelis. Primarily a boycott movement, the *intifada* leadership called on all Palestinians to render the Israeli military occupation inoperative through acts of economic boycotts and general strikes. It is in the context of this continuing national agitation that Um Khalil's philanthropy can be understood. Her organization developed into a model of self-help and national resistance. "Funding is a political issue," she once confessed to an interviewer. She added:

> I have been approached by a number of American charitable organizations offering financial aid. I always ask where they got their money from. If it comes from the Congress of the United States, I reject it. I refuse to take money from the enemy of my people on principle. It is the same Congress that gives billions of dollars a

year to Israel in military aid and for funding illegal settlements on stolen Palestinian land.[37]

In'ash would only accept funds from neutral and peace-loving American groups, such as the National Council of Churches. The rest of her foreign funds came from donations by Arab-American groups, from a well-known London-based Palestinian millionaire, Zein al-Mayyasi, from the Norwegian Agency for International Development, and the Association Medicale Franco-Palestinienne. Um Khalil was not only the most economically nationalistic among the female social welfare leaders, but she was also a consistent nationalist. Unlike the younger Western-educated leaders of the women's work committees, Um Khalil championed causes with a distinct anti-feminist twist. Although conceding that having many children is a burden and a hardship for women, she often preached that national survival demanded releasing women's natal potential to the fullest. Her society actually advertised that it will give two hundred prizes to women who produced the greater number of children.[38] Um Khalil's pro-natal views, though quite controversial, never determined the success or failure of her organization. Instead, all the women's organizations, the old and the new, were mostly judged by their overall contribution to the economic survival of the occupied population.

THE DEVELOPMENT DEBATE

The women's organizations in the West Bank and Gaza, nevertheless, did not dominate the field of philanthropy. First, there was the oldest charitable agency serving Palestinian refugees wherever they were found, and not only in Palestinian lands, the United Nations Relief and Works Agency. UNRWA was created in 1948 specifically to provide humanitarian assistance to those Palestinians who were officially considered refugees. Aid was extended to the original three-quarter million Palestinian refugee population and to their descendants. UNRWA began with food rations and eventually established schools, training centers, and health clinics in the middle of refugee camps. The publications of UNRWA clearly demonstrate two crucial aspects of its operating philosophy. The first of these was UNRWA's traditional approach to development, favoring males with income-generating training. The second visible characteristic of UNRWA was the absence of any visible nationalist orientation in its projects. Purely charitable relief work, UNRWA's operations focused on eliminating poverty exclusively. The stated objective of this agency's four training centers in the West Bank and Gaza in 1986, for instance, was to find employment abroad for their graduates. These programs trained 359 male university graduates as teacher trainees for employment in the Arab Gulf states. UNRWA also began expanding its programs that year to include male and female physiotherapy training, construction technicians' training, computer courses, business and shorthand, as well as laboratory work. The organization determined that the greatest demand in Saudi Arabia was for teachers first, then for people in the medical profession and in technical fields.[39] Clearly, UNRWA did not subscribe to the ideology of *sumud*, or survival on the land, motivating the women's social welfare projects. Um Khalil's nationalist aspirations, by contrast, focused on projects which strengthened Palestinians' will to struggle, persist, and remain on the land, and to resist joining the army of well-to-do expatriates in the Arab oil states.

UNRWA's services for the female sector of the refugee population were also devoid of the rhetoric of empowerment and female liberation. Unlike the women's work committees which focused on income-generating projects and grass roots building as means of strengthening nationalist resistance, UNRWA was satisfied with teachers' and nurses' training programs. Women employees of UNRWA who ran these female-training centers also reflected the genteel upbringing of Palestine's old classes but none of the radicalism of the younger generation of the 1970s.[40]

The West Bank and Gaza were also served by a large number of foreign NGOs. These were estimated to be 130 European and 40 North American NGOs. Local NGOs in the occupied West Bank and Gaza were estimated to be between 850 and 2,500. The foreign organizations developed programs in support of local Palestinian groups or implemented their own projects directly. The foreign NGOs have undertaken health, education, and rehabilitation programs, but have moved in recent years in the direction of agricultural, business, and community development projects. Both the local and foreign NGOs have attempted to fill a serious gap resulting from the absence of state institutions and government programs.[41]

The conservative figure of 850 local NGOs does not include trade unions or professional organizations. Palestinian charitable societies account for almost 300 of these NGOs. Of this number, around 174 organizations are women's NGOs, mostly specializing in income generating activities such as sewing and handicrafts. The women's NGOs include 82 voluntary societies, 58 committees, 13 cooperatives, and 22 productive projects.[42]

The foreign NGOs are expected in most cases to transfer their skills and administrative knowledge to the Palestinian NGOs, particularly to women's associations. This expectation has not always been met, although some cooperative experiences between these groups proved to be very successful. The Central Committee of the American Mennonite Church in the West Bank, which established a women's sewing cooperative in the village of Surif in the Hebron district, is such a case. The Mennonites are among the most experienced in this line of work, having created one of the oldest NGO projects in the West Bank in 1953, the Palestinian Needlework Program. The project was intended to provide Palestinian women refugees with an income-generating activity. By the mid-1970s, five hundred women were employed turning out embroidery in six villages in the Hebron area. Initially, the project was run from the Mennonite Committee's Jerusalem offices, and the output was marketed from shops in Jerusalem, the USA, and Canada. In 1976, however, a Palestinian female worker submitted a proposal to transfer the management of this program to the women employees. The committee then chose the village of Surif as a pilot for this proposal. The Surif cooperative was given the duties of distributing work orders, overseeing production, inspecting and dispensing monetary compensation, and keeping records. The Mennonite Committee retained control over marketing outlets. Village women apparently hesitated before undertaking this responsibility, but after a brief orientation program and visits to two nearby villages with similar projects, they plunged ahead. After awhile, women began to demand higher salaries and better equipment, two requests that were met with an explanation of the economics of such a cooperative venture. More importantly, the experience of managing a cooperative produced an inevitable process of social transformation. The women began to travel alone to other villages and to do their own banking. Many reported a new attitude of respect for their labor on the part of male family members.[43]

Most foreign NGOs, however, were criticized for their higher salaries and failure to transfer skills and technology to local agencies. Palestinian women's NGOs, on the other hand, have been criticized by development experts for several shortcomings. Among these are the lack of administrative training and, more importantly, serious marketing strategies. These weaknesses became painfully apparent when the Gulf War deprived Palestinian NGOs of most of their Arab sources of funding and forced a scramble to enhance their marketing efforts to compensate for lost funds. The women's NGOs, which always depended on external funding, whether Palestinian or foreign, were criticized for ignoring the market dynamics of their economic activities. The women's NGOs generally relied on exhibits and appeals to nationalist sentiment to market their products and overlooked the imperative of cost-effective production. On a separate note, the women's NGOs were also taken to task for centralizing their activities around the personality of the founder. These women, referred to collectively as *shakhsiyat* (prominent figures or stars) such as Um Khalil, dominated the life of their agencies but failed to nurture a second generation of managers.[44] Um Khalil, nevertheless, was so revered for her acts of resistance and dedication that she was able to run in January 1996, as a candidate for the position of President of the Palestine National Authority.[45] Arafat's easy victory over Um Khalil does not diminish her nationalist and feminist credentials. Indeed, it is arguable whether or not these fragile social welfare agencies dedicated to the survival of women would have thrived without the leadership of such flamboyant, charismatic, and nationalist women such as Um Khalil.

Finally, even though Palestinian women's activism, both social and nationalist, never met with male resistance, it should be analyzed in light of the historic changes which are transforming Palestinian society today. Resistance to Jordanian and Israeli oppression has forced these agencies to play the role of civil society and fill a void created by the utter lack of state social services. With the conclusion of the Palestinian-Israeli peace settlement and the emergence of the Palestine National Authority as the quasi-government of the Arab population, Palestinian civil society will inevitably weaken. Experts predict that the Palestine Authority's inevitable rush to institute a new set of government regulations; NGOs expected dependence on official Palestinian funding sources will diminish the political power and gender effectiveness of women's social agencies. Both the cause of Palestinian democracy and the feminization of Palestinian society will suffer. Had the Palestinian struggle for nationhood and statehood lasted longer, it would have allowed women greater opportunities for development and political maturation. Now, they will have to contend with a national authority preoccupied with enormous problems and a general public indifferent to issues of gender mobilization.

THE ROOTS OF WOMEN'S PHILANTHROPY IN EGYPT

Egypt underwent extensive social change at the beginning of this century. Some of this change resulted from massive national agitation against the British occupation, accompanied by the mobilization of women. Egypt's first feminist campaign was led by bourgeois women, both Muslim and Coptic, who sought to enhance feminist consciousness through involvement in nationalist agitation. Thus, the demands of the first Egyptian feminist organization to emerge on the scene in 1923, the Egyptian Feminist Union, mirrored this intermixing of nationalism and feminism. The Feminist Union continued to present the Egyptian parliament with such demands as the retention of Egypt's control over the Sudan and the withdrawal of British troops from the Suez Canal Zone. The women's first agenda reflected feminists' demands for political rights, such as voting rights, membership in parliament, and access to institutes of higher learning. The Feminist Union also agitated for the cancellation of polygyny and the restriction of the male privilege of summary divorce.[46]

If the social origins of the early generation of Egyptian feminists predisposed them toward the political and social objectives of middle-class women, philanthropy remained an assured avenue for public prominence. The career of Egypt's foremost feminist and founder of the Feminist Union, Huda Sha'rawi, illustrates this inevitable experimentation with social welfare projects as a means of breaking the pattern of women's isolation and domestic confinement. Even when Sha'rawi's earliest ventures were viewed as a feminine form of *noblesse oblige,* they were also valuable as a sure way of acquiring organizational and agitational experience. Sha'rawi came into her work with the Feminist Union after establishing Mabarat Muhammad 'Ali (Muhammad 'Ali's Institution) in 1908. This agency, which was co-founded with Princess 'Ayn al-Hayat, provided sewing classes and a clinic for needy women and children.[47]

Islamic organizations, however, always recruited members of the working classes and Egypt's peasant population in the cities. These required services that were rarely provided by the state; women, as always, were among the neediest in the slums of major cities. The woman who led Egypt's first Islamic charitable organization, ironically, received her training earlier within the ranks of the secular Feminist Union. This was Labibeh Ahmad, who founded the women's auxiliary of the Muslim Brotherhood in 1937, known as the Muslim Sisterhood, or Al-Akhawat al-Muslimat. Barely eight years after Hassan al-Banna founded the Muslim Brotherhood, an organization bent on Islamizing society and the state, the need for recruiting women and gaining their support became apparent. Ahmad herself was attracted to the Brotherhood because of its resources and charitable works. In addition to the Brotherhood's educational and recruitment programs, such as five hundred educational projects, fifty scout troops, and twenty athletic clubs, the organization built ten textile shops to train the orphaned and the poor. The Brotherhood also opened a health clinic to serve its membership, as well as a medical dispensary supplying free medicine. These projects, although primarily targeting the brotherhood's male following, spilled over to the female relatives of the Muslim Brothers.[48]

Although Islamic groups normally ignore gender issues, the Muslim Sisterhood was founded especially to spread religious education among women and to instruct them in the ideal ways of raising and educating Muslim children. The Sisterhood reinforced Islamic social norms by creating a system of home visitation for secluded women who were unable to attend public meetings. The Muslim Sisterhood was founded simply as a committee made up of the wives of Muslim Brothers at Cairo and Isma'iliyah. Ahmad became President of the Sisterhood's Cairo headquarters. By 1948, 50 branches were established throughout Egypt. The committee of each Sisterhood elected a female president, a vice-president, a secretary, and a treasurer. The Supreme Guide of the Muslim Brotherhood, Hassan al-Banna, however, remained the general director of the Sisterhood and was responsible for naming a male secretary as an emissary to the female organization. Guidelines governing the charitable projects of the Sisterhood needed the approval of the Brotherhood's main office. The Sisterhood trained its recruits in food processing and canning, as well as sewing, the products of which were marketed by the committees of the organization. In the provinces, the committees of this women's agency undertook the task of improving health conditions for the poor by directing them to public health facilities and other charitable organizations. Not enthusiastic about issues championed by other feminists, such as the removal of the veil and its negative impact on women, Ahmad preached obedience to husbands and dedication to the family. Her only pro-feminist views called for repealing Islamic divorce laws and forcing the sterilizations of poor women.[49]

THE ISLAMIC ORGANIZATIONS FACE STATE REPRESSION

Women's philanthropy along the lines of Labibeh Ahmad's Sisterhood was a traditional form of charity provided by the male parent organization and under its direction. During the late 1940s and 1950s, however, the Brotherhood entered a phase of deadly confrontation with the socialist regime of Jamal Abd al-Nasser. This struggle ended up with the massive destruction of the Brotherhood's infrastructure and the imprisonment of its officers. Remarkably, what saved the organization from total demise was the determination of the president of another Islamic women's association to remain independent of the Brotherhood. This was the renowned Islamic activist and political leader, Zeinab al-Ghazzali who founded in 1937 the Society of Muslim Women, Jama'at al-Sayyidat al-Muslimat. Al-Banna asked her to merge her organization with the Brotherhood, but she and her executive committee refused. The independence of the Society of Muslim Women was appreciated later when the government decided to dismantle the Brotherhood in 1948 and seize all its assets. When state repression of the Brotherhood and all its branches intensified during the Nasserite period, Zeinab al-Ghazzali's charitable agency became a convenient refuge for the survivors of the repression. The society also played a crucial role as the emissary to their wives and families of the imprisoned Brothers. Following the trials of 1954, which targeted the active male members of the Brotherhood, Ghazzali and female relatives of other prominent Brothers organized relief efforts to assist the suffering Islamic families. Al-Ghazzali's efforts benefited all members of the beleaguered Brotherhood, especially the males who were released after severe interrogation.[50]

Part of Al-Ghazzali's organized campaign to rescue this important sector of the Egyptian polity entailed coordinating efforts with the government of Saudi Arabia. The Saudi regime, which feared the destabilizing effect of Nasser's pan-Arab socialism, opened its doors to the persecuted Brotherhood. Al-Ghazzali led an all-female delegation to perform the Islamic pilgrimage in Saudi Arabia in 1957, in a bold effort to relocate many of them in this friendly Islamic state. While there, she submitted a memorandum to the Saudi monarch, asking that the daughters of the imprisoned Brothers be educated in Saudi Arabia.[51] This turned out to be the first wave of a massive Islamic migration from Egypt to the Arab oil-rich states, a migration of enormous significance in later years. It was in this Islamic cultural milieu that exiled Egyptian Islamic activists adopted the values of Islamic capitalism, acquired habits of Islamic dress such as the veil, and began to associate financial success with Islamic observances. When these generations of exiled Egyptians, beginning with the female students of Al-Ghazzali, returned home in the 1970s, the Islamic revolution began in earnest.

Upon her return to Egypt in 1957, Al-Ghazzali continued with her community-wide relief effort, which raised funds from the faithful to support the children and wives of the imprisoned and martyred Brothers. This humanitarian campaign was coordinated by women in the mistaken belief that no state apparatus would victimize society's weaker elements. The effort was so massive that she described extensive bookkeeping and funds spent not only on sustaining the families, but also on educating their children. Fund-raising and the distribution of resources had to be done secretly under the gaze of the security agencies. In time, state repression caught up with her and she suffered imprisonment and torture. The most serious charge directed at Al-Ghazzali while on trial was the disbursement of four thousand Egyptian pounds to the families of the imprisoned Brothers, for which she was sentenced to twenty-five years at hard labor.[52]

The new phase of Islamic revivalism, which began in the 1970s, witnessed a successful campaign to create exclusive Islamic investments
and a social-welfare structure alongside those of the state. Egypt began
to experience the phenomenon of Islamic banking and Islamic corporations financed by the activities of the exiled Islamic leaders in the
Arab oil states. Beside al-Rayyan and al-Sa'ad companies, Muslim groups
founded a successful monthly magazine named *Al-Da'wa,* which also
benefited from advertisements by other Islamic companies.[53] The magazine's circulation reached 78,000, and its Islamic advertisers included
bookshops, food companies, and foreign car dealerships.[54] The new Islamic social welfare network included clinics which were located in or
near mosques, schools, day-care facilities, and youth clubs. Of these, the
most heavily used by Egypt's lower middle-class and the urban poor
were the health clinics. The clinics were staffed by dedicated doctors
and nurses and offered services that were often superior to those available at government facilities. Charging modest fees and supported by the
community, these clinics were used regularly by families and by women.
The total number of Islamic NGOs, according to the registration files of
the Ministry of Social Affairs, is 8,000, out of a total of 14,000 NGOs
operating in Egypt today. The Islamic clinics serving the public at large
are around 1,000 to 2,000 throughout the country, and between 300 and
350 in Cairo alone. Situated generally within Cairo's poorer sections or
in the less costly outlying suburbs, the clinics range from those operated
by two doctors and one nurse to those employing 200 doctors and 200
nurses and clerical staff. The average-sized clinic employs ten doctors
each. The clinics offer extensive medical services, including surgery, gy-
necology, dentistry, and x-ray services. Preferred by the general public
to government's free health services, the Islamic clinics boast better-paid
doctors, more hygienic conditions, and a highly motivated staff.[55]

The clinics are supported by community donations, which are collected as *zakat,* and particularly by large sums given by wealthy entrepreneurs. It is also clear that decisions are made by members of freely
elected community assemblies who are predominantly male. The clinics are not run by women, for the benefit of women. Muslim female
doctors and nurses who work in these clinics, however, are expected to
be veiled and adhere to accepted standards of Islamic behavior. A researcher discovered that the clinics have no Christian doctors, although
there is no policy which prohibits their hiring, and Christian families in
need also patronize these centers for a simple fee. Male and female doctors offer gynecological services, and there is no special effort to cater
to women's needs exclusively. Some doctors and directors of these clinics claim that the clinics are in the secular philanthropic tradition of

Mabarat Muhammad Ali, founded by Princess Ayn al-Hayat. All overt Islamic fundamentalist propaganda is avoided.[56]

Although religious proselytization within these clinics is kept to a minimum, the clinics' very existence, let alone their efficient performance, exposes the inadequacy of the government's social infrastructure. But women are neither mobilized by these Islamic services, nor given a leadership role. This is not surprising in view of the general Islamic philosophy regarding the activation of women. Zeinab al-Ghazzali shed some light on this in the 1960s, when she was interrogated by the police prior to her imprisonment. In response to her interrogators' questioning as to the extent of her leadership role within the Islamic Brotherhood, she vehemently denied any ambitions for high office if the Brotherhood ever came to power. She emphasized that when the Islamic state finally emerges, women will be happy to return to their natural kingdom to raise the future generations of the nation's men.[57] Clearly, women's activation and mobilization was not an open-ended principle, but an emergency measure for emergency times. In Egypt of the early 1970s, with the influx of Islamic wealth from the oil-rich countries of exile during the 1950s and 1960s, and under the benign gaze of the Sadat regime, Islamic activities were tolerated. There was no need to disrupt the natural order of things and thrust women onto the public arena.

When Islamic organizations accelerated their activities on the campuses of Egyptian universities during the 1970s, however, the need to mobilize female students became obvious. This mobilization was accomplished through charitable works in the form of badly needed services designed to ease the dismal conditions surrounding university life. Because of these services offered by Jama'at Islamiyya, an organization particularly active in student circles, student organizations between 1975 and 1979 were dominated by Islamic activists. By 1979, the Jama'at succeeded in defeating the previously powerful pro-Marxist and pro-Nasserite student organizations. Much of this success was due to the Jama'at's ability to respond to the rising congestion at the universities resulting from the availability of free public education. Female students, particularly those from the provinces, had to contend with packed buses, dismal lodging facilities, and constant harassment by male students. The Jama'at provided bus services exclusively for the use of veiled female students and successfully demanded separate lecture-hall seating of female students by row. Veiled students, nurtured and strengthened by these Islamic organizations, became a visible presence on campuses, especially at election time and during political demonstrations.[58]

CONCLUSION

Naturally, these all-male Egyptian efforts on behalf of women did not spawn the kind of Islamic feminist leadership exemplified by Zeinab al-Ghazzali during the 1950s and 1960s. As the Islamic movement in Egypt grew stronger, males assumed leadership in all aspects of public organizational life. Even acts of philanthropy, whether Islamically sanctioned, like the *zakat* — based activities, or politically driven, like the services of Jamma'at Islamiyya, were either directed at the Islamic family or were politically motivated. Ironically, despite denials of any feminist ambitions, the female-dominated philanthropy of al-Ghazzali's era brought forward a certain leadership cadre whose influence and effectiveness cannot be denied. The male-dominated activities of the Sadat era, however, produced the phenomenon of controlled female mobilization. Paradoxically, Islamic philanthropy strengthened women's roles in the universities and as members of the new Islamic organizations without necessarily empowering them.

Palestinian women, on the other hand, were strengthened through adversity and because of the absence of males. By creating a badly needed social infrastructure, the Palestinians were able to direct their philanthropy toward women. More importantly, Palestinian charitable organizations responded to changing political conditions with agility and foresight. Remarkably, the Palestinian feminist movement was able to transform itself from pure acts of charity, to organized acts of political and economic resistance. Their goal became increasingly the empowerment of women, and they attempted this through economic activities. But there is no question that the superimposition of a feminist agenda on their social agenda was tolerated by male society because of its relevance to the nationalist struggle. Perhaps the greatest challenge for Palestinian women's associations today is how to retain their leadership role within Palestinian society when both their philanthropy and independence are threatened with political stability and male-takeover.

NOTES

1. Fatima Mernissi, *Beyond the Veil: Male-Female Dynamics in a Modern Muslim Society* (New York: John Wiley and Sons, 1975), xviii–xix.

2. Ahmad Faraj, *Al-mu'amarah 'ala al-mar'a al-Muslimah* (The conspiracy against the Muslim woman). (Al-Mansoura, Egypt: Dar al-wafa' lil tiba'eh wa al-nashr, 1985), 49–54, 135–38, 174–78.

3. Orayb A. Najjar, *Portraits of Palestinian Women* (Salt Lake City: University of Utah Press, 1992), 176–77.

4. Ghada Talhami, "The Human Rights of Women in Islam," *Journal of Social Philosophy* 14, no. 1 (Winter, 1985): 3–4.

5. Mona Rishmawi, "The Legal Status of Palestinian Women in the Occupied Territories" in Nahid Toubia, ed., *Women of the Arab World* (London and New Jersey: Zed Press, 1988), 85.

6. Muhammad al-Ghazzali, *Turathuna al-fikri fi mizan al-shar' wa al-'akil* (Our intellectual heritage on the scale of the Shari'a and the mind). (Cairo: Dar al-shuruq, 1991), 48–49, 51, 160–61.

7. Muahmmad al-Ghazzali, *Qhadhaya al-mar'ah bayn al-taqalid al-rakidah wa al-wafidah* (Women's issues between current and future traditions). (Cairo: Dar al-shuruq, 1990), 15–16, 38–39.

8. 'Abd al-qader Ahmad 'Abd al-Qader, *Al-gharah 'ala al-usrah al-Muslimah* (The raid on the Muslim family). (Cairo: Dar al-nasr lil tiba'ah al-Islamiyya, 1991), 119–20.

9. As'ad al-Sahmarani, *Al-mar'ah fi al-tarikh wa al-Shari'a* (Women in history and the Shari'a). (Beirut: Dar al-nafa'is, 1989), 153–63.

10. A. H. Mahmoud Muhammad, *Huquq al-mar'ah bayn al-Islam wa al-diyanat al-ukhra* (Women's rights in Islam and in other religions). (Cairo: Maktabat Madbuli, 1990), 78–87.

11. Hassan al-Turabi, "The Real Islam and Women," *The Message* (July 1993): 24.

12. Rosemary Sayigh, "Encounters with Palestinian Women under Occupation," *Journal of Palestine Studies* (Summer 1981): 9.

13. Ghada Talhami, "Palestinian Women: The Case for Political Liberation," *Arab Perspectives* (January 1984): 6–7.

14. Talhami, "Women under Occupation: The Great Transformation," in Suha Sabbagh and Ghada Talhami, eds., *Images and Reality: Palestinian Women under Occupation and in the Diaspora* (Washington, D.C.: The Institute for Arab Women's Studies, Inc., 1990), 21.

15. Issam Abdel-Hadi, "From Nablus to Beirut: The Story of GUPW Head Issam Abdel-Hadi," *Al-Fajr* (March 8–14, 1981): 9.

16. Talhami, "Women under Occupation," 20.

17. Abdel-Hadi, 9.

18. "Al-Ittihad al-Nisai Hospital: Two Years of Emergency," *Tanmiya* (Development) 16–17 (December 1989): 1–3.

19. "Maternity: High Risk in the West Bank," *Readings on Palestinian Women, Al-Fajr* (March 8, 1985): 208.

20. Rishmawi, 86.

21. "Maternity," 206–7.

22. Abdel-Hadi, 9–11.

23. Talhami, "Palestinian Women," 7–8.

24. Talhami, "Women in the Movement: Their Long, Uncelebrated History," *Al-Fajr* (May 30, 1986): 8–9.

25. Amal Kawar, "National Mobilization, War Conditions, and Gender Consciousness," *Arab Studies Quarterly* 15, no. 2 (Spring 1993): 62–64.

26. "Al-Filastiniyoun wa al-madares al-Kuwaitiyah," (The Palestinians and Kuwaiti schools), *Filastin al-Thawra* no. 539 (January 5, 1985): 17.

27. Talhami, "Women under Occupation," 16–18.

28. "Palestinian Woman Unionist Finds Organizing Tough Going," *Al-Fajr* (March 3, 1986): 13–14.

29. Nehaya al-Helou and Karen Lende, "Women's Activism in the West Bank and Gaza," *Al-Fajr* (March 3, 1986): 10–11.

30. Najjar, 121–23.

31. "An Interview with Rita Giacaman: Women, Resistance, and the Popular Movement," *Palestine Focus* (July–August 1987): 3.

32. Ibid.

33. Sayigh, 11.

34. Najjar, 45.

35. Sayigh, 11–12.

36. Ibid., 12.

37. Najjar, 45–46.

38. Ibid., 46–47.

39. "Economic Squeeze Hits Refugees in West Bank, Gaza," *Palestine Refugees Today*, UNRWA Newsletter no. 116 (October 1986): 3–4.

40. "Pioneer in Education for Palestinian Women," *Palestine Refugees Today*, UNRWA Newsletter 112 (October 1985): 2–3. This article celebrates the twenty-three-year career of a prominent British-trained educator, Saba' Arafat, who served as Field Education Officer of the West Bank. Another prominent UNRWA educator was In'am al-Mufti who directed the women's teacher training center in Ramallah and later became the first female cabinet minister in Jordan.

41. "The Role of Foreign NGOs," *Tanmiya* Issue 38 (March 1995): 2–3.

42. "Palestinian NGOs Face the Future: The Welfare Association Program," *Tanmiya* Issue 37 (December 1994): 2–3.

43. "Village Women Take Over Cooperative," *Tanmiya* Issue 2 (March 1986:) 2–3.

44. "Palestinian NGOs Face the Future," 3–5.

45. Storer H. Rowley, "Palestinians' Historic Vote Nears," *Chicago Tribune* (January 14, 1996): 4.

46. Ahmad Taha Muhammad, *Al-mar'ah al-Misriyah bayn al-madhi wa al-hadher* (The Egyptian woman between the past and the present). (Cairo: Matba'at dar al-ta'lif, 1979), 61–63.

47. Amal al-Subki, *Al-harakah al-nisa'iyah fi Misr ma bayn al-thawratayn, 1919 wa 1952* (The feminist movement in Egypt between the two revolutions, 1919 and 1952). (Cairo: Al-Hay'a al Misriyah al-'aameh lil kitab, 1986), 101–02.

48. Ibid., 72, 116–17.

49. Ibid., 118–19, 140, 147–48.

50. Zeinab al-Ghazzali, *Ayyam min hayati* (Days of my life). (Cairo: Dar al-Shuruq, 1991), 23–29.

51. Ibid., 30–32.

52. Ibid., 41–56, 178–81.

53. Tareq al-Mahdawi, *Al-Ikhwan al-Muslimin 'ala mathbah al-munawara*, 1928–86 (The Muslim Brotherhood on the altar of deception). (Cairo: Dar Azul, 1986), 133–34.

54. Giles Kepel, *Muslim Extremism in Egypt: The Prophet and the Pharaoh.* (Berkeley: University of California Press, 1984), 103–09.

55. Janine A. Clark, "Islamic Social Welfare Organizations in Cairo: Islamization from Below?" *Arab Studies Quarterly* 17, no. 4 (Fall 1995): 11, 13–6.

56. Ibid., 17–21.

57. Zeinab al-Ghazzali, 144.

58. Kepel, 129–44.

– 10 –

Women and Philanthropy in India

PUSHPA SUNDAR

INTRODUCTION

Although the Indian state plays a major role in meeting welfare and development needs, its reach — in terms of need or geography — is limited. The gap between need and state provision has been met by philanthropy: the giving of time, effort, and money for promoting the public good, without expectation of return. Until the break-up of self-sufficient village communities began under British colonial rule (1757–1947), individual welfare was primarily the responsibility of the family and of the village community. Although the state began to play an increasingly important role in people's lives as British rule progressed, alien government and limited resources ensured that provision of welfare services remained dependent on private charity, albeit more formally organized in charitable institutions. These charitable organizations, endowed by the wealthy and dependent on volunteers and donations, worked both for the relief of distress and for lasting social improvement. They mark the beginning of modern philanthropy in India.

Unfortunately, although the practice of philanthropy is almost as old as Indian civilization, serious scholarship has concerned itself hardly at all with this topic. This is even more true of women's role in philanthropy, where the field of women's studies has yet to make any inroads. Recent studies of the Indian women's movement (e.g. Shah, 1984; Gandhi and Shah, 1991; Kumar, 1993) have touched on women as "doers," and some historians of social work have glanced at voluntary social work by women, but there are no historical studies, theoretical analyses, or empirical surveys of women as philanthropists.

This is a revised and extended version of a paper originally published in *Voluntas* (vol. 7, no. 4), the International Journal of Voluntary and Nonprofit Organizations and the official journal of the International Society for Third-Sector Research (ISTR). The authors gratefully acknowledge *Voluntas* and ISTR for their permission to reproduce this paper.

Despite the low socio-economic status of the Indian woman, and contrary to popular perception, women's philanthropy has deep roots in India, and women have made significant contributions to social progress even while remaining outside the formal power and profit structure. The examination here is chronological, treating somewhat separately the colonial and post-Independence periods. Women are considered as donors, as volunteers/social entrepreneurs, and as beneficiaries. These categories are not exclusive: a woman may be both donor and volunteer, and when the organization's work improves the position of women generally may also be a beneficiary. The focus is on middle- and upper-class women, for historically only these women had money for donation or time for volunteering. Only since the 1960s have poor women organized themselves into self-help and support organizations, contributing money (often as membership dues) and volunteering for organizational work.

THE RELIGIOUS BASIS OF PHILANTHROPY

In India charitable giving was a social obligation nurtured and sustained by religion. Intrinsic to Hinduism are the concepts of *dharma* or sacred duty expressed in right behavior, and *karma,* the law of moral and physical cause and effect which brought the good and bad results of behavior. Compassion or *karuna* was a virtue, and the Hindu was enjoined to undertake *yajna* (sacrifice), and *dana* (charity). Social obligation is also engendered by discharging the three debts or *rina: rishi rina* or debt to the sages (discharged by advancement of knowledge), *deva rina* or debt to the gods (discharged by service to humans), and *pitra rina* or debt to the ancestors (discharged by propitiation of ancestor spirits).

In the Vedic period (c. 1500–500 B.C.) *dana* and *yajna* were prescribed to acquire religious merit and a place in heaven. The Upanishads and the Bhagvat Gita, the most sacred Hindu texts, modified this motivation; the Gita enjoined selfless service to fellow humans to realize the Divine in oneself and to experience the unity of Life. The Gita's recasting of *yajna* and *dana* into the ideals of *loka sangraha* or universal human welfare became the basis for all subsequent Hindu social work (see Lokeshwarananda, 1968, 75–81; Ranganathananda, 1968, 46–52). Buddhist and Jaina religious canons had analogous prescriptions for charity. Islam, which came to India in the twelfth century and preached similar ideas about charity, brought with it a system of *zakat,* which required individuals to pay a certain percentage of their income to charity.

According to the ancient texts, the most precious gifts were those which enhanced spiritual knowledge, followed by secular knowledge; the least meritorious giving satisfied physical needs. Thus, in pre-British times, the most popular gifts were land, housing, or money to build or maintain temples, and endowments for maintenance of monasteries and educational institutions. Giving to Brahmin teachers, maintaining poor students, and presenting copies of manuscripts to schools and monasteries were popular gifts of secular knowledge. Other charitable activities included provision of food and drink to pilgrims at sacred places, and the care of the sick.

Women, no less than men, were motivated by religious ideals to donate time and money in the service of the needy. That they did so is clear from legends, inscriptions, and religious texts. While the charity of the average woman in pre-British times was probably limited to almsgiving to mendicants and students, there are several instances on record of wealthy women, especially queens and wives of wealthy merchants, giving wealth and houses to monastic orders, endowing temples, and building tanks and wells for public use.

SHIFTS IN TRADITIONAL VALUES

The British introduction of Western ideas and Christian ethics, new land and judicial systems, and modern industry and commerce dramatically affected traditional philanthropy. Missionary educational and charitable institutions established to spread the Christian message of service to humankind both reinforced and transformed indigenous charitable traditions. Liberals in the new elite were also influenced by English utilitarianism and evangelism, which stressed education as a panacea for India's problems. Thus, education became the most favored field for philanthropy in the colonial period. This was not a departure from traditional values, but instead of supporting temples and Brahmin priests, philanthropy was directed to modern secular schools. Imperialist theory held that "moral and material progress" was only possible through British institutions. Public resources could not support such institutions and, moreover, the British were proud of their charitable institutions which stood "as a monument to the superiority of voluntary action"(Owen, 1964, 164). British civil servants in India endeavored to create the same ethos by encouraging prominent Indians to donate to "productive" causes.

Although they continued the older forms of giving, both the traditional merchant elite and the new Western educated elite took to new philanthropic ventures, which not only gave them social prestige but was also good for their business and social advancement (see Haynes, 1987). These shifts in general philanthropic attitudes and values inevitably influenced women as well as men, so that those who could endowed or donated to new institutions, especially educational institutions. Most, however, were constrained in their giving by having no independent economic means. Many therefore turned to volunteering.

WOMEN AND REFORM

Of greater consequence to women's philanthropy than shifts in traditional values was a change in belief about women's social position, as the rights of women became an issue in the nineteenth century. Almost up to the beginning of the Christian era, Indian women enjoyed a high social position, but by then women were beginning to be pushed to a subordinate status. Manu, the famous Hindu law-giver of the early Christian era, decreed that:

> By a young girl, by a young woman, or even by an aged one, nothing must be done independently, even in her own house. In childhood a female must be subject to her father, in youth to her husband, when her lord is dead to her sons; a woman must never be independent (*Manusmriti, v,* 147–56, quoted in Sarasvati, 1888/1984, 58–59).

Girls began to be denied education, and were married off in childhood. If widowed they could not remarry and led such a harshly austere life that many preferred to commit *suttee* (immolate themselves on their husband's pyre), which came to be considered an act of meritorious devotion. Wage work was taboo, so women of the upper castes and class had no economic independence, and had limited property rights. Most of India followed a patrilineal system: a joint family with common property ruled by the eldest male was the norm.

Even where women enjoyed some rights in property, they had only a life interest; they did not enjoy full ownership rights and could not alienate, sell, or mortgage it. After the death of her husband, a widow had only a right of maintenance and could not claim any other rights in joint family property. A widow's right of usufruct over her husband's landed property was also subject to her not remarrying. But there was one class of property over which women had full control: the *stridhana* (women's wealth) given at the time of marriage. A woman was considered the absolute owner of such property and could dispose of it any way she liked. It usually went to her daughter after death. Theoretically, a woman had absolute control over her *stridhana,* but, in practice, it was often managed by the husband and used for the family.

In contrast, Muslim women in India enjoyed full property rights, although their share in the property was limited to half the share of the male of the same degree, and a widow's share was limited to one-eighth.

A woman was entitled to a dower from her husband which she could, theoretically, dispose of as she wanted, whereas she could dispose of her other property only up to a third (see Mehta, 1987; Singh, 1989). Although they had better property rights, Muslim women suffered many of the same disabilities as Hindus — limited social mobility due to confinement within purdah and lack of education — so that the property rights were again more apparent than real. With such restrictive property rights, it is not surprising that there were few women donors. Although a strong religious motivation to philanthropy would have prompted women to engage in philanthropic activities, their low position in society would have decidedly restricted their ability to act in the public domain. Only women with a sizeable *stridhana* could indulge their philanthropic impulse on any significant scale; it is noteworthy that many of them did devote their wealth to good purposes.

With the spread of Western education, the emergent bourgeoisie found Indian religion and society wanting in many respects, particularly regarding the position of women. The subsequent reform movement campaigned against polytheism, caste, idolatry, and the exploitation of women. The early campaigners for education of women, for abolition of child marriages, and for removing the disabilities suffered by widows were *men;* significantly, most were more concerned with improving the position of women in the family than their position in society.

The most important measure for improvement of women's rights was education. The first missionary girls schools opened in the 1810s in Bombay and Bengal, and thereafter education of girls became an important plank of reform. In 1854 only 25,000 girls were enrolled in schools; by 1902 the number had risen to 256,000 (Shah, 1984). The impact of education was quickly visible. The mid-century organizations to educate women, to ameliorate the lot of widows, and so on were almost entirely at the initiative of male reformers. By the late 1800s women began to form their own organizations. Several Christian missions — among them Bengal's Serampur Mission and Bangalore's Good Shepherd Convent — set up welfare organizations for destitute women, and in Pandharpur one of the first homes for abandoned babies was set up in 1875. D. K. Karve, one of the leading male reformers campaigning for widow remarriage and women's education, set up the first university for women in 1916.

More significant from the point of view of volunteering was the emergence of a new public activity: social service by widowed women for themselves and for the country. One of the most remarkable of these was Pandita Ramabai (1858–1922). In 1882 she formed a women's organization in Pune, and in 1889 started Sharada Sadan, a home and school for widows where they were taught skills to rehabilitate themselves (Kumar, 1993). In central India, Kamlabai Hospet, herself a child widow, trained herself as a nurse and started the Matru Sewa Mandir in 1904 to serve the maternity and other medical needs of poor women. Many widows themselves became volunteers in such organizations and helped run them. For instance, the widows' home set up by Karve expanded largely due to the efforts of his sister-in-law, Parvatibai Athavale, who was widowed at the age of twenty. In her autobiography she describes her travels throughout India to raise money for the Home. In all, she collected some 70,000 Rupees (a large sum for the time) in twenty years, a difficult feat since more public attention was given to political causes, and non-female institutions, than those for women (Athavale, 1928).

In Bengal, too, women were setting up associations to rehabilitate destitute women. One notable woman philanthropist was Swarnakumari Debi of the elite Tagore family. In 1886 she founded the Ladies Association to promote a spirit of service among Indian women, and to help widows and orphans by educating them. She raised money by holding women's handicraft fairs at which products made by women were sold to women. Later, she set up the Hiranmoyee Widow's Industrial Home (Kumar, 1993). Among the few women who endowed institutions for charitable causes was Maharani Chimnabai of Baroda State. She was actively involved in welfare activities for women and set an example for aristocratic philanthropy by founding several women's health, political and education organizations.

Until the late 1800s, women's agendas were largely welfare-oriented and non-political. Between 1880 and 1930, a women's movement emerged (Kumar, 1993), interwoven with the dominant events and ideologies of the day. In particular, the question of women's emancipation became enmeshed with emergent nationalism. On the one hand, women were concerned with the subordinate social condition of women. On the other, they saw themselves as mothers of the nation with a responsibility to emancipate the country from political bondage. Therefore, action by women took two forms: welfare work, and struggle for political rights and social reforms through legislation. The early twentieth century saw a proliferation of widow's homes and orphanages with an emphasis on education and training for employment. Women also expanded their role in relief work during plagues, famines and floods. At the same time, several significant national organizations were established to provide a political platform for women.

Women were realizing the importance of influencing the political process to make larger and lasting changes in women's position. Inspired by the Western suffrage movement, Indian women's organizations campaigned for the vote and for representation in legislative bodies, and once this was achieved they lobbied for legislative reforms from within and without political bodies (see Basu and Ray, 1990; see also Shah, 1984). Many of the women leaders of the day were involved both in politics and social work. They thus ensured that women and children's needs would be on the national agenda. But few women held political power, and women had more impact upon the national agenda through demonstrations and filing of memoranda. Women also moved into the newly available avenue of publishing opened up by the nationalist struggle. Many started or funded the publication of journals with a view to raising the self-awareness of women.

Most of the women's associations were privately funded from individual donations and gifts by the wealthy, and hardly any funding was offered by the state. The state's attitude towards such organizations was ambivalent. On the one hand, it encouraged women's volunteering, the formation of women's organizations, and their participation in public life as signs of women's awakening and the success of its education policy. Wives of rulers were active in founding or in volunteering in women's and other charitable organizations, such as the YWCA, industrial homes, and the Red Cross, and this provided an example to other Indian women. At the same time, since women's emancipation and the agendas of women's organizations were inextricably bound up with the freedom struggle, it viewed them with disfavor, especially those with a more political agenda.

WOMEN AND GANDHI

With the entry of Mahatma Gandhi on the Indian political scene in the 1920s, women's philanthropy entered yet another phase. Gandhi's emphasis on non-violent means of struggle inevitably made him turn to women to participate, both in the freedom struggle and in the task of reconstructing and regenerating Indian society. He sought to achieve both national freedom and emancipation of women by encouraging women to take an active part in social and political life, but as purely volunteer and not paid work. He believed the primary duty of women was to raise the next generation of the nation. Equally, he believed that they should become self-confident and develop their full potential through volunteer work. He therefore advocated women's social education, self-direction, and self-help.

The result was a tremendous unleashing of woman power. Many women were inspired to found new organizations and to involve themselves in work, not only for other women but also for all the underprivileged and the disabled in society. Among those influenced by

Gandhi were several women from wealthy families. Janaki Devi Bajaj, widowed wife of a leading industrialist, became a great worker in the Bhoodan movement for more equal land distribution in rural India. The Sarabhai family, leading mill owners in West India, were also deeply influenced by Gandhi, and both women and men took to philanthropic work, each contributing to their own field of interest.

Gandhi cast his spell not only on the aristocratic but also on the average Indian woman. Although it is impossible to record the names of the many Hindu and Muslim women who contributed or raised money to found charitable organizations for women in pre-Independence India, mention needs to be made of Durgabai Deshmukh who raised women's volunteering to new heights. After an initiation in the freedom struggle, Durgabai became a lawyer and fought many cases on behalf of women. She simultaneously founded one of the biggest women's welfare organizations, and as member of India's Planning Commission influenced government policy and set up the Central Social Welfare Board to co-ordinate, help, and develop existing voluntary social work in India.

It is important to note that all these social entrepreneurs and philanthropists accepted the Gandhian ideology that women's prime function and responsibility were to be housewife and mother and that, while men and women had equal rights, their duties were different. The organizations they belonged to believed in a complementary ordering of gender relations in society and were not seeking a radical change in these. Women's volunteering was an extension outside the home of their traditional role of nurturing and caring, and charitable giving by women followed a similar pattern in the types of organizations endowed and assisted. To summarize several points of interest about philanthropy in the colonial period:

- The period represents a transition from individual charity to organized philanthropy distinguished by a faith in collective action to bring about social change.

- Although the period was rich in the development of women's philanthropy, it was not necessarily distinguished by endowments of large fortunes by women for charity. Women's organizations, both activist and welfare, were funded almost entirely from private funds since no largesse could be expected from an alien government, especially for nationalist causes. This means that the bequests and donations which funded women's organizations during the period came largely from *stridhana.*

- The most distinctive characteristic of philanthropy during this period was the emergence of volunteering and social entrepreneurship. A generation of educated women took on social responsibility in the public domain for the first time, and collected funds and volunteered time in large numbers.

- In the emancipation of women, men played a significant role. Even when women began to take charge to fight for their rights, there was no overt or organized gender confrontation or conflict as in the Western world at the time, although undoubtedly women in the vanguard faced some opposition or criticism at home and in society.

- Philanthropic effort was largely concentrated in three areas: the education of women and girls; the relief of distress, especially of vulnerable women such as child widows, unmarried mothers, orphans and deserted women through provision of shelter and schemes for economic independence; and the political and legal emancipation of women.

WOMEN AS DONORS IN CONTEMPORARY INDIA

The nationalist and Gandhian fervor that motivated women's philanthropy ceased to be a strong motive force after Independence (1947). Centralized planning was adopted in the 1950s to foster modernization. As the state increased its role in welfare and development activities, there was a corresponding decrease in both voluntary action and philanthropic giving, accelerated by urbanization which diminished the sense of kinship and community responsibility. Inflation, the rise of consumerism, and the high tax regime instituted to finance government programs all reduced private wealth and donations. Taxes were considered akin to charitable contributions by many wealthy families. Misuse of funds by some charitable organizations and the use of trusts as tax dodges by some businesses also discredited philanthropy. Disinterest in philanthropy extended to women as well; immediately after Independence, women largely stopped taking an active interest in social issues.

In the late 1960s, however, the picture changed. There was a growing impatience not only with the government's inefficiency and ineffectiveness, but also with the apathy and dependent mentality of the masses. People turned once again to charitable activity as an instrument of social change. There was a notable growth of non-governmental organizations (NGOs) to undertake relief and developmental work. Once again, businesses and wealthy individuals began to support voluntary action with donations, especially once tax policy developed exemptions for philanthropy. Women's philanthropy, however, remained lethargic. The 1956

Hindu Succession Act greatly enhanced women's property rights but left important loopholes which perpetuated women's inequality. The 1975 National Committee on the Status of Women reviewed these loopholes and the inferior status of women of other religions. The committee made proposals to remove discrimination, but the picture has not changed substantially. The net result is that in practice women have not been able to inherit and bequeath family fortunes.

Whether women's charitable donations would have increased if property laws were more favorable is difficult to say, but the fact is they are still scant. With rare exceptions, no trust, foundation, or institution of any size has been endowed by women in contemporary times. The tradition of philanthropy for women by male benefactors has continued. The first women's university in India, started by D. K. Karve in 1916, was endowed by the wealthy Sir Thakersay in memory of his mother, and is today known as the Srimati Nathibai Damodar Thakersay (SNDT) University. More recently, the Chameli Devi Foundation was set up to give scholarships to deserving women journalists, and the Neerja Bhanot Foundation to give awards to women of exceptional courage in memory of an air hostess who died in a hijacking. But women-exclusive institutions commemorating female relatives are still rare.

WOMEN AND VOLUNTEERING

Women's volunteer work was dominated by Gandhi-influenced traditional women's organizations, and remained listless until the 1960s. In the late 1960s and early 1970s there was a sudden mushrooming of women's organizations, very different from the earlier ones, in response to a sudden acceleration of women's interest in social and economic issues. Women began to participate in public campaigns to protest inefficiency and corruption in government, and the failure of the development model to ease poverty and inequity. The Western women's liberation movement, the human rights movement, the International Women's Year in 1975, and the National Committee on the Status of Women, which highlighted the disadvantaged position of Indian women, all led to a radicalization of women. The 1975 National Emergency and the repression it caused led to a focus on civil liberties, in particular violence against women. The focus of campaigns to improve women's lives shifted from needs to rights; not only the right to parity but also to self-determination (Kumar, 1993, p. 3).

Initially the struggle was led by women activists working with progressive, radical, and leftist organizations fighting caste and class domination, and was more anti-state than anti-patriarchy. Women activists soon saw that progressive organizations' concerns did not extend to gender discrimination, and formed independent autonomous organizations of women. A further development was the growth of participatory groups of poor and low-caste women who realized that self-help would bring more enduring results than handouts. The result was a proliferation of women's organizations, in three broad categories:

- *"Women in development" organizations,* which sought to introduce new skills and technologies for women's employment and strategies to see that women were not exploited by forces of caste, class and patriarchy. The emphasis was on empowerment and development.

- *Radical social action groups,* which asserted that the gender-based division of labor and inheritance laws oppressed women. They concentrated on protest, and political and social pressure to achieve their objectives.

- *Support groups,* which offered legal aid and advice, credit, research and documentation, counselling and relief during crises.

Women have also been volunteers in a number of other welfare and development agencies working with and for the poor and disabled, such as the Red Cross and the YWCA. No discussion of contemporary women's philanthropy would be complete without mention of Mother Teresa and her workers, a majority of whom are women. Women also constitute a large part of the paid employed staff of the non-profit sector. The jobs are relatively lower paid than comparable jobs in the government or in the for-profit sector, but women have gravitated to them in part because of the flexibility they offer them to combine home and career.

It is impossible to estimate with any degree of accuracy the current number of women's organizations in India. The Indian Social Studies Trust estimates nearly fifty thousand women's organizations, in India, although it lists only fifty as being significant in degree of participation and outreach among women. The directory of NGOs published by the Industrial Development Bank of India (IDBI) numbers less than 144 exclusively women's NGO's, but if charitable welfare organizations, for women are included, the figure is likely to be much higher. There are also no statistics on the number of women volunteers or paid employees working in women's or other non-profit organizations, and therefore there is no way to quantify the value of women's volunteer or paid work. Nor is it possible to estimate the charitable contributions which women's organizations represent, or identify the favored fields of donation.

The new women's organizations are as much an expression of women's philanthropy as the older organizations, but there are important differences between them. In the pre-Independence period, many of the women's charitable organizations were the result of one outstanding personality who either donated her own money or collected funds from different sources. Although some new organizations are also born of the vision and leadership of one individual, many are the result of collective effort by students and professionals motivated by feminist ideology, rather than by religion, liberal ideals, or nationalism. They view themselves not as charitable workers but as members in a common cause with a shared ideology* (Kumar, 1993, 144).

In contrast to the earlier women's groups which were confined to the urban middle and upper classes, the new women's groups mobilize and sensitize women at all class and caste levels to the realities of women's lives, and have created in them a desire to challenge social and legal conventions. The new volunteers are not necessarily urban, or upper class and caste, although many wealthy women donate their time and money to charitable organizations.

The newer groups also differ from those of the earlier period in the pattern of their funding. While the earlier groups depended almost entirely on private contributions, the sources of funding today are more varied. Unfortunately, there are few detailed studies on how women's organizations are funded. An exception is a study by Gandhi and Shah (1991), who examine funding as an important issue for sustaining the women's movement, although there are no quantitative comparisons of different funding sources. On the basis of conversations with some women's groups and the Gandhi and Shah work, it is clear that outright and regular donations or bequests count for less than other means of funding. In general, women's groups rely on raising funds from membership fees, from special charitable events and sale of goods, and from government or foreign funding organizations.

There are no overall figures to indicate the total size of government or foreign funding of NGOs, either general or for women, nor of their relative importance in the sector, or relative to individual giving. Impressionistically, the importance of different sources of funding appears to vary from organization to organization, depending particularly on its ideological stance and its skill in accessing one source or the other. Women's welfare and development agencies seem to depend more on government and foreign funding than do radical social ac-

---

*For this insight I thank members of Jagori, a Delhi women's activist organization, and of the Center for Women's Development Studies.

tion groups, who are more particular about their sources of funds since these can influence the direction of programs. Largely due to fear of ideological subversion, most radical organizations prefer to forgo government and foreign money and to generate funds from membership dues, fundraising events, and the sale of goods or services.

Gandhi and Shah point out that there is a positive side to this mode of fundraising since it ensures active involvement and participation of donors, and also acts as political education and consciousness-raising. A problem is that it takes much time and raises limited amounts of money (Gandhi and Shah, 1991, 298–99). Moreover, although there are no supporting data, it appears that the average woman does not necessarily want to give to women's causes alone and is drawn to general welfare-oriented charities, especially those concerned with children. Although men also endow and donate to institutions in memory or in honor of women, they are less enthusiastic about contributing to women-exclusive organizations or causes, especially if they are considered radical in any way. From Gandhi and Shah's study, it appears that business donors are less likely to favor radical women's organizations and vice versa, although businesses contribute more readily to traditional anti-poverty programs for women. The study observes that, in general, women's groups find that businesses are interested in getting political mileage through their funding and are uninterested in small "non-aligned" groups and their alternative development models (Gandhi and Shah, 1991, 300–301).

CONCLUSION

In many societies, religion is an enabling factor in philanthropy, opening "space" for women and legitimizing their role in the public domain. In India, however, religion has played an ambiguous role. While Hinduism and Islam have motivated women to be more charitable in the sense of donating money for the public good, they have restrained women from acting in the public domain, limiting their mobility and independence of action. The superimposition of a Christian ethic has been somewhat different. It encouraged women's volunteerism and enabled the emergence of women's volunteerism outside the home, but its values were patriarchal and did not encourage women to play a more active role in other spheres, especially where this was likely to lead to changes in gender relations in society. Moreover, for the younger generation of urban, upper- and middle-class women, religion is beginning to count for less than a secular humanitarian ethic. Among lower-class and caste women too, participation in women's organizations represents more a secular desire for self-betterment and an expression of sisterly solidarity than religious belief.

Given that their existing disabilities were sanctioned by traditional and religious influences, it was not unnatural that women gravitated towards "maternalist" agendas, in the institutions they supported with time and money, and in the causes they lobbied for change in laws and policies. Although both men reformers and the government — colonial and national — showed concern for women's plight and welfare, this was, and continues to be, paternalistic concern within a patriarchal framework. For this reason women are likely to continue to focus on issues of women and children, though not exclusively. With more secularization and greater mobility, their agendas are likely to become more diverse, especially since even in the past Indian women have served not only women's interests but also wider causes such as freedom from colonial rule, maintenance of civil liberties, and elimination of government corruption and inefficiency.

In both the colonial and post-Independence periods, the state has represented strong centralized authority, but this has not made much difference to women's philanthropy either directly, or indirectly through affecting public policy. The different political conditions made a difference of degree rather than substance in the nature of women's philanthropic activities. Since there is no point of comparison, it is difficult to prove the thesis that women's organizations have more authority in weak states than in centralized ones. If one talks of authority relative to men's, then in neither period can women's organizations be said to have had more power, political or otherwise, than other national organizations in India, and it is improbable that they would have had relatively more power with a weaker central authority.

It is not necessarily through direct political participation that women have made an impact on national agendas, especially on women's matters. If anything, the presence of women at the head of government or in legislatures has counted for less than their organized presence outside. By exercising their vote in large numbers, women — especially poor women in rural and urban areas — have voted out governments they did not like. And through research, use of the media, public demonstrations and lobbying, they have brought women's issues to center stage. At the same time it cannot be denied that women's achievement in the social and political sphere would have been greater if they had had direct access to political power.

The history of women's social entrepreneurship also shows that women in India, as elsewhere, have used multiple organizational strategies to carve out a niche for themselves, and to exercise power indirectly, in the absence of direct access. They have created women-exclusive organizations and women's political parties, trade unions, and so on, but equally they have worked through gender-neutral non-profit organizations like the Red Cross. But clearly it is women-exclusive organizations which not only enable women to exercise more power both within and without the organization but also allow *more* women to exercise or share that power. The women-exclusive organizations confer an identity, a sense of worth, and a feeling of solidarity on numbers of women and enable some leaders to move on to other more important positions, elected or appointed. In this sense, women's volunteering or social entrepreneurial activity enables them to create alternative or parallel power structures and to use them for politicizing and socializing women, either directly or indirectly.

It is also clear that, in their struggle for recognition of their rights and needs by the state and society, Indian women have been influenced and helped by liberal and feminist movements outside India, as well as by foreign funding. Although one cannot go so far as to say that these have played a crucial role in opening a "space" for civil society, undeniably they have contributed ideas and helped women sustain causes or organizations until their acceptance by the government and society. More importantly, perhaps, they have been instrumental in setting up pressures on the government to move in the desired direction.

REFERENCES

Athavale, P. 1928. *Hindu Widow: An Autobiography,* trans. from Marathi into English by Rev. Justin E. Abbot, 1930. New Delhi: Republished by Reliance Publishing, 1986.

Basu, A. and B. Ray. 1990. *Women's Struggle: A History of the All India Women's Conference, 1927–1990.* New Delhi: Manohar Publications.

Gandhi, N., and N. Shah. 1991. *The Issues at Stake: Theory and Practice in Contemporary Women's Movement in India.* New Delhi: Kali for Women.

Haynes, D. E. 1987. "From Tribute to Philanthropy: The Politics of Gift Giving in a Western Indian City," *Journal of Asian Studies* 46:339–60.

Kumar, R. 1993. *The History of Doing.* London and New York: Verso; New Delhi: Kali for Women.

Lokeshwarananda, S. 1968. "Charity and Charitable services," *Encyclopaedia of Social Work in India,* vol. 1. Planning Commission, Government of India, New Delhi.

Mehta, R. 1987. *Socio-legal Status of Women in India.* Delhi: Mittal Publications

Owen, D. 1964. *English Philanthropy, 1660–1960.* Cambridge, Mass.: Belknap Press.

Ranganathananda, S. 1968. "Philosophy of Social Work: Traditional," *Encyclopaedia of Social Work in India,* vol. 2. Planning Commission, Government of India.

Report of the Committee on the Status of Women in India (1975) Government of India, New Delhi.

Sarasvati, P. R. 1888. *The High Caste Hindu Woman.* Philadelphia. Republished 1984 by Inter-India Publications, New Delhi.

Shah, K. 1984. *Women's Liberation and Voluntary Action.* New Delhi: Ajanta Publications.

Singh, I. P. 1989. *Women, Law and Social Change in India.* London and New Delhi: Sangam Books.

Women and Philanthropy in South Korea from a Non-Western Perspective

HYE KYUNG LEE

INTRODUCTION

"Philanthropy" is one of the few English words that is still waiting for an appropriate translation in Korea. For most Koreans, love toward humankind is not associated with the practical forms of down-to-earth historical experiences, such as the works of Andrew Carnegie, John D. Rockefeller, and Henry Ford. It is an imported notion that is heavily loaded with Western connotations of enlightened individualism, plural- ist democracy, civic culture, and advanced capitalism. The difficulty in its translation, however, does not necessarily mean that the concept itself is not accepted in contemporary Korea. (For similar reasons, the Japanese use the English word and write it in Katakana.) On the contrary, the no- tion is already quite widely received and is becoming more and more of an important part of Korean society. In particular, recent democratiza- tion and economic achievements, as well as the fall of the Berlin Wall, have combined to increase the interest, both academic and practical, in the makings of the civic sector in Korea.

As is well known, Korea had been one of the poorest agrarian econo- mies in the world until the early 1960s. Within one generation or so, it has grown into a strong candidate for membership in the Organiza- tion for Economic Cooperation and Development (OECD), with a per capita GNP of $10,000. Ever since the liberation from the Japanese occu- pation, many forward-looking Korean leaders have aspired to transform the society, to inculcate pluralist democracy instead of authoritarian dictatorship, civic culture instead of subject culture, and enlightened capitalism instead of jungle materialism. But the change has been slow and the reality has always been dynamic and dialectical: competition among contending values, usually old and new, traditional and mod- ern, has ended up in complicated compromises unique to Korea. This is the process of indigenization of the new and transformation for the old. Women's philanthropy represents a new requirement of the changing Korea, which is also invariably in the process of indigenization, that is, Koreanization.

This paper has three objectives: first, to analyze the concept of women's philanthropy from a Korean perspective; second, to identify and examine the factors that have encouraged and discouraged its development and thereby shaped its making; and, third, to delineate the evolution of women's philanthropy in Korea. After all, this is a case study of the development of women's philanthropy in a country where the age-old authoritarian and patriarchal culture has interacted with the democratic, egalitarian demand of rapid industrialization and its concomitant social changes, particularly of women. In the second section of this paper, the definition and the various ways of classifying women's philanthropic activities are discussed. The third section provides the context of the evolving philanthropy of women in Korea with a number of its potential determinants. Discussed are the nature of the relationship between the organic state and the civic sector in Korea and three other conditions that are deemed to have a direct impact upon women's social position — that is, women's education, women's employment, and the changing family life cycle. The profile and evolution of Korean women's philanthropy is presented in section four. The paper closes with brief remarks on future prospects and directions.

WOMEN'S PHILANTHROPY:
THE CONCEPT AND CLASSIFICATION

Although the term "philanthropy" is still searching for a proper translation in Korea, it is defined in this paper as voluntary giving of money and time for a public purpose. All non-remunerative activities, not for self-interest but for a public purpose, are to be called philanthropy, to cover the wide range of activities of nongovernmental organizations (NGOs), foundations, volunteers, corporate giving, individual donations, nonprofit organizations, and so forth. By this definition, women's philanthropy is a concept much broader than the feminist movement.

The notion of women's philanthropy presupposes a few conditions. Women's voluntary giving of money and time for a public purpose implies, first, women's free will to decide what to do; second, women's possession of money and time; and, third, recognition of women's activities outside the home in connection with public affairs, perhaps with men. These are the conditions that could hardly be met in a Confucian traditional society.

Indeed, considering the age-old patriarchal frame of Confucian culture, which emphasizes women's subordination to men, the idea of women's voluntary giving of time and money for a public purpose is quite revolutionary in itself. Women, under the old Confucian order in Korea, were taught the virtue of the Three Obediences: obedience to parents in childhood, to husband after marriage, and to children (sons) in old age. Absolute obedience to one's husband was held to be an essential virtue of all women. Moreover, there were the so-called Seven Deadly Sins for married women, which could be cited as grounds for divorce: (1) refusal to obey parents-in-law, (2) failure to bear children, (3) adultery, (4) jealousy, (5) contracting a serious malady, (6) garrulity, and (7) theft. It may be noted that except for the last offense, all the other grounds for divorce originated in the requirements of the feudal family system. Divorce was a punishment almost like excommunication, which brought unbearable disgrace not only to the woman but to her family. The wife was taken as a functional asset, not as an individual, for fulfilling various duties in relation to other members of the family. She could not lend anything to others, even to her own father and mother, without her husband's permission. Often she was not allowed to visit her parents without her husband's permission. She was expected to do only household work. The segregation of man and woman was so strict that a married woman was not supposed to expose her face to other men in the street. Consequently, there was no social interaction between men and women, whether married or single.

Lives of Korean women today are incomparably free and independent. They are more educated, many of them are now in paid jobs, occupy high public positions, and participate more in associations than in the past. When compared to the men in Korea, however, gender equality is still more an aspiration than a reality. Women's philanthropic organizations are increasing in number and influence, but they are still very much underfunded and understaffed. The conditions of women's philanthropy mentioned above — that is, the social recognition of women as independent human beings, women's right to property, and gender equality of opportunity in social participation — are still in formation in Korea, circumscribing the contours of women's philanthropic activities.

In order to understand the uniqueness of women's philanthropy in Korea, various dimensions and classificatory criteria might usefully be considered. First, the definition of this study includes both volunteers and donors as philanthropists. Women philanthropists in Korea are mainly the volunteers rather than the donors. Women can give money for a public purpose as philanthropists typically when they are permitted to have inheritance; if they do not donate their inheritance they make themselves women of fortune. The image of women philanthropists as donors is closely associated with advanced capitalism. With the development of capitalism, and perhaps with the decreasing influence of familism in Korea, there will be an increasing opportunity for more women donors, but Korea today is at the stage where male tycoons have just begun to show an interest in corporate philanthropy. Now and then the stories of women who bequeath their life savings to the universities appear in the newspaper. But they are mostly those who do not have children or other relatives.

Second, philanthropic activities can be differentiated by their functions: the service functions versus representational advocacy functions. Some provide services such as health, education, personal services, and arts and culture, but others have an essentially representational role, advocating particular causes or on behalf of certain groups. Women's philanthropic organizations in Korea have had both service and representational functions. But their activities have been very poorly documented. Particularly women's voluntary services for the poor and sick have been provided through various organizational networks that are mostly initiated under religious auspices, usually male-dominated. Advocacy-oriented women's philanthropy has been led by women intellectuals and women leaders and has been far louder.

The general relationship between the state and civic sector signifies much of the varying nature of philanthropic activities. Particularly in societies of authoritarian state culture, it is the state that decides what these civic groups can do. The government, with its authorities of financing, regulatory, and service functions, can have one set of relationships with respect to the service functions and another with respect to the advocacy functions of philanthropic organizations. One of the most commonly applied criteria to differentiate the women's philanthropic organizations has been this relationship with the government — that is, whether they are pro-government or anti-government. Under the authoritarian developmental state, much of the freedom and civil rights of dissenters was curtailed in the name of security and international competition. In the meantime, there was rapid growth not only in industry, but also in civic social groups that demanded a reduction in the state's relative autonomy. Civic group activities in this period were actually classified by the government into two categories: advocacy-oriented activities for the promotion of social justice, democracy, and human rights on behalf of workers, farmers, and other alienated people in society; and mainly education- and service-oriented groups. While the latter were often actively supported, sometimes initiated, and at other times left relatively less-controlled by the government, the former were labeled as "anti-government" and severely repressed, many eventually being forced into the underground.

For those who opposed the dictatorial regimes, being pro-government meant supporting the government, which they believed to be corrupt, dictatorial, repressive, illegitimate, and unjust, while the anti-government dissident forces were regarded as representing social justice, progressiveness, righteousness, egalitarianism, and democracy. It was a distinction that led to oversimplification, but it is quite unique to the Korean situation, reflecting the low level of its political development. This sort of characterization has been gradually losing its power with political democratization after 1987. Still, the civic leaders in various new and old organizations are asked which camp they belonged to under those authoritarian regimes, as are the leaders of women's organizations.

A more analytic classification can be made according to the choice of strategies, as suggested by Kathleen D. McCarthy (1994), who distinguished three philanthropic strategies that American women have used: separatism, assimilationism, and individualism. In separatism, women work together with other women to develop nonprofit organizations and social reform movements. In the assimilationist strategy, they work within male-controlled organizations, generally as donors. The individualist approach is adopted by independent and wealthy women who wandered away from both men's and women's groups to create institutions and foundations of their own, on their own. The individualist approach is rarely found in Korea. As a variant form of this approach, there have recently emerged a number of art museums established by the big conglomerates and headed by CEOs' wives. (There is no gift from the CEOs' wives involved.) Endowment comes usually from both the company and the owner of the company; the art museum is typically represented by his wife. This type of approach represents the case of another gender division of labor within the families of tycoons in Korea. Very few assimilationists are found as donors to male-controlled nonprofit organizations, except a few women who bequeath their life savings to the universities, as mentioned above.

The major strategy of women's philanthropy in Korea seems to be separatism in the sense that women work together with other women mainly as volunteers, sometimes as entrepreneurial organizers. Although the number is not well known, there should be many assimilationist women volunteers who have been working in organizations, institutions, and associations where men work together. Female factory workers participate in the labor movement, women volunteers help the handicapped in rehabilitation centers, housewives organize green community movements — the examples are endless. Sometimes they establish a women's chapter as a subdivision of the larger organization of the labor movement, environmental movement, consumer movement, and so forth. But other times, women's separatist organizations incorporate various causes including gender equality and democracy, modernization, and reunification. Thereby they collaborate closely with male-dominated higher-order civic organizations. This is a peculiar aspect of the Korean women's strategy that requires further elaboration. The Korean women's separatist strategy is often within the framework of collaborative support from higher-order social movements.

From earlier days, Korean women leaders have tended to participate in higher order social movements for causes broader than women's development, such as patriotism, national independence, reunification, the urban poor, industrial workers, human rights, the environment, and so forth. Many of them coordinate with larger male-dominated organizations. Thus far, these organizations tend to gain more organized support and have better social standing in Korea. But, as can be seen in the later pages of this paper, feminist voices are raising questions regarding the possible detrimental effects of the assimilationist strategy.

Five dimensions of women's philanthropy have been discussed, and for each dimension, a number of alternatives are identified. As for the mode of participation, one may be a volunteer, donor, or entrepreneurial organizer. As for the strategy, choices include separatism, assimilationism, and individualism. As for the main function of the activities, a service orientation and advocacy orientation can be differentiated. As for the issue commitment, a specifically feminist commitment and a broader commitment to general social causes can be differentiated. The dimension of the relationship between the state and philanthropic sector is useful particularly when the society has a history of a strong authoritarian state.

WOMEN'S PHILANTHROPY:
KOREAN CONTEXTS AND DETERMINANTS

Two of the most striking features of contemporary Korea are its phenomenal economic growth since the early 1960s and its recent democratization. In 1960, per capita GNP was only $80, one of the lowest in the world. In 1995, it reached $10,000. In 1996, Korea became a member of the world's rich countries' club, the OECD. Many scholars have attempted to answer the puzzle of why Korea has grown so much faster than most developing countries. Needless to say, many different explanations have been generated. The commonplace observation is that the miracle has been orchestrated by a strong, ubiquitous, interventionist state. By this success case, the orthodox or neoclassical economic theories that stress the economic benefits of the minimalist regulatory role of the state are severely challenged. All the socioeconomic, politico-cultural changes that Korean society has undergone incorporate dynamic interactions with overarching political authoritarianism. This section depicts the changing relationship between the state and the civic sector in general during recent decades, as well as the changing conditions of women through the examination of three major government policy areas.

Two modes describe the relationship between the state and society: the liberal pluralist model and the organic model. Liberal pluralist theorists contend that the state is what the civil society makes of it. The state's governing structure takes its forms and functions from the diverse groups of various interests and their government. The major state organ through which group views are formulated and negotiated is the legislature. The direction of influence is from society to the state, not vice versa. The state is society-determined and should remain so. The central purpose of the state is to guarantee individual freedom, equality, and happiness as proclaimed in the constitution. The overarching philosophy of the liberal pluralist state is the belief in the primacy of the individual.

On the other hand, the so-called organic theorists of the state contend that the state derives its legitimacy from the very nature of what it ought to be, a provider or a precipitator of a common good, a moral and just order. It moves by its inner ethical and moral imperatives, not necessarily by what the society wills to it. Under the organic state, the relative state autonomy is considerable, though by no means absolute, because an organic state does not negate basic elements of civil society. The state's primary interest is that these elements conform to work toward common goals and objectives for the collective good.

While the United States is said to be a prime example of the liberal pluralist state, though not without organic features, the state of contemporary Korea comes close to an Asiatic Confucian version of the organic state, although it aspires to move gradually toward the liberal pluralist model. In the Confucian tradition, there is no distinction between the state and society. The role of the state is to cultivate moral values through its rites. It is the state that should educate and by so doing transform the behavior of the rules, not the other way round. People do not determine the role of the state.

Indeed the Korean state during the few decades preceding 1987 may be described as a de facto authoritarian organic state, one that could make vital decisions, essentially ignore their political and social implications, and then implement them with precision. But this state had to suffer from legitimacy crises, having trouble with the growing civic sector claiming the primacy of the individual and pluralist democracy. Ever since a modern state with a parliamentary form of government was born in 1948 in Korea, several cycles of constitutional and military regimes can be discerned that have swung back and forth. Initially a new regime made an attempt to realize a constitutional democracy, but as time passed it sought to remain in power by repressive measures. Opposition forces and students carried out violent demonstrations to challenge what they perceived to be a dictatorial regime. And as Chalmers Johnson (1988) states, the Olympics with which Chun tried to sponsor Korean nationalism proved to be a great challenge, opening a window of opportunity for protests. He was driven to make concessions, and the Sixth Republic was ushered in by the presidential election of 1987 and the parliamentary election of 1988, inaugurating parliamentary democracy. It survived to be succeeded by the civilian president Y. S. Kim as head of a democratic regime.

Throughout these years, the independent civic sector has been able to develop only in the limited sociopolitical space left by the authoritarian state for legitimate activity. In fact, its roles and functions have been grossly downplayed by the state. Nevertheless, the 1987 Declaration of Democratization itself signified the failure of the authoritarian state and the success of the civic forces, particularly of the opposition coalition forces.

With the abrupt end of the authoritarian regime in June 1987, there emerged increasingly effective and sophisticated civic groups led by the younger generation emphasizing progressive advocacy functions. This positive development within the civic community was accompanied by a remarkable upsurge of public, scholarly, and business attention focused on the role of NGOs and philanthropy, not only as alternative providers of public services but also as a vehicle for active citizen participation. Particularly important is that the new democratic government, of which many leaders were themselves active in opposition groups during the Yushin period, is inclined to appreciate the role of the civic sector not as an adversary but as an ally. This change may contribute to the development of a more effective mechanism to improve cooperation between the state and the civic sector, and perhaps cooperation among civic organizations. Women's philanthropy in Korea has grown along with the recent history of modernization.

CHANGING STATUS OF WOMEN AND DETERMINANTS

The concept of women's philanthropy makes sense only when women are regarded as independent human beings and are entitled to the same opportunity for self-expression as men. Foundations for women's philanthropy in this sense began to be laid in Korea when the Confucian hermit kingdom of the Yi Dynasty began to meet with capitalist Western culture. Individualism as opposed to familism and democracy as opposed to centripetal authoritarianism came into contact with Western technology, Western medicine, and the modern school system, first introduced by Christian missionaries in the nineteenth century. The process of modernization thereafter contributed to the liberation of women in Korea. Three of the many potential determinants of women's social status today are examined in this section. One is women's education, initiated by the early Christian missionaries; the second is family planning policies since the 1960s; and the third is the increasing employment of women that accompanied economic growth.

Modern Education of Women

Education increases a woman's ability to participate in society and to improve her quality of life and standard of living. It enables her to raise her productivity in both market and nonmarket work and improves her access to paid employment and higher earnings. Educated women have more control over the time they spend in child-rearing — and thus have more time for productive work outside the home and for leisure. They are more likely to use contraceptives and to have smaller families.

The modern education system was introduced by Christian missionaries and survived the occupation period and on into the post-liberation years. A compulsory public education system at the elementary school level was initiated by forward-thinking Korean educators before independence, and was formally adopted by the government established in 1948. The fundamental enthusiasm for education that lay in the traditional culture itself was increased by the decline of the landlord class after independence. In order to maintain their former social status, many of the former landlords were obliged to invest their residual resources in the education of their children.

From 1953 to 1963, the literacy rate rose from 30 percent to 80 percent. The number of college students rose about eighteen-fold during the same period. This exceptionally successful educational development is often cited as one of the most important factors that has generated the economic success of the 1960s by promoting productivity and technology and by increasing mobility and adaptability for economic change. Moreover, this relatively advanced development of modern education in Korea laid the groundwork for the growth of counterforces that have rejected the state ideology of authoritarianism as well as the ideology of male primacy.

Table 1. School Enrollment Ratio by Level and Sex

	1980		1985		1993	
	Male	*Female*	*Male*	*Female*	*Male*	*Female*
Primary	102.9	103.7	100.0	100.1	101.5	102.1
Middle	95.1	92.5	100.1	99.6	97.0	97.4
High	63.5	56.2	79.5	75.5	89.2	87.9
College and University	11.5	5.8	25.0	14.8	29.6	19.4

During and after the 1960s, education continued to expand with the growing resources available. Enrollment rates at all levels of education increased. That at the elementary level reached 97 percent in 1966 and has registered 100 percent ever since 1970. The same is true for middle and high schools, which increased from 72 percent in 1966 to 92 percent in 1980. As for the gap between men and women in enrollment ratios, at the level of elementary school and middle school the ratios reached 100 percent for both boys and girls as of 1985. At the middle school level, the male enrollment ratio increased from 95.1 percent to 97 percent, while the female rate changed from 92.5 percent to 97.4 percent. The female ratio has not only caught up with the male's but has slightly surpassed it. A similarly accelerated rate of increase in the female enrollment ratio was found at the high school level where the male enrollment ratio moved from 63.5 percent to 89.2 percent while the female ratio increased from 56.2 percent to 87.9 percent. At the college and university level, the female enrollment ratio more than tripled from 5.8 percent to 19.4 percent while the male's rose by two and a half times from 11.8 percent to 29.6 percent. In other words, the 1992 female ratio at the college and university level still lagged behind the male's by more than 10 percent.

As shown in Table 2, Koreans still expect a lower educational attainment of their daughters than of their sons. Whereas 86.5 percent of the respondents expected to have their sons finish college in 1993, only 79.4 percent expected their daughters to finish college. The difference in 1993 is far narrower than that (23 percent) in 1972.

The education policy in Korea has been a great success in extending access. Thereby, women's educational status has been improved to a great extent. Schools in Korea do not explicitly underwrite gender discrimination. As far as admission policies are concerned, the principle of equal opportunity is honored. But schools seldom take further steps to redress sexual inequality, that is, to take affirmative action for disadvantaged female students. On the contrary, in educational objectives,

Table 2. Expected Level of Education for Children

		1977	1982	1987	1993
	Middle	7.5	0.2	1.6	1.4
Son	High	36.2	11.5	12.1	12.1
	College	55.2	70.7	61.9	64.6
	Graduate +	0.8	17.6	24.4	21.9
	Middle	23.7	2.9	3.9	3.0
Daughter	High	42.7	33.8	20.4	17.6
	College	33.3	55.1	61.3	64.8
	Graduate +	0.3	8.2	14.4	14.6

the curriculum, textbooks, and all aspects of schooling, the prevailing traditional views on women are taken for granted.

Family Planning and Changes in Family Life Cycle

The Third Republic (1961–69) was convinced that the control of population growth was a prerequisite for fast economic growth. So it launched a rigorous family planning program. The state's policy objective of the Korean Family Planning Program, 1962–71, was to decrease the annual population growth rate from 2.9 percent in 1961 to 2.0 percent by 1971. The program target was later revised to an even lower growth rate of 1.5 percent by 1976, and the growth rate indeed slowed to less than 1.0 percent by 1992. This performance is often quoted as the success story of population control among developing countries.

The state policy of family planning is one of the most obvious means of state intervention into the private area of family life, especially of women. The success of the family planning programs — that is, birth control programs — in Korea has created profound changes in the lives of women. First, fewer children meant overall changes in the life cycle of women, one of whose primary functions was to raise children. Table 3 on the following page shows the changes in the life cycle of three different cohorts of married women as suggested by the recent research of the Korean Institute for Population and Health. The 1935–44 marriage cohorts, who were sixty-one years old on average as of 1985, married at the age of sixteen with a husband five years older and had six children. It took forty years for them to raise and marry all their children. They became widows at fifty-five, that is five years after the last child got married.

The life cycle of the younger women is quite different. As is demonstrated in Table 3, the 1975–85 marriage cohort, whose average age was twenty-eight as of 1985, married late, is expected to have fewer chil-

Table 3. Changing Family Life Cycle by Marriage Cohorts

Family Cycle Events	Marriage Cohorts of		
	1935–44	1955–64	1975–85
First marriage	16.1	20.4	22.6
(husband's age)	(20.8)	(24.3)	(26.4)
First child's birth	20.2	22.3	23.8
Last child's birth	35.7	31.4	36.0
First child's marriage	45.0	48.5	50.0
Last child's marriage	50.5	57.6	52.2
Husband's death	54.7	58.0	67.2
Death of self	60.6	66.0	74.4
Number of children	6	4	2
Years from first child's birth to last child's marriage	40	36	28
Years of empty nest	1	8	23
Years from marriage to death	45	46	52
Average age as of 1985	61	46	28

dren, spend a shorter period in child-raising, and live longer. At the average age of thirty-six, her last child is born. By the time her second child enters college, she is about forty. Being better educated and having more facilities and machines to help her with domestic work, compared to her elder generation, she is in the better position practically to seek opportunities for self-expression outside the home.

Second, the implementation of the family planning programs involved not only technical actions but also the inculcation of changes in values and attitudes regarding family size, the spacing of children, and sex roles. During the 1970s, the family planning slogan was "No distinction of Daughter and Son, Stop at Two and Bring Them Up Well." The slogan flooded newspapers, magazines, radio, and television. The idea was identified with the forward-looking, change-oriented character of national development. The hidden significant message was something very close to sexual equality, whether the government realized it or not.

Third, the nationwide family planning movement brought about the creation of an immense national network of Mothers' Clubs. Since 1968 the Mothers' Clubs had been organized on a voluntary basis in order to promote motivation and participation in family planning among members. By 1971, they had grown into a nationwide movement with a membership of twenty to forty women in each of nineteen thousand villages. It has become a basic multipurpose organ for the nationwide new village movement. Thereby the Mothers' Clubs at the village level have helped in integrating the family planning program into the broader aspects of community development. It is arguable to what extent these Mothers' Clubs were instrumental for more effective population control, but it is significant to note that this organization provided a precious window for women's social participation, especially in rural villages.

Job Creation and Double Burden

There has been a positive relationship between the progress of economic development and women's participation in the world of work outside the home. Not only in terms of an absolute and relative increase in the number of working women, but also in terms of the increasing variety of jobs open to them, economic growth during the last few decades has indeed brought with it unprecedented opportunities for Korean women. No line of work is completely closed to women, and even the deeply seated taboos against women entering the mines or boarding ships have been broken down.

Such a seemingly smooth picture, however, obscures certain peculiarities characterizing the pattern of women's participation in the nation's overall work force. The first peculiarity, and of overriding importance, is the fact that the women's labor force is heavily concentrated in the unskilled, low-paying sectors of the economy. For the two decades between 1960 and 1980, the largest improvement in the women's participation ratio occurred in agriculture, forestry, and fishing, where it jumped from 30.4 percent to 44.9 percent. Women's participation in the manufacturing sector also increased sharply, from 26.7 percent to 36.2 percent, reflecting an eight-fold increase in absolute terms. But here, too, most of the women were concentrated in the production lines of the textile industry, the leader in the rapidly expanding export economy, which was banking on the readily available pool of cheap but high quality labor that women provided. As the economy expanded, women's participation in white collar work also registered a steady rise. But most of these women were found in a limited variety of low-skill or unskilled jobs — receptionist, typist, or telephone operator. Men, by contrast, exercised a near monopoly on middle management and supervisory positions.

The second feature to be pointed out in the labor force participation of Korean women is the double load of domestic work and market-oriented activities that a large segment of them bear. In 1970, of the women engaged in agriculture and forestry, 87.8 percent were married, and 75.5 percent of them worked without pay. In the tertiary sector, the highest ratio of women's participation has been in the service segment, in which small businesses employ fewer than two persons and are run on the family premises. Here, women are expected to carry their normal load of work as housewives in addition to producing goods and services for sale. In each case, women's work outside the home, although it makes a vital contribution to the household economy, is looked upon as a secondary activity, never to be offered as a grounds for neglecting women's traditional responsibilities as homemakers. Support systems such as child care facilities or husbands sharing the housework are still almost totally absent.

The third anomaly, closely related to the second, is that the women's labor force participation ratio is higher in the lower educational bracket and in rural areas. Since it is the man who is traditionally looked upon to provide for the family, even when he is actually incapable of doing so, the fiction has to be carefully maintained for the peace of all concerned. This means that women have to engage in income-producing activities, making themselves as inconspicuous as possible, and forego better employment opportunities even when they present themselves. This negative attitude toward work, in turn, breeds a negative attitude toward working women, which further limits women's chances of obtaining favorable opportunities.

These characteristics indicate that the dramatic rise in the proportion of women working outside the home has not been accompanied by an equally impressive improvement in the relative economic status of women. The relationship between women's paid employment and unpaid philanthropy is moot because there is no information available regarding exactly who are the women volunteers, women donors, and women entrepreneurial philanthropists.

Women's philanthropy in a given society is determined by numerous variables. Some are favorable, and others are unfavorable; they also interact with each other. Confucian values of the organic state that downplay the role of the pluralist civic sector, Confucian values of authoritarian patriarchal familism that presuppose women's subordination, and the traditional gender division of labor both in the public and private spheres are the factors that limit women's participation in philanthropic activities. Advancement of women's education and self-consciousness, increasing labor market participation, and the changing family life cycle due to successful family planning policy are some of the forces that push women from the traditional roles within the family into the broader society and encourage women's philanthropy. Of course, the reality is far more complicated. Each factor interacts with the others and does not necessarily correlate in a simple linear way with the dependent variable with the same strength. The dynamism of the gender division of labor, gender discrimination, and male supremacy interacts with the forces that demand women's minimum dignity. The most painful devaluation of women is the physical and psychological violence that stalks women from cradle to grave. Sexual abuse, domestic violence, and rape represent the major elements of discrimination and the unacceptably low status of women in Korea. In the following section, Korean women's philanthropy is portrayed together with its achievements.

WOMEN'S PHILANTHROPY: EVOLUTION AND ACHIEVEMENTS

Women's status and the conditions of the society determine women's philanthropy, but women's status is also influenced by women's philanthropy itself. In other words, women's status, women's philanthropy, and the conditions of civic society are all closely interrelated, influencing each other. Korean women's status, both within and outside the family, is still very low. The Confucian value of familism, which takes women's subordination for granted, is still strong. When compared to the old days, however, improvement has been phenomenal. How much of this improvement can be ascribed to women's actions is difficult to answer. There is still much to be achieved, but the leading women philanthropists have been very effective. In addition to the factors discussed above, one more factor to be emphasized is the role of Christianity in the modernization process in Korea. Very special recognition should be given to the early Christian missionaries who taught the first Korean schoolgirls, their provision of leadership training for church women, and the Christian community that has led the Korean civic sector throughout its modern history. Christianity has not comprised the entire civic sector in Korea, but it has always been a large part of it. As will be shown in the following pages, bases of Korean women's philanthropy were laid by the education of women that was started by Christian missionaries at the same time as that of men, and those bases worked with, if not within, the Christian civic community.

The evolution of women's philanthropy in Korea is divided roughly into three stages. The first is the period from the early twentieth century to the early 1960s; the second, up until the late 1980s; the third, from 1987 to the present. This discussion will be followed by an analysis of a few achievements in the form of legal and institutional changes.

Evolution of Women's Philanthropy

It is known that the first women's underground network was the Songjuk-hoe, formed in 1913. Its establishment signaled the beginning of an organized movement by women. The Songjuk network acted as a consumers' organization for women's retail shops, promoting patriotism in the minds of the people. It played an important role in the March 1st Movement in 1919. Underground activities extended abroad until the end of Japanese rule. The detailed background of the members is not known, but by 1909, there were 605 schools established by the Presbyterian Church and 200 schools established by the Methodist Church, with an average of twenty to thirty students per school. Ewha Hakdang, the first girls' mission school in Korea, already had a thirty-year history. Christian educational activity had indeed made an important contribution to the modernization of Korea.

Early Christian missionaries discovered Hangul's (the Korean alphabet) superior effectiveness in communication and thereby helped the people, both men and women, become literate in their own language system. Korea was by no means without an education system or without zeal for education; on the contrary, the traditional aspiration for education is well known. But while the Confucian tradition is perhaps responsible for the high regard for learning, it was Christian missionaries who laid the foundation for a Western-style education system. The first Western-style schools opened by the missionaries were Ewha and Paichai, one for the girls and the other for the boys. In providing modern education, there was no time lag unfavorable to women. The girls' mission schools in particular accelerated the changes in process, and it is fair to say that the participation of women in every level of social life, although limited, came with Christianity.

Protestant missionaries stressed the cultivation of Christian women, encouraged their participation in Bible classes and church activities, and sought, above all, to make them keepers of Christian homes, devotedly rearing Christian children. This was the early missionaries' response to the greater resistance encountered among men in general, and upper-class men in particular. The modern Christian injunction against polygamy gradually abolished concubinage. The Christian worship place provided a forum where men and women were able to associate, although a heavy curtain usually divided the sexes. It was the first opening of the women's place outside the home.

In fact, Christian churches offered women historic new opportunities for growth and self-expression, which no Korean religion had offered before. To prepare them for leadership positions in the church, girls' schools were founded. These quickly grew and developed into modern institutions, which in turn opened careers for women as well, in higher education, medicine, and other technical fields. There women learned to read and solve problems; they learned history, English, and democratic principles; and their senses were sharpened to the issues of justice and opportunity for women. The Confucian tradition placed and still places women at a disadvantage in many aspects of life, but the progress made possible for them within and through the Christian church was nothing short of revolutionary.

It is logical to expect that the first woman who would satisfy the fundamental conditions for women's philanthropy in Korea would be a Christian woman who had been directly or indirectly exposed to the education and leadership training provided by the churches or mission schools, outside the home for the first time. Under Japanese colonial rule, the Christian church became a center of an anti-Japanese national independence movement. Christianity gathered strength and support from Koreans who used church institutions as havens from Japanese oppression. In other words, Christianity enabled Korean believers to feel both patriotic and modern at the same time. Many of the Christian women leaders, a cornerstone of the Korean church, organized a women's movement that was affiliated with the anti-Japanese movement.

In the 1920s, the socialist movement of political activism attracted quite a number of women intellectuals, but it could not survive for long. The mainstream of the women's movement was the educational and cultural movement and led mostly by Christian liberals. Of the Christian liberals, the part of the women's movement focused on education was sustained throughout the colonial period. Various activities were organized by many elite women of Christian faith to educate women to be literate and to help them adapt to a new way of life. The Korean YWCA was an important organization at that time.

In the years from liberation to independence, civic groups of varying ideological preferences blossomed. After independence, the state was preoccupied with maintaining security as its primary national goal, the civic organizations were mostly service-oriented, and the women's organizations were instrumental to the task of nation-building. After the war, many civic organizations emerged to provide welfare services or to implement development projects for the poor, and they were mostly supported, if not established, by foreign aid.

The second stage was set with the de facto authoritarian developmental state, which lacked political legitimacy but achieved remarkable success in export-oriented economic growth. It lasted from the early 1960s until 1987 when it fell with the Great Workers' Struggle (June to September). As already mentioned, during this period the authoritarian developmental state curtailed much of the freedom and civil rights of dissenters in the name of national security and international competition.

There developed two different but related lines in the women's movement. One came from the forceful democratization and labor movements of the 1970s. The other was intimately related to the visible increase of women's participation in the public sphere and the rise of new consciousness stimulated by the women's liberation movement in the West. The former represents the assimilationist strategy, even though women participated in these movements mainly through the economy of time. The latter is more clearly a separatist approach. The woman question from the point of view of democratization and the labor movement focused on women as revolutionary agents and laborers. Most activists working along this line were Christian activists in the labor movement in the beginning stage, ex-student activists and female workers themselves in the later stage. Factory women workers who had been in the harsh labor struggle of the 1970s formed groups to continue their struggle.

In another setting, a large number of female students joined in the struggle against the dictatorial regime of the 1970s, leading to the organization of female activists. The first grassroots organization of this kind was PyongU-hoe (Women for Equality and Peace), which was established in 1983 by a group of female college graduates. Most of the group members were university professors, lecturers, and graduate students in social sciences. Their aims were to eliminate sexism, to build a humanistic society for men and women through the common effort of men and women, and to overcome the tragedy of national division. Specifically the group was engaged in the fight for political democratization along with the established Nationalistic Democratic movement, and they also wanted to promote gender equality independently from the movement. This group dissolved in 1986. Some of the founding members of PyongU-hoe mapped out a plan to form a coalition of grassroots organizations of women. This led to Korean Women's Associations United (KWAU) launched in 1987, in the middle of the highest tide of the political democratization movement.

Another stream of the women's movement clearly originated from women's specific experiences. News of the women's liberation movement in the West contributed a great deal to the circulation of the issues of gender equality. Liberal ideology and a feminist perspective underlay this stream of the movement. There are now several grassroots organizations of this kind. The Women's Hotline was established in 1984 by a group of housewives with liberal Christian backgrounds. They were members of the women's studies group organized by Christical Academy. One group specialized in battered women's problems with a firm belief that women's oppression could not be a secondary concern. The first weekly feminist newspaper, the *Women's News*, was started in 1988.

The 1980s were a time of extraordinary growth in the women's movement in Korea. Groups and organizations that identify with the women's movement were formed in major cities, and increasing numbers of women participated in the labor, urban poor, environmental, consumer, community child care, democratic education, and various cultural movements. They tend not to make distinctions between the feminist movement and the broader social movement. Their charters typically incorporate both gender equality and broader causes like reunification, democratization, nationalist populist democracy, social justice, and so forth.

It should be noted that the formal structure of cooperation between the government and the civic groups was also established during these years. All civic groups and NGOs were expected to register with competent ministries either for establishment as a legally recognized organization or for mere recognition as a public body. As the number of registered NGOs increased and the issues came to require more professional information and management, the ministries began to establish quasi-governmental organizations as intermediate institutions between NGOs and the government. Also during this period, the women's movement expanded, and their organizations became active. For instance, the Ministry of Health and Social Affairs established the Korean Women's Development Institute as a quasi-governmental organization as early as 1983. This was a gesture by the government of support for the women's movement and was not regarded as a challenge to the regime. KWDI activities include not only policy research and support of women's organizations, but also direct services to the community.

The third stage began with the abrupt end of the authoritarian regime in June 1987. New to this stage of evolution of Korean women's philanthropy was the emergence of increasingly effective and sophisticated civic groups led by the younger generation emphasizing progressive advocacy functions, including efforts to broaden public debate and participation in the formulation of public policy, safeguarding or expanding the domain of human rights, and safeguarding public goods such as the environment against the pressures of economic growth. To name only a few very effective NGOs established after 1987, the Citizen's Coalition for Economic Justice, established in 1989 by five hundred founding members as a citizen's organization to express opinions on general policy issues with a broad focus on economic justice; Korea Action Federation for Environment, established in 1994 by former opposition movement leaders who view environmental issues as related to the more fundamental questions of people's right to life; the anti-nuclear movement; the anti-Chaebol movement; and most of the listed organizations for human rights. These and other relatively new organizations are new additions that are in fact leading components of the contemporary civic sector in Korea.

Another important feature of the third sector in post-1987 Korea is the flux of the business sector's interest in the notion of corporate citizenship. It is related to the new progressive civic leaders' anti-Chaebol movement, as well as the new government's transparency policy for fair competition and for severing the old symbiotic relationship between the state and big business. The largest conglomerates are now competing with each other for social philanthropic programs for various reasons. The number of corporate foundations has increased rapidly during the last few years. The art museums mentioned above are a part of this trend. Civic volunteerism has been promoted by the media, and by the revision of the Education Act in 1996, all schoolchildren are required to have volunteer experience.

The map of the third sector in Korea is changing rapidly. Korean women's age-old voices for gender equality have been heard, and a number of important legal and institutional achievements have been recently made. Before going into these achievements, a brief description of the actual status of women's organizations in Korea is useful.

As stated already, women's philanthropy is indeed a poorly documented area. It was in 1988 that the KWDI published the first book of women's organizations in Korea, listing 2,200 groups. In the second book, published in 1994, 4,050 women's organizations were identified and listed. An increase in numbers does not necessarily represent an actual increase, but it might represent improved efforts of seeking out the organizations. It provides a picture of only separatist organizations. The current status of these women's organizations has seldom been studied empirically. It was in 1991 that the KWDI conducted a survey of these organizations concerning their organizational structure, staffing, purpose of establishment, financial status, and other characteristics. Out of 2,200 identified women's organizations, 303 responded to the study. And only 80 responded to the budget-related questions. Assuming that the respondents represented the most active organizations, the survey shows how poorly they are financed and staffed. Most of the organizations were dependent upon annual membership fees, which ranged from $15,000 to $75,000. Most of them had either only one or no full-time paid clerks or secretaries. Financial support from the government was concentrated on a few politically strategic organizations such as the Korean War Dead Soldier and Police Widows' Association (Veterans' Administration), the National Conference of Housewives for Betterment of Home Life (Ministry of Human Affairs), Korea Legal Aid Center for Family Relations (Ministry of Justice), and the National YWCA (Ministry of Health and Welfare).

Recent Achievements

Despite their poor financing and staffing, the perseverance of Korean women's organizations achieved important institutional changes. As has been stated above, it is difficult to carve out the exact impact of women's philanthropy or the women's movement on the status of women in the society. But it has been since the 1980s, particularly after 1987, that a broad range of laws has been revised to remove gender biases or was newly enacted to introduce institutional adjustments for women's advancement.

One of the oldest issues for the women's community has been the revision of the Family Law (Domestic Relations and Inheritance Clauses of the Civil Code). The Family Law, in its 1958 version, contained many traditional elements contrary to the principle of gender equality, especially with respect to marital, divorce, and inheritance rights. The law was revised in 1990 to remove discriminatory elements and to accord women a status almost equal to men's. Thus it introduced an egalitarian family system with the husband and the wife at its center as equal partners. The revised Family Law granted women the right to head a family, something previously unthinkable in the country's heavily Confucian culture, and severely opposed by the orthodox Confucianists in contemporary Korea. It also removed male privileges in inheritance and gave women the right to claim their share of family property even without formal title to it. Furthermore, it granted divorced women the right to guardianship over their children. In support of the revised Family Law and its full and speedy implementation, the government took steps to adjust related tax laws and to legislate the Domestic Litigation Act. For instance, the Inheritance and Gift Tax Act, revised in 1990 and again in 1994, upwardly adjusted the level of tax exemption for the wife's inheritance from her spouse's estate. This came in clear legal recognition of the right of the housewife to her share in the family property even when she had not contributed to it directly through gainful outside employment. The Property Tax Assessment Regulations, used to check the source of funds for acquiring property, previously contained gender-discriminatory definitions of taxable sources of funds and gender-differential tax deduction ceilings. Such inequalities were removed by the June 1991 revision of the regulations.

The Family Law Revision movement started in the 1960s and was led by the first woman lawyer in Korea, who established the Legal Aid Center for Family Relations in the early 1960s, which has now become an institute with more than 150 staff and extension offices nationwide.

Another important area of legal enactment and revisions actively sought by women's organizations has been sanctions for the equal treatment of women at the workplace. It was in 1987, after the Great Workers' Struggle, that the Equal Employment Opportunity Act was first legislated to realize the principle of gender equality in employment opportunities and conditions and to protect motherhood in the women's work context as stipulated in the Constitution. It is also aimed at developing women's occupational potential and thereby advancing their socioeconomic status. This act codified the principle of gender-equal treatment of all workers and the maternity right of working women. It has also made it possible to impose sanctions against employers engaging in gender-discriminatory personnel practices.

While the 1987 Equal Employment Opportunity Act was the country's first legal instrument for enforcing the equal treatment for equal work principle and for protecting women's maternity rights, there was a need for making these provisions, as well as the nondiscriminatory recruitment and employment requirements, more explicit. Accordingly, the act was revised in April 1989. The revised act, inter alia, provides for the extension of unpaid child care leave for up to one year and for counting the leave period as part of a consecutive work period. Furthermore, in labor disputes, the burden of proof has been shifted from the employee to the employer.

To strengthen its powers of enforcement, the revised act stipulates penalties of up to two years in prison or a fine of up to 5 million won ($6,250), and fine of up to 250 million won ($312,500) for violating the equal recruitment, training, placement, and promotion requirements and the child care leave provision.

In a similar vein, the Labor Standard Act of 1953, based on Article 32, Item 4 of the Constitution, was also revised to ensure equal treatment of working men and women (Article 5) and to protect women's maternity rights in the work context (Chapter 5). Previously, a limited range of employers were bound by the Labour Standard Act. Following its revision on March 29, 1989: (1) all business/industrial establishments with five or more employees are bound by it; (2) penalties for noncompliance are stiffer; (3) the employer is required to grant menstrual leave even without the employee requesting it; and (4) the employer now must seek the consent of female employees for their overtime work, whereas, previously, only the permission of the Minister of Labour was necessary. To encourage its speedy implementation by concerned employers, the revised Labour Standard Act stipulates harsher penalties for noncompliance. A fine of up to five million won ($6,250) has been set for violation of the equal treatment for equal work clause and up to five years' imprisonment or a 30 million won ($37,500) fine has been set for violation of the maternity rights protection clause.

In the same year, the regulations governing the national civil service examination were revised, and in the following year, regulations governing the employment of local civil servants were revised, so that there is no longer gender-based discrimination in the recruitment process of civil servants at either the national or the local level. Some local governments have gone further to adopt a goal of increasing the proportion of women civil servants.

To support women's gainful employment, the Infant and Child Care Act followed in 1991. This law came in response to urgent child care service needs brought about by a rapid rise in the number of women entering the labor market and participating in civic activities. Under the act, a comprehensive child care service system, with priorities for the children of low-income families with working mothers, is in the process of being established. The act contains, inter alia, the requirement that all business/industrial firms with more than five hundred female employees must establish at least one day care facility each within their respective premises, or, alternatively, subsidize external child care service charges incurred by their female employees.

The act has not only established a legal foundation for systematizing and expanding child care facilities and services required by women's entry into the social and economic fields but has succeeded in bringing the state, local governments, and legislative bodies into the effort as major partners. At the same time, it has helped to establish, in the public mind, the fact that child care issues are public as well as domestic issues bearing simultaneously on the advancement of women and that of the Korean society as a whole.

The most recent achievement has been the passage of the Law for Punishing Sexual Offenders and Protecting Victims of Sexual Assault. This law provides for strict punitive measures for offenders and medical treatment, temporary shelters, and counseling services for victimized women, but many difficulties are being discussed in its implementation. In addition to these legal revisions, it was in 1988 that the government appointed a woman as the Minister of Political Affairs (II) in 1988 and empowered her to coordinate all governmental and nongovernmental activities directed toward the advancement of Korean women. The Ministry, in consultation with other sectoral ministries concerned, identifies issues and problems relating to women and develops and recommends policy measures to address them. Where activities of the concerned ministries and agencies overlap or come into conflict, the Ministry intervenes to bring about the necessary adjustments. All government ministries and organs at various levels are required to consult the Ministry in advance when drafting new laws or planning new programs with implications for women. The Minister of Political Affairs (II) is assisted by a Vice Minister, an Assistant Minister, and four Coordinators for Political Affairs. The women's community in Korea demands this Ministry to develop into a full Ministry of Women's Affairs.

CONCLUDING REMARKS

Lives of Korean women today are relatively free and independent. They are more educated, many of them are now in paid jobs, more of them occupy high public positions, and they participate more in associations. But this is true only when compared to the past. When compared to the men in contemporary Korea, gender equality is still a myth, not a reality. Women's philanthropic organizations are increasing in number and influence, but they are still very much underfunded and understaffed. The conditions of women's philanthropy mentioned above — that is, the social recognition of women as independent human beings, women's right to property, and gender equality of opportunity in social and economic participation — are still on the way to formation in Korea, circumscribing the contours of women's philanthropic activities in Korea.

This is part of the general picture of the Korean philanthropic community. In all the voluntary organizations, women predominate in number. This is because of the absolutely small size of the third sector in this country. Volunteering is not a part of our daily community lives. But male donors are coming along. Though the Inheritance Tax Law has been revised recently, many female counterparts are hardly expected to come along soon. Nevertheless, the recent achievements of institutional changes for women's development are quite impressive. How was it possible? One plausible answer is that despite the poor financial condition of the women's organizations, the leadership of a number of organizational entrepreneurs was extremely effective. Many of them were educated in segregated women's colleges and trained as women leaders at the churches. But in pursuing their goals of institutional changes, they gathered support from the broader male camp because of their assimilationist strategy.

Now the two policy issues have come to the fore. One is the question of the place of women. The other is philanthropy's relationship with the government. These are the two out of five dimensions of the concept of women's philanthropy discussed in the second section of this paper. As mentioned above, contemporary Korean women have more opportunity to participate in the philanthropic sector than before. The KWAU consolidated further, having united most grassroots women's organizations. KWAU is known for its assimilationist causes, incorporating not only gender equality but also reunification and rationalization of society. The feminist question is only secondary for most of these effective new associations. Now, with the expansion of the civic sector, feminist leaders are facing the choice between separatism and assimilationism. And this issue is being raised by feminist women scholars and active philanthropists.

But the Korean women's movement emerged along with the need for the nation's independence. This character is shaped by the context of national history. Korean history has been interspersed with the experiences of colonialism, economic backwardness, division of the nation, and authoritarianism. Such historical circumstances have led women in Korea to participate in the movement for national liberation, modernization, reunification, and democratization of Korean society. Since the women's movement has developed around issues related to socioeconomic structures, women's rights issues, especially in the private sphere, have been the subject of benign neglect in the movement. In many cases, women have been asked to put aside their own demands in order to support a struggle for independence or democracy. This historical heritage is still predominant, and the question remains unanswered. The concern is that this approach, not identical but similar to the assimilationist strategy, may yield unintended consequences, strengthening the institutions and professional aspirations of men to the detriment of other women, as the experiences of the advanced countries show.

The second issue is related to the government's policy toward the third sector. The new democratic government wants to play an explicit conducive role for the development of philanthropy. Each department is so anxious to help the voluntary sector that departmental competition is severe to become competent authorities for voluntary activities and civic organizations. Given the age-old tradition of organic statism in Korea, the relationship between the government and the philanthropic sector is expected to evolve in unique ways.

Notes on Contributors

Beth Baron is Associate Professor of History, City College and the Graduate School, City University of New York. She is author of *The Women's Awakening in Egypt* and coeditor with Nikkie Keddie of *Women in Middle Eastern History.*

Susan M. Chambré is a Professor of Sociology at Baruch College, City University of New York. Her publications focus on the link between adolescent pregnancy and welfare dependency, the social and cultural factors that influence volunteerism by elders, the changing nature of Jewish philanthropy and the role of New York City's AIDS Community in designing and influencing HIV policy. Her research has been supported by the PSC/CUNY Faculty Grant Program, the AARP/Andrus Foundation, the Aspen Institute, the Indiana University Center on Philanthropy, and the Baruch College Fund.

Evelyne Diebolt is a historian who specializes in the history of the French associative movement in the twentieth century. She has taught at Stanford University and is presently working on a study for the Secretary of State for Women's Rights of decision-making by women in the associative field in France.

Amani Mohamed Kandil is Executive Director, Arab Network for NGOs in Cairo, Egypt. She holds a Ph.D. in Political Science from Cairo University. She is a board member of International Committee for the Preparation of the International Year of Volunteers (2001) and a former board member of the International Society for the Third Sector (ISTR). Her publications include: *The Socio-Economic Contribution of NGOs in Arab Countries, Defining the Non-Profit Sector in Egypt,* and *Democratization in Egypt (1981–1993).*

Leilah Landim is Professor at the Federal University of Rio de Janeiro and Research Coordinator of the Project "Citizenship and Philanthropy in Brazil," at ISER — Institute for Religious Studies, in Rio de Janeiro, Brazil, where she lives. She is also Associate Researcher for Brazil in the Comparative Nonprofit Sector Project of the Johns Hopkins Center for Civil Society Studies.

313

Hye Kyung Lee received a Ph.D. in Social Welfare from the University of California at Berkeley. She is a Professor of Social Welfare at Yonsei University and serves as president of the Korean Academy of Social Security. She is a member of the Premier's Commission on National Policy Evaluation and other bodies, and has written extensively in the areas of poverty, inequality, women's policy, non-profit sector, and social security.

Maria Luddy is a Senior Lecturer in History at the University of Warwick, England. She has written extensively on the history of women in Ireland. Her works include*Women in Ireland, 1800–1918: A Documentary History* and the award-winning *Women and Philanthropy in Nineteenth-Century Ireland.*

Per Selle is Professor in the Department of Comparative Politics, University of Bergen; and Research Director at the Norwegian Centre in Organization and Management, Bergen. Among his English-language books are *Government and Voluntary Organizations* (with Stein Kuhnle), *Women in Nordic Politics: Closing the Gap?* (with Lauri Karvonen), and *Cultural Theory as Political Science* (with Michael Thompson and Gunnar Grendstad).

Pushpa Sundar is the Founder-Director of the Indian Centre for Philanthropy, New Delhi. She was a Senior Fellow under the International Fellows in Philanthropy program of the Johns Hopkins University in 1995. She is author of *Patrons and Philistines: Arts and the State in British India* and *Beyond Business: From Merchant Charity to Corporate Philanthropy.*

Shurlee Swain is a Senior Lecturer in History at Australian Catholic University and a Senior Research Fellow in the History Department at the University of Melbourne. She is the author of several books and articles in this area, the most recent of which was *Single Mothers and their Children: Disposal, Punishment and Survival in Australia* (Cambridge University Press, 1995).

Ghada Hashem Talhami teaches courses on the Middle East and African politics and on women of the Third World at Lake Forest College, where she is D. K. Pearsons Professor of Politics. She is the author of three books on Egypt, including *Palestine and the Egyptian National Identity* and *The Islamic Mobilization of Women in Egypt.*